Loyola University Chicago
Family Business Center
820 North Michigan Avenue
Chicago, IL 60611-2196

Glossbrenner's Guide to
Shareware for Small Businesses

Alfred Glossbrenner

Windcrest®/McGraw-Hill

FIRST EDITION
FIRST PRINTING

© 1992 by **Alfred Glossbrenner**
Published by Windcrest Books, an imprint of TAB Books.
TAB Books is a division of McGraw-Hill, Inc.
The name "Windcrest" is a registered trademark of TAB Books.

Library of Congress Cataloging-in-Publication Data

Glossbrenner, Alfred.
[Guide to shareware for small businesses]
Glossbrenner's guide to shareware for small businesses / by Alfred
Glossbrenner.
p.   cm.
Includes index.
ISBN 0-8306-3377-4   ISBN 0-8306-3375-8 (pbk.)
1. Business—Computer programs. 2. Small business—Computer
programs. 3. Shareware (Computer software)   I. Title.
HF5548.2.G593   1992   92-5330
650'.0285536—dc20   CIP

TAB Books offers software for sale. For information and a catalog, please contact
TAB Software Department, Blue Ridge Summit, PA 17294-0850.

Acquisitions Editor: Brad Schepp
Book Editor: David M. McCandless
Director of Production: Katherine G. Brown
Book Design: Jaclyn J. Boone
Cover: Sandra Blair Design and Brent Blair Photography,
Harrisburg, PA   LHP3

Contents

4 Software basics: DOS, Windows, and applications *59*

Part II   Buying equipment and programs

Part III Shareware in your business: The "Big Four" applications

9 Word processing 149

Part IV   Shareware: Beyond the basics

13   **Accounting and money management**   *265*

14   Printer productivity tools and techniques   *281*

15   Business forms and graphics   *305*

Introduction

THIS BOOK WILL SAVE YOU *MONEY*. IT WILL ALSO SAVE YOU *TIME*. YOUR CASH savings will range anywhere from under $100 to well over $1000. Your time savings will be worth even more. The actual savings in both cases will depend on how much you plan to do with your computer. But, believe me, with this book in your hand, you will be able to do so much more than you ever dreamed. And you'll pay a lot less for it.

Computer power for everyone

The book is aimed at small business owners and professionals. It is designed to tell you what *we*—myself and Emily, my wife and business partner—know and have learned in over a decade of using computers in *our* small business.

Our business happens to be writing how-to books about computers and distributing a highly selective collection of shareware software through the mail. So when I tell you that one of the things we've learned is that no small businessperson today can afford *not* to use a computer, you have a right to be skeptical. If not downright suspicious.

But the statement is true, nonetheless, and in Chapter 1 I'll show you why. I can give you a one-word hint here, however, and that word is *competitors*. Whether you computerize your business or your office or not, the people who are out to take away your customers, clients, or patients are doing so right now. And the reason they are doing so is that the cost is so low and the benefits are so great.

Dirt-cheap hardware

Computer hardware is so cheap today that, even if you computerize only one task, it can often pay for itself within just a few months. There's just one problem: as thoroughly as most small business owners and professionals know their own fields, most don't have any idea of how computers work, what they can do, or what to look for when buying a system.

Chapters 1 through 6 will fix that. These chapters will give you everything you need without telling you more than you want to know. They will take you from Ground Zero in computer knowledge to a state of true enlightenment. As you will discover, a computer is just a machine, and like any other machine, it's not difficult to understand once it is explained properly.

By the time you reach Chapter 5, "How to buy the system you need," you'll be comfortably slinging the jargon with the experts. But, unlike many "experts," you will really *know* what you're talking about. Chapter 6 presents a quick rundown on the features to look for when buying add-on equipment (equipment not included in your initial computer system package). And Chapter 7 tells you where to get "support." That's computerese for "Help!"

Costly business software

You will find that buying smart and saving money on your hardware is a continuing theme of ours. But no matter how good a deal you get, your computer will be useless without software to make it do its stuff. It is at this point that many small businesspeople and professionals encounter another problem. What programs should I get? Can they be serious charging $595 for a single package? Where in the world should I begin?

The answer is revealed in Chapter 8, "The shareware concept: High quality, low prices." Shareware is computer software offered on the honor system. If you don't like it, you don't pay for it. Indeed, even if you do like it, nothing but a guilty conscience will force you to register a shareware program by sending its author the requested fee.

The fees are low—usually between $10 and $75—and the benefits are substantial. Free updates, professionally printed manuals, and, most important of all, personalized support from the programmer who wrote the program! Imagine calling up the guy who wrote Lotus 1-2-3 and asking him to add a feature to his spreadsheet. Yet that kind of personal dialogue between user and programmer takes place all the time in the shareware field.

You've got a friend in shareware

Though you may never have heard of it, shareware has long been a vibrant force in the computer field. Magazines don't talk about it much—they've got their hands full reviewing commercial packages. Sometimes it almost seems as though you've got to know someone to get tapped in. But once you enter this world, you'll find that literally tens of thousands of programs are yours, free for the asking. Or at least for the price of a floppy disk and postage.

Shareware and its cousin, public domain programs (for which no fee is asked), cover all the bases. There are scores of word processors, accounting, database, and spreadsheet programs, plus thousands of games, helpful utility programs, music and education software, investment and tax software, real estate managers, desktop publishing programs, and typefaces galore.

It is no exaggeration to say that whatever you want to do with a computer, you can find a shareware program that can do it. Unfortunately, as with commercial software, not every shareware package is a winner. So which word processor do you choose? Which accounting program? Which business forms package?

There are only two ways to find out. The first is to order a bunch of shareware disks and laboriously work your way through each program until you find the best of the lot. In most cases, the best will be so good that it can go toe-to-toe with any equivalent commercial package. But you will have spent so much time finding it that you'd have been better off buying a well-reviewed commercial program.

Only the best!

The second way to discover the best shareware packages is to have someone else survey the field and evaluate the software for you. That's exactly what Emily and I have done. Parts III and IV of this book present the results. There isn't a program discussed in these pages that isn't absolutely top-drawer.

How good are they? You won't really know until you try them yourself. But a number of the programmers involved have built multimillion dollar companies on the strength of these packages. Many of them receive licensing fees from Fortune 500 companies. A number of them have licensed their products to commercial software firms. The NDOS module supplied with the best-selling Norton Utilities, for example, is actually a version of the shareware program 4DOS.

Shareware can save you MONEY

In our own business, we use shareware almost exclusively. I do all my word processing with PC-Write (Chapter 9). Emily keeps track of book sales with File Express (Chapter 10). I do all of my communicating with ProComm (Chapter 12), and Emily does all of our financial projections, income statements, and the like with As-Easy-As, the Lotus 1-2-3 clone covered in Chapter 11. We're also constantly using shareware utility programs because they offer features you simply can't find in commercial products. (And every now and then, we kill an hour or so playing a game like Hugo's House of Horrors or Commander Keen.)

All of these business programs come with ready-to-print on-disk manuals, each of which is 100 to 200 pages or more. There is certainly no dearth of information. The problem is that if you are a new user, you have no way of knowing which specific techniques are crucial and which you can save for another time.

That's why Chapters 9 through 12 in Part III take you step-by-step through the process of installing and using the "Big Four" applications: word processing, database, spreadsheet, and communications. These are the programs you will use everyday, but there is no need to start out by trying to absorb all of their features.

The chapters in Part III will show you what's most important and get you using this software for productive purposes literally within minutes.

Part IV, "Shareware: Beyond the Basics," is designed to expand your range even further. The chapters in this part of the book profile the best shareware accounting and money management software. They cover programs to produce business forms on your printer, graphics and CAD/CAM software, and the utilities that can make any computer easier to use while saving you tons of time. Finally, since neither man nor woman lives by work alone, we close with a look at some of the best games and education programs.

Powerful programs on the disk

But, as the saying goes, there's more! The disk bound in with this book contains our personal selection of programs every computer user should have. You'll find a summary in Appendix A, and once you install the software, you will wonder how anyone can use a computer without them. If you know a little bit about running a PC, you may want to turn to Appendix A right now for a quick preview. Otherwise, you'll just have to trust me: This is really prime stuff!

At the back of the book you'll also find the Glossbrenner's Choice Order Form in Appendix B. Chapter 8 will tell you about all the many sources of shareware (mail-order firms, local computer user groups, online systems like Compu-Serve, etc.). It will also show you the best ways to tap in. But since everyone's so busy these days, and since we've got all of these programs cited in the book anyway, we'd be happy to send them to you. The programs cited in the book are part of a collection we call "Glossbrenner's Choice." Individual disks are available for a small fee to cover postage, handling, and the cost of the disks themselves.

Finally, in keeping with the book's money-saving theme, you will find a selection of really good coupons at the end of the book. Each of them is for a product or service that Emily and I use ourselves. We have no relationship with the companies making these offers. We simply felt that they are so good that you should know about them too. If you decide to take advantage of just a few of the special offers included here, you can save enough to nearly pay for this book.

Conclusion

Our ultimate goal is to help you get into personal computing as easily and as inexpensively as possible. The book is thus designed to supply all the missing links. If you are a brand-new or prospective computer owner, it will tell you what you need to know to understand your system and feel comfortable using it. It will tell you what to buy, where to buy it, and give you the tools you need to fend for yourself in the marketplace.

Then it will show you how to save big bucks—with no sacrifice in power or performance—by following the shareware route. But it doesn't stop there. It also identifies the specific shareware programs that are the best in their class, and tells you exactly what software to get. But it doesn't stop there either. It goes on to show you how to install and actually *use* the Big Four applications programs.

Then it shows you how to move beyond the basics and explore the best shareware programs for other applications.

   With this book and the hardware and software it recommends, you'll have everything you need to harness the power of the personal computer and put it to work in your business or profession. And you'll save a great deal of time and a great deal of money in the process. Emily and I know it works, because we've done it. Now you can too.

Part I

Understanding computer hardware and software

1

Get a competitive edge

Computerize!

THERE'S BEEN A LOT OF NONSENSE WRITTEN ABOUT PERSONAL COMPUTERS over the years. But that's only natural. PCs have been the subject of so much verbiage—day after day, week after week—during the last decade, it simply stands to reason that a lot of it is pure poppycock. In the early days, for example, many a magazine article seriously suggested that keeping track of your recipes or balancing your checkbook was a perfectly sensible reason for investing over $5000 in a "home computer."

Never mind that a pack of 3×5 cards, or a pocket calculator and a pencil, cost virtually nothing and let you do the same jobs much faster. The industry was desperate to sell hardware and software and would do anything to come up with a reason, any reason, for you to buy.

Not surprisingly, the nonsense quotient has remained constant ever since, though the nonsense itself has become more sophisticated and seductive. Today, for example, the party line is that *every* small business should computerize as many of its operations as possible, as soon as possible. Buy that hardware! Install this software! And hook up everything in sight to a Local Area Network (LAN)! All you've got to do, apparently, is buy a system, plug it in, and put your feet up as instantaneous productivity gains and profits rain down from above.

The frustration flashpoint

Well, ladies and gentlemen, this simply isn't true. There is much more to "computerizing" than some magazines and books would have you believe. Yes, the

3

hardware is cheap. In fact, it's unbelievably cheap to anyone who has watched this industry grow over the years.

But computer hardware is the *least* of your costs. You can easily pay as much for just two or three commercial software packages as you did for your entire computer system. But even commercial software isn't your biggest expense. The greatest cost involved in installing any computer system, be it ever so humble, is *time*. Your time, and the time of your employees or associates.

A personal computer is an incredible tool. But like any powerful piece of equipment, both hours and effort are required to gain the skills needed to put it to use. On the plus side, as with any skill, once it's yours, it's yours for life. And the payoff can be so huge as to make your initial investment of time and effort pale to insignificance. But that initial investment *must* be made, and when you are just starting, there is no way to tell whether the payoffs will indeed materialize.

My point is simply this: Don't take everything you read about personal computing as gospel. Don't assume that you must computerize your business simply because everyone seems to be saying that you should. If your business is humming along with things the way they are, don't change. Leave well enough alone—and leave this book on the bookstore shelf for someone else to find.

On the other hand, if you are dissatisfied in some way with your current operation, if your instincts tell you that you've got to work faster, smarter, and more efficiently to survive and prosper, then you're probably ready to take the plunge.

There is a simple test you can apply. Ask yourself if you have ever thought or said: There's got to be a better way to do this! If you have, then more than likely, it is time to seriously consider getting a computer. That's because a computer will probably be able to do the job faster and better.

But wait until you reach this "frustration flashpoint." Only then will you have the motivation needed to make sure your new system doesn't end up as an expensive desktop sculpture and dust collector. This book is designed to make the task of computerizing your business as easy and inexpensive as possible. But you've got to be willing to apply yourself. The work is not difficult—and I promise you, we'll have some fun along the way—but it is work that must be done, and you're the one who must do it. Make sure you're ready to sign up for the duration.

Why buy now?

That said, if you are ready to acquire a system, there is no better time than the present. Hardware prices have never been lower than they are right now. That's something I can say in full confidence, regardless of the calendar year. The fact is that, historically, computer hardware prices always go down. At times, prices may fall as much as 5% per month or more on some pieces of equipment. With other hardware, the rate of descent is not as dramatic. But the price trend is always in the same direction—downward.

Certainly there's a bottom somewhere. And certainly some time periods offer marginally better values than others. But how long do you want to wait? Regardless of when you buy, you will almost always be able to get the same equipment for less money six months later. That's simply the way the computer hardware business works. There's no point in fighting it or in delaying and delaying, hoping to get the ultimate lowest price.

In short: Don't fool around. Buy what you need, when you need it, and don't worry about the deal that might come along some future day. Fortunately, the price of what we can call an "entry-level, small business system" today is so low that nearly everyone with a small business can afford it. As I said, hardware is cheap. Once you reach the frustration flashpoint, the sooner you get started, the sooner you can begin reaping the benefits of computerization.

What computers do best

And just what are those benefits? What can a computer system do for you? Can it really give you an edge on your competition?

It's impossible to say. I don't know your business, after all. But I know a lot about the kinds of things computers do, and I know that many small businesses can benefit by using them. I also know that computers can do many things that can be done faster and more efficiently by hand.

Managing inventory

So let's talk in generalities for a moment. Computers are very good at finding and manipulating information. Whether you're a butcher, baker, or candlestick maker, if you've got a lot of things to keep track of, a computer can be a crucial tool.

Consider the most obvious example—inventory management. Nearly every small business has an inventory of parts, products, or materials it needs in order to do what it does. If you keep your inventory records in a *database* on a computer, you can use the machine to instantly locate any information you may need about any item or class of item in your storeroom.

You can tell what you have ordered, when, how much, what you paid, and how much is left in stock. And you can do it in *seconds*. When it is time to re-order, you do not have to guess or otherwise fly by the seat of your pants. When you want a summary of what you've paid for a given product during the last six months, you do not have to spend your time copying figures from file cards or supplier invoices.

The computer can deliver the information you need, instantly. That puts you in control, and it gives you a competitive advantage. Among other things, it means that you will be less likely to tie up precious capital and credit in inventory.

Don't get me wrong. I'm not saying that you should disregard everything you have learned about your business and blindly follow what the computer says. If the machine indicates that you should order only 10 gross of a product, but you sense that the item is likely to be a big seller in the coming months, by all means order more.

The computer isn't your master. It is simply another tool. As a tool, it can give you a clearer picture, a better handle on what you're doing. As a result, you're likely to have more flexibility than the guy or gal down the street who is competing with you using traditional "guesstimate" methods. Thanks to better inventory management, you might have the spare cash to take advantage of a supplier's promotional offer or to earn special discounts not available to your non-computerized competitor—who's got too much working capital frozen in the storeroom.

Riding herd on receivables

Of course, inventories aren't limited to goods and products. In a sense, every professional or small business also has an "inventory" of clients or customers. A computer's power to find and manipulate information is as crucial here as it is in tracking pork bellies, flour, tallow, and other raw materials. Consider receivables as your "inventory" of unpaid bills.

With the possible exception of those dealing in illegal substances, there isn't a small business operator going who doesn't have a list of people who owe him for goods or services rendered. Receivables are our lifeblood, and we all know that not every customer or client pays promptly. A computer can help keep that lifeblood flowing.

If you record the customer's name and address, the product or service purchased, and the date of the transaction in a database, you can tell the machine to instantly produce a report listing all overdue accounts, the number of days they are overdue, and the total amount owed. The action you take on each account is completely up to you. Once again, the computer is merely a tool, not a machine that is going to take over your business. Its job is merely to tell it like it is. The action taken, if any, is totally up to you.

But if you decide that perhaps a gentle reminder note is required for some accounts, while a personal phone call is indicated for others, the computer can make both of these jobs easier. At your command, it can automatically generate a "Past Due" reminder letter addressed to the customer. Or it can produce a list of customers to be called, including their phone numbers and crucial account information.

A computer, in short, can give you better control over your receivables. As we all know, that translates into money in your pocket. How many times have you called a customer who is 60 days overdue and, as a result, gotten a check for the full amount a few days later? Sometimes even the best customers simply forget or really do misplace your bill. In such cases, there's a good chance that you could have had your money 30 days sooner if you had been able to send a reminder note as soon as the bill was past due. A computer can give you that power. By so doing, it can put you in a better position than your competitors.

The quickest path to payback

Reduced to its bare essentials, a small business is nothing if not money going out and money coming in, with enough convenience or value added in the process to generate a profit. If you don't take in more than you pay out, you will eventually fail. So if someone comes along and says, "There's a tool that can give you much better control over the supplies you buy and the accounts that owe you money," it is only smart to pay attention. In the most basic, fundamental sense, those businesses that can control their inventory and their receivables most effectively are going to have a competitive edge over those who cannot.

If you do nothing more with a personal computer than use it to manage your inventory and ride herd on your receivables, you will be ahead of the game. Those two applications offer the quickest path to a measurable payback on the $1200 to $2500 you invest in a system. You don't *have* to do anything more. The hardware can pay for itself in as little as a month or two, simply by giving you a better handle on your inventory and receivables.

But this only scratches the surface of what one of these machines can do for you. In addition to being exceptionally good at finding and manipulating information, computers are absolute demons at crunching numbers. The most obvious example is using a PC to balance the books, handle your payroll, and manage your finances. A computer will *not* replace a skilled accountant or bookkeeper. But it can make his or her job much easier, with the result that you will get a higher level of service, possibly for less money.

But accounting—essentially simple arithmetic—is child's play for a modern PC. It is with electronic spreadsheets that a computer's number crunching ability really shines for most small businesses. Many small business owners are familiar with paper-based spreadsheets and their components. If the term is new to you, a simple example will make the concept clear.

Spreadsheets and "What if . . ."

Spreadsheets are designed to pull together all of the many financial elements involved in making a decision or in determining where the business will be at some time in the future. The focal point of most spreadsheets is, quite literally, the bottom line. When all of the expenses are considered, what will it cost to build this plant? If revenue and expenses follow this 12-month projection, where will we be financially at the end of the fiscal year? And so on.

The most familiar "spreadsheet" of all is the tax return each of us fills out the night of April 15th. Add this, subtract that, multiply by the number on line 23a, etc.—all of which leads to the amount of tax we owe. The information on the IRS's Form 1040 usually comes from several other forms and schedules, each of which involves subsidiary calculations. So the "bottom line"—the one reading "Attach check or money order . . ."—depends upon many individual figures and items.

Now, imagine that your tax return—all the schedules and forms—are on a computer. And imagine that the various figures and calculations are *linked* via a spreadsheet program. You are finally finished with the return and are about to print it out when you discover a deduction you somehow missed.

If you were using a traditional paper-based system, you would sigh, groan, and curse as you reached for your eraser and pocket calculator. But with a computer at your command, you can simply change a single figure on your Schedule C (or whatever), and every number that depends on that figure will change *automatically*! Presto: a new bottom line. This is what an electronic spreadsheet is all about.

That's why it is often said that spreadsheets let businesspeople play "what if" games. For example, assume that you are thinking of moving to a new location, but you are not quite sure that such a move will be in your best interests. If you have incorporated all of the variables into an electronic spreadsheet (lease payments, taxes, telephone and utilities, assumed increase in walk-in traffic, advertising to let the public know that you've moved, etc.), you can easily "ask the computer" questions like: What if the tax bill increases by three mills? What if walk-in traffic is ten percent greater than I'm currently projecting? How will that affect my bottom-line profit? Or, how much more would each average customer have to buy for the bottom line to be $X?

With a spreadsheet, you can make a single change in a line item, and every figure that depends on that item will automatically change to reflect the new value. Most spreadsheet programs, including the shareware Lotus-compatible program recommended in Chapter 11, can present their information graphically as a pie chart, bar graph, or in some other visual form.

Once again, better information and better control can give any small business a significant edge over its competitors. Electronic spreadsheets offer you a handle on where your business or professional practice is, where it is going, and what needs to be done to reach desired goals in the future.

Instant electronic information

In addition to finding and manipulating information and crunching numbers like crazy, computers also offer specialized powers. One of the most useful of these is the ability to talk to other computers via the telephone. Why, you might ask, would any small businessperson or professional be interested in that? The simple answer is that those other computers your machine would be talking to contain information that you can use.

We can start with an easy example. Imagine that you're a doctor with a patient who has a certain condition. It is not a condition you've seen before, though you think you know what it is. To get more information, you fire up your computer, tell it to dial the phone, and use it to search the National Library of Medicine's online database, Medline.

In seconds, the distant computer will have located all the most recent medical journal articles on the condition. You tap a few keys, and three minutes later, your printer is producing the last of five articles you have requested from the distant database. Your total cost for this computerized search and information: less than $3.50.

The remarkable thing is that the online system I have in mind here, Knight-Ridder's Knowledge Index, is available to anyone, and Medline is but one of the nearly 100 databases it offers. Topics covered include agriculture, arts, biology, chemistry, computers, economics, education, engineering, environmental sciences, food science, legal information, mathematics, religion, and social sciences.

There is also a great deal of corporate information provided by Standard & Poor's, *Who's Who*, *Consumer Reports*, the National Technical Information Service (NTIS), the *Harvard Business Review*, newspapers like the *Los Angeles Times* and the *Philadelphia Inquirer*, plus databases to help you locate any book currently in print or any U.S. Government publication. The cost is a flat rate of $24 an hour, rounded up to the nearest minute.

Knowledge Index is only one of over 500 online systems which, together, offer over 4000 individual databases. It is only a slight exaggeration to say that you can find out just about anything you might want to know by tapping the keys of your personal computer, once it is hooked up to the phone line.

Access to experts and friends

You will almost certainly use your system to tap some remote database every now and again. But for many small business owners and professionals, it is the people-to-people communication PCs make possible that is most useful of all. For example, suppose you and your spouse run a bed and breakfast (B&B) operation out of your rambling, historic home in Vermont. Like all businesspeople, you've got a host of concerns and problems.

Friends, neighbors, and others can be helpful. But there's nothing like comparing notes with other B&B operators. What do you do about guests who cancel at the last minute? Is it worth installing Jacuzzis in every room, and, if so, what's it likely to cost? Would anyone be willing to swap a recipe for blueberry muffins for a dynamite cinnamon bun recipe?

We've all got questions like these—questions only someone else who knows the business can answer. Traditionally, conventions and trade shows have provided the only opportunity to really get together and swap tips and tricks. But now, with a communicating computer, you can "meet" with your friends and fellow laborers in the vineyard every day.

Systems like CompuServe and GEnie, for example, offer areas called special interest groups (SIGs) where people who share a common interest can meet. (Both of these systems have SIGs devoted to small business concerns.) Regardless of your geographical location, you can tell your system to dial a local number and check in at your favorite SIG. You can post messages and questions for others to answer; transmit or obtain files from the SIG file library; and "chat" in real time with any number of people, almost as if you were on a CB radio.

Word processing

We've talked about inventory management and receivables control using a database program. We've touched on the "what if" projections one can do with an electronic spreadsheet. And we've taken a brief peek at the vista that opens up to you once you begin using computer communications. The last of what we can call "The Big Four Computer Applications" is word processing.

Word processing was the first real personal computer application. Long before "the two Steves" (Steve Wozniak and Steven Jobs) created the Apple I in the Jobs family garage, and long before Dan Bricklin and Bob Frankston created VisiCalc (the spreadsheet program that gave Apple computers their initial success), there were machines called "dedicated word processors." These were actually personal computers optimized for text creation. They did not do *data* processing; they "processed" words.

Technically, word processing software takes advantage of a computer's ability to manipulate information and to crunch numbers. But in laymen's terms, a word processing system (computer, software, and printer) replaces a typewriter. It is thus no surprise that word processing is the most popular of all PC applications. You may not need a spreadsheet, and your paper-based inventory management procedure may be perfectly fine. But, by golly, every business needs a type-writer—or a word processor.

Once around the block

More than likely, you're familiar with word processing in general. But for those who aren't, let me take just a moment to describe what word processing software can do. You load the program; type whatever it is you want to write; and press a button to send a copy of the text to your printer. If you want to print out another copy, just hit the button again, and a second copy will be printed.

If you need to make changes as you write, you can make entire paragraphs, sentences, or words disappear by pressing a few keys. If you need to insert a word or a phrase, you can do so and let the program automatically adjust the text to the margins you have set. At the press of a few other keys, you can tell the program to check the spelling of every word in your document.

You can also quickly and easily produce a whole batch of customized form letters. The first letter might begin "Dear Bob," while the second letter begins "Dear Allison," even though the body copy is identical in both cases. What's more, to perform this magic, you need only create one master copy of the letter. Then, using a "mail merge" option, you can tell the program to fill in the blanks using name, address, and other information from your database program.

A database program like File Express (Chapter 10) and a word processing pro-gram like PC Write (Chapter 9) make it easy to send a personalized letter to every one of your customers, thanking them for their business and expressing hope that they are enjoying the specific product they last purchased from you.

You can send a gentle note to everyone who is 30 days past due and a some-what sterner letter to everyone who is 60 days or more behind, plus a personal-ized "private sale" announcement to your very best customers. Believe me, this is not difficult to do. Once you get it set up, the system will run like clockwork.

Of course, you will also use word processing for routine business correspon-dence. If you've got "boilerplate" paragraphs listing your terms and conditions, you will only need to type those paragraphs once. From then on, they can be "word processed" into any document by tapping a few keys.

As with all the applications discussed here, you will find much more about how to benefit from this "Big Four" application in the chapter devoted to it. But I can't leave the topic of word processing without sharing what I think is one of the neatest things about having most of the documents you create on a computer disk.

A personal note

A lot of words get entered at this keyboard, primarily by me. But whether you do the document creation yourself or have someone to help you, we all share the same problem—finding the information we need when we need it. The traditional answer is a filing system, or, in my case, a "piling system" in which documents are stacked around the office or in spare rooms until they fall over or I find time to file them, whichever comes first.

The problem is, whether they are piled or filed, some documents simply resist being found. But I've learned that often the computer holds the answer. If the document I want is on my hard disk, I can find it in seconds using a little shareware program like Chris Dunford's FGREP.

All I've got to do is run the program, point it at the desired section of my hard disk, and tell it what keyword or phrase I want it to look for. Within seconds of turning it loose, it will show me the name of the file, the keyword or phrase I have told it to look for, and several sentences worth of surrounding words. It's not quite like having all of my filing cabinets on disk, but it's close, and the productivity benefits are enormous.

The competitive edge

In this chapter we have glimpsed the kinds of things you or any other small business owner can expect from a personal computer system. To avoid overwhelming you, the discussion has been limited to the basic topics that apply to every small business—inventory and receivables, financial projections and accounting, text creation, and online information and communication.

The chapter has focused on the Big Four applications of database, spreadsheet, word processing, and data communications, and it has only lightly skimmed the surface of each. As we'll see later, there are many other things you can do with these applications and many other things a computer can do for you and your business.

Still and all, there is no way to definitively demonstrate that acquiring a computer system and learning to use it will give you an edge over your competitors. Indeed, you would be amazed at the number of learned articles that have been written over the past few years on the subject of PCs and productivity gains. Most focus on large corporations, and most conclude that the productivity impact of personal computers is difficult to measure. Any number of explanations are offered, but none of them applies to us, the small business owners of America.

In my opinion, we should forget about all the studies and quantitative analyses and apply a little common sense instead. The facts are these: Personal computers can do all kinds of things faster and more efficiently than you can do them by hand. They are not the best solution for every task, but they have a role to play in even the smallest of small businesses. And, thanks to plummeting hardware prices, every small business worthy of the name can afford a system. Indeed, the shareware discussed in this book makes the hardware even more affordable.

But will a computer give you a competitive edge? Will it help you increase profits? Hold onto your customers? Improve your cash flow? Leaving all the hype aside, the answer is almost certainly "yes," regardless of the business you happen to be in. The only question is one of commitment.

We must all remember that the sun shines on our competitors just as brightly as it does on us. The same hardware and software is available to everyone. So, with hardware prices so low, you can assume that many of your competitors have already acquired systems or are on the verge of doing so. If you don't follow suit, you could easily be left behind.

In a phrase, the game is moving to a new level. I don't want to scare you into getting a system. I have no advertising pages to fill. I'm simply telling it like it is. Wait until you reach the frustration flashpoint. But sooner or later you are bound to conclude that you probably cannot afford *not* to have a computer handling some of your work if you expect to compete effectively.

On a playing field where *everyone* either has a computer or is in the process of buying one, the competitive edge is not going to go to the person who has the hottest machine. The computer itself is not going to make the major difference. What's going to make the difference is *you*.

Those who win the new game are going to be the ones who are committed to doing the most with what they have. The incredible shareware recommended in this book can help you preserve your resources. Its high power and low cost can enable you to buy a more powerful machine or free up money for other needs.

But only *you* can give yourself a competitive edge. I can give you the tools. I can tell you what to get and where to get it. I can give you the fundamental understanding of systems and software you need, without telling you more than you really want or need to know. But only you can apply this information to your own business. No one else can do it for you.

So, with the sermon out of the way, let's get started. Let's look at computer hardware and at the basic information you'll need to get the system that's right for you and your business.

2

Hardware basics

Computer equipment
and how it works

I KNOW THIS IS GOING TO SOUND LIKE COMPUTER GOBBLEDY-GOOK, BUT HERE is a list of the computer hardware components I think you should look for in a system today:

- 386DX 33-MHz (or faster) CPU or a 486-based system
- 4 megs of RAM on the motherboard, expandable to 16 megs or more
- 16-bit Super VGA (SVGA) card and non-interlaced (NI) color monitor
- 120-megabyte 18ms IDE hard drive (or larger)
- 1 high-density (360K/1.2M) 5.25-inch floppy drive
- 1 high-density (720K/1.44M) 3.5-inch floppy drive
- 1 parallel port and 2 serial ports
- HP laser printer or compatible
- Mouse (optional)
- 2400-bps external modem (optional)
- DOS 5.x

At this writing, you can have just such a system, excluding the mouse and modem, for about $2200. You'll pay about $1400 for a 33-MHz 386DX-based computer system and about $800 for the printer. Add a total of about $100 more for the mouse and the modem and you're at $2300 for everything.

Those are the "street" prices at this writing. As you read this, the cost of a system like this will have fallen further still. Indeed, there is every likelihood that you will be able to get a system built around the even more powerful Intel 486 processor for the same amount of money. At this writing, the price difference between identically equipped 386DX and 486SX systems is about $380. In the

13

very near future, according to the market research firm International Data Corporation (IDC), that gap should narrow to about $150.

If the prospect of getting a system like this for $2300 doesn't exactly thrill you, it will by the time you finish reading this and the following chapter for at that point, you will know what the terms ''386DX'' and ''486DX'' actually mean. You will know what all of the terms used above signify. You will be able to translate the typical computer ad. And you will be able to walk into a computer store with confidence.

Battle plan for understanding

Since I don't know how familiar you are with computer hardware, I'm going to present the necessary information in two phases. This chapter is the first phase. Here you will find an overview of the major components of a computer system and learn, in general, how they work. We'll cover the basics here and try to avoid burdening you with confusing details. Chapter 3, ''What to look for in a system,'' is the second phase. It builds upon what you will learn here and goes into the specific features you should look for in each component.

If this is your first exposure to personal computing, take it nice and slow. Read this chapter through the first time without trying to understand everything. Then read it through again and see if things don't start falling into place for you. Then go on to Chapter 3. When you are ready to actually begin shopping for a system, use the summary of all the various features and specifications provided in Chapter 5, ''How to buy the system you need.'' We've called it, logically enough, the Computer Shopper's Guide.

Software considerations

There is one other point to make while laying out this battle plan for understanding, and that has to do with software. You will find software basics like DOS and Windows and system memory management programs covered in Chapter 4. It is impossible to separate hardware and software completely, however. Thus, you will encounter some software references in these two hardware chapters.

If this is your first encounter with the field, you need to know two things about software at this point. First, DOS (pronounced ''doss'') is the operating system software that ties all of a computer's hardware components together. DOS is always loaded first. And, in general, the only way either you or an applications program can get to the hardware is to go through DOS. The version of DOS current at this writing is DOS 5.0, though 5.1 is expected shortly. You should insist on nothing less than DOS 5.0 or higher.

Second, Microsoft Windows is an operating ''environment'' that loads in on top of DOS. (In the future, Windows is likely to become a full-fledged operating system itself.) Windows is designed to let people use their computers by moving a pointer around the screen with a mouse and ''clicking'' on little pictures called *icons*.

Windows uses lots of memory and hard disk space and requires the kind of hardware components listed above for effective operation. In general, Windows is designed to make IBM-compatible computers imitate an Apple Macintosh.

The case for IBM-compatible clone computers

Speaking of which, we owe it to you to explain why we've recommended buying an IBM-compatible "clone" computer. Certainly anyone looking at equipment today has to consider Apple's Macintosh. And, for that matter, what about IBM's PS/2 line?

Let's take a look at these topics now.

Why not a Macintosh?

As you may know, the personal computer marketplace is divided broadly into two camps: Those who use IBM-compatible "DOS" machines and those who use the Apple Macintosh. There are far more of the former than the latter, but it is certainly a fair question to ask why a small business owner should opt for an IBM-compatible over a Mac.

The answer is in the last part of that sentence. You'll frequently hear the term "IBM-compatible," but you will never hear of "Mac-compatible" machines. That's because there aren't any. The Macintosh is a fine computer. Indeed, if your small business is rooted in the graphic arts or if you plan to do a great deal of desktop publishing, you absolutely must give the Mac line very strong consideration.

In fact, if you had a large company with many different needs, you would probably get Apple equipment for some departments and IBM-compatibles for others. As good as they are with graphics, for example, Macintoshes are notoriously slow with spreadsheet applications, unless you add a chip called a "math coprocessor," and not all Macintosh models can accept such a chip.

For a small business owner, however, there simply isn't a choice. In plain language, the Macintosh is a monopoly. Apple, the company that has long portrayed itself as fighting for "the rest of us" against the dictates of an all-powerful Big Brother (IBM), has vigorously quashed any attempts to produce Macintosh clones. If you want a Mac, you've got to go to Apple, and you've got to pay whatever price they choose to charge.

Why not an IBM PS/2?

In the IBM-compatible marketplace, in contrast, there is so much competition that commodity pricing rules the day. In classic Big Brother fashion, IBM attempted to correct this situation by introducing its PS/2 line of equipment several years ago. The original PS/2s were not compatible with the IBMs that had come before. Most models still aren't today.

IBM's concept was to introduce a new standard that incorporated a number of improvements over the original design. But, unlike the original design, the new standard would be heavily protected by copyrights and patents. IBM would license the design to anyone who wanted to produce compatible equipment. But IBM would control things, much as it had long controlled things in the mainframe world.

Unfortunately for IBM, a funny thing happened on the way to getting the horses back into the barn. For some perverse reason, users balked at the idea of throwing out perfectly good add-on cards and other computer equipment—none of which could be used with the new standard—to voluntarily return to the tender mercies of a newly proprietary IBM. Particularly since the benefits offered by the new PS/2 design, while real, weren't really important to most users.

Summarizing the case for clones

By getting a so-called IBM clone computer of the sort recommended at the beginning of this chapter, you will not only get a great deal for your money, you won't have to give up a thing. Today, there is nothing you can do on a Macintosh that you can't also do on an IBM clone. As for the Macintosh's much-advertised ease of use, it is worth taking that claim with a large dose of salt. There is a certain basic quantum of knowledge one must have to use a computer, and at that level, the two machines aren't all that different.

If you're intrigued by the possibility of using a mouse to move around the screen and "click" on various pictographic icons, take a look at Microsoft's Windows operating environment for IBM-compatible machines. It is no accident that Windows makes an IBM-compatible look like a Mac—so much so that Apple has sued Microsoft over this very point.

The IBM PS/2, like the Mac, is a monopoly. IBM has succeeded in pushing large numbers of these machines into its corporate accounts, but very few hardware manufacturers have taken the company up on its offer to license the technology. At this writing, several years after the PS/2 design was introduced, there is absolutely no movement in the market toward the PS/2 standard. (The IBM PS/1 being sold through Sears and other mass market retailers is generally underpowered and overpriced. It is not something one can recommend for business use.)

A strange combination

Apple and IBM are the two companies that founded the personal computer business, but the role they will play in the market in the future has never been more uncertain. The breathless pace of technology and the relentless decline in prices and margins, combined with a large assortment of management blunders, have driven the two firms, if not to the wall, then at least into each other's arms. In 1991, Apple and IBM agreed to begin joint development of new computer designs and operating system software. It isn't clear what the issue of this marriage will be, or even if the marriage itself will last.

What is clear, both now and for the foreseeable future, is that you can't lose by getting an IBM-compatible "DOS machine" of the sort recommended here. For $2300 (or less) you'll have a system with power to spare. By the time something else does come along, the machine will not only have paid for itself many times over, you will have written it off or fully depreciated it. And, since computer equipment tends not to wear out, it will still be as good as new.

Laying the foundation

This chapter is designed for people who know little or absolutely nothing about personal computer hardware. Its goal is to convey general concepts of how computer hardware works and how the various components work together. You'll find that computers are really a lot simpler, in general terms, than you imagined.

We will look at the central processing unit that really is the essence of any computer, the data bus circuitry it plugs into, memory and built-in BIOS software, the keyboard, video equipment, and hard and floppy disks. Then we will discuss printers, particularly laser printers, modems, and mice. In other words, we're going to go right down the list of components recommended at the beginning of this chapter.

The one item on that list we are not going to cover here is DOS 5.x. We'll get to that and the other software you may find "bundled" with a system in Chapter 4. The chapter closes with a look at the various options open to you regarding your system's "form factor" (case size and design).

Think of this chapter as a general sketch to show you the lay of the land. Think of it as a foundation for understanding the more detailed information presented about these same topics in Chapter 3.

The microprocessor or CPU

The heart of every computer is a chip called a *microprocessor*. This is a tiny sliver of silicon no bigger than your fingernail that has been packed with nearly 300,000 to over a million transistors. Like the vacuum tubes that preceded them, transistors control the flow of electricity. All microprocessors have certain configurations of transistors "hard-wired" into them that are designed to produce certain results when activated. The chips also have many transistors that can be turned on or off, depending on the state of other transistors.

A microprocessor is essentially a collection of switches, some sequences of which are hard-wired into a particular pattern and some of which can be opened or closed at will to produce different results. Thus, in the most basic sense, what a microprocessor "processes" is electricity. You pour in one pattern of electrical on/off pulses, turn the processor's crank, and out flows a different pattern.

The pulses themselves are two different voltage levels, each of which exists for a set amount of time determined by a clock of some sort. The amount of time a pulse exists is measured in nanoseconds (billionths of a second), and the microprocessor's clock rate is measured in megahertz (millions of cycles per second), abbreviated MHz.

A computer's processor is usually called its *central processing unit* or CPU. CPUs differ in many important ways. Some operate faster than others. Some have more capabilities hard-wired into them. And each has its own unique way of doing things. This is important because the CPU really *is* the computer. Everything else in the machine, from hardware to software, must be designed to work with it.

The two leading makers of personal computer CPUs are Motorola, which manufactures the line of processors used in Macintosh machines, and Intel, which makes the CPUs used in IBM-compatible equipment. Intel has licensed IBM to manufacture some CPUs, and a company called Advanced Micro Devices (AMD) has successfully cloned some Intel chips. Other companies (NexGen, Chips and Technologies, and Cyrix Corporation) are trying their hand at creating clone chips as well. But Intel is far and away the market leader.

Though it would be possible to give every machine a different kind of CPU, doing so would eliminate compatibility. So CPU chips are produced in "families." The original IBM/PC was built around the Intel 8088, a member of the Intel family founded by the 8086 processor. Succeeding generations included the 80286 (AT-level machines), the 80386, and the 80486. The Intel 80586 is on the way at this writing, and an 80686 is already being designed. The family as a whole is referred to as the "80x86 architecture." The "x" here stands for anything from nothing (8086) to 2, 3, 4, or some other single digit. Often, the line will be referred to as the "X86" family.

It is a small point, but 8088 and 8086 are pronounced "eighty eighty-eight" and "eighty eighty-six," respectively. However, in the model numbers that followed, the "80" is pronounced "eight-oh," as in "eight-oh-three-eighty-six." Typically, though, computer users drop the "80" and refer to chips as a 286, 386, 486, etc.

Each new chip generation offers more speed and power, but all maintain "downward compatibility" with the family members that came before. That means that you can run the same programs designed for an original IBM/PC on the latest equipment, though you may not be able to run programs designed for the latest equipment on an old PC or XT.

The motherboard

The CPU is normally located on a large circuit board called the *motherboard*. The motherboard has "expansion slots" into which you can plug other circuit boards, like the circuit board or "card" that drives your monitor. Motherboards also have sockets designed to accept various add-on chips. Today, many motherboards also have sockets into which you can plug not only your keyboard, but your printer, modem, disk drive cables, and even your color monitor.

The advantage of building more and more functions into the motherboard is that it keeps *OEM* costs (and presumably the prices they charge) down. "OEM" stands for "Original Equipment Manufacturer," the industry's term for mail order companies and others who assemble computers. The more functions each component can provide, the fewer the number of components, and the lower the labor costs in assembling an OEM machine.

Table 2-1. All in the Intel 80x86 family.

The following table is designed to help you make sense of the Intel processor numbers you will read about. The table includes only some of the leading members of the family. I've left out all the math coprocessor chips designed to work with many of these members, for example. So I will simply note that anytime you see an Intel chip ending in `` 87,'' as in 8087 or 80487, it's a good bet the chip has something to do with math processing.

The chip's birth year is important because it shows you how old some of the ``latest technology'' being pushed today really is. In the computer field, a year is like a decade to other industries. Power, speed, and features increase that fast--while the prices keep going down. And they say there are no more American success stories!

Official Name	Nickname	Birth Year	Comments
8088	none	1978	IBM/PC and IBM/XT models; can use only 1M of memory. Top speed: 4.77 MHz.
8086	none	1978	Some clone XTs; PS/2 Models 25 and 30; essentially a bit faster version of the 8088.
80286	286	1982	IBM/AT and AT clones; PS/2 Models 50 and 60; a stop-gap chip that experts have called ``brain dead.'' Avoid it.
80386DX	386DX	1985	The new minimum business standard. A major step forward. PS/2 Models 70 and 80, and lots of clones. Can use 4 gigabytes of memory. Current top speed: Intel version--33 MHz; AMD clone version--40 Mhz.
80386SX	386SX	1988	Current ``entry'' level chip. Limited to 16M of memory; but not really much cheaper than the 386DX. Will probably disappear soon, except for use in laptops.
80486DX	i486, 486DX	1989	The business standard to come, if it isn't already here as you read this. Far more power than most small businesses need, but irresistible when cheap enough. The ``i'' in the name simply stands for ``Intel.''
80486SX	486SX	1991	A 486DX chip with the math section disabled or removed. As discussed in Chapter 3, this is probably the chip you should start with today.
80586	586	coming	More speed; more power; but, as with the 386 and 486, there is no software to take advantage of it all! (Yet.)

The disadvantage of this kind of integration is that it reduces your flexibility. If you later opt for better video performance than is provided by your motherboard's built-in circuitry, you will have to disable that feature and buy a separate add-on card. You will thus sacrifice one of the capabilities you paid for when you bought the system. You might have to follow the same approach if one of the built-in features conks out on you. Or you may find that you will have to replace the entire motherboard.

I'm not saying avoid systems with highly integrated motherboards. Indeed, if you opt for a "slim-line" system that takes up a minimum amount of space on your desktop, you may have no choice. But I think it's important to be aware of the dangers of having most of your eggs in the same basket.

The data and memory buses

The motherboard also contains the "data highways" the CPU uses to communicate with the system's various components. In computer terms, these highways are called the *data bus* and the *memory bus*. We'll have more to say about data and memory buses in Chapter 3. Right now, you need to know that a key characteristic is the width of the bus—the number of lanes in the highway.

Microprocessors are designed to process a certain number of electrical pulses simultaneously. These are the on/off pulses mentioned earlier. They are called *bits*, a contraction of the phrase "binary digit." Bits are what travel to and fro along the data and memory buses, and they always travel in parallel formation, like a squadron of jets streaking across the sky.

Early microprocessors were designed to process eight bits simultaneously. That meant the motherboard had to have buses eight-bits wide, like an eight-lane highway. The processor in the original IBM/PC could handle 16 bits at a time. But, to keep costs down, IBM used a version of the chip designed to plug into an eight-bit bus. In technical terms, that meant that two clock cycles—two separate operations—were needed to supply the CPU with 16 bits.

The next advance was a machine with both a 16-bit processor, the Intel 80286, and 16-bit-wide data and memory buses. This was the IBM/AT, introduced in 1984. It is the AT that is responsible for the most popular bus design used today. But technology marched on and produced the Intel 80386, a processor designed to handle 32 bits at once.

For reasons we don't need to get into right now, the 386 was a major step forward, so significant that I'm not sure I could ever advise you to use a machine based on a lesser chip, even if someone wanted to give it to you free of charge. In marketing 386 systems, IBM and Intel used essentially the same trick used with the original PC.

Two main versions of the 386 exist. The 386SX is designed to plug into a 16-bit bus system and bring information into itself as two 16-bit chunks. (The "SX" in its name actually stands for "sixteen.") The 386DX, in contrast, is designed to use a 16-bit data bus and a full 32-bit-wide memory bus. Internally, both chip models are identical. Systems based on the 386SX are a little slower due to the two-step data fetching operation and a little cheaper due to the use of 16-bit circuitry.

The next step forward was the Intel 80486. This chip is even more incredible than the 386. "The raw CPU performance of the i486 is comparable to the raw CPU power of the 3090 IBM mainframe," according to Intel official Bill Rash [*Lotus*, August, 1989]. It's got 1.2 million transistors, a built-in 8K cache (explained in Chapter 3), and a built-in math coprocessor. At this writing, versions of the 486 exist that run anywhere from 16 to 50 MHz, but even faster models are on the way.

There are two main versions of the 486. The 486DX is the chip complete with math coprocessor. The 486SX is the chip without the math coprocessor or with the coprocessor disabled. Due to the increased efficiency of its design, a 486 can accomplish more during each clock cycle than can a 386. Consequently, at least when running software designed to take advantage of its 32-bit architecture, a 486 can be as much as 45 percent faster than a 386 of the same speed.

You'll find more details in Chapter 3. But the bottom line will remain the same. Most small businesses can get by with less than a 386, but there are sound technical reasons to accept nothing less. Similarly, few small businesses need or will ever really use the power of a 486. But prices keep coming down.

All indications are that Intel plans to make 486-based systems very, very attractive. If at the time you're shopping for a computer, a 486 system is only $200 or so more than a comparable 386 system, I'd say buy it. The extra performance is worth it, and you will be well-positioned for the next wave of software that is on the way. You'll also be able to take advantage of the 486 processor upgradability (see Chapter 3 for more details on this).

Megabytes and memory

The 386 and 486 are true 32-bit chips. I should emphasize that both chips talk to most system components along an AT-style 16-bit data bus. However, they use a 32-bit bus to converse with the system's random access memory or *RAM*. "Full-bore" memory access is crucial because a processor spends most of its working time moving information in and out of memory.

Computer memory is like a seemingly endless wall of tiny pigeonholes, each of which accommodates a single bit of data. In broad technical terms, each memory cell is a switch that can be set on or off, depending on the pattern of current that most recently moved through it. The resulting settings preserve the pattern of voltage pulses. That's how "information" is stored.

Memory capacity is usually measured in kilobytes or megabytes. A *byte* is a unit of eight bits. No one is quite certain where the term came from. But a collection of eight bits is a natural unit since, under the coding system computers use to communicate with human beings, eight bits are required to represent an alphabetic or numeric ("alphanumeric") character. There are other reasons as well, but, in general, you can't go far wrong if you think of one byte as equivalent to one alphanumeric character.

A kilobyte (K) is actually 1024 bytes, but think of it as one thousand bytes. And think of a megabyte (M) as one million bytes. More important still, think of your system's RAM as the CPU's storage area. This storage area is used to hold both programs and data.

Thus, when you load a program from disk, you are actually copying on/off bit patterns from the disk into RAM. When you run a program, you tell the CPU to treat these particular patterns as instructions and to behave accordingly. As a result of following these program instructions, the CPU typically processes the data you give it when you tap keys at your keyboard or use some other "input" device.

That processed data has got to be stored someplace, and the CPU certainly doesn't have room for it. So the data is stored in RAM, prior to being saved to disk. Some programs automatically save processed data to disk; others require a command from you.

Admittedly, this is a simplistic explanation. But the point is clear: The more RAM you have, the more programs and data you can load into your system at one time. In very general terms, that means convenience and speed. In some cases, it means you can switch from one application to another instantly—at the speed of light—with no requirement to close down one program before starting another.

That's just about all you need to know about system memory at this point. But I should note here that one of the things that distinguishes CPU models is the amount of memory they can use or "address." Also, one of the things that distinguishes motherboards is how much memory they can hold. The software, particularly the operating system software, is also a crucial factor.

To cut to the chase, memory is cheap—about $40 per megabyte. But a 386DX processor can directly address more memory than you can afford to stick into your computer, even if there were room to hold it all. With a 386 or 486 processor, four megabytes of RAM, and Microsoft's DOS 5, you are likely to have all the power and capacity you need.

Most motherboards today can hold at least 16 megabytes of RAM, while some can be expanded to 32, 64, or even 96 megabytes. Older motherboards are limited to 4 to 8 megabytes. Though you can almost always add memory via a separate add-on card, it just makes good sense to get a system with a motherboard with room for at least 8, and preferably 16 or even 64 megabytes.

A word about the BIOS

At this point you've got a pretty good basic understanding of personal computer operations. You know that the CPU is the heart of the matter, and you have a general idea of what it does and the role it plays. Before moving on to the other major system components, however, it is important for you to know about the "basic input/output system" or *BIOS*.

The BIOS is a set of rudimentary programs frozen in silicon and socketed into a computer's motherboard. It has a number of responsibilities. Chief among them is coordinating the activities of all the various hardware components, including the CPU. Indeed, one can almost say that the BIOS provides a harness for the raw horsepower of the CPU. It lets your software drive the system and make it go where it is supposed to go.

As you may have noticed, throughout our discussion so far I have repeatedly referred to bits and voltage pulses. Voltage pulses are the only "language" that CPUs and other computer hardware understand. The gulf between an on/off pulse and a human command like "COPY" is enormous. It is filled by layer after layer of software, and the BIOS is a crucial step along the way.

Thus, the programs frozen in the BIOS chips on your motherboard "plug into" system hardware. The operating system software, like Microsoft's DOS 5, "plugs into" the BIOS. And applications software like PC-Write or File Express "plugs into" the operating system software.

It's like the famous Tinker-to-Evers-to-Chance triple play combination that so wowed baseball fans many years ago. You tap a key to send it to PC-Write, PC-Write passes the signal to DOS, DOS passes it to the BIOS software, and the BIOS tells your video hardware to display the character on the screen. The BIOS can do this because it knows all the nitty-gritty details of how to put a character on the screen.

PCs operate so quickly that this combination of software layers causes no delay in most cases. But it exists all the same. This is an important concept because it means that an applications programmer does not need to worry about hardware specifics. All he's got to do is write a program designed to talk to the operating system: "Here, DOS, put this character on the user's screen." The operating system tells the BIOS what to do, and the BIOS takes care of the specific details.

The key benefit of this modular "adapter plug" approach is flexibility. For example, if everyone who wrote a word processing program had to worry about the details required to address every video card, very few word processing programs would be written. They would be horrendously expensive, and they would have to be rewritten every time a new piece of video equipment was introduced. Multiply this situation by all the other hardware components and the tens of thousands of computer programs, and you can see what a mess things would be.

With a modular approach, accommodating hardware changes is fairly simple. Only the affected modules need to be modified or changed. As long as the modified module presents the same interface to the module that plugs into it, no one will be the wiser. In other words, there is no need to forge a completely new chain when you can modify a single link.

Keyboard considerations

Now let's look briefly at how the other equipment in a standard computer system fits into the picture. Keyboards are essentially a non-issue—virtually all systems today come with a "101" keyboard that sports 101 keys, instead of the 83 or fewer keys used in the past. Basically, this means you'll have 12 function keys (F-keys) and a set of cursor-control ("arrow") and paging keys that is separate from the numeric keypad. Earlier keyboards used the keys on the numeric keypad for both adding-machine-style number entry and cursor control. Incidentally, the little bump on the 5 key serves as a reference point for those who can use a keypad without looking at the keys.

To switch between number and cursor control functions, you toggle the NumLock key on or off. The 101 keyboards continue to offer this keypad/cursor control option. But they also include the dedicated cursor control keys that can be found between the typewriter and numeric keypads.

Keyboard design is fairly standard. The only major variation among them is the location of the function keys. Some designers string all 12 function keys across the top. Others place them in a double row down the left side. Personally, I prefer to have the function keys in two rows on the left side, where God intended them to be. But then again, I use my keyboard so much that I tend to be very particular about its layout and "feel."

You may have no feelings one way or another. Which is a good thing, since usually you don't get any choice in the matter of keyboards when you buy a system. Frankly, some of them can be a bit junky. Fortunately, if you find the keyboard supplied by your vendor is not up to snuff, you can buy a really good keyboard as a separate component.

I've found the OmniKey keyboards from Northgate Computer Systems [(800) 828-6125] to be exceptional, for example. I've also heard good things about Data-Desk equipment [(800) 328-2337]. These companies can sell you a top-quality keyboard for less than $100. And, while you would never want to choose a computer system package on the basis of the keyboard, if your vendor specifies that a Northgate or other brand-name keyboard is included, it could be a sign that he really cares about quality components.

The video equipment jungle

Video equipment—your video card and monitor—used to be simple. It used to be that you bought an IBM monochrome display adapter (MDA) and monitor, which offered great one-color text resolution but could not do graphics, or you bought a color graphics adapter (CGA) which did color and graphics but was less than ideal for text. Then a company called Hercules Computer Technology, Inc., introduced a monochrome card that offered both sharp text and graphics.

IBM's Enhanced Graphics Adapter (EGA) standard was next. Then came the Video Graphics Array (VGA) standard, introduced with the PS/2. And the Multi-Color Graphics Array (MCGA), a subsystem originally built into PS/2 Models 25 and 30 that supports the old CGA standard and part of the VGA standard (but not EGA). These days, the standard is Super VGA (SVGA), though the term is loosely applied to any system offering better resolution and more colors than VGA. Beyond that, there are the 8514-compatible systems that offer even more resolution and color, and IBM's XGA standard for high-end PS/2 models.

If you think all this is confusing, wait until you plunge into the mysteries of aspect ratio, frame rate, bandwidth, and horizontal retrace delay. Not to mention the difference between digital, analog, and multi-frequency monitors. In a word, video equipment isn't simple anymore.

Pixels and dot pitch

Monitors operate like televisions. An electron gun at the back fires a beam at the front of the picture tube. The inner surface of the tube is coated with phosphors which glow in different colors when stimulated by the incoming electrons.

The phosphors, of course, are not applied at random. Indeed, the entire screen is divided up into discrete triads of red, green, and blue phosphor dots. The smaller the dots, the sharper the resolution of the monitor. For reasons we don't need to get into, dot size is referred to as *dot pitch*. A dot pitch of 0.31 millimeters (.31mm) is the minimum acceptable. For resolutions of 1024×768, you will need a monitor with a dot pitch of 0.28mm or smaller.

Video resolution is measured in picture elements or *pixels*. A pixel (or "pel" in IBM-speak) is the smallest screen area that can be independently controlled. Resolution is measured in horizontal and vertical pixels. VGA resolution, for example, is 640 horizontal pixels by 480 vertical pixels. Super VGA, it is generally agreed, offers at least 800×600, but the term may also be used to describe equipment offering 1024×768.

There is much more to it than this. Among other things, most video cards can operate in a variety of modes or resolutions. The number of colors they can display varies with the mode and with the amount of memory on the card. But, regardless of a card's capabilities, you won't be able to fully benefit from them unless your monitor is capable of displaying everything the card puts out.

Table 2-2. A quick guide to the video jungle.

For your convenience, here is a quick run-down of the main video adapter cards and formats you will hear bandied about. I've deliberately left out many of the resolution figures since, frankly, who cares? It is impossible to really know what they mean anyway.

The key thing, at this writing, is to get a Super VGA system (video card and monitor)--unless you have a genuine need (and some serious money) for "1024x768" resolution equipment.

Blasts from the Past

MDA   *Monochrome Display Adapter*
The original 1981 IBM/PC video card; good text; no graphics.

CGA   *Color Graphics Adapter*
Your other option in 1981; state-of-the-art color and graphics at the time; but lousy text resolution.

HGC   *Hercules Graphics Card*
The leading third-party solution in the early Eighties: An MDA clone with graphics.

MCGA   *Multi-Color Graphics Array*
Found on PS/2 Models 25 and 30; kind of a combination of the CGA and VGA. VGA resolution, but only with no more than two colors.

EGA   *Enhanced Graphics Adapter*
Introduced in 1984. Can emulate CGA and MDA, with other modes. Forget it.

Today's Leaders

VGA   *Video Graphics Array*
The minimum standard today. Sharp text, great graphics, lots and lots of colors (depending on how much memory you put on your VGA board).

SVGA   *Super VGA*
What you should start with if you are buying your first system. Does everything that VGA does, plus at least one mode of even higher resolution. Some SVGA equipment goes even higher than that. There is no clearly defined "Super VGA" standard. It is whatever the marketplace currently says it is.

8514/A   *Coprocessor-equipped "video accelerator" card*
A video board sporting its own microprocessor that boosts speed by taking some of the burden off the CPU; named after a product introduced by IBM. Offers 1024x768 resolution with 256 colors.

XGA   *Extended Graphics Array*
Currently available only in IBM PS/2s equipped with a 386 or better. Uses a coprocessor for speed. Offers 1024x768 resolution, but, at present, only in the flicker-prone ``interlaced'' video format discussed in Chapter 4.

In my opinion, you can save yourself a lot of trouble and endless frustration if you simply opt for a Super VGA system and let the vendor be responsible for making sure card and monitor match. Color is such an essential part of computing today that I wouldn't consider a monochrome system, even if I could save a hundred bucks or so. The only real issue is whether to get a VGA or a Super VGA.

The video cards themselves are cheap—about $125 for a basic SVGA card with one megabyte of RAM at this writing. An SVGA monitor, "non-interlaced" (which means no flicker), capable of displaying 1024×768 pixels costs about

$390. At this writing, you can save about $120 by opting for a plain VGA monitor (640×480), but that might be penny-wise and pound-foolish. Plain VGA is very, very good but you're going to have your monitor for a long time, and that extra "super" resolution can make a difference, particularly if you decide to use Windows or some other graphics-based program.

Besides, if you buy your Super VGA monitor as part of a package, as is likely, you won't have to worry about the technical details of matching monitors and video cards for some time to come. If your budget is really tight, you might consider a monochrome VGA monitor for about $125. This kind of equipment usually is not offered in a mail-order package, but a good computer dealer will be able to include it in a package you buy from him.

Finally, the one thing you will want to be sure to ask about is whether the video card is an 8-bit or a 16-bit card. This refers to the width of its data bus. You can plug an 8-bit card into a 16-bit data bus, and it will work just fine. In fact, many systems include one or more add-on card expansion slots on their motherboards that only offer an 8-bit connection. The problem is that an 8-bit video card is noticeably slower than a 16-bit card, since the data "opening" is only half as wide. Most systems today come with 16-bit cards, but it doesn't hurt to ask.

Information storage

Remember the CPU and the patterns of electrical pulses it processes? Remember RAM chips and how they store patterns of pulses by being either "on" or "off?" Well, the problem with RAM is that when you turn the power off, the patterns it holds disappear. That proposal you just prepared with your word processing software exists only as a pattern of on/off switch settings in RAM. If you ever want to see your proposal again, you had better find a way of storing that pattern in a more permanent fashion. "Permanent" storage is what hard and floppy disks are all about.

Now I want you to think about this for just a minute. Don't worry about exactly how a computer translates an eight-bit byte of on-and-off pulses into an alphanumeric character that you and I can make sense of. We humans have our ways; computers have theirs. So take this capability as a given.

Now make a conceptual leap. All that matters to a computer is that you feed it a pattern consisting of two and only two elements. Black dots and white dots; punched holes and spots where no hole has been punched; pits and level spots; or spots of magnetic tape that are either magnetized or not magnetized.

Computers, in other words, are not limited to dealing with electrical voltage levels. With the proper hardware and software, they can read and save information in many different ways. Only two things matter. The first is that at any given moment the computer is looking at a specific area, and the second is that the condition of this narrow area of focus be either one thing or the other.

The process works because we all agree that the area of focus *must* be either this or that. There is no in-between. There are no shades of gray. Either a hole has been punched in the focus area or it hasn't. Either the focus area consists of a pit or it is level with the surface. Either the focus area has been magnetized or it hasn't. And so on.

Believe it or not, you now know how all computer storage systems work. Punched cards, magnetic tape, punched paper or Mylar tape, CD-ROMs, floppy disks, and hard disk drives—one way or another, all of them preserve the "either/ or" patterns computers use to store information.

Hard drive and floppy disks

Thus, as I said earlier, when you load a program from disk, the machine reads the patterns the disk contains and duplicates those patterns in random access memory. And when you record something on disk, the patterns in RAM are duplicated on the disk's magnetic media. In RAM, the patterns exist as on/off switch settings. On disk, they exist as magnetized or non-magnetized focus areas. But the means and media don't matter. All that matters is the pattern.

The advantages of storing programs and information on disk are obvious. Disks are permanent, at least until they are erased or re-recorded, and they are portable. Conceptually, the only qualities that separate disk storage alternatives are capacity and access speed. Thus floppy disks can hold anywhere from 360K to 720K to 1.44M or more. Hard disks can hold anywhere from 10 megabytes to 1 gigabyte (one billion bytes) or more. And every hard disk is faster at reading and writing information than any floppy.

How hard disks work

At the beginning of this chapter, I suggested a "120 megabyte IDE hard drive." I'll explain why you should have a drive of this size and what "IDE" means in Chapter 3. What you need to know right now is that drives of this sort, indeed any hard drive, consist of a stack of platters coated with a magnetic substance. The platters are on a spindle that turns them at 3600 revolutions per minute or more, and they are in a sealed unit to prevent dust, pollen, and smoke particles from entering.

Information is read from and written to the platters by a comb-like arrangement of read/write heads. These heads are conceptually similar to the heads in a tape deck. There is at least one head on the tip of each tooth of the "comb." Each head mates with one side of a platter, and the comb arrangement darts in and out of the platter stack to move its heads to specific parts of the disks. The heads literally fly above the platters, becoming airborne once the spindle gets up to speed. The heads are so close to the platter surface that even something as tiny as a smoke particle can act as a roadblock.

Floppy considerations

Floppy disks operate on the same general principle, but they are much slower and hold much less information. Two sizes and four formats are in general use. Size-wise, there are 5.25″ and 3.5″ floppies. Sometimes the former are called "disks," while the latter are called "diskettes," but few people in real life make that semantic distinction. Both sizes consist of floppy circles of Mylar or some equally tough plastic coated with a substance similar to that used for audio tape. The 3.5″ size, introduced a couple of years after the 5.25″, has the advantage of being less destructible (because of its hard plastic case) and can actually hold more data than a 5.25″ floppy.

There are two types of 5.25″ disks and two types of 3.5″ disks, each of which is usually designated "high" and "low" density. If you buy a high-density 5.25″ drive and a high-density 3.5″ drive, you will be able to read and write all four formats, since the drives are downward compatible. Low-density 5.25″ disks can hold 360K; the high-density version can hold 1.2M. Low-density 3.5″ disks can hold 720K, while the high-density version can hold 1.44M.

Disks that are designed for high-density storage actually have a thicker coating of magnetic substance than low-density media, though you cannot tell by looking at the plastic disk itself. Indeed, there is no way to tell that one 5.25″ disk is designed for high-density storage and another is not, unless you have a disk label to tip you off. In contrast, a low-density 3.5″ disk has only one hole in its plastic case, while the high-density version has two. This makes it easy for both you and the drive to tell the difference.

Printers, laser and otherwise

Viewed from one perspective, a printer is nothing more than a translation device. A printer receives a pattern of voltage pulses from your system unit, and it translates them into alphanumeric characters. There are all kinds of ways this can be done, but the result is always text printed on paper. Printers can also produce graphic images by duplicating on paper the on/off patterns (bits) stored in your system's video memory.

Dot-matrix and ink-jet printers

There are at least three technologies currently used to produce printed output. The first is *dot-matrix* printing. A dot-matrix printer forms letters with a printhead that consists of a tower of wires. At any given moment, some of the wires are pushed forward and some remain in hiding. When the printhead is hit from behind by a hammer, the protruding wires are forced into a ribbon and dots are made on the page. In most cases, several wire or "pin" configurations and several hammer hits are required to form a complete character as the printhead moves across the page.

The quality of the output depends on the number of wires/pins/dots used to form each character. The goal is to produce letters that are at least as crisp as those produced by a typewriter, a device that produces a fully formed letter with each strike of the key. Thus, the more wires or pins the printer uses, the smaller the dots, and the more like "letter quality" typewriting the result appears.

The second technology is *ink-jet* printing. An ink-jet printer makes its dots by spraying tiny droplets of ink on the page. In general, ink-jet printers tend to produce better quality output than dot-matrix printers. But both technologies rely on the inability of the human eye to see the separate dots they use to make their characters.

Laser printing

The third technology is *laser printing*. Here, a laser draws characters on a revolving drum that is nearly identical to the drum used in a photocopier. The drum conveys a charge to the paper passing beneath it, and the charged areas of the paper attract oppositely-charged toner particles. The process finishes with a heat treatment that fuses the particles in place by melting them into the paper.

Laser printing is the most flexible technology and the one that produces the highest quality output. Naturally, it is also the most expensive. But it is not *that* expensive anymore, which is one of the reasons I recommend it. Hewlett Packard (HP) has set the standard in laser printers—it is the one standard that all software programs support—and you can get an HP laser printer (with a toner cartridge) for as little as $790. An HP ink-jet printer sells for about $390 at this writing, and a no-name 24-pin dot-matrix printer can be had for under $200.

Each of these is a viable alternative. But nothing is quieter, faster, or more flexible than a laser printer. And nothing produces a higher quality output. I'm a great believer in what one can call, for lack of a better term, "presentation" on the part of a small business owner. For business correspondence, ink-jet and 24-pin dot-matrix printers are at least marginally acceptable. But one can usually distinguish their output from the output of a laser printer.

It is strictly my opinion, but if you don't need to impress anybody and don't plan to work with detailed graphics, save yourself $600 or so and get a 24-pin dot-matrix printer. Ink-jet printers are very good, but I would save my money until I could afford an HP or HP-compatible laser. When you do get a laser printer, the dot-matrix printer won't go to waste. In most cases, there is no reason why you can't hook both printers up to your system and use each for the most appropriate task. You might use your laser to produce business letters and your dot matrix to pump out continuous form labels, for example.

Parallel and serial ports

Most printers are designed to connect to a system's *parallel port*. As you may have guessed, a parallel port sends out eight bits at a time, in parallel formation. Loosely speaking, eight wires are required to perform this feat. Generally, computer systems can support up to three parallel ports, designated LPT1, LPT2, and LPT3. The "LPT" stands for "line printer," a holdover from mainframe days. Basically, if an ad says a system comes with one parallel port, it means that you can plug in a parallel printer without buying an add-on printer card or "I/O" (input/output) card. This is not a big deal, since I/O cards cost only about $25.

The opposite side of the coin is a *serial port*. Imagine a one-lane tunnel in the middle of an eight-lane highway. Eight cars approach the tunnel at the same time. There is a car in each lane, and they are travelling in parallel formation, eight abreast. But the only way to get through the tunnel is one at a time.

A traffic cop directs the cars into the tunnel, starting with the car in Lane 1, followed by the car in Lane 2, and so on. The eight cars travel through the tunnel as a series, one after the other. On the other side, another traffic cop directs them into eight lanes again, and they continue in parallel formation.

That's how a serial port works. Eight-bit patterns of voltage pulses whiz around in parallel formation along the data bus. But when they are directed to exit through a serial port, a special chip acts as a traffic cop to change their formation into a *series* of bits. The bits travel down a single wire plugged into the serial port. When they reach their destination, another traffic-cop chip gets them organized into a parallel formation again for the rest of their journey. (The other wires in a serial cable are used for printer control signals.)

Serial ports can be used to connect printers. In fact, my HP LaserJet Series II can be configured to accept either parallel or serial input. The most common use for serial ports, however, is to connect mice and modems. Thus, if a system has two serial ports, you should be able to connect one mouse and one modem. IBM-compatible computers can typically support up to four separate serial ports, COM1 through COM4. The "COM" stands for "communications."

Incidently, you will occasionally see systems that include a "game port." This is a port into which you may plug a joystick, a trackball (essentially an inverted mouse), or some other input device required or used by some game software. If you need this capability and the system you want does not have it, you can add a game port card for as little as $25 sometime in the future.

Mice

A mouse is essentially a pointing device. Mice are designed to be held in one hand and moved about the desktop. An arrow or other symbol on the screen tracks with the mouse movement. When the on-screen symbol is located over a particular spot, you click the mouse by pressing the leftmost button, and something happens. If you "double click" (click twice rapidly), something else may happen. The mouse pointer will only show up on programs designed to accept mouse input.

You will need a mouse if you plan to run Windows, a graphics "paint" program, or a desktop publishing program like Ventura. All of these programs can be operated from the keyboard, but a mouse makes them so much easier that the device is nearly essential. Some other programs, both commercial and shareware, will respond to mouse input, if you happen to have one and if you have activated it.

But no program of any sort can completely eliminate the need to use the keyboard. You might be able to "mouse" into your word processing program, for example, but you can't "mouse" the words you intend to type.

There are two ways to connect a mouse to a computer. A serial mouse can be plugged into (what else?) a serial port. A "bus mouse" plugs into a separate mouse add-on card. There is no difference in performance and no difference in the hardware itself, save for the connecting interface.

Most people who run small businesses don't really need a mouse. It's nice if it happens to be included in a package, but it certainly is not essential. The same might be said of modems.

Modems

A modem is a black box with a single purpose. It is designed to convert the voltage pulses whizzing around inside your computer into sound that can be transmitted over the phone lines. It also transforms incoming sound signals into voltage pulses for your machine to process. In a word, a modem provides the interface necessary for one computer to talk to another over the phone lines. The term itself is a contraction of "modulator/demodulator."

Although communications is without a doubt one of the Big Four computer applications, it is the least essential for most small business owners. I say this as the author of several books on the subject. Computer communications and the worlds it opens are two of my favorite subjects. But, realistically, I cannot say that a modem is required equipment for small business.

On the other hand, if communications is an interest, or if a modem is included in the package you plan to buy, there are one or two things you should know. First, modems are rated by the top speed at which they can communicate. Today, I wouldn't consider a modem that operated at less than 2400 bits per second (bps). That's the current standard, though many hobbyists use equipment that operates four or more times faster.

Personally, I like an external modem because most have LED indicator lights that show you what's going on. External modems can also be used with any computer of any type that has a serial port. The difference between an external modem and an internal modem is that an external unit consists of a circuit board in a separate box. An internal unit is essentially that same circuit board designed to be plugged into an expansion slot on your motherboard.

Connecting an external unit involves running a cable from one of your system's serial ports to the modem and plugging the modem box into the phone line. With an internal unit, you plug the phone directly into the end of the card that is accessible via the back of the computer.

In Chapter 12, I'll go into much greater detail about modems and what you can do with them. For now I would simply say that if a modem comes with the hardware package you want to buy, don't worry if it is internal or external. Just make sure that it is rated at 2400 bps or "baud." On the other hand, if you have the option, keep your costs down and do *not* opt for a modem at this time. With very few exceptions, most people who run small businesses can put off learning about communications until they master more basic functions. And, as is always the case, the longer you wait, the lower the price.

Getting down to cases

Finally, there's the matter of the case your computer comes in. In the industry, computers are referred to as "boxes" and "tubes." A *tube* is the display monitor, of course. A *box* is a system unit—the container that holds the motherboard, memory, and disk drives, and into which everything else plugs.

I did not include a box size in my recommendation at the beginning of this chapter because your choice is largely a matter of available office and desktop space and your personal preference. There are four basic styles, or as the industry likes to put it, "form factors": traditional desktop, slim-line, tower, and mini-tower. Naturally, there are slight variations within these main groupings.

Desktop units: traditional and slim-line

In the beginning was the desktop system. It measured about 20″ left-to-right, 15″ front-to-back, and about 5″ top-to-bottom. The system unit had room inside— "drive bays"—for two full-height 5.25″ floppy drives or one full-height hard disk and one 5.25″ floppy drive. There are variations, and disk drive units have shrunk continuously, but all full-sized desktop systems are based on this original model.

The advantages of a full-sized desktop system are plenty of interior room, lots of expansion slots on the motherboard, and easy access to the floppy drives. The disadvantage is the amount of space such boxes occupy. Most are at least 5″ wider than the monitor, and, with their keyboards in front, most occupy a full segment of the typical 30″ deep desk.

The compromise today is the slim-line or "small footprint" system unit. Most are not much wider or deeper than the monitor that sits atop them, and most are less than five inches high. Slim-line system units typically save space by using motherboards with many functions built in. That reduces the need for expansion slots, so they typically do not offer as many as a full-size system. Indeed, slim-line systems often have their add-on cards mounted horizontally instead of vertically to save on height.

Towers and mini-towers

A tower system is a box that is designed to stand on the floor. Imagine rotating a full-size desktop system 90 degrees and standing it on its side, and you will have the concept. Many people do exactly that with their desktop system units, in fact, placing them in the kneehole of a desk. Tower systems, however, usually have room for lots of drives (six to 10). Those drive bays may be occupied by floppy units, an internal tape system for backing up your hard drive, a CD-ROM drive, one or more hard drives, and so on. The motherboards supplied with tower systems also have lots of expansion slots (eight to 12) for add-on cards. They will have heftier power supplies and, often, two fans to keep things cool.

Finally, there are the mini-towers. These cases are designed to sit on the desktop but take up even fewer square feet than a slim-line. They work this magic by building up instead of out. If you were to put most regular tower cases on a desk, you'd have to stand up to insert floppy disks. But with a mini-tower, the drive bays are still easily accessible from your desk chair.

My personal preference is for a full-sized tower system. If such a system were not available, I would opt for a full-sized desktop system and stand it on its end as a pseudo-tower. But then, when I'm in the middle of a project, I make full use of the desktop real estate that I have, often supplementing it with fold-away tables. I want the expansion capacity and room of a large box, but I do not want to have to work around it on my desk. As it is, with either my tower or my up-ended full-size system, I simply lean back and reach down by my right knee to use the floppy drives or the tape backup.

Conclusion

I'll tell you a secret. If you have read this far, you now know more about PCs than 80 percent of the small business owners buying systems today. With the information presented here, you really could go out and buy the system I've recommended and be very satisfied with your purchase, even though we have not gone into all of the details.

However, I want to make sure that you have the tools you need to stand on your own and make your own well-informed decisions. So wait until you have digested Chapter 3 before actively pursuing buying a system. Indeed, if any of the information presented here is unclear to you, wait a day, and then come back and read this chapter again. Make no mistake—there is a lot to absorb. But once you do, you'll be slinging the jargon and speaking computerese with the best of 'em. And, you'll really know what you're talking about!

What to look for in a system

THE PREVIOUS CHAPTER PRESENTED AN OVERVIEW OF THE MAJOR COMPONENTS of any computer system and showed you how each works. In this chapter, we're going to move in for a closer look and present more specific details. This will give you a better understanding of what to buy and why.

It goes without saying that you should have either absorbed or already know the information presented in Chapter 2. If you have any doubts, please go back and read that chapter again. We have a lot of ground to cover here, building on the information presented earlier.

By the time you finish this chapter, you will understand why you should get a 386DX or 486-based machine instead of a bargain-basement 286 or—I cringe to say it—an even cheaper PC/XT-style model. You will know a bit about bus designs, co-processors, SIMMS and SIPS, IDE versus everything else, dots per inch (dpi), and FCC Class B certification. In short, you will have the tools you will need to stand on your own in the PC marketplace.

Let me be the first to say that I wish it were not necessary to be familiar with these terms and the technology behind them. But I'm afraid the market doesn't leave us much choice. Those with bushels of money can afford to call in an electrician, carpenter, or plumber whenever something needs to be done. Those of us who have to watch every dollar must become do-it-yourselfers much of the time.

Fortunately, you do not have to become an expert in computer technology to buy a system. In fact, you'll probably find that most so-called computer experts are merely large egos endowed with the gift of gab. Let them talk. Be humble. Get everything you can out of them. But be skeptical, even if the "expert" is doing his or her talking in a magazine or in a book. Remember, this field is too big and things are moving too fast for anyone to be an expert on everything.

Concentrate instead on the basic information you read here. Then combine it with the articles and reviews of current equipment you will find in leading magazines like *PC, PC Computing, PC World, Computer Shopper*, and others. These two components will give you everything you need.

System components and details

We're going to look at processors, memory, motherboards, and data bus designs. We will discuss monitors and video equipment. We will give you the specs you need to get a truly fast hard disk drive. We will also look at printers. Our focus is a basic computer system, but, of course, there are many other pieces of "peripheral" equipment you can add. For quick, "buyer's guide" information on mice, CD-ROMs, tape backup systems, and other add-on equipment, please see Chapter 6.

Before we begin, it is important for you to know that there is light at the end of the tunnel. Both in this chapter and in Chapter 5, "How to buy the system you need," I'm going to tell you what I think you should do. But before we can get to that point—before you can understand the recommendations and learn to make your own decisions—there are more than a few things you have to know. Don't worry if it doesn't all sink in the first time through. Simply take a break, and then go back and read the chapter again.

Unavoidable measures

We can start by re-visiting the kind of key specifications that computer people typically call "speeds and feeds." Doing so will give you a better understanding of what you're buying and why.

As we look at various components, keep in mind that everything is designed to serve the CPU. Indeed, all of the other parts of a computer are designed to do one of three things: they are all related to input, output, or storage.

Your keyboard, your mouse, your trackball, and your joystick, for example, are designed to get information into the CPU. The printer, video screen, and speaker are designed to present or "output" information the CPU has processed. Disk drives are designed to store information the CPU has processed and the instructions (programs) it may need in the future. A modem is designed to let a CPU input and output information over the telephone.

Viewed from this perspective, the main qualities that characterize input, output, and storage devices are speed, quality, and capacity. Laser printers, for example, produce higher quality printing than do dot-matrix or ink-jet printers. Some video equipment lets you view complex images in a higher resolution or scroll through text faster than others. Some hard disk drives not only hold more information, they also deliver it to your system's memory faster than others.

The point here is to help you begin making sense of megahertz, megabytes, milliseconds, and all the other technical terms used to describe various computer components. Modem speed, for example, is measured in bps (bits per second).

Laser printers are judged by ppm (pages per minute) and dpi (dots per inch). Dot-matrix printers are measured in cps (characters per second). Video resolution is reported in pixels (picture elements). Hard disk speed is typically measured in milliseconds (ms) of average access time. RAM chip memory is measured in nanoseconds (ns). And so on. And on and on.

Bad news—good news

These various measurements of speed, quality, and capacity are confusing, to be sure. But there is no way to avoid them. It is the price we must pay for having access to hardware that continues to dramatically improve while prices dramatically drop.

That's the bad news. The good news is that you do not really have to know precisely what each of these measurements means. All that matters is that you can compare them and the significance of their actual performance. For example, suppose a 28ms (millisecond) hard drive sells for X, while a 15ms drive of similar capacity sells for X+$200. You don't have to know what a millisecond is to compare this equipment. The 15ms unit is nearly twice as fast as the 28ms drive.

But what's the actual significance? Will a difference of 13 milliseconds make $200 worth of difference in your daily work? Will you save a noticeable amount of time? The answer is often a qualitative judgement call—what seems fast to you may be unacceptably slow to me, while a magazine reviewer who has looked at a dozen or more drives may rate the unit as about average.

There is no easy answer to this problem. The best course I can recommend is one of listening to people you trust, particularly those familiar with how you use your system. Also, try to test different equipment whenever you have the opportunity. There is ultimately no way to avoid megabytes, milliseconds, megahertz, and all the other criteria.

But these criteria are far less crucial than you may think. You need them to be able to compare the features and benefits of various computer system packages. But unless you are a hobbyist or computer expert intending to build your own system, you really don't have to know much about, say, hard disk access time, other than that it is measured in milliseconds and that some drives are faster than others.

In the chips

Now let's look at your choices of CPU chips. Since this is the most crucial choice you will make, it is worth spending a little time on the topic. We will look at your main chip choices and show you why either a 386DX or some version of the 486 is likely to be the best alternative.

As you know, the main computer decision any small business owner today must make is whether to get an Apple Macintosh or an IBM-compatible "DOS machine." Each type of system is built around a particular family of microprocessors, so there are really only two families to choose from. You might thus conclude that there are basically two ways to build a personal computer.

Chips as "products"

If you stop to think about it, however, you will quickly see that there are really an infinite number of ways to do the job. There is absolutely no scientific reason why personal computing must be based on either the Intel or Motorola chip design. The fact that computing is indeed based on the products of these two companies is simply a marketplace reality.

I bring this up because I want you to realize that personal computing is not graven in stone. No Voice From On High commanded Motorola and Intel to do things in a certain way. Nor did any Superior Power tell Intel to make the 80286 one way and the 80386 another.

Microprocessor chips are *products*, and like all products, each model is designed to offer certain features. The only iron rule is that each new generation of a manufacturer's chip be backward or "downward" compatible with the chips that came before it. Engineering and physics play an important role. They are repeatedly providing new answers to the question: How many transistors can dance on the surface of a silicon chip? But ultimately, it all comes down to product positioning and marketing.

As with anything else, the question for you is, "Which product offers the features I need at a price I can afford?" Forget about the magic and the mystique. That's the bottom line.

Benefits of the 386/486 design

Realistically, at this writing, there are four main chip choices if you're a small businessperson: 386SX, 386DX, 486SX, 486DX. I'll tell you about two additional 486-based chips in a moment. For now, we'll keep things simple.

"But, wait a minute!" you say. "What about all those bargain 286 systems I see advertised in *Computer Shopper* and other publications? What about a used PC or XT? Why is the 386/486 design so great?"

In the first place, by the time you equip a 286 or lesser system with everything you need to use it in business, you'll find that it isn't all that cheap. The prices advertised in magazines are often for stripped-down, "bare bones" systems or for systems with small hard disk drives and monochrome monitors.

But leaving that aside, without getting technical, there are three main qualities that separate the 386/486 design from the 286 and lesser chips: effective operating speed, memory addressing, and additional capabilities.

Operating speed

Because they are more efficient, 386/486 chips accomplish more during each clock cycle. And because they represent newer technology, they are available in versions that operate at higher speeds. Most 286 systems, for example, operate at 8 or 12 MHz, while 386 chips are available with speeds as high as 40 MHz. Before long, there will be 486 chips operating at 100 MHz.

Qualitatively, you will really notice the extra speed and better performance of 386/486 chips when using graphics and paint programs, desktop publishing software, Microsoft Windows, and any other application that puts complex images on your screen. But I find that the extra speed is important even when using a word processing or database program.

Memory addressing

As for memory addressing, the 386/486 design can handle much more RAM than the 286 and it does so in a much more capable way.

A 286 can address up to 16M of memory, but it does so in an ungainly fashion. For technical reasons, if you want to be able to use more than one megabyte of memory, you must add not only memory chips but also a special memory-management circuit board. In some instances, if you want to reconfigure your memory, you will have to disconnect the system, remove its cover, and attack its innards with a small screwdriver.

The 386/486 architecture, in contrast, has all the memory management circuitry you need built right in. You can reconfigure memory with a few commands from your keyboard. This can be important because some programs run better with different memory configurations.

For example, with Microsoft's DOS 5, any 386/486 user can make more conventional "640K" memory available to any PC program. DOS does this by loading both itself and many of your resident programs into memory located beyond the 1M limit. That gives your applications programs, almost all of which were written to run within the confines of 640K, much more memory to work with.

On one of my 386 systems, for instance, I've got 606K of free conventional memory for programs to use. The reason I've got this is that I have used DOS 5 to load a total of 306K of software into the memory that extends beyond the 1M mark. If I did not have a 386, almost all of that software would be loaded into conventional memory, taking up room and giving my application programs only 334K to work with.

Additional capabilities

Finally, there is the matter of additional capabilities. The 386/486 design actually offers three modes of operation: real, protected, and virtual 8086 (V86). The technical details are not important here. All you need to know is that, for all intents and purposes, if you want to run Windows 3.1 or OS/2 2.0, you will need these features.

The 386/486 chip design, in short, places the power of a 1970s era mainframe computer at your feet (or on your desktop). It is a major advance over previous generations in the 8086 family, a far greater advance than the 286 chip was over the PC and XT chips.

386SX and 386DX differences

Now, let's get more specific. Let's look first at your 386-based options and then turn the focus to the 486.

There are three primary differences between the 386SX and 386DX designs. The first has to do with the total amount of memory each chip can address. The

SX has the ability to address a total of 16 megabytes of memory; the DX can address 4 gigabytes (G) of memory.

The second difference concerns the width of the bus the chips use to access that memory. Internally, both are 32-bit processors. But, as you know from Chapter 2, the SX plugs into a 16-bit bus. It must thus make two calls to memory to get its 32 bits. The memory bus on 386DX-based machines, in contrast, is 32 bits wide, allowing the chip to fetch 32 bits of information in a single pass.

Qualitatively, the difference is effective speed of operation. There are many ways to stack the deck in one direction or the other. But, all things being equal, given an SX and a DX operating at 25 MHz, the DX will finish a task faster because it can get more done during each cycle of the system's clock. It's reaching for memory with two arms each time instead of just one.

The third difference between the two chip designs is in processor speed. The top speed available in 386SX chips is 25 MHz. The top speed of an Intel 386DX is 33 MHz. This is more of a marketing decision than anything else. The current AMD clone of the 386DX runs at 40 MHz.

As for price differences, in today's market, there is almost no difference in price between a 386SX and a 386DX. I'm looking at an ad right now placed in a local business paper. The retailer has a 386SX/25 MHz system for $1420 and a 386DX/25 MHz system for $1570. That's a difference of $150. (These prices do not include a printer.)

But it's not the CPU chip alone that is responsible. For that additional $150 you get a 64K cache instead of a 32K cache. (I'll explain caches in a moment.) You also get four megabytes of RAM on the motherboard, instead of just two, and a 100M hard disk drive, instead of an 80M unit. Both systems come with a VGA monitor offering 1024×768 resolution with 0.28mm dot pitch.

In a case like this, I believe that opting for the lower-priced 386SX package would be a bad decision, to say the least. Remember, this stuff doesn't wear out. If you assume a useful life of five years, that $150 difference works out to only $30 per year. And it brings you so much more in speed, power, and capacity.

As you read this, the price difference is likely to be even less. In fact, I wouldn't be surprised if 386SX-based desktop systems disappeared altogether. The chip may still be used in laptop machines due to its small space requirements. Or a version that consumes less power (386SL) may take its place in that market. But I don't think you're going to find the 386SX on the desktop much longer.

What about a 486?

That leaves the 386DX and some version of the 80486 as your main choices. So let's look at the 486 to see what it offers.

Historically, hardware always outruns software. But rarely has hardware development run so far ahead. The software available today doesn't even scratch the surface of 386 power, yet already 486s are becoming the chip of choice.

The reasons are complex. But they have nothing to do with any current, widespread need for 486 power and everything to do with free market competition and marketing. As I said at the beginning of this chapter, we must never forget that microprocessor chips are *products*. They are introduced, marketed, positioned, differentiated, and sold like laundry soap, cars, or VCRs.

For many years, Intel held a virtual monopoly on the CPU chips used in IBM-compatible machines. Then Advanced Micro Devices (AMD) cloned Intel's 386 and offered a 40 MHz version. Indications are that AMD took 20 percent of the 386 business away from Intel as a result. Chips and Technologies (C&T), NexGen, and, according to some reports, a host of Asian firms, are joining the clone carnival as well.

Intel has retaliated by aggressively cutting prices on its 486 line, moving up the introduction of its 586 processor by more than a year, and spending millions in advertising. The company has hired Lucas Films (of "Star Wars" fame) to produce a series of stunning television commercials for the 486. It has also established a cooperative venture with computer makers. Every company that includes the "Intel Inside" logo in its ads, for example, receives rebates on its CPU purchases from Intel.

Under the circumstances, the suggestions in the trade press that Intel is trying to kill off the 386 must be taken seriously. As one analyst puts it, "The 386 business just doesn't bring in the profits it used to as a result of AMD and other clones."

486 features

The fact that few of us *need* a 486, the fact that no software yet exists to tap its power, is irrelevant. A marketing war is raging above us that, in my experience, is unprecedented. (Much the same thing is going on in the operating system software arena, as we will see in Chapter 4.) It's a good time to keep your head down. But if you play your cards right, as a computer user, you can emerge as the ultimate winner.

Let's briefly look at the 486 and see what it offers. The chip is based on the 386 design. However, it includes some potentially significant enhancements. For one thing, its internal design is more efficient. That means it can do more with each tick of the clock than can a 386. It should be noted, though, that most of the software available today—so-called 16-bit software—cannot take full advantage of this feature. Everyone is waiting for true 32-bit operating system software to appear.

The 486 also includes a built-in math coprocessor, also known as a "floating point unit" (FPU). There has been a math coprocessor available for all Intel chips from the 8088 on. The difference is that in the past, the coprocessor has been packaged as a separate chip that plugged into a special socket on the motherboard. By incorporating the coprocessor circuitry on the main chip, Intel says that the 486 can perform 40% more efficiently than an 80386 and its math coprocessor mate, an 80387.

The catch is that, regardless of the chip or chips you use, the software you run must be designed to take advantage of a coprocessor. Otherwise it does you no good. Lotus and other commercial spreadsheet programs, commercial desktop publishing, and computer-aided-design (CAD) programs typically have this power.

But a math coprocessor is not likely to be of much use for word processing, database, or communications applications.

The 486 also includes a built-in 8K cache and a cache controller. At this writing, it is available in models that run as fast as 50 MHz. A 66 MHz version will be available as you read this. (Indications are that Intel will not produce 386 chips operating any faster than 33 MHz.)

The 486SX and 486DX

As with the 386, there are two basic versions of the 486 chip: the 486DX and the 486SX. The difference between them has nothing to do with the width of their memory addressing path, however. As one trade journal puts it, "If you thought 'SX' meant '16-bit bus' and 'DX' meant '32-bit bus,' then it's time to update your vocabulary. Apparently 'SX' simply means 'cheaper.'"

Both the SX and DX versions of the 486 use a 32-bit memory bus. The difference is that the math coprocessor on 486SX chips has either been disabled or removed. If the software you run doesn't need or doesn't recognize an FPU, then you will never notice the difference.

According to Intel, a 486SX running at 20 MHz offers higher performance than a 386DX running at 33 MHz. And a 486SX running at 25 MHz will easily outperform a 386DX running at 40 MHz. I know this is confusing. We'll work on straightening things out in a moment.

The quick bottom line, however, is this: A 33 MHz 386DX system will almost certainly provide you with more than enough power to run your small business. But if you find that when you're ready to buy your system, market forces have pushed the prices of 486 computers down to within a couple of hundred dollars of a 386 machine, you should probably buy the 486.

CPU upgradability

I know that sounds contradictory. Why buy a 486 when there's no software around yet to take advantage of it? Why spend even two hundred dollars more when a 386DX/33 will more than meet your needs?

A hundred here and a hundred there can add up when you're buying computer equipment. But ultimately I have to come down on the side of the 486 for one simple reason: processor upgradability.

This is not a new concept. Over the years, various companies have offered products designed to replace your computer's original CPU with something more powerful. I once used an Orchid Turbo card to turn my old XT into an AT, for example. There's even a product called the All ChargeCard designed to effectively turn a 286 into a 386 by adding memory management circuitry to the CPU. Kingston Technology Corporation [(800) 835-6575] takes a different approach—it completely replaces your 286 with a 386SX (20 or 25 MHz) for about $350.

As useful as they are, however, these third-party solutions ultimately amount to clever work-arounds. With the 486, things are different. This time processor upgradability is an inherent part of the design. At Intel's urging, most computer makers today are producing 486-based systems that are specifically designed to let you remove the CPU chip and replace it with a more powerful model. Either that, or they include an empty socket on their motherboards for the same purpose.

The Orchid Turbo, All ChargeCard, and other third-party solutions notwithstanding, in the past, if you wanted a faster, more powerful machine, there were two main options. You could either buy a brand new system, or you could buy a new motherboard (containing a more powerful chip) and have it installed in your current system's case. These are still viable options, but the option of simply changing the CPU may end up being the best alternative of all.

The key point is that the processor upgrade option is only available with 486 systems. You can buy a 386DX and be perfectly happy for years to come, possibly forever. But should you ever want to upgrade such a system, you will either have to buy an entirely new computer or install a new motherboard. At this writing, the CPU chip in most 386-based systems is soldered in place and not designed to be removed.

If you buy an upgradable 486 system, in contrast, you will be able to boost its performance by simply inserting a more powerful version of your 486 processor. In fact, you may be able to do even better than that. There is every indication that Intel plans to offer its next processor, the 586, in a version that can be inserted into a 486 socket. Due out in late 1992 or early 1993, the 586 is a 64-bit chip that is expected to offer three times the performance of a 50 MHz 486DX chip.

486DX2 and OverDrive clock doublers

At this writing, the 586 is in the future. What upgrade options are available today? Well, here's where things get really interesting—and confusing. According to industry reports, Intel plans to introduce no fewer than 31 versions of its 386 and 486 processors. As one authority puts it, "The company is trying to cover every possible price point to help stave off the competition." The chips will vary on the basis of their use of an internal cache, internal FPUs, power management features (for laptops and portables), and most of all, on the basis of processing speed.

If all of this makes you suddenly feel like you're drowning, take a deep breath and relax. I'll show you how to sort it all out. The first thing you need to know is that the 486SX and 486DX are just the beginning. There are two more major versions of Intel's 80486. These are the 486DX2 and the 486 OverDrive chip. Both of these chips include a fully functional math coprocessor (FPU) and an 8K internal cache.

Most important, both operate internally at *twice* the speed of the system they are plugged into. This is crucial because it gives you high-speed performance without the extra cost of high-speed support chips and hardware.

Empty sockets and special levers
The OverDrive chip is the one that is being marketed to consumers who want to upgrade a computer they already own. For example, suppose you have a 20 MHz 486SX-based system. The 486SX chip that came with your system operates at 20 MHz internally and talks to the rest of the computer's components—memory, data bus, etc.—at that speed as well. Now you want to upgrade, possibly to be able to

more easily run Windows, a multi-media package, or some other power-hungry program.

So you buy a 486 20/40 OverDrive chip and insert it into the special vacant "performance enhancement" socket on the motherboard. This is the socket some magazines refer to as the 486 "math coprocessor socket." Once inserted, the new chip disables the original chip. If your motherboard does not have a vacant socket, it probably has a special built-in lever to release the original CPU. Replace the original with your new OverDrive chip, and use the lever to lock it in place.

The entire process takes about five minutes. And, although it is too soon to tell at this writing, you may find that you can sell that original chip or return it to your computer maker for credit against the OverDrive. One way or another, a market for used 486 CPUs is certain to develop.

When you turn the computer on again, none of your other components will notice the change. The processor is still talking to them at 20 MHz. But internally, the processor is operating at double that speed (40 MHz). That's what "clock doubling" is all about. The result is a performance boost of between 35% and 70%, depending on the software and other hardware you are using.

At this writing, OverDrive chips are available with external/internal speed ratings of 16/32, 20/40, and 25/50. The cost is about $700, though that price is expected to quickly drop to $500 or less.

The OEM channel

Intel is making the 486DX2 available only through the OEM channel—that is, only to companies that build computers.

Thus, at this writing, you can buy computers built around 486DX2 chips with external/internal speed ratings of 25/50 and 33/66. A 486DX2 chip operating at 50 MHz externally and 100 MHz internally may also be available as you read this. Once again, clock doubling lets computer makers offer high-performance at a low cost since they don't have to spend money on high-speed memory chips and other support hardware.

The lowdown on upgrades

We cannot leave the subject of 486 processors without emphasizing several special points. First, make sure when you buy your 486 system that it is indeed designed to be upgraded. Many 486 computers were produced before Intel's chip upgrade strategy was fully developed. Consequently, unless the ad or the literature describing the computer specifically says the chip can be upgraded, be suspicious. Do not take a salesperson's word for it.

Sometimes a salesperson will tell you whatever you want to hear. Sometimes the individual just does not know. For example, soon after the DX2 and Over-Drive chips were announced, I called a number of stores that advertised 486 systems. None of them had even heard of clock doubling chips, and none could say whether the equipment they were selling could be upgraded. One sales rep said, "I think the chip is soldered in place."

The second point concerns the way the upgrade is implemented. As noted above, some upgradable systems have motherboards with vacant performance enhancement sockets. Others are specifically designed to let you remove and replace the original CPU. In my opinion, the removable CPU option makes the most sense.

Inserting an OverDrive chip in a performance enhancement socket disables the original CPU, but the original chip remains on the board doing no one any good. That's like locking several hundred dollars away in a drawer you never plan to open. Again, it is too soon to tell what kind of market will develop for used 486 CPUs. But one thing is clear: If you want to benefit from it, you must be able to easily remove the original CPU chip without damaging either it or the motherboard.

Finally, there is the matter of multiple upgrades and complete flexibility. As you can imagine, regardless of the chip's core (internal) speed, it is crucial for the speed of its bus interface to match the speed of the bus itself. Thus, if you buy a 20 MHz system with a 20 MHz 486 chip and decide to upgrade, the external speed of your upgrade chip had better be 20 MHz. Otherwise it won't match up with the other motherboard components. Unless . . . unless it is also possible to change the bus speed at the same time that you change the chip.

As it happens, two companies at this writing offer systems that do indeed let you change the bus speed as well as the chip. These are Northgate [(800) 828-6125] with its Elegance ZXP line and The Acer Group [(408) 432-6200] with its ChipUp technology. With these systems, you can start out with a 16 MHz and upgrade to anything from a 16/32 to a 33/66 using the same motherboard.

This approach makes so much sense that it seems likely to become the industry standard. It offers the customer maximum flexibility while enabling the computer maker to use the same motherboard for an entire range of systems. Acer and Northgate representatives assured me that users do not give up any measure of performance, although you might want to wait until their machines are tested and compared with others by *PC Magazine* or by some other trustworthy publication.

Cache time savings

Now, what about this "cache" thing? All 486 chips have 8K internal caches, and most 386DX/33 chips are supplied in systems with external caches. The cache concept is applied in various ways in almost all computer systems. The goal is always to increase performance.

A cache is a chunk of memory that has been set aside to serve as a temporary holding tank for information. The idea is that information can be delivered to the CPU faster from the cache than from its "home" location, whether that home location happens to be on a hard disk or in a bank of dynamic RAM chips (DRAM).

In the old days, the speed of the CPU and the speed of RAM chips more or less matched. There was no need for memory caches to smooth out inequalities. The problem today is that memory chip technology and pricing have not kept up with CPU advances. Memory chips come in two flavors: static RAM (SRAM; pronounced ''Es-RAM'') and dynamic RAM (DRAM; pronounced ''Dee-RAM''). SRAM is much faster, but DRAM is much cheaper.

Ideally, a system built around a 33 MHz CPU would have nothing but SRAM matched to the speed of that CPU. But such a system would be horrendously expensive since SRAM is so costly. As a compromise, computer makers originally introduced the idea of CPU ''wait states'' to slow down the chip's performance to the point where it more closely matched the speed of the DRAM that served as its storage area. A wait state is basically an idle period during which the CPU is doing nothing.

Today's solution involves CPU caching. Instead of inserting wait states into the CPU's operation or offering an expensive all-SRAM system, computer makers offer motherboards with fast CPUs, fast DRAM, and a small cache of super-fast SRAM. This is an external cache, and it is controlled by a special chip, usually an Intel 82385. This chip tries to second-guess the CPU and load the cache with the information it thinks the CPU will want next. That way, the CPU gets its information from the cache at SRAM speeds.

As noted, all 486 chips have an internal cache of 8K. The cache control circuitry and the cache space are all part of the CPU itself.

A cache controller's guesses are not always on the mark, but they are accurate enough of the time to make a CPU cache a viable solution to the speed mismatching problem. At this writing, the typical 386 CPU cache consists of 64K of 20 or 25 ns (nanosecond) SRAM chips. You may have the option of expanding this to 256K or more, but you will probably be better off putting your money into some other feature, since the increase in speed from a larger than standard cache may not be noticeable. As for the DRAM in your system, its speed should be 70 ns or less. Be sure to ask.

You may also hear the term ''shadow RAM'' used in ads for 386 and 486 systems. This is a speed-improvement feature built into the motherboard. It is designed to boost the performance of eight-bit add-on cards and 16-bit BIOS chips by copying the software they contain in their ROM chips into 32-bit memory.

Motherboard makers

With the all-important CPU more or less under control, let's move on to ''the mother of all systems''—the main circuit board onto which the CPU is socketed and into which all your add-on cards and peripherals plug. Let's talk about motherboards.

If you want to, you can build a computer system from scratch. You can read the reviews of various individual components—much as you might read the reviews of various stereo system components—and assemble a system of perfectly matched components, each of which is the ''best'' in its area. The assembly itself is not hard to do, and it is a lot of fun.

If you decide to try this option, I've got a great book to recommend: Aubrey Pilgrim's *Build Your Own 80486 PC and Save a Bundle* from Windcrest/McGraw-Hill. The book applies to 386 systems as well, and at $16.95, it is a genuine bargain.

The problem is that, as small businesspeople, most of us don't have the time to indulge ourselves this way. We need a system that works reliably and that is more or less ready to go when it arrives. Nevertheless, when shopping for such a "turnkey" system, it wouldn't hurt to ask the vendor who makes the systems' motherboards.

A number of big-name PC manufacturers design and produce their own motherboards, but most purchase them from outside vendors. Among the leading U.S. 386-based motherboard manufacturers are American Megatrends, Inc., (AMI) of Norcross, GA; Hauppauge Computer Works, Inc., of Hauppauge, NY; and Micronics Computers, Inc., and Mylex Corporation, both of which are based in Fremont, CA.

An economical upgrade

I bring this up first because you may indeed want to ask whomever you decide to buy from who makes the motherboards in his systems. Second, I have found that, in the past, at least, swapping out motherboards can be the most economical way to upgrade computing capability. For example, I had a 286-based system that I decided to upgrade to a 386DX. So I had my computer dealer pull out the 286 motherboard and replace it with a 386 AMI motherboard. At the time, the new board, with four megabytes of RAM, was about $400. The labor charge was $35.

Later, I had the same 386 AMI motherboard transferred to a large tower case. In the first instance I bought a new motherboard. In the second, a new case. But everything else remained the same. As I have said from the beginning, computer hardware is very much a commodity business. You can swap this out and swap that in pretty much whenever you want. In simple terms, computers today are like the Tinker Toys we all grew up with.

So, even if you have no power to select the makers of the components you buy as part of a complete system package, you are not locked in, in most cases. If your system later needs to be upgraded, you can almost certainly do so at a minimal cost by swapping out boards or otherwise buying additional, single components. If you buy a 386DX/33 to start out with and later want to move to a 486 of some sort, you will almost certainly be able to do so by installing a new motherboard.

That's when you'll want to really look into the quality of the components. For example, according to Clyde Washburn, owner and principal of Washburn & Co., a computer products distributor in Pittsford, New York, "A quality motherboard exhibits a certain amount of physical integrity. If you take an oscilloscope and look at the bus signals, the higher up you go in board quality, the more pristine the signals look."

Mr. Washburn adds, "The least expensive boards have inexplicable incompatibilities—say, an add-on board works in slot 3 but not in slot 5 . . . Another dimension to a quality motherboard is whether the manufacturer actually designs the product. If there is a problem with a particular board, its maker will have engineering change records to help identify the source of the problem."

In general, it is best to go with "name brand" motherboards, if at all possible, even if they cost a bit more. "With AMI, all of our engineering is done internally," says Scott Magnes, national sales manager for AMI. "The guy who wrote the BIOS is in this building; the guy who designed the board is right here, too. We can optimize the [BIOS] software to take advantage of the hardware, so that it operates as fast as it possibly can."

Other leading motherboard makers have similar comments. The point is, you may find that it is worth more to get a system built around a motherboard made by a leading manufacturer. This is certainly not a deal breaker. But it is not something to ignore.

So, when you are shopping for a system, ask the vendor who makes the motherboard. How long have they been in business? What kind of support do they offer? Good vendors will be happy to tell you because they will use good equipment. After all, vendors who plan to be in business for the foreseeable future don't want to push inferior equipment on their customers. It will only come back to haunt them.

Four key questions

There are at least four other questions you should ask. First, find out if the video, floppy, and hard drive controller circuitry is built into the motherboard. As noted in Chapter 2, built-ins like these can be convenient, but if something goes wrong with these areas, you may have to replace the entire motherboard.

The alternative is a motherboard designed to accept add-on cards that handle these functions. This is the traditional way of doing things. It gives you maximum flexibility and control. And, replacing a dead add-on card is cheaper than replacing the main board.

Second, ask the vendor how many add-on slots the board offers. Conventional boards typically offer eight slots or more. Some of these will be designed to accept 8-bit add-on cards and some, 16-bit cards. There will probably be at least one slot designed to accept a 32-bit card of the sort used to add more memory to a 386DX system. An 8-bit board can be used in a 16-bit slot. And a 16-bit board can be used in a 32-bit slot.

Plan to use one slot for your video adapter and one for your combined floppy/hard disk controller card. This card is often abbreviated in ads as "FDD/HDD," which stands for "floppy disk drive/hard disk drive." These days, given the popularity of IDE drives, the "FDD/HDD" card doesn't actually do much "controlling." That is done by the electronics located on the hard drive unit itself.

You will also use one slot for an I/O card that can handle your printer and your modem, and possibly a joystick or game paddle. That leaves you five for future expansion.

Third, ask how much RAM the board can accommodate. It will probably be a long time before you go beyond 4M, but it is worth knowing whether the board is limited to a maximum of 8, 16, or 32 megabytes. For a 386DX or 486SX, you should insist on a board that can be expanded up to at least 16M.

Finally, make sure that your system has an *FCC Class B* rating. This rating is mandatory for all 386/486-based computers. It specifies maximum allowable radio emissions and is granted for a particular CPU with specified clock speeds. The rating is based on a specific combination of case, power supply, and mother-board. The FCC Class B rating is ten times as stringent as "Class A," and without it, you cannot legally use a computer in your home.

The government requirement is so demanding because all CPUs give off radio emissions that can interfere with nearby television reception, cellular-phones, garage-doors, or two-way-radio operation. Since all reputable dealers sell systems with FCC Class B rating, this should not be a problem. But it doesn't hurt to check.

More about memory

As you know by now, computers use memory as storage areas. Memory stores programs and data loaded in from disk or created by you and the CPU. In general, the more memory you have, the more you can do.

Computer memory is a fascinating and exasperating topic. A complete discussion is well beyond the scope of this book. If you need more information, see the Random House book *DOS 5* by Alfred Glossbrenner or *MS-DOS Beyond 640K* by James Forney from Windcrest/McGraw-Hill. Here, we will cover only the basics.

Everything, of course, goes back to the CPU. The microprocessor at the heart of the original IBM/PC, the 8088, could address one megabyte of memory. So the system designers divided up this "1000 kilobytes" (one megabyte). They pre-served 360K for system hardware addresses—your video and printer card have to have memory addresses somewhere, after all—and left 640K for general use. The operating system (DOS) was written to work with 640K, and all applications programs had to follow suit.

In contrast, today's 386/486 chips have the ability to address up to four giga-bytes of memory. That's four *billion* bytes. Since a billion is a thousand million, we can say that 4G is equal to 4000 megabytes. Even assuming that you could fit it all into your machine, at the current market price of $50 per megabyte, 4000 megabytes of memory would cost you $200,000.

DOS, the program that is to software what the CPU is to your computer, is still limited to using only addresses within the first megabyte of memory to run programs. It can make additional memory available to programs that know how to use it, but DOS itself is still limited to working within a 640K space. More on this in Chapter 4.

So why do you need "4 megs" of memory? The simple answer is that you need four megabytes of RAM if you want to run Microsoft Windows effectively. The popularity of Windows is the reason so many packages today include that much memory.

But what if you don't plan to run Windows? Do you still need that much memory? You probably don't *need* all of it, but you are definitely going to need more than a "one megabyte" system, which for technical reasons, is often much less than it seems. And you're probably going to need more than two megabytes, the next bump up. If a package comes with 4M, there is no point in quibbling.

Forget about Windows and its ability to actually run programs in all that memory. The key point is that more and more garden variety applications programs have the ability to use memory above the 1M mark for storage. For example, if you've got the extra memory, a program like File Express (Chapter 10) will recognize and use it automatically. That means it may be able to load your entire customer database into memory, enabling you to locate any record instantly— instead of waiting for the program to read it in from disk. And that will make you more productive.

DIPs, SIPs, and SIMMs

DRAM is typically supplied in three main physical configurations. The DIP (dual-in-line-package) memory chip is the original. It looks like a rectangular caterpillar and is rapidly fading from the scene. The SIP (single-in-line-package) chip vaguely resembles a squashed transistor, with all of its leads protruding from one side of the "package." It, too, is fading from the scene.

Today's RAM chip of choice is the SIMM (single in-line memory module). This is basically a small circuit board designed to accommodate surface-mounted memory chips. SIMMs take up much less space than other types of memory, and they are very easy to insert and remove. This is what you should insist upon. If you don't, you may find that you will not be able to get the chips you need to expand your memory in the future.

A typical motherboard these days incorporates four to eight SIMM slots, each of which can hold 1M of memory (one SIMM circuit board). As noted, there is usually a 32-bit expansion slot as well for an optional memory-expansion card. The total amount of memory a board can hold is also determined by the capacity of the memory chips it can accept. With a different set of memory chips, the same SIMM slot that holds 1M might be able to hold a 4M board of identical size. If possible, your system should have a motherboard that can accept *both* 1M and 4M SIMMs.

Quick takes: The other components

Here, for your convenience, is the same list of components I recommended you look for in any computer system package at the beginning of Chapter 2:

- 386DX 33-MHz (or faster) CPU or a 486-based system
- 4 megs of RAM on the motherboard, expandable to 16 megs or more
- 16-bit Super VGA (SVGA) card and non-interlaced (NI) color monitor
- 120-megabyte 18ms IDE hard drive (or larger)
- 1 high-density (360K/1.2M) 5.25″ floppy drive
- 1 high-density (720K/1.44M) 3.5″ floppy drive
- 1 parallel port and 2 serial ports
- HP laser printer or compatible
- Mouse (optional)
- 2400 bps external modem (optional)
- DOS 5.x

Hopefully, by now, this list of terms doesn't look so formidable. We've covered the processor and the memory in detail. The rest is crispy lemon duck, or duck soup, if you prefer. Indeed, with the exception of the size of your hard drive and the laser printer, these items are pretty much standard. Consequently, we will cover them quickly.

16-bit Super VGA card and color monitor

You need 16 bits for the speed. In fact, the most important thing you can do to upgrade the performance of an old system is to replace its 8-bit video card with a 16-bit card. "Super VGA" means at least 800×600 resolution. If your package offers 1024×768 as well, so much the better.

Make sure, however, that the "dot pitch" of your color monitor is 0.28 mm. As you know from Chapter 2, this refers, roughly, to the size of the individual dots that make up your screen. The dot pitch of my NEC MultiSync 2A is 0.31 mm, and it is quite good, even in Super VGA mode. However, the monitor cannot display 1024×768, even though my video card can generate such images.

Analog, digital, and muti-synch

You should also know that there are at least three categories of monitors: analog, digital, and multi-synch. In the beginning, PCs used video cards that output digital signals. So if you have an MDA, CGA, or EGA card, you will need a digital (TTL) monitor.

For VGA, SVGA, 8514/A, XGA and high-resolution cards, you will need an analog monitor. Multi-synch monitors can accept either analog or digital signals, but they don't make economic sense in these days of VGA and SVGA. In short, get an SVGA system with an analog monitor. The standard size these days is 14″, measured diagonally. The so-called "flat-screen" monitors reduce glare and virtually eliminate the distortion that can occur at the sides of images on non-flat-screen monitors.

Multi-scan and interlace

Multi-synch monitors may no longer be needed. But "multi-scan" is another matter. This refers to a monitor that can use a variety of horizontal (left-to-right) scan rates. These rates can vary with the video mode. A monitor for a Super VGA or higher resolution card needs to be a multi-scan monitor with a range of horizontal scan frequencies including VGA's 31.5 KHz, and the rate required by the card for its SVGA 800×600 mode and 1024×768 mode.

In general, you can assume that a monitor sold as part of a package that offers SVGA resolution will have the necessary capabilities. However, this is not the case with the "interlace." To be able to display 1024×768 resolution screens, a monitor needs a large "bandwidth." Bandwidth literally determines the amount of information a monitor can accept at once.

However, the wider the bandwidth, the more expensive the monitor. Thus, to cut costs, the technique of interlacing was developed. An interlaced display compensates for its narrower bandwidth by building up a full screen's worth of pixels in two sweeps of the electron gun. It interlaces odd and even-numbered rows and relies on the persistence of the screen phosphors to fool the eye into thinking they are constantly being refreshed. The result, in a word, is screen flicker when in 1024×768 mode.

I've seen ads from leading OEMs that try to make this sound like a benefit by saying a package includes a monitor with "long persistence phosphors." Ideally, a monitor should have the bandwidth to refresh the screen at 72 Hz (or faster) when in 1024×768 mode. A monitor that can handle this is "non-interlaced" and typically costs about $100 more than its "interlaced" cousins.

Often computer vendors offer you a choice of an interlaced or non-interlaced monitor. Naturally, I think you should go with the non-interlaced equipment. But I have to note that it is usually relevant only in 1024×768 mode. The key thing is to be sure to ask the vendor whether the monitor is interlaced on non-interlaced before you buy.

Video card memory

Finally, there is the matter of how much memory is on the video card. This is definitely something you should ask about. The amount of memory on the card governs the maximum resolution of the board and the maximum number of colors it can display at one time. A standard VGA card with 256K memory has a maximum resolution of 640×480, with 16 colors chosen from a palette of 256. Super VGA boards must have more than 256K memory to produce "super" VGA. SVGA cards require a minimum of 512K on the board to produce 800×600 resolution with 256 colors. Some boards can accommodate as much as a megabyte or more of "VRAM" (video RAM) for faster screen scrolling.

Also, you may want to ask about any software "video drivers" supplied with your system. Often the quality your board delivers when running Windows, Ventura Publisher, or some other graphics-intensive software depends on the driver software supplied with the board and how well the two have been optimized to work together.

Hard and floppy drives

Floppy disk drives are a non-issue. As discussed in Chapter 2, you need one of each: a high-density 3.5" drive (720K/1.44M) and a high-density 5.25" drive (360K/1.2M). That way you will be able to exchange disks with anyone.

The hard drive is another matter. Next to the CPU, the hard drive is the most important component in the system. As I said in *Glossbrenner's Complete Hard Disk Handbook* [Osborne/McGraw-Hill], you *live* on your hard drive. Floppy drives are used only to transfer files to and from a hard disk. You never run a program from a floppy. Not that you can't, of course. It's just unbearably slow.

I have long recommended that people buy the biggest, fastest hard disk drive they can afford. Practically speaking, I don't think a business can get by today with anything less than a 120M drive. The average "access time" should be 18ms or less, and it is important to ask, since many ads quote only the hard disk size.

Some systems include a "caching" hard drive controller to speed things up even more. Typically the cache controller reads ahead, assuming that if you have asked for the first part of a file now, you will want the next part of it later. The cache controller tucks that next chunk of information into RAM located on the hard drive controller board, from which it can be delivered instantly if asked for.

This is a nice extra, but you can do much the same thing with the right piece of software.

As with all of the recommendations presented here, you are free to follow this one or not. If you choose a smaller drive, you won't be up a creek later. Most drive controller cards (or motherboard drive circuitry) can accommodate two hard drives. So you can add another drive later, assuming there's space in your case.

The reason I'm so insistent on getting a 120M or larger drive has to do with both personal experience and the size of the software that is popular today. Personally, when my 80M drive died after three years of service, I was glad. I was getting tired of constantly having to move files to floppy to free up space.

Since it was an old-style 5.25″, full-height drive, it completely filled the drive bay, making it impossible to add a second internal drive. But as long as it was working, I could not justify replacing it. When it died, however, I quickly installed a 200M, 15ms IDE drive.

Part of the reason I had to struggle so with the 80M unit relates to the second reason: the size of software today. DOS 5 occupies nearly 3M of disk space if you want to have access to all its files. Windows comes in at more than 4M. So that's 7M just for the operating system and Windows. Many other applications are also in the multi-megabyte range.

As you can see, it doesn't take long to fill up 10 to 20 megabytes, and that's just for openers. Wait until you start creating letters and text files and databases. Wait until you start downloading shareware from online systems.

Listen to the voice of experience: Don't even consider less than 120M, and get a 200M or larger drive if you can afford it. Your hard disk is your home, and you will be much more comfortable if you have a little elbow room.

IDE, ESDI, and SCSI

In almost every case, the hard drive in your system will be an "IDE" hard drive. These letters stand for Integrated Drive Electronics, a phrase that means most of the controller circuitry is mated to the drive unit itself. Unlike older models (MFM, ST-506, RLL, etc.), IDE units arrive from the factory almost ready to go. That saves labor and simplifies the connections required for a company to assemble a system. It also yields better performance, due to the close mating of the controller electronics and the drive itself.

Other hard drive interfaces are available, however. They include ESDI (Enhanced Small Device Interface) and SCSI (Small Computer System Interface). If your system needs are complex or if you need a really gigantic drive, ask your local computer dealer about these options. However, I advise being particularly cautious about installing SCSI ("scuzzy") drives since there are indications that not all the bugs have been worked out in using this interface in the DOS world.

Ports, mice, and modems

One parallel port and two serial ports are also part of the standard PC configuration today. As noted in Chapter 2, you plug your printer into the parallel port. And you plug your modem into one serial port and, often, your mouse into the other. DOS and the standard PC BIOS can support more of each type of port—you might want to hook up two printers, for example—but most users will never need more than this.

A mouse really is an optional piece of equipment, unless you plan to run Microsoft Windows, a desktop publishing program, or a paint/drawing package. Many vendors either include a mouse as part of the system or throw one in for free. That's fine. If you have a choice, opt for a Microsoft Mouse since it has the best contour and feel. Be aware that most mouse-supporting software—both commercial and shareware—requires only one button (the left button). Unless you have some special application, a mouse with more than a right and a left button is not likely to be of much use.

As for modems, 2400-bps ("baud") units are nearly a commodity. If one is included in your system, fine. If not, also, fine. As you will discover in Chapter 12 when we look at the shareware program, ProComm, a 2400-bps unit is a great way to get your feet wet. In fact, it may be all that you need. However, units that handle data up to six times faster are also available at relatively reasonable prices.

Why a laser printer?

There are two reasons why I recommend a laser printer. First, the output is so good, so professional and businesslike. Second, prices have fallen to around $790, including toner cartridge, at this writing. That's for an HP (Hewlett Packard) Laser-Jet IIP+ that produces 300 dots per inch (dpi) and four pages per minute (ppm). You can pay much, much more for other models, of course. But, while the output speed may double to 8 ppm and the unit may have more whiz-bang features, the resolution will still be 300 dpi in almost every case. (Some 600 dpi units are available.)

The main difference among laser printer models, regardless of manufacturer, is speed. In addition to higher ppm rates, more advanced models have more internal memory (as much as 4M) that lets them produce complex graphic images faster. The number of built-in fonts (software in silicon that lets the laser create different styles and sizes of fonts) may vary. And keep an eye on the paper tray. A capacity of 100 to 200 letter-sized sheets is the minimum, though some vendors sell a "standard" system with only a 50-page capacity. (An upgrade is available for more money. Of course.)

A complete explanation of printer alternatives is far beyond the scope of this book. But it is possible to offer some general guidelines to help you in your evaluations. Fortunately, most vendors do not sell printers as part of computer packages, so you will not have to take something you do not really want to get the system you do. You will be free to shop around.

Making an impact

Let's start at the bottom. The main reasons for getting a dot-matrix printer today, whether 9-pin or 24-pin, are that they are cheap and that they use impact printing.

This means that if you have forms that require multiple "carbons," a dot-matrix printer can produce them since the printing element actually hits the page. Nine-pin printers are acceptable only for personal or in-house use, though there are at least two excellent shareware programs (LQ and ImagePrint) that can make a 9-pin printer produce 24-pin output.

A 9-pin printer today costs about $160. Twenty-four-pin printers sell for about $230 and tend to be both faster and produce higher quality output. Dot-matrix printer speeds are typically measured in characters per second (cps). They might range from 330 cps for draft quality to 60 cps for "near letter quality" (NLQ) to 40 cps for even higher quality. Both come in "wide carriage" models measuring about 16 inches, compared to the standard size of 11.7".

If there are 75 characters per line and 28 lines per double-spaced page, the total number of characters is 2100. So, at 60 cps, a printer could produce a page every 35 seconds, or about two pages a minute. That's a rough calculation, of course, since many of those 2100 characters are spaces.

In general, dot-matrix printers do not produce acceptable business correspondence output. But they are excellent at running off a large batch of labels. You can do wonderful labels on a laser printer, but for speed and low-cost, nothing beats continuous form, pin-fed, pressure-sensitive labels.

Ink-jet printers are nice, but not for business use. They produce 300 dpi, but they are not as fast as a laser printer and not nearly as flexible. Admittedly, they are about half the price of the lowest priced laser. But I'd rather see you get an inexpensive dot-matrix printer as an interim solution and save your money until you can afford a laser printer.

Saving money on laser printing

If—or when—you do buy a laser printer, make sure that it is truly Hewlett Packard (HP) compatible. The best way to do this is to buy a genuine HP printer. However, this does not mean that you are locked into using HP equipment from then on. A company called Pacific Data Products, for example, offers a single font cartridge that includes all of the fonts you will find on *several* of the font cartridges sold by HP, all for about what you would pay for a single HP cartridge. Pacific Data Products also offers a PostScript cartridge, should your software need it. And Pacific is only one of many companies making HP-compatible font cartridges. Pacific Data Products can be reached at (619) 552-0880.

The same philosophy applies to toner cartridges. All HP and many other laser printers use the same Canon laser engine. It is essentially the same equipment found in Canon personal copiers. The photo-sensitive drum and the toner supply are self- contained. So when printed pages begin to get faint, you pull out the old cartridge and insert a new one in a process that takes less than five minutes.

The trouble is, new cartridges sell for $70, including sales tax. But there is a simple trick that can cut that cost by $30. A company called The Laser Group, Inc., can sell you a fully-loaded Super Cartridge with a lifetime guarantee for $70. When you've used up the toner it contains, simply send it back to The Laser Group for cleaning and refilling. The cost is about $40, including all shipping charges. The Laser Group and similar firms will even buy your spent HP cartridges for between $7 and $10, in most cases. [For more information, contact The Laser Group at (800) 527-3712.]

The one thing that no computer printer does a really good job on, at least not by default, is envelopes. Some dot-matrix printers have "by-pass" slots that let you feed a business envelope without removing the continuous form paper you have loaded. All laser printers have a provision to let you feed a single envelope at a time, and some can be equipped with separate envelope paper bins. But many people print their letters on the computer and type the envelope addresses on a typewriter.

Fortunately, there are software solutions. A shareware program called GRAB, for example, can clip an address off your screen and easily print it on an envelope. See Chapter 14 for more on GRAB, LQ, and ImagePrint.

Different bus designs

Finally, we should say a word or two about the competing computer bus designs available today. This is really just a point of information. Normally the bus is not an issue, and it is not usually mentioned in equipment ads. But there are some things you should know.

ISA, MCA, and EISA

There are three bus designs sold for 386/486 systems: ISA, MCA, and EISA. The ISA (Industry Standard Architecture) bus is the one introduced by the IBM/AT. It is far and away the most common, even though it is the least capable. It is plain, inexpensive, and nearly everything works with it. It is, quite simply, the current standard.

Next is IBM's Micro Channel Architecture (MCA) bus, introduced with the PS/2 series. This was IBM's attempt to get the horses back in the barn. MCA is technically superior to the ISA bus. But most users have yet to display a demand for its features.

The MCA bus has the ability to automatically detect a given add-on card and configure itself and the card accordingly. Unfortunately for IBM, MCA add-on cards cost more than corresponding ISA cards and are not as widely available. MCA bus slots don't accept ISA cards, so if you switch to a PS/2 with MCA architecture, you will have to pitch all your old cards and buy new MCA-compatible replacements. Which is one of the main reasons the horses refused to return.

IBM's "bring 'em back" strategy did not go unnoticed by leading clone manufacturers, particularly Compaq, Zenith, and the seven other computer manufacturers who constituted the "Gang of 9." They countered with the EISA (Extended Industry Standard Architecture) bus.

Technically, EISA systems offer all the advantages of MCA, but they also accept ISA cards. EISA cards have longer connectors to reach deeper into expansion slots than the ISA cards. Unfortunately for the Gang of 9, EISA system units cost between $500 and $1000 more than ISA systems, and EISA cards are not widely available.

Which one for you?

Basically, it is safe to say that the trusty old ISA bus provides all the capabilities most users need today, so that's what most systems offer. As for IBM's MCA, companies are not lining up to license it. Impressive as it is technically, it is "too much, too late." You won't lose anything by buying an EISA system (other than money), but most users won't gain anything either.

I should note here, however, that both MCA and EISA are full 32-bit buses. So, technically, there is no question but that they offer a better platform for 486 processors than ISA. The 486, for example, has a special "burst-mode" memory transfer function that works best on EISA/MCA machines. These two designs also support "bus-mastering" processors. These are subsidiary processors designed to share the memory and data buses intelligently, taking much of the burden off the CPU and thus maximizing throughput.

That might be important if you are using a 486 as a network file server or in some other truly demanding situation. But, unless you've got some special application like that, most authorities agree that the ISA bus is your best bet, regardless of the CPU you choose.

Conclusion

At this point, you should have a very good idea of what computer hardware is, how it works, and how its performance is measured. I have tried to avoid giving you more information than you need. It still amounts to a lot, I know, but I have used the ads you will encounter once you start shopping for a system as a guide— ads from Dell, Zeos, Austin, Northgate, Gateway, and many other less famous firms. Believe me, if you want to be able to make sense of these ads, you need all the information presented here.

Mastering this material will take a little effort. You may want to take a break and then read this chapter again. But your efforts will pay off, both in confidence and in hard dollars. Once you're comfortable with the information presented here, you won't need a computer salesperson. You'll be able to buy a system through the mail and save.

We'll look at how to actually buy a computer in more detail in Chapter 5. Right now, there is one more piece we've got to move into place before your understanding can be complete. Hardware is useless without software, and software is the focus of the next chapter.

4

Software basics

DOS, Windows, and applications

I'VE SAID IT BEFORE, AND I'LL SAY IT AGAIN: COMPUTER HARDWARE IS USELESS without computer software. It's like a top-of-the-line table saw, router, sewing machine, food processor, or any other piece of equipment you'd care to name, without a human hand to operate and guide it.

As crucial as it is, however, software is not magic. Software is simply a set of instructions—instructions created by human beings—that tells the hardware what it should do when it receives a particular signal. I emphasize the word *human*, because like any product of the human brain, software varies greatly in quality.

Think of the last few movies you've watched. Think about how you reacted to them. A few of them were undoubtedly superb—the kind of movie that leaves you saying, "Yes! By golly, that was good!" Some of them, I'm sure, were real stinkers. Movies that you watch for ten minutes or so and then press the "Stop" button on your VCR clicker or get up and leave the theater. I'm also sure that some of them were fair to middling, movies you sit through to the end because they are at least tolerable.

The same is true of software. Some programs are so good, so well thought out, that you want to tell the world about them. Some are simply awful. And, as with everything else, a lot fall into that middle range of acceptable but unspectacular.

The shareware programs recommended in this book are all of the "tell the world" variety. Each is simply superb. And each can not only save you a great deal of money, but a great deal of time and effort as well. Yet, like all "applications programs," all must work with DOS, the "disk operating system" software that serves as gatekeeper to your computer hardware.

59

We will start with some information on what DOS does and where it fits in the scheme of things. Then we'll tell you about Microsoft Windows and where *it* fits.

There are only about ten DOS commands you need to know to operate a computer. The DOS Quick Tutorial section of this chapter will show you how to use them. The tutorial assumes that you are sitting at a computer, ready to tap out the commands at the keyboard. Therefore, if you have yet to buy a system, skip ahead to Chapter 5, ''How to buy the system you need.'' Once you have your system, return to the tutorial section of this chapter.

After the DOS Quick Tutorial, we will tell you what steps to follow to configure your system for maximum power and ease of use. We'll show you how to make the most of your memory, how to prepare your CONFIG.SYS file, and how to set your ''path.'' Here again, if you haven't bought a system yet, don't worry about any of this now. Wait until you get your system and are sitting at the keyboard.

''DOS'' as in ''Boss''

DOS (''doss'') is nothing but software. Like all human creations, it has its pluses and its minuses. People in the business may carp about the features it lacks or the way it implements various functions. Companies like Digital Research Incorporated (DRI), now a subsidiary of Novell, may offer ''improved'' alternatives like DR DOS. But no one can escape the fact that some sort of operating system software is essential to every computer on the market.

Something has to tie all the various pieces of hardware together and get them functioning smoothly. And for some 90 million computer users worldwide, that something is Microsoft's MS-DOS. All IBM-compatible machines are designed to work with it, as are the overwhelming majority of applications programs (programs that do word processing, database management, communications, and so on).

This is why Bill Gates, the thirty-something Harvard dropout who founded Microsoft, is a multi-billionaire. If you want an IBM-compatible machine that runs IBM-compatible software, you've got to buy Microsoft's MS-DOS, or the IBM version, IBM DOS. (DR DOS, while impressive, holds only a tiny fraction of the market.)

In this chapter, we're going to look at DOS from a purely practical, small business perspective. We're going to tell you what you've got to know to get up and running as quickly as possible. For a complete treatment of the subject, see *Glossbrenner's DOS 5* from Random House Electronic Publishing.

DOS: The role of a lifetime

We can begin by helping you understand the role DOS plays in your system and how it interacts with your applications programs. Here are the kinds of things that operating system software does for your computer:

- Coordinates computer hardware internally.
- Makes the hardware available for applications software to use.
- Organizes and oversees the storage of data and programs.
- Gives you, the user, control over your system's hardware and stored information.

The bootstrap loader

If you were to hook up your hardware and turn it all on without an operating system, nothing would happen. There would be nothing to tie your various hardware components together. Every component would be shouting for the CPU's attention. And there would be pitched battles for the computer's resources. You need software to tell the hardware what to do, when to do it, and how to respond if certain situations come up or if certain conditions are met.

That's what operating system software does. And it does it through the modular approach outlined in Chapter 2. Every computer maker or OEM includes a BIOS (basic input/output system) in his machine. The BIOS is like an adapter plug. One end of the plug is customized to meet the needs of a specific OEM's hardware design. The other end is standard, the same across all makes and models of systems.

The BIOS is software frozen in silicon chips called *ROM* (Read-Only Memory). BIOS chips are socketed right into the system's motherboard. Among the programs in the BIOS collection are little pieces of computer "code" (programming) capable of raising the system to a certain point.

Though comparatively feeble, the BIOS programs are capable of getting the system going and sending the read/write heads of your hard disk to a particular spot on the disk. The little program responsible for this is called the "bootstrap loader," a reference to the notion of the system pulling itself up by its bootstraps.

If the bootstrap loader does not find what it's looking for at this special spot on the hard disk, it checks the floppy A drive. If it still does not find what it needs, it shuts down and gives you a "Non-system disk" error message on the screen.

Searching for "the system"

What the bootstrap loader program is searching for is broadly called "the system." More specifically, it is searching for two very special files. On MS-DOS machines these files are called IO.SYS and MSDOS.SYS. On IBM brand machines, the files have different names. These files mate with the code already loaded into the computer's memory by the bootstrap loader and take your machine to a higher level. One module mates with another until, before you know it, your computer is at full power and capacity and ready to accept your commands.

Many of the machines sold today come with DOS pre-installed on their hard disks and ready to go. So, when you turn your machine on, you may well be greeted by the "C>" prompt. That means that the computer is currently focusing on Drive C.

However, it is crucial for you to know how that "C>" got there. If something should happen to those special "system" files on your hard disk, you will need to be able to replace them. The quick solution is this: Put the DOS "system disk" that came with your system in Drive A, close the drive door, and turn the machine on. Then consult your DOS manual for information on using the SYS command.

The Chief of Staff

Now, let's assume that your computer is up and running. The operating system is in control, and the "C>" prompt is on your screen. From this point on, the operating system software will perform like the White House Chief of Staff. Like the President, the microprocessor is the engine that makes things happen. But like the President's Chief of Staff, the operating system controls who (which piece of hardware) has access to the CPU. It also sets up schedules and establishes priorities. And it manages emergency hot lines called "interrupts" that let peripherals (like the keyboard) and programs demand immediate CPU attention.

The operating system does much more as well. It helps the processor achieve its full potential by enabling and responding to its built-in features. As you know, 386 and 486 processors can address and use megabytes of memory, but it is the operating system that makes this memory useful.

POST (Power On Self-Test)

We now know a lot about what an operating system is and does. Next, let's look at the experience each of us has almost every day. Let's look at what happens when you "power up." That is the computer user's term for turning the machine on. Turning it off is called "powering down," naturally.

As soon as you power up, electricity begins flowing into the computer, and shortly thereafter a little program in the ROM BIOS begins to run. The procedure is called the power-on self-test or "POST" for short. It involves a series of diagnostic routines to make sure that your memory chips and everything else are functioning normally. These routines also configure various support chips and get the add-on adapters initialized and ready to go to work.

The bootstrap loader then kicks in and starts looking for the system files. Once found, the loader turns control of the computer over to "the system," and the system starts looking for a file called COMMAND.COM. This is the program that is responsible for acting on the commands you issue from the keyboard. Thus a "boot disk" must contain two things: The two "hidden" system files, each located in its proper place on the disk, and COMMAND.COM. On a hard disk, COMMAND.COM must be located in your "root directory," a term we'll explain later.

Files, files, and more files

Okay. The operating system is in control, and you are ready to go to work. Now what?

Now you're ready to run programs. This is one heck of a lot easier to do than most people imagine. But a little background information is essential.

The first thing you need to know is that a program is nothing but a series of instructions designed to tell the CPU what to do. At your command, a program will be loaded into memory and the CPU will be told to begin following its instructions.

The procedure is so simple, I'm almost embarrassed to tell you how easy it is. There are really only two things you need to know. The first is how to find out what programs are available on your disk, a topic we'll discuss in a moment. The second has to do with the tags that identify a given file as a program that can be run.

Computers, like most small business owners, store everything in *files*. Computer files are discrete collections of information. One file might contain your list of customers. One might include a letter you are sending to a client. Another might contain the CPU instructions needed to run a particular program.

If you ever take a course in how to use a personal computer, your instructor is likely to say, "There are data files and program files." That is absolutely true. But for our purposes, we can say that there are program files and everything else.

So the key questions are how do you determine what is a program file and how do you get it loaded and running? The answers to both questions are very simple. Let's take the first one first.

Crucial extensions: .COM, .EXE, and .BAT

Computer files are normally given names that consist of two parts. There is the name, a dot, and the file extension. The entire package is called the *filename*. Thus, in the filename COMMAND.COM, "COMMAND" is the name and "COM" is the extension. Extensions are used to tell both the operating system and human beings what type of file they're dealing with. An extension of ".TXT," for example, almost always indicates a "text" file. An extension of ".HLP" indicates a "help" file. And so on.

Program files always have one of three extensions: .COM, .EXE, and .BAT. Translated, this means "command," "executable," and "batch." Here's the key point: Anytime you see a file ending in .COM, .EXE, or .BAT, you can type in the name of the file, and something will almost always happen. Thus, if you happened to see the file FE5.EXE on your disk and you keyed in **FE5**, the program File Express v.5 would load and run. If the file FORMAT.COM is on your disk and you key in **FORMAT**, you would activate the DOS disk formatting program.

There is a technical distinction between .COM and .EXE files, but that needn't concern us. Both consist of what can loosely be called "machine language" created when some programmer's English-like instructions were assembled or compiled into a .COM or .EXE file.

A batch file, on the other hand, is a text file containing a batch of DOS commands. When DOS runs a .BAT file, it starts at the top of the file and begins executing each command in turn, just as if you had typed them at the keyboard. Indeed, when DOS boots up, it looks for a file called AUTOEXEC.BAT in the root directory of your boot drive. If it finds a file by this name, it immediately begins to act on the commands the file contains. AUTOEXEC.BAT thus eliminates the need to key in the commands needed to get your system set up the way you want it each time you boot up.

You may not be aware of it, but we've just given you the keys to the kingdom. With the knowledge of the magic of the file extensions .COM, .EXE, and .BAT, you can run virtually any computer program—if you can find it. We'll show you how to do just that with the DIR command in the tutorial section of this chapter.

Applications programs and DOS

Before taking a brief look at how applications software interacts with DOS, let's summarize what we know so far. We know that the operating system is the software responsible for coordinating all of the various components of your computer and placing them at the service of both you and the CPU. We know that it consists of several modules: the ROM BIOS, the two hidden system files (IO.SYS and MSDOS.SYS), and the command interpreter (COMMAND.COM)

That's the essence of it. All of the other files that come with your DOS package are utility programs or special tools. They can be quite handy at times, but none of them is required to boot up a computer.

Now, as noted in Chapter 2, the key thing about an operating system as far as your word processing, database management, and other software is concerned is that it present the identical interface in every case, regardless of the make, model, or configuration of the machine. This is called the Applications Program Interface or API.

If you would like more detail on exactly what DOS's API consists of, see Peter Norton's *Programmer's Guide to the IBM PC & PS/2*, from Microsoft Press. Otherwise, take it on faith that there are all kinds of commands a program can issue to DOS to tell it to put a character on the screen, to read a character from the keyboard, to check the status of the serial port, and so on.

As long as a programmer knows what these commands are, he or she can write a program that will run on any DOS machine. The programmer does not have to worry about how to manipulate your particular video card to get a character to appear. All he's got to do is tell DOS to do it, and DOS will take care of it.

Variations and modifications

It is probably fair to say that the vast majority of programs available today do things this way. That is, they work with the hardware solely through DOS. These programs are said to be "well-behaved." However, some programmers go around DOS and manipulate the hardware directly, usually to get more speed. Years ago, Lotus 1-2-3 and Microsoft's Flight Simulator were notorious for directly manipulating the video hardware to make the program respond faster. These programs became a de facto test of how "IBM-compatible" a given machine was. If it could run Lotus and Fight Simulator, it could run anything.

Compatibility and speed of this sort are far less significant issues today. Still, it is important to be aware that it is possible to go around DOS and that some programs do it. All of the programs recommended in this book are well-behaved.

They'll run on any DOS machine. But someday you may encounter "misbehaved" software that will not run.

You should also be aware of a technique programmers use to ensure maximum compatibility with a wide variety of hardware. Many programs these days provide what we can loosely call software "drivers." These are small bits of code or special configuration files designed to support given makes and models of computer equipment.

A software driver lets you customize a program for optimum performance using your particular hardware. Drivers are thus frequently used to customize a program to use a particular printer. For example, when you install the word processing program PC-Write (Chapter 9) or the database program File Express (Chapter 10), you will be asked to make a selection from a long list of printer makes and models. In response to your selection, the correct printer driver will be copied to your hard disk as part of the installation process.

Similarly, when you install ProComm (Chapter 12), you will be asked to select from an extensive list of modem makes and models. The ProComm installation program will then make sure that ProComm is automatically set up to work with your modem.

DOS versions and DR DOS

It is important to note at this point that Microsoft/IBM DOS is not the only operating system available for your computer. Indeed, DOS 5.x isn't even the only version of DOS available. DOS 3.3 and DOS 4.01 are still being sold. In fact, at this writing, many OEMs and system vendors give you a choice among these versions of DOS 5. (Don't settle for anything less than DOS 5.)

In the software field, major revisions or re-writes of programs are signified by a change in the number to the left of the dot. Minor revisions are indicated by the number to the right of the dot, and maintenance versions to fix bugs are indicated by the number to the right of that. An "x" indicates that any number can fill a spot. Thus, when I say, "Get DOS 5.x," I mean DOS 5.0, which is available as of this writing, or DOS 5.1, which may be available as you read this.

There are no hard and fast rules or standards about what constitutes a major or a minor revision. It's up to the software company to choose a designation, though the computer press can usually be relied upon to keep them honest.

There is not much point in rehearsing the differences among the main DOS versions available today. All you need to know is that any program that runs with an older version will also run with a newer one. And DOS 5 offers so many more features that the only reason I can see for 3.3 and 4.01 still being offered by computer vendors is that they bought a lot of copies some time ago and need to reduce their inventory.

Nor is there space to discuss how Digital Research's DR DOS differs from the Microsoft product. It is a fine product offering a number of imaginative features, but, as one computer commentator put it, "The realities of the marketplace are such that, good as it is, DR DOS will always be 'Brand-X.'" You can be certain that absolutely everything will work with Microsoft's DOS. Even though I don't know of any incompatibilities with the DRI product, I could not say that about DR DOS. I mean, they had to make *some* changes to avoid infringing on Microsoft's copyrights, after all.

Microsoft Windows and other "environments"

The real competition today, however, is not in the DOS arena. The real competition is between Microsoft's Windows and IBM's OS/2. ("OS" is computer-talk for "operating system.") It's being called the "Battle for the Desktop," and the outcome is far from certain. The personalities, the politics, the historical relationship between Microsoft and IBM—all make for fascinating reading. Someday, after the dust has settled, perhaps Tracy Kidder or some equally talented journalist will tell the tale. Meantime, pick up a copy of Mr. Kidder's Pulitzer Prize-winning book, *The Soul of a New Machine*. This non-technical, dramatic account of the creation of a new computer is must reading.

Here, we'll concentrate on telling you what's going on and what, if anything, it is likely to mean to you.

Back from the grave

In a nutshell, Windows and OS/2 are designed to make a PC look like an Apple Macintosh. That's a very broad characterization, I know, but it does get to the heart of the matter. Both "interfaces" spring from the same root.

Years ago, Xerox set up an R&D group it called PARC (Palo Alto Research Center). The company assembled some of the best minds in computerdom and paid them to dream about the long-term future of computing. One of the things they came up with is what we today call a *graphical user interface* or GUI (pronounced "gooey").

The GUI screen would be designed to be analogous to a desktop, and as on a desktop, various papers ("windows") would overlap one another. At any given time you might be working in only one window, but you could see enough of the other windows to know what they were. Switching among windows would be nearly as easy as reaching for a different set of papers on your desk.

Instead of keying in filenames to their word processing software, for example, users would see a tiny picture (icon) of a fountain pen or other writing device on their screens and simply "click" on it with their mouse.

That would load the program. And the program would be written so that it used essentially the same interface and commands as the main GUI screen. This common interface would eliminate the need to master a completely different set of commands for each program. Once you have mastered the GUI basics, you're more or less able to run any piece of software, almost without a manual.

This is the goal Apple co-founder Steve Jobs was aiming at when he came up with first the Lisa and then the Macintosh. Xerox had tried to bring this technology to market with its Star system dedicated word processor in the early 80s. (The ads looked great, and I might have bought one if I didn't already have a different system.) But the world wasn't ready. Nor was the world ready when Apple bet the company on the Macintosh several years later. Indeed, even two years after its introduction, the Mac looked doomed to extinction.

For their part, Microsoft and IBM were not sitting idle. With Microsoft's help, IBM developed a windowing environment called TopView. Part of TopView evolved into Windows—which Bill Gates announced at a special party held at the Windows on the World restaurant atop the World Trade Center in New York City. Then the first version of Windows was shipped. The date was November, 1985.

No, that's not a typo. Windows has been kicking around for nearly seven years at this writing. And it was going absolutely nowhere. That's one of the reasons why IBM and Microsoft agreed to work together on a brand-new product, OS/2. The idea was to draw on the best stuff from TopView and Windows to create a completely new operating system.

In other words, Windows was nearly as dead as the Macintosh and appeared to be following that machine to the grave. Then the Mac began to revive as corporations began to take it more seriously. And, in May, 1990, Microsoft released Version 3.0 of Windows, and the product began to win a host of awards.

All of a sudden, here we are today. The drums beating for Windows are incessant. At this writing, Version 3.1 has appeared, and major computer publications are running cover stories offering "first looks" at it. What in the world is going on?

The cost of commitment

I've given you this whirlwind historical tour for a reason. If you are a new computer user, no one can blame you for getting caught up in the hoopla that currently surrounds Windows. That's why it is important for you to realize that, although the software was much improved with v3.0 in 1990 and v3.1 in 1992, Windows is not a new idea or a new product. The concept of overlapping windows and pictographic icons has been around since before there were personal computers, and the initial version of the product dates from late 1985.

So the question is this: If Windows is so great, why has it taken nearly seven years to reach its current popularity? Why wasn't there a mass stampede to Windows a few years after it came out? Is it possible that there's less here than meets the eye?

These are the questions everyone should ask before making a commitment to Windows or any other new operating system. And make no mistake, it is a commitment. Windows requires substantial hardware resources. Windows itself, for example, occupies nearly 5M of hard disk space. Also, to get the most out of Windows, you must buy versions of applications programs specifically designed to work with it. As a new user, opting for Windows also adds significantly to the amount of information you must master. Since it is impossible today to operate with Windows exclusively, you will have to learn both Windows and DOS, instead of just DOS.

The emperor's new clothes

The answer to these questions, in my opinion, is "Yes, there is a lot less here than meets the eye." For one thing, despite all the computer magazine cover stories and columns about working with Windows, there is no mass stampede. Writing in *PC Week* [December 16, 1991], industry watcher William Zachmann notes that if every copy of Windows Microsoft says it has sold is actually being used, Windows had "only 8.3 percent of the market" in 1991. But many of the people who get Windows, often as part of a computer package, never install it. If you correct the figures to allow for this, Zachmann says, Windows actually had only 5.5 percent of the market in 1991.

In a follow-up column on January 13, 1992, Zachmann said, "Windows penetration is still in single digits and won't dominate anything at recent growth rates." After working through the numbers, Zachmann concludes that if Windows really has the momentum claimed for it, shipments in 1992 should be "somewhere in the range of 15 to 20 million copies."

We'll all have to wait and see. But that would be quite a feat, considering that Microsoft shipped only five million copies in 1991. To put this into perspective, you should know that Zachmann estimates there were 90 million PC-compatible systems in use at the end of 1991, and he estimates a growth rate of 20 million systems per year.

Not even close

Clearly, while there is a lot of dust, there *is* no stampede to Windows, and Windows isn't even close to dominating the market. Yet the cover story review of Windows 3.1 in *PC World* magazine [February 1992] concludes with the suggestion that even users who aren't keen on Windows should buy a copy and "join the rest of the PC world." If it didn't happen so often, this kind of off-the-wall hyperbole would be considered outrageous. As we have just seen, using Microsoft's own numbers, this statement has no basis in fact. Even by the most generous estimate possible, only ten percent of PC users owned copies of Windows at the time that magazine issue appeared. That's hardly the "rest of the PC world."

Of course it is always possible that Microsoft *will* succeed in making Windows the leading operating system package in fact as well as in fiction. Maybe a stampede really will develop. Maybe its main competitor, IBM's OS/2, will self-destruct. (The latest version of OS/2 can run Windows, incidentally.) Maybe IBM and Apple really will jointly produce the killer operating system they have talked about. There is no way to know.

Overkill

Still, given all the hype and publicity, you've got to ask yourself why there has been no mass movement to Windows. Again, it is not as though Windows in one version or another hasn't been around for the last seven years or so. The answer, I think, can be summed up in the word *overkill*. There is no question that PCs need to be made easier to use, if only so that more people can use them.

But that doesn't necessarily mean they must be operated with a mouse, Super VGA-resolution icons, and half a dozen screen fonts. Windows icons are quite clever. But, to tell you the truth, I look at many of them and wonder "What the heck does that mean? What's that supposed to be anyway?" Indeed, if Windows icons are so intuitively obvious, why is it that every icon in Fig. 4-1 carries an explanatory tag like "File Manager," "Clipboard," or "Fonts"?

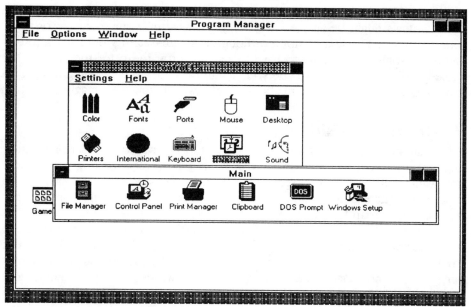

Fig. 4-1. A sample Windows screen.

The little pictures are cute. But I would much rather look at an English phrase on a menu and "click" on that to launch a program. As we'll see later in this book, there are many ways to make a system present you with a menu of programs and utilities each time you reboot. It may not be all that sexy, but for many people, a menu provides all the "ease of use" they need.

Making PCs easier to use doesn't mean "multi-tasking," either. Multi-tasking refers to the ability to actually run two or more programs at once. This is a much ballyhooed Windows feature. But somehow all the hype sounds familiar. It sounds suspiciously like people urging me to buy a computer so I can balance my checkbook or keep track of my recipes.

For example, I'm a heavy computer user. But the only time I can imagine benefiting from Windows's multi-tasking abilities is when I'm downloading a large file from a remote system. If the download is going to take more than a minute or so, I'd like to be able to load a different program and have the download continue in the background. That's multi-tasking.

But I can live with this small inconvenience, particularly since eliminating it is not worth the price I'd have to pay to do everything in Windows. Besides, only a small percentage of computer users regularly download files from remote online systems. There may be other clear benefits to multi-tasking, but I've yet to find them.

Finally, I know DOS and I have more than a passing acquaintance with Windows. And I can tell you that if you thought Windows would eliminate the need to know about files, hard-disk subdirectories, and many of the other things about computing that are less than intuitive, you're going to be sadly disappointed.

Windows might be an ideal way for your assistant, your secretary, or some other employee to use a computer (though a menu system would work just as well.) But someone is going to have to set the software up for them. And that someone is probably going to be you. To fill that role, you're going to have to learn a lot more about DOS and about Windows than you ever imagined.

On the plus side

Fair is fair, however, and I have got to say that Windows does present a pleasant face. You can move icons around until you get your screen looking just the way you want it. You can easily expand, contract, or reposition windows with your mouse. And there is no question about it, Windows *is* sexy. Much more interesting than the spartan DOS prompt.

You should also know that switching to Windows does not cut you out of using shareware. You can run any DOS program from Windows, of course. But the number of shareware programs for Windows, like the number of Windows versions of commercial programs, continues to grow. Also, it is important to note that, while Windows 3.1 fixes bugs and answers most previous user complaints, a totally new Windows is in the works.

This is Windows NT (New Technology). It will look the same on the surface, but underneath it will be almost completely different. Today's Windows, for example, loads in on top of DOS. You boot the system with DOS and then load Windows as an "operating environment." Windows NT will incorporate the operating system and, in effect, eliminate DOS.

The NT version is also expected to expand on the Windows promise of letting you cut and paste items from one program into another. The feature is called Object Linking and Embedding (OLE); versions 3.0 and 3.1 can do this now, but only on a limited basis.

When fully implemented by Windows and by applications programs, this feature will let you produce a graph in your spreadsheet program, clip it out, and insert it into a report you are preparing with your word processor. If you later change the spreadsheet numbers upon which the graph is based, the change will appear the next time you print your word processor-created report. You can also look at the graph in your report, enter a command, and be taken immediately to your spreadsheet program to make any changes.

Bottom-line time

My point here is not to slam Windows. It could very well be the new wave of the future. But it's important to have a little perspective. One can easily get caught up in the fever, once the drums have begun to pound. If you've heard the drums beat for other products over the years, it is easy to be more than a little skeptical.

So let me summarize things briefly. Neither Windows nor DOS nor OS/2 nor anything else is going to eliminate the need to master a certain quantum of knowledge about personal computing. If you want to play, you've got to pay.

Windows is sexy, and even in its current version, it has some attractive features. But when you opt for Windows, you automatically surrender a large measure of control over your system. That may or may not be important to you, though surrendering control over your wallet may hit closer to home. Things could change, but at this writing, by committing to Windows you are committing yourself and your company to a path that could end up costing you a lot more in the long run without delivering benefits commensurate with the expense.

If you are worried that an employee won't be able to use the computer, type up a list of step-by-step instructions to get him or her into and out of the target program. If you or your employees need easy access to several programs, prepare a menu using the shareware program Marx Menu. It doesn't have cute little icons, but it's colorful, fast, and remarkably easy to set up.

Finally, I cannot recommend actually buying Windows at this time. As for Windows NT, we'll all have to wait and see. Maybe it will be spectacular. On the other hand, if Windows happens to come with your machine at no extra charge, by all means give it a try. You will find the built-in solitaire game to be a real treat. Give Windows a good workout. But don't feel you have to study the manual. Get your DOS legs first. Then return to Windows if you feel the urge.

The hardware-software industrial complex

The Windows marketing, promotion, and publicity machine is truly exceptional. It may be that no one but Microsoft could create the impression that everyone is using Windows when only ten percent of users have copies. But the company has not done it alone. And that leads to a much larger truth all new personal computer users should be aware of.

We must never forget that there is a very large industry out there interested in moving computer products. Nothing wrong with that. As businesspeople, it's something we all understand. But we should also understand that this industry has never been shy about hype. If enough momentum can be created for a product, lots of people benefit. And if Microsoft can really get the Windows bandwagon rolling, absolutely *everybody* in the industry benefits.

Microsoft gets you to buy something in addition to DOS, be it Windows alone or Windows and several Windows versions of Microsoft applications programs. Hardware companies of every sort benefit due to the need for better monitors and bigger, faster hard disk drives to hold Windows and Windows applications. Microprocessor companies benefit because running Windows comfortably requires faster CPUs and lots of memory.

The magazines we all rely on for our information benefit from increased ad revenues from all the companies trying to sell you Windows-related products. And, of course, writers and book publishers benefit due to the need for more books on these new products.

In short, the computer industry today is characterized by a de facto hardware-software industrial complex. Like the military-industrial complex we used to hear so much about during the Cold War, each participant benefits from the success of the others. Of course, both complexes rely on us to supply the fuel in the form of cash. And both must persuade us to do so. During the Cold War it was the Soviet threat. In the computer industry it is usually the hyping of a category of software—desktop publishing comes to mind—or a particular piece of hardware (portables, notebooks, networks, etc.)

I don't for a moment suggest any impropriety. In fact, a synergistic arrangement like this is perfectly natural. After all, what would you do if you were selling a product that just doesn't wear out? And what if you knew that a basic, ten-year-old IBM/XT and a few shareware programs provided all of the power and capability that most people and small businesses need? You'd try your darndest to find some reason to get people to trade up.

As consumers, however, we are very much in the position of taxpayers trying to decide among a raft of complex weapons systems in years past. What do we know about throw weights, basing modes, and MIRVs? Maybe Windows really will dominate the desktop in the future. Maybe multi-media PCs with superb sound, CD-ROM drives, and lots of wonderful software really will take the market by storm. There is no way to tell.

The best course, I believe, is to take everything with a grain of salt. Don't rush into anything. Don't be swayed by the hype.

But when you decide to get into personal computing, don't hesitate. Check the market, and get the best system you can afford. Windows or no, you can never have enough speed, capacity, or power—even if you don't *really* need it. And at today's prices, I think it would be foolish to buy anything less than the type of system outlined in Chapters 2 and 3.

Buy your computer following the guidelines presented in Chapter 5. Then learn to use it, starting with the DOS Quick Tutorial offered next. The key thing to remember about a personal computer system is that it is not a discrete unit like, say, a television set.

A PC is much more like a stereo system. You can always buy additional components or individually upgrade the ones you have. And there is a nearly endless supply of "software" (records, tapes, and compact disks) to try. There's no hurry. The PC is going to be a part of your life from now on, and the hardware and software industry isn't going to go away. On the contrary, its products keep getting better, while many prices keep getting smaller. There's plenty of time to buy add-ons, upgrades, and new operating system software later.

DOS quick tutorial

As noted at the beginning of this chapter, we are going to assume that you have bought your computer, that it is turned on, and that you are sitting in front of it. We are also going to assume that the last line displayed on the screen consists of the C> prompt with a little blinking block next to it. The blinking block is called the *cursor*.

If the C> prompt is not on the screen, check your *documentation* (the instructions that came with the computer) for information on how to make it appear. Look for the term "DOS command line" in the documentation. If you have no joy, call your vendor's customer support number and ask them how to get to the DOS command line. It is possible that the vendor has set the system to automatically run Windows or some other program on boot-up.

Finally, you should view this tutorial as a quick introduction. It will have you using the top ten DOS commands immediately, but you will certainly want more information. So consult your DOS manual. For a quick, on-screen summary of any of these commands except Ctrl-Break, get into your DOS subdirectory and key in **HELP** followed by the command (i.e., **HELP DIR**, **HELP COPY**, etc.) This instant help information was one of the features added with DOS 5.

The ten most crucial DOS commands

As you know, one of the main functions of operating system software is to give you, the user, access to the computer's hardware. You issue orders to DOS by keying in commands at the command line. The command line always begins with the letter of the drive you are focusing on, a "greater-than" sign, and a blinking cursor (C>, A>, etc.)

DOS offers what it calls *internal* and *external* commands, but there is an easier way to describe this distinction. When DOS boots up, it loads a file called COMMAND.COM. This "command interpreter" software is designed to respond to the most frequently used DOS commands. Since it is loaded into memory, you can use one of these "internal" commands regardless of the disk drive you happen to be focusing on.

To conserve memory space, however, the people who created DOS opted not to include all possible commands in COMMAND.COM. Instead, they created a series of little programs like FORMAT.COM or SYS.COM. These are the external commands, and when you issue them, you actually tell DOS to run a program. The trick is that DOS must be able to find these files in order to run these programs. If DOS is focusing on Drive A and the programs are on Drive C, it won't find them, for example. (The PATH configuration command offers a way around this, but I don't want us to get ahead of the story.)

Only two of the DOS Top Ten Commands are "external" commands requiring access to program files. These are FORMAT and UNDELETE. All the rest are part of COMMAND.COM and available at any time. Here is the complete list:

- DIR
- MD or MKDIR ("Make Directory")
- CD or CHDIR ("Change Directory")
- RD or RMDIR ("Remove Directory")
- COPY
- DEL
- UNDELETE
- TYPE
- Ctrl-Break
- FORMAT

The DIR command

You know that computers store information and programs in files and that many filenames are significant. But how do you find out what files you have to work with? The answer is the DIR command.

Once DOS is in control, you can use DIR to discover the contents of any disk or hard disk subdirectory. If your on-screen prompt reads "A>," you can key in **DIR** and DOS will give you a list of all the files on the disk in Drive A. Any of those files ending in .COM, .EXE, or .BAT are programs that you can run.

If the prompt on your screen reads "C>," you can enter the same DOS command. That's what you should do right now. You will probably see something like this:

```
Volume in drive C is DISK C   Volume Serial Number is
3A2F-1DF5
Directory of C:\

DOS              <DIR>                12-13-91   11:33a
AUTOEXEC BAT                   43    01-12-92   11:28p
COMMAND    COM              47845    03-22-91    5:10p
CONFIG     SYS                427    01-29-92    4:05p
     3 file(s)               48315  bytes
                          77547520  bytes free
```

Now, change to Drive A by keying in **A:** and hitting your Enter key. The prompt will change to read "A>." Put a disk in the drive and close the door. Then key in **DIR**. You should see a list of files on the screen. Move back to Drive C by keying in **C:** and hitting Enter. Do another **DIR**.

The MD (Make Directory) command

The DIR command lets you discover what files are available in your current area of focus or, in DOS-speak, the "drive or directory you are currently logged onto." The MD (see MKDIR in your DOS manual) command is used to create the equivalent of file drawers on your hard disk. The DOS subdirectory shown in the screen listing above is one such "file drawer." You can create hundreds of others.

I've deliberately intermingled the terms "directory" and "subdirectory." The DOS manual may make a distinction, but real people don't. There is a distinction that is important, however, and that is between the *root directory* and the subdirectories branching off it. If you think of a subdirectory as a file drawer, the root directory is the room that contains all the drawers. The "room" can contain individual files as well, as is the case in the root directory shown above. Note that it contains the DOS subdirectory and three files (AUTOEXEC.BAT, COMMAND .COM, and CONFIG.SYS).

The key thing about directories is that any given directory can have an unlimited number of other directories branching off it. (The root directory does have a limit, but it is in the hundreds and need not concern us.) This is DOS's built-in file management system, and the biggest mistake most new users make is not taking advantage of it. Many, many new users pile everything into the root directory, where all of the program and data files get intermixed and it soon becomes impossible to find anything. Imagine an office room with no file drawers and stacks and stacks of manila folder files, and you will have an idea of what I'm talking about.

The MD command is the answer. Use it right now. Key in **MD TEST** and hit Enter. (Whenever I say "key in" from now on, assume that you should hit Enter to send the command to DOS.) Then do a **DIR**. You will see that the TEST directory has been added to the root directory.

The CD (Change Directory) command

So far, so good. You have just created your first "file drawer." Now how do you get down into TEST to see what's there. The answer is the CD (CHDIR in your DOS manual) command. This lets you "change directories." To move down to TEST, key in **CD \TEST**. Then do a DIR. The screen will tell you that you are now in C: \ TEST, and you will see two filenames, the "dot" and "double dot" files. These two files are for DOS's use, so don't worry about them.

Now, how can you get back up to the root directory? Use the CD command again, only this time, key in **CD **. Do a DIR to make sure you have landed where you expected. The single backward slash (\ ) is the "name" of the root directory as far as DOS is concerned.

The RD (Remove Directory) command

Okay, we're tired of TEST, so let's get rid of it. Use the RD (RMDIR in your DOS manual) command like this: **RD TEST**. As long as two conditions are met, DOS will happily oblige. The first condition is that you must be "above" the directory you want to remove when you use the command. In our case, we are at the root directory of Drive C and TEST branches off it, so we are "above" TEST on the directory tree. Second, the directory must be empty. As a safety measure, DOS won't let you remove a directory if it contains any files.

The COPY command

Now that we know how to create a file drawer (directory), let's see how to fill it. Use the MD command to make a directory of your choosing, TEST, BOZO, JUNK, whatever. Then use the COPY command to copy some files into it. We'll assume you have created a directory called TEST. Key in **COPY COMMAND.COM \TEST**. Log onto \TEST and do a **DIR** to see if the copy operation was successful. You should see the two dot files and COMMAND.COM.

Notice that we told DOS what to do (COPY), what to do it to (COMMAND .COM), and where to put it (\TEST). This three-part structure appears again and again in DOS commands. Here we would only point out that you do not have to specify one file at a time. If you like, you can tell DOS to act on a whole bunch of files at once by using *wildcards*. See your manual for details.

Briefly, the "star" (asterisk) stands for "anything." Thus **COPY *.BAT** would copy all files ending in .BAT to your selected destination. **COPY JUN.*** would copy all files beginning with JUN. A question mark can be used to stand for any single character. **COPY J??.BAT** would thus work on JUN.BAT, JUL.BAT, JAN.BAT but *not* on JUNE.BAT.

The DEL and UNDELETE commands

The DEL (delete) command is the one you use to remove files from your disk. If you keyed in **DEL *.BAT**, for example, you would tell DOS to delete every file in the current directory ending in .BAT. If you keyed in **DEL *.***, you would delete all files. Since this is considered a drastic step, DOS will prompt you first to make sure you're sure. Of course, you may also delete a single file: **DEL TEST.TXT**.

Prior to DOS 5, deleting a file was a more serious matter than it is today. In fact, Peter Norton Computing, now a part of Symantec, was founded on a program designed to recover accidently deleted files. In DOS 5, Microsoft finally offered an "undelete" program (licensed from the folks who produce PC Tools). This is an external command, so you will need access to the DOS program file UNDELETE.EXE.

You will want to consult your manual for more details, but briefly, when you **DEL** a file, DOS does not wipe it from the disk. Instead, DOS changes a single character in the filename to say, in effect, "This Space Available." The UNDELETE program changes that character back to signify "Occupied." There's more to it than this, but that's the basic idea. The key thing is to make sure that you **UN-DELETE** a file as soon as possible after erasing it. Otherwise, there is a chance that some new file will be put into its space and its data really will be destroyed.

The TYPE and Ctrl-Break commands

The TYPE command lets you see the contents of a file. You're not going to hurt anything if you TYPE a program file, but the command is designed for text files. Thus, you might use the DIR command to locate filenames ending in .TXT or .BAT or some other extension signifying a text file. Then key in a command like **TYPE AUTOEXEC.BAT**. The contents of the file will be displayed on the screen.

The only thing you need to know about it is how to use it to display long (more than one screenful) files. The command to enter is **TYPE filename.ext ¦ more**, where **filename.ext** stands for the actual name of your target text file. This sends the output of the TYPE command through the DOS MORE filter, which displays one screen of text at a time and prompts you to hit a key to see the next screen.

In Chapter 16 I'll show you how to make this easier still, using either Mark Hersey's FANSI-CONSOLE or Vern Buerg's LIST, two of the most valuable shareware programs you will ever encounter.

At this point you should know that DOS's "all stop" command is the key combination Ctrl plus Break (Ctrl-Break). If TYPE, for example, is merrily displaying a continuous stream of text, and you don't want to wait for it to finish, hold down your Ctrl (control) key and hit your Break key. On most keyboards, Break shares a key with Pause. Entering a Ctrl-C will have the same effect. Whatever is taking place will stop, and you will be returned to the DOS prompt.

You can use Ctrl-Break to break out of batch file programs and many BASIC programs as well. But if all else fails, do a Ctrl-Alt-Del to reboot the machine, or hit the red reset button on the front of the system unit if you have one.

The FORMAT command

Finally, there is the FORMAT command. You will want to consult your DOS manual for complete details, but here is what you need to know, in general. All disks, whether floppy or hard, are completely blank when they roll off the assembly line. Conceptually, they are like the world before the invention of latitude and longitude—one vast, uncharted open space. Before DOS can store files on one of these disks, it must apply the magnetic equivalent of latitude and longitude lines.

It must build a framework, in other words, so that every point on the disk can be described by a set of coordinates. That's what the FORMAT command is all about. It prepares a blank disk for DOS to use. And it does it by laying down concentric circles of magnetic signals called *tracks* and dividing each track into *sectors*. FORMAT does some other things as well, but that's the basic idea.

Once a disk has been formatted, DOS can break a file into chunks and tuck one chunk into each disk sector, almost as if it were filling pigeonholes in a mailroom. Since each sector has a specific address, DOS can easily load the complete file into memory again (or copy it to some other location) by going to each pigeonhole in sequence and literally picking up the pieces of the file.

FORMAT is an "external" command, so DOS must have access to the program FORMAT.COM. As your manual will tell you, it is capable of formatting everything from a single-sided 5.25" floppy to a huge hard disk. Fortunately, DOS will not let you apply FORMAT to a hard disk without issuing a warning that all data will be destroyed.

System memory and configuration

We can't leave the subject of hardware and the operating system without saying a word or two about memory and system configuration. For reasons of space, it will have to be a very brief word. PC memory optimization is such a broad topic that *Glossbrenner's DOS 5* devotes three chapters to the subject. I will give you "cookbook" instructions on what to do here, but you will undoubtedly want to consult your DOS manual as well.

The first thing you need to know is that in addition to looking for COMMAND.COM and AUTOEXEC.BAT when it boots up, DOS also looks for a file called CONFIG.SYS. All three files must be in the root directory of your boot drive. CONFIG.SYS is a text file, and it contains your instructions on how you want your hardware to be configured.

Here is the CONFIG.SYS file I suggest you start with:

```
DEVICE=C:\DOS\SETVER.EXE
DEVICE=C:\DOS\HIMEM.SYS /machine:1
DEVICE=C:\DOS\EMM386.EXE i=e000-efff ram 1000
DOS=HIGH,UMB
STACKS=0,0
BREAK=ON
BUFFERS=20
FILES= 80
SHELL=C:\DOS\COMMAND.COM C:\DOS\ /e:512 /p
```

The key assumptions here are that you have a directory branching off Drive C called \DOS, and that it contains all of your DOS 5 files, as well as a copy of COMMAND.COM. Finally, it assumes that you have two to four megs of memory or more, and that you want to allot one meg of it to EMS memory and the remainder to XMS or "extended" memory.

At this point, I may have lost you completely. But, in for a dime, in for a dollar. If you do not have a word processing program, you can create this file directly from the keyboard by following these steps. First, key in **COPY CONFIG.SYS ORIGFIG.SYS**. That will save any original CONFIG.SYS file that came with your system. Should things go wrong, you can restore your present situation by keying in **COPY ORIGFIG.SYS CONFIG.SYS**. Whenever possible, always build yourself an escape hatch. That's what we have done here.

Now you're ready. Key in **COPY CON:CONFIG.SYS**. Then key in each line you see above. Finish by hitting your F6 key and Enter. DOS should say "1 file copied." Reboot your computer to put this new CONFIG.SYS file into effect.

I don't think you'll have any problems, but if you do, use your escape hatch and restore the system to its original state. It isn't likely, but you may find that you will have to reboot by putting your DOS system disk floppy in Drive A, instead of booting from Drive C. Then use the escape hatch.

Three types of memory

We're going to limit the discussion here to memory. That's what the recommended CONFIG.SYS file above is all about. The key to understanding PC memory is to visualize a vast array of pigeonholes. Those are the system's memory cells and, as you might imagine, each cell has a unique address number.

Memory is used by the CPU to hold programs and data. And it just stands to reason that the amount of memory any given CPU can use is limited by the number of memory "pigeonhole" address numbers it can write. The Intel 8088 chip upon which the first IBM/PC was based could write enough addresses to access one megabyte of memory. This was at a time when 64,000 bytes (64K) was considered normal.

The PC's designers divided up that megabyte into two sections. There was a maximum of 640K for programs and data—the 640K "work space"—and 360K of addresses for add-on cards like the video card, the printer card, and so on. The original version of DOS was written to work with these restrictions. And all applications programs were necessarily written to use no more than 640K of work space.

That worked fine for a while. But new chips came along that were able to address 16 megabytes worth of memory. And, as applications became more elaborate, they began to bump up against the 640K barrier. DOS could have been rewritten to take advantage of memory above the one-megabyte mark, but there are all kinds of reasons why this was not done.

Two techniques were used to solve the problem and provide more memory to applications programs. They were and are called EMS and XMS memory. This stands for the Expanded Memory Specification and the Extended Memory Specification, respectively. Both assumed a system that had more than 640K of memory. (Remember, the remaining 360K of the first megabyte was actually 360K of reserved address numbers. There were no actual memory pigeonholes associated with these addresses until you added a card that occupied them.)

Extended memory is memory that extends beyond the one megabyte mark. If you think of memory as a column and draw a line at "1M," extended memory is every address above that mark. Expanded or EMS memory, in contrast, is like a balloon attached to that column someplace below the 1M mark.

The EMS technique says in effect, "You can only address 1M of memory? Okay, fine. I'm going to cut a window into that column and swap additional memory in and out of that window as needed." An EMS window might show only 64K worth of memory at any given time, but the contents of that 64K would vary, depending on when you looked at the window.

There are thus three categories of memory in PCs today. There is "conventional memory," the 640K work space. There is EMS or "expanded" (remember the balloon) memory. And there is XMS or extended ("extends" beyond 1M) memory. A 286-based computer can use all three types, but it does it in an awkward fashion. For example, it requires a separate add-on memory board with special control circuitry to use EMS memory.

The 386 chip (SX or DX) has memory control circuitry built in. So too does the 486 line of CPUs. These chips can easily make extended memory emulate expanded memory, allowing you to select any amount of EMS memory you want. That's what the line `DEVICE=c:\dos\emm386.exe i=e000-efff ram 1000` is all about in the CONFIG.SYS example shown above. The `1000` at the end of the line tells the EMM386.EXE driver to allocate 1000K (1M) of extended memory for EMS memory.

And why would I want to take one of my four megabytes and turn it into EMS memory? Because I run any number of programs that are designed to automatically detect and use EMS memory. File Express v.5 (FE5), is one example. FE5's use of expanded memory lets it load an entire database into memory, instead of leaving part of it on disk. That makes it run faster and perform better.

Try the MEM command

The sample CONFIG.SYS file above also activates the "HMA" (High Memory Area)—that portion of extended memory that lies immediately beyond the 1M limit—and loads most of DOS into it. If you are a more experienced user, you may have TSRs and other programs that you would like to load into extended memory as well. See the DEVICEHIGH= and the LOADHIGH commands in your DOS manual for more information on how to do this.

Please don't feel bad if you do not understand all of this. I have given you a very, very quick explanation. Try the above CONFIG.SYS file on your system, adding to it anything that may already be in the version of the file that came with your system. If it doesn't work, use the escape hatch to restore your system to its original configuration. Then get a book about DOS or call your vendor's support line.

If it does work, assuming you've got four megs of memory and a 386 or 486 system, you can probably leave it alone. You will have close to the maximum amount of free conventional 640K memory, one megabyte of expanded "EMS" memory, and the remainder in extended memory. Almost every program, whether it recognizes memory beyond the 640K mark or not, will run better. If you do not want EMS memory, delete **RAM 1000** and replace it with **NOEMS**. That way, all of your extra memory will be configured as XMS extended memory.

Finally, be sure to check your DOS manual for instructions on using the MEM command. This command, particularly MEM /C will show you your memory and what programs are loaded where.

The PATH command

There is one final configuration tip you should know about. It's a small matter, but it can make an enormous difference. It is called the PATH command. You will want to consult your DOS manual for the fine points, but here is some information that will help the manual's explanation make more sense.

The PATH command lets you tell DOS "where else to look." Normally, DOS focuses only on whatever disk drive or directory you happen to be logged onto. If you key in **FORMAT**, for example, DOS will look in your logged drive/directory for a file called FORMAT.COM, FORMAT.EXE, or FORMAT.BAT. If it does not find a file by one of those names, it will report "File not found" or a similar error message.

The PATH command lets you tell DOS, "Okay, if you don't find a program file where I am at the time, check these places as well." Thus, if you key in **PATH=C:\DOS**, you will have told DOS to add that directory (C:\DOS) to its search list. If FORMAT.COM is in C:\DOS, you can key in **FORMAT** at anytime, regardless of where you are in your system, and DOS will find and run the program. Similarly, if your word processing program is in D:\ED and is called

ED.EXE (as PC-Write's main program is called), you can key in **PATH=C:\DOS;D:\ED**. If you are over on Drive B and you key in **ED BILL.TXT**, DOS will look for ED.EXE on Drive B. Not finding it there, DOS will look in C:\DOS. Not finding it there, it will look in D:\ED, and, bingo!, PC-Write will load and you can start the file creation process.

A "path" in DOS-speak is a file's full address. Thus, the path for the FORMAT program is C:\DOS\FORMAT.COM. By including the directories containing your most frequently used programs in your PATH command, you can have access to those programs at any time. No need to actually move to their locations and operate from there.

Lastly, once you have decided upon the directories you want to include in your PATH command, you can make the entire line a permanent part of your AUTOEXEC.BAT file. That way, the PATH command and your specifications will be entered automatically each time you reboot the system. You won't have to do it by hand every time.

Conclusion

I know we've only skimmed along the surface in this tutorial. But, hopefully, the information presented here will direct you to the right places in your DOS manual and make what you find there more understandable. Some points may seem very complicated. And, frankly, some of them really are. The key thing is to be aware of the really important aspects and commands DOS offers. And that is definitely what has been presented here.

If there is something you want to understand, but can't quite make out, ask a computer-knowledgeable friend for help. Check your DOS manual. Or get a book on the subject.

As spare as these explanations may seem, I have every confidence that if you use this chapter and this tutorial as your guide, you will be off to an excellent start. Once you've zeroed in on and mastered the points raised here, you will be ready to move on to tap even more of DOS's power.

Part II
Buying equipment and programs

5

How to buy
the system you need

IN THIS CHAPTER, WE'RE GOING TO TELL YOU HOW AND WHERE TO BUY A computer system for your small business. Or, more accurately, we're going to lay out the alternatives and options open to you. Aside from the possibility that your brother-in-law will suddenly decide to move to Moscow to help the Russians rebuild their economy and leave you with his system, there are generally three ways to acquire a computer. You can buy from a computer retailer in your area. You can order a system through the mail. Or you can buy used equipment from a friend or through an organization like the Boston Computer Exchange (BoCoEx).

The avenue you choose will be determined by your specific needs, and I don't mean *computer* needs. You can get comparable equipment through all three channels, so makes, models, and megabytes are a non-issue. The needs I'm speaking of have to do with dollars and cents, service, support, warranties, and all the other issues that surround the purchase.

Through careful shopping, you can save a few dollars here and there. But the price competition is so brutal that you may be surprised at how small the savings will be. Shopping around is definitely worthwhile, however, and I strongly advise it, if only to develop a sense of the market. The one thing you must never forget, though, is that no one is going to suddenly suspend the laws of economics for you.

You are not going to get something for nothing. If one store's price is significantly lower than another's, there is a reason. In all likelihood, the store offering the lower price offers less customer support and service. Few things are more irritating than to hear a computer owner brag about getting the lowest price and then complain bitterly that the vendor does not provide the hand-holding, help, and support he needs.

This attitude defies all logic. It's on a par with the notion that under a national health insurance program each of us will receive all the health care we want and somehow not have to pay for it. As a small businessperson or professional, I'm sure you've encountered customers or clients who expect you to deliver the moon to their doorsteps but are outraged when you charge them for the freight.

Don't be such a customer yourself when you set out to buy a computer. Realize that there is a cost for everything. Realize, too, that your biggest cost is time. For example, the best way to save money on a system is to buy the individual components and build a system yourself. But that also involves the highest expenditure of time. At the opposite end of the spectrum, you can go to a computer store in your area right now, buy a machine, and have it in place and ready to go a few hours later. You may pay a few hundred dollars more than you have to, but your time expenditure is close to zero.

The middle area between these two extremes is broad indeed. But it's this middle area that we will concentrate on here. I don't think most businesspeople should be spending their time building a system from scratch, but I don't think you should automatically buy from your nearest computer dealer either.

Accordingly, we'll look at the two main channels for buying new equipment—retail and mail-order—and offer some advice to help you decide which is right for you. Then we will touch briefly on the used computer channel and explain what you can expect if you follow this route. Finally, at the end of the chapter, we'll present the Computer Shopper's Guide, an encapsulated summary of the hardware components discussed in Chapters 2 and 3 and the questions you should ask when buying this equipment.

The retail route

Computer mail-order companies are fantastic. The leading firms—Dell, Zeos, Northgate, Gateway, PC Brand, and the others singled out for praise in magazines like *PC* and *PC World*—offer wonderful price-performance deals with all the warranties you could want, on-site service, leasing and credit terms, and speedy delivery. They have solved their biggest problem: The automatic hesitation we all feel when we contemplate buying a piece of high-tech equipment—costing thousands of dollars—through the mail.

But there's one thing no mail-order firm can offer, and that's a personal relationship. Only a computer retailer can do that, and only the right retailer. In my opinion, every small business owner or professional should try to develop a relationship with a trusted computer retailer.

This can take some doing. You may have to branch out beyond your own town. But if you live in a reasonably well-populated area, the chances are that you will be able to find the person you're looking for without too much trouble.

The "right" retailer

If you have no luck finding the "right" retailer, you can turn to the mail-order option. Indeed, you should always keep mail-order in mind, particularly for the components you find you want to add in the future. But when you are just starting, get yourself a "main man" (or woman or whatever). Find a retailer you can talk to, someone who takes an interest in what you're trying to accomplish with a computer, and buy your system from him.

You may or may not end up paying a bit more. (I should note here that I was surprised to find a retailer in my area offering a 486DX/33 system for $5 less than comparable mail-order systems.) But if there is a difference, it won't be great—no more than one to two hundred dollars—and the benefits can be enormous. Besides, you will easily save many times that amount by using the shareware discussed later in this book.

The right kind of retailer will set up your system for you and spend some time showing you how to use it. He won't be able to give you a full tutorial course without charging for it, but if you've got questions after you get the thing installed, you'll be able to pick up the phone and call him.

Equally important, in years to come, if there is something you want to do with the machine, you can call your guy and ask what he recommends. A good computer retailer, like a good accountant, stays on top of what's happening in his field. That is part of the service he or she provides, and it means you don't have to spend the time and effort yourself.

Nor will a good retailer ever knowingly steer you wrong. You have a relationship, after all. He values your business, just as you value his expertise. He will have a service department, usually staffed by one or two "techies." They may or may not make house calls, but, of course, you can always bring the system in should it need an upgrade or repair. And, you may be able to request "rush" service at no extra charge. It's all part of the relationship.

How to find the right retailer

I realize that what I've described here sounds almost too good to be true, particularly if you have already been out shopping for computers. But retailers like this do indeed exist—you just have to know where to look for them. Start by consulting the "Computers—Dealers" heading in the Yellow Pages for your area and eliminating anyone who is an "authorized" IBM or Macintosh dealer. Next, eliminate anyone with more than two locations.

Make a list of the dealers who are left. Arrange the names by proximity to your place of business, if you like. Then call each one of them. Ask to speak to the owner. When the owner picks up the line, introduce yourself, explain that you want an IBM clone, and ask what he or she would charge for a system like the one detailed at the beginning of Chapter 2 or in the Computer Shopper's Guide presented here.

Ask what warranty the store provides on the systems it sells. Ask what the warranty covers: parts only, or parts and labor? A one-year limited warranty is standard. In most cases, I would advise against any "service contract." If your computer works for the first 90 days, it will work nearly forever. The only wear points are the electro-mechanical devices like disk drives and printers, and they should last for years with no problems whatsoever.

The purpose of this initial interview is to gather factual information, so be sure to take notes. Equally important, however, is the sense you get from the person. Is he knowledgeable and sincerely interested in helping you? Or is he someone who simply wants to move tubes and boxes? What you're looking for, in short, is personal chemistry. As when selecting a doctor, dentist, attorney, or accountant, what you're really buying is the *individual*.

In line with this, you might also ask how long the firm has been in business. How did he or she get into computer retailing? What did he or she do before? Get to know the person, in other words.

The next step is to visit those retailers you called who gave you "good vibes." Phone them and tell them you'll be in the area on such-and-such a date. When would be a good time for you to stop by the store? No need to commit to a definite appointment, unless you want to. Your goal is to make sure you'll be able to meet in person the man or woman you spoke with on the phone.

Meet with the people on your list. Tell them about your business. Use the information presented in Part I of this book. Get quotes from several promising dealers, if possible. Then pick the one you feel will be best for you.

You should also buy a copy of *Computer Shopper* magazine (which we'll describe in a moment) and let your fingers do the shopping. If your chosen dealer's price is higher than some other store or a mail-order firm, level with him. Tell him you can get a comparable system from Dealer X or Mail-Order Company Y for however much less. You want to do business with him, but money is tight. Is there anything he can do?

The dealer may or may not be able to see his way clear to lower his price or otherwise sweeten the deal. But if he is the right retailer for you, he will at least be able to explain why he charges what he does.

This is something you have to play by ear. As a businessperson yourself, you know he's got expenses, and he's got to be able to make a living. So if he says he simply can't cut his price any further, if your personal chemistry is good and you can live with his quote, give him the benefit of the doubt and give him your business.

Again, your main goal is starting what you hope will be a long-term relationship. You've got to let your dealer make an acceptable profit. Otherwise he won't be in business very long. At the same time, you do not have to buy absolutely everything from him. If you want a genuine Hewlett-Packard laser printer, for example, and he is not an authorized HP dealer, get your printer through the mail.

Similarly, I don't recommend buying any applications software from the dealer at the time you purchase your system. Your dealer knows that you will need software, and as a good businessperson, he or she will try to sell you a word processing program, at the very least. Explain that you want to ease into things gradually. Tell the dealer that you'd like to play with DOS for awhile before addressing larger issues.

The shareware programs featured in this book and the information provided in Part III can fill all your needs and save you big bucks besides. If you need a commercial package, you will almost always do better ordering it through the mail. Important as it is to patronize a good computer dealer, there is almost never any advantage to buying commercial software from him.

Some dealers will offer to install the programs you buy from them and show you how to use them. But in most cases, the main advantage a retailer provides when it comes to software is instant availability. Very few provide any kind of training or support, and almost none offers these things for free. If you can wait a day, most mail-order firms can ship you the same product via Federal Express.

The mail-order approach

There are two reasons for taking the mail-order route. One is if you cannot find what I've called the "right" retailer in your area. The other reason is purely a matter of price. We'll look at both topics here.

Where I live, on the New York-Washington corridor, there are lots of places to buy a PC. I could go to one of the ubiquitous locations of the nation's leading electronics store franchise operation. But their machines have a reputation for quirkiness and slight incompatibilities, and I have never been impressed by the quality of the sales staff.

I could go to the discount office supply store where I buy almost everything I need for my office. This national chain has begun to carry Dell computers, but the staff, while friendly, knows next to nothing about personal computing.

In the same strip shopping plaza is one of a dozen stores operated by a local chain. I know the founders and used to buy from them back when they were a one-store, Mom-and-Pop operation. But I wouldn't buy from one of their stores today.

I admire the nimbleness and marketing savvy of this mini-chain. But the last time I went into one of their stores, I found it staffed by appliance salesmen who stuck to you like Velcro. They knew how to figure their commissions, but little else. Thanks, but no thanks.

As it is, I do all of my computer business with a one-store firm in a new shopping center located in a town 20 minutes away. The two owners are there every day, along with a technician I've known since he worked in a similar store in another town. For me, this is the "right" retailer. The vibes are excellent, and I trust these three gentlemen completely. Nevertheless, I also buy hardware and software through the mail.

They've got it covered

My point is simply this: Anyone can locate a computer retailer, but if you can't find the "right" retailer, you might as well buy through the mail. If your local salesperson would be more comfortable selling you a phone or a stereo system (as is the case with the national chain), or if the company's main interest is getting salespeople to push tubes and boxes (as is the case with many other computer chains, large and small), then you might as well order your system through the mail.

I believe it is worth paying a couple hundred dollars more to the right retailer if there is the promise of building a long-term relationship. But I wouldn't pay even a dollar more for the marginal convenience of buying from the local outlet of some national chain or warehouse operation.

"But," you say, "what about service?" The mail-order companies—at least the leaders in the field—have got that covered. Many of them have contracted with TRW, RCA, and other large companies with computer service operations to provide on-site service during the first year you own the machine. That means that when you've got a problem, a person actually comes to your place of business to fix it. Not even most "right" retailers can offer that, and the national electronics chains and warehouse operations may not even have service available at their store locations. So much for "local" convenience.

How to shop by mail

The downside of the mail-order route is that the field is so crowded. The ads you may have seen in *PC Magazine* or *PC World* represent only the tip of the iceberg. For a truly comprehensive view, pick up a copy of *Computer Shopper*. Published by Ziff-Davis, this sister publication of *PC Magazine* presents page after page of ads from mail-order firms, most of which you've never heard of. You can find *Computer Shopper* at most Waldenbooks and B. Dalton stores.

I'm sure that the vast majority of companies advertising in *Computer Shopper* and other magazines are reputable. But I'm also sure that at least some of them consist mainly of some guy ordering parts and assembling PCs in his garage. As I have said before, computer hardware is a commodities business.

The "built with loving hands at home" machine may be every bit as good as the one offered by a leading mail-order firm. In fact, it probably uses a few of the same parts. But the few hundred dollars you'll save by buying one of these beauties won't make up for not having a toll-free support line, a real warranty, on-site service, and all the other benefits of a truly professional operation.

Most local computer stores can service most mail-order clone machines. So getting service isn't really an issue. Paying for it is, however. You may save a few hundred dollars buying from Phil's Computer Bargains someplace in Oklahoma, but if your machine goes on the fritz, you'll have to pay a local computer store to have it repaired. And that will reduce your savings.

Fortunately, there is a common-sense solution. In recent years, mail-order firms and the computers they offer have crossed a threshold. They are now taken seriously by the computer press. Mail-order equipment is routinely included in computer hardware reviews. Therefore, you can greatly simplify the task of deciding which system to buy by consulting *PC Magazine*, *PC World*, or *InfoWorld*, three of the leading computer magazines.

The testing labs at these three publications beat the dickens out of every machine they review. They know what they're looking for, and they know where to look. If there is some internal difference, or if an OEM has used cheap materials, they will report it.

So, read the reviews, and use them to narrow the mail-order field. *PC Magazine*, for example, periodically does exhaustive "roundup" reviews of 386 or 486 systems. The systems judged best are given the "Editor's Choice" designation, and all reviews are summarized in a table somewhere within such articles. If you are not a subscriber, check for copies of *PC Magazine* and these other publications at your local library or bookstore.

Mail-order questions

If you deal with a leading mail-order firm, one whose products have been reviewed in a leading magazine, you probably won't have much to worry about. Still, to make sure you are getting the whole picture, you may want to ask the following questions:

- Is there an extra charge for using Visa or MasterCard?
- What will the actual bottom line—including shipping—be?
- How does the on-site service feature work? Can I call the service company directly, or do I need authorization from you?
- Is there a "re-stocking" fee? If I decide to return the equipment within 30 days, will I get all my money back? (Be sure to save your original boxes and packing materials.)
- What about support? Is there a toll-free support (help) number, and if so, is there any kind of limit on the number of calls I may place? Is there a support bulletin board system (BBS) I can access with a modem?

As I have said, I think everyone interested in buying a computer should experience *Computer Shopper*. There is no better way to get an overview of the current market. Chapters 2 and 3 contain all the information you will need to make sense of the ads. So plunge in for an evening and take a look around. The quantity of ads is overwhelming, but there is no better way to get an overall sense of the mail-order market.

As to which mail-order firm to choose, I can recommend nothing less to a brand-new user than buying from a company whose products have been favorably reviewed in leading computer magazines. In years to come, after you've had some experience, you may be able to save some money buying from little-known mail-order companies. But don't start out this way.

The used computer market

You're probably tired of hearing this by now, but computers simply don't wear out. Only the components with moving parts are truly vulnerable, and this means the floppy and hard drives and the printer. Everything else will last the way a television set lasts—nearly forever.

But technology marches on. Consequently, there are always people eager to shed slightly older systems and use the money they receive from selling their equipment toward the purchase price of the latest stuff. That's what the used computer market is all about.

Check the classifieds

There are all kinds of ways to buy a used computer. You might start by checking the classifieds of your local newspaper. You know what to look for from Chapters 2 and 3. If you're buying the machine for your business, under no circumstances should you settle for anything less than a 386SX, no matter how good the offered price.

Use the ads in *Computer Shopper* and other magazines to gauge the seller's price. The seller will probably want to get rid of his entire system, but you should definitely bargain hard over the printer. Explain that you're concerned about wear and tear on the unit and ask what the price would be if you bought only the system unit, keyboard, and monitor.

This effectively makes the printer a non-issue in the negotiations. If the seller wants to throw it in for a token amount, you will oblige him. But you can always get a brand-new printer, with full warranty, from a mail-order supplier. So (shrug) you don't really care one way or another.

As when buying a used car, you should automatically assume that you'll have to put some money into a used computer. If that turns out not to be the case, so much the better. But start your bargaining with this assumption foremost in your mind. And make it clear to the seller.

Explain to the seller that you will probably have to replace one or more floppy drives (at about $60 each), and you really were looking for a system with 50 to 60 megabytes more on its hard drive. And, by the way, is it an IDE hard drive and is the access time close to 15 ms?

It's not? It's an MFM/RLL drive with an access time of 28 ms? (Draw in a deep breath over your teeth so the seller hears it on the phone here.) Gee, that's too bad. Explain that performance is important to you and you're not really too happy about buying a 386SX 16 MHz machine (or whatever) in the first place.

Finally, the seller may try to sweeten the deal by throwing in a ton of commercial software. Don't be swayed by this. More than likely, the software he provides will be older versions of commercial programs, and the manuals may or may not be included. In any case, it's a good bet the seller has registered the programs with their producers under his own name. (Each copy of a commercial program typically has its own unique serial number for purposes of registration and support.) There is also the possibility that the seller may not be legally entitled to provide you with the software.

The *new* hardware market is such that you can drive a very hard bargain when buying used equipment. Just remember to be kind. And don't forget: Someday you may be the person interested in unloading older equipment so *you* can buy something new.

Check local users groups

Classified ads are probably the most convenient way to buy a used system. Indeed, if no "For Sale" ads have appeared in your paper, you might consider placing an ad in the "Wanted" section of the classifieds. You never know—such an ad might get some people off the fence and stimulate them to call you.

A second route is to buy from someone in your local computer user group. We'll have more to say about computer user groups in Chapter 7. For now, you should know that all across the country there are non-profit organizations staffed by enthusiastic volunteers that are dedicated to helping people get into computing. Membership fees are typically around $25 a year, and most user groups publish a monthly newsletter, sent free to all members.

To find a group in your area, ask at your local computer retail store. If the sales staff does not know of any group, ask the store's service and repair technician. Of all the people in a typical computer store, the technicians tend to be the ones most interested in computers. They're the ones most likely to know about, and belong to, computer user groups.

Most groups meet one Saturday a month, often at a local school, community college, or even in someone's home. So ask around. If there's an active group in your area, you are sure to find it.

People join computer user groups for any number of reasons. But you can bet that at least some proportion of the membership will be men and women interested in the latest technology. These are the folks most likely to want to sell older systems so they can afford the latest hardware. They may place an ad in the user group newsletter. Or they may simply let it be known that they are interested in selling their systems.

Again, ask around. Attend one of the group's meetings and let it be known that you are new to the field and are interested in acquiring a system. By their very nature, user groups are friendly organizations. Many members are "tapped in" to the computer field and the computer community in your area. Something is bound to turn up.

Computer brokering firms

As with any market, brokers have emerged over the years to bring buyer and seller together. The leading used computer broker in the country is Alex Randall's Boston Computer Exchange (BoCoEx). In the spirit of full disclosure, I should tell you that Alex Randall and I were classmates in college. Over the last ten years or so, he has brought the same organizing abilities to the used computer market that he brought to organizing rock concerts when we were in school. Alex holds a PhD., and among other adventures, studied anthropology with Margaret Mead.

He and his wife, Cameron Hall, started the BoCoEx in 1982. The firm gets uniformly favorable reviews and counts General Electric, Sun Oil, Kodak, and even the White House among its past and present customers. It maintains what is possibly the world's largest database of computers and related equipment for sale.

The process starts when someone wants to sell his or her machine. BoCoEx handles virtually every kind of computer equipment, from modems to minicomputers, though Dr. Randall advises that name-brand computers and IBM clones tend to sell best.

BoCoEx adds the listing to its database free of charge. Each week, the company publishes its current list of equipment for sale. Prospective buyers can purchase this list for about $10 a copy or subscribe on a weekly or monthly basis.

When you see a system you want, you contact BoCoEx and it puts you in touch with the seller. BoCoEx brokers will also advise you on the current range of prices for the system and guide you through the transaction. When you and the seller come to an agreement, the seller ships you the system and pays the brokerage firm ten percent for its services. As a buyer, using BoCoEx costs you nothing.

The Boston Computer Exchange can also direct you to companies that write service contracts, should you wish to purchase one for your "new" used system. For more information, contact:

Boston Computer Exchange Corporation
Box 1177
Boston, MA 02103
(617) 542-4414

Incidentally, if you are interested in buying a used system, look for *Alex Randall's Used Computer Handbook*, $14.95 from Microsoft Press. The prices cited are inevitably a bit out of date, but the advice is timeless, and you will get a kick out of the many anecdotes Dr. Randall weaves into his text. Each is both pointed and entertaining.

The Computer Shopper's Guide

The Computer Shopper's Guide presented here is intended to serve as a crib sheet. It is built around the components outlined and discussed in Chapters 2 and 3 and is meant to more or less "pull it all together." It offers a handy way to assimilate the information presented in Part I of this book, and you will find it useful when you actually set out to shop for and buy your system.

Here, once again, is the list of the components I think any small business person should look for when buying a system today:

- 386DX 33-MHz (or faster) CPU or a 486-based system
- 4 megs of RAM on the motherboard, expandable to 16 megs
- 16-bit Super VGA (SVGA) card and non-interlaced (NI) color monitor
- 120-megabyte 18ms IDE hard drive (or larger)
- 1 high-density (360K/1.2M) 5.25" floppy drive
- 1 high-density (720K/1.44M) 3.5" floppy drive
- 1 parallel port and 2 serial ports
- HP laser printer or compatible
- Mouse (optional)
- 2400 bps external modem (optional)
- DOS 5.x

And here begins the crib sheet:

386DX 33-MHz (or faster) CPU or a 486-based system

Get the fastest 486-based system you can afford. Remember, the 486DX includes a built-in floating point unit (FPU) math coprocessor. The 486SX does not. If the software you plan to run is not designed to take advantage of an FPU, you'll never notice the difference. Therefore, you will probably want to start by focusing on 486SX systems and buy a 486DX only if the price difference is minimal.

The original Intel 486 design includes an 8K onboard cache. There are indications that AMD and other cloners may double this to 16K for a claimed 20 to 30 percent performance boost over the Intel product. But Intel may respond with a bigger cache of its own.

Whatever you do, make absolutely certain that the 486 system you buy is specifically designed to let you easily upgrade the processor in the future. The preferred option, in my opinion, is a system that lets you remove and replace the original CPU chip and adjust the bus speed at the same time. This combination of features offers maximum flexibility for future upgrades.

However, a system with an empty "performance enhancement socket" on the motherboard is also acceptable. If the system you are considering has such a socket, ask whether and how the original CPU can be removed. This can be important because you may be able to sell or trade in that chip once you upgrade. Ask if the bus speed can be changed as well.

Under no circumstances should you settle for anything less than a 386DX/33 (or a 386SX/16, if money's extremely tight). Systems with 386DX/33 processors should have at least 64K of external cache SRAM memory operating at 20 to 25 nanoseconds (ns).

It is true that lesser machines can handle most small business tasks quite well. But you will have to work harder to use them. You will not be able to easily run the latest software. And you will not be well positioned for the future.

Most systems sold today use the ISA bus. Do not opt for a system with an EISA bus unless you need exceptionally fast internal transfers of lots of data (as might be the case in a system used as a network server). At this writing, neither IBM's MCA (PS/2) bus nor EISA have much to offer most small business owners and professionals.

Finally, be sure to check with your accountant before deciding on a system. In many cases, computer equipment does not have to be capitalized and depreciated. You may find that you can write off up to $10,000 of the money you spend on computer equipment for your business or profession in the year of purchase. That's like getting up to a 31% discount at today's tax rates.

4 megs of RAM on the motherboard, expandable to 16 megs

Memory handling and configuration is easy with 386 and 486 CPUs. Machines of this level can effortlessly allocate memory above the 1M mark to be extended or expanded memory. No need to start with more than 4M (4 megs) on the motherboard. But allow for expansion. Ask about the maximum amount of memory the motherboard can hold. (Today, a capacity of 16M is fairly standard.) Insist on SIMM-style memory (not SIPs or DIPs) operating at 70 ns or faster. Ask about the procedure for adding more memory, should you need it, in the future.

Shadow RAM can be useful if you plan to use old eight-bit add-on cards. But, since you're starting fresh, most of your cards will be 16-bit cards. If the system includes a shadow RAM feature, make sure you can disable it or turn it off.

16-bit Super VGA (SVGA) card and non-interlaced (NI) color monitor

Accept nothing less than a 16-bit SVGA card. And pay the extra $70 or so for a non-interlaced monitor, even if you don't think you'll be using 1024×768 resolution. Standard VGA is 640 pixels horizontal by 480 pixels vertical. SVGA is at least 800×600 and may include 1024×768.

How much VRAM (memory) is on the video card? A memory of 256K is the base point. Fine for most small business users. But ask if and how this can be boosted to 512K or 1M in the future. More memory means more available resolutions, more colors in all modes, and faster screen scrolls.

Also ask about the "drivers" that come with the card. Is there driver software to optimize the card's performance with software like Ventura Publisher, PC Paintbrush, Windows, and other packages.

Features to ask about regarding the monitor:

- 14-inch (measured diagonally); today's standard size.
- Analog; no need for multi-synch.
- Flat screen to reduce distortion and glare; nice, but not essential.
- Dot pitch of 0.28 mm (or smaller) for 1024×768.
- Dot pitch of 0.31 mm is fine for SVGA 800×600; the smaller the dot pitch number, the better.
- Multi-scan (able to handle different video modes).
- Vertical scan refresh frequency of 70 Hz, 72 Hz, or faster; at 50 Hz screen flicker becomes quite noticeable.
- Non-interlaced; eliminates flicker in hi-res modes. If the ad doesn't say NI or "non-interlaced," assume the monitor is interlaced. Ask if you can substitute.

120-megabyte 18 ms IDE hard drive (or larger)

The bigger and the faster the hard drive, the better. With today's software, 80M is simply too small. A size of 120M is the absolute minimum for a business system. If a 200M unit is available, and if you can afford it, give it strong consideration. Be sure to ask if there is room in the computer case for a second hard drive, should you wish to add one later.

The interface should be IDE. Access time should be around 15 ms. Today, a 28ms drive is considered slow.

Floppy disk drives

Not much to say here. You absolutely must have one each: a high-density (360K/1.2M) 5.25″ floppy drive and a high-density (720K/1.44M) 3.5″ floppy drive. Teac makes an excellent drive, and has done so for many years. If the system you are interested in has Teac drives, it's a good sign. But there are many other excellent floppy drive makers.

Parallel and serial ports

Pretty much a non-issue. You need one parallel port to connect your printer. You will use one serial port for a modem and one, probably, for a mouse. If you need more in the future, you can always buy an add-on I/O card for about $25.

HP laser printer or compatible

Few, if any, mail-order or retail computer packages include a printer. So you'll have a lot of discretion in this area. I don't think a businessperson or professional today can afford to be without a laser printer. Hewlett Packard is to printers what IBM is to computers and Hayes is to modems. All software supports HP equipment. At the very least, you should settle for nothing less than a 100-percent HP-compatible laser printer.

Resolution of 300 dpi is standard. Minimum throughput is 4 ppm. Ask about the size of the paper tray. You need 100 to 200 sheet capacity. Ask about add-on printer memory. How much can the printer hold and what does each megabyte cost? Buy extra printer memory only if you will be doing a lot of desktop publishing or graphics work.

Buy your add-on font cartridges from someone like Pacific Page, not HP. Cut supply costs by having your toner/cartridge units refilled. If you can't afford a laser printer at this time, fight a holding action. Spend $150 on an Epson-compatible nine-pin (wire) dot-matrix printer and save up your money. If you need 24-pin output from a 9-pin printer every now and again, consider the shareware programs LQ and ImagePrint.

Of mice and modems

Neither a mouse nor a modem is essential. If your package also includes Microsoft Windows, however, then a mouse is crucial. If possible, try to get the Microsoft Mouse. Ask if it is a serial mouse (plugs into one of your serial ports) or a bus mouse (comes with its own interface card). No difference in performance, but you may want to use that serial port for something else later, so opt for a bus mouse.

Modems are the least essential component of all. If you can get the package you want without a modem at a lower price, great. But under no circumstances should you pay more to get a system with a modem—unless you already know how to use it. There will be time to get into communications later.

DOS 5.x

At this writing, many mail-order firms offer you a choice of DOS 3.3, 4.01, or 5.0. There is simply no question, however: You should insist on Microsoft DOS 5.0 (or 5.1, if it's available at the time). DOS 5 is a major advance over earlier versions, and it includes many crucial features that can save you time and money.

You may also find that the system package you want comes with Microsoft Windows. At this writing, the current version is 3.1. If Windows is part of the package, insist on version 3.1. And make sure that the package includes a mouse.

Other questions to ask

If you deal with a reputable company, it should go without saying that you will also receive a DOS 5.x manual. However, it wouldn't hurt to ask. If a manual is not included, then the company is almost certainly engaged in pirating software and should be avoided.

A good company will take good care of you. However, if you have special needs or concerns, you may wish to ask the following questions:

- How many expansion slots are on the motherboard? How many are 8-bit, 16-bit, and 32-bit?

- Will there be room in the case for a tape backup unit, a second hard drive, and a CD-ROM drive? You will definitely want to add a tape backup unit in the future since it offers the fastest, most efficient way to back up your hard drive.

- What is the size of the power supply? Today, 200 watts is fairly standard. Will the power supply allow for everything you may wish to add to the system in the future (more memory, additional drives, etc.)? If you have a choice, get the larger power supply, even if it adds $50 to the package price.

- Is a higher quality, name-brand keyboard available with the package, and if so, what is the extra charge?

- Does the unit have FCC Class B certification? This really is a must since it means the system won't give off radio frequencies that can cause interference. Without the Class B certification, you cannot legally use the system in your home.

Conclusion

There is no simple, cut-and-dried way to buy a computer system. The best path for a small business owner or professional is to find a local retailer with whom you can develop a relationship. Such establishments are neither easier nor more difficult to find than a good attorney or accountant. It's the individual who counts, and you should expect to have to look for the right person.

If you opt to follow the mail-order route, make sure that you buy only from companies whose equipment has been well reviewed by the computer press. After you've had some experience, you can branch out to "no-name" firms to buy additional systems and equipment. But start with first-tier companies.

The used computer market is also a possibility. You will have less flexibility, since used systems are sold "as is." You will not be able to order a "bespoke" computer, and, of course, there are no guarantees. But, since you now know what to look for in a system, you could do very well indeed by checking the classifieds, user groups, or the Boston Computer Exchange.

The next chapter offers brief, "buyer's guide"-style information about add-on equipment. This will give you an idea of the kinds of other things you can do, once you get a system. In closing, however, I would leave you with a single thought: The computer you buy today will not be the only system you ever buy.

This is not a once-in-a-lifetime purchase. So relax. The equipment available today is so powerful that even the least capable system can easily handle all of your needs. As long as you stick with a 386- or 486-based system, the worst that can happen is that you will end up with a system that isn't quite as fast as something else.

The stuff is so cheap that we're not talking about a tremendous amount of money. As I have said before, if you can't afford to invest $2500 in computer equipment for your business, then you should forget about small business computing altogether. Or at least until your business grows larger.

I don't think you can go wrong if you follow the guidelines I've laid down, though you will want to season them with your own sense of the market at the time you are ready to buy. If you get a system and later hanker after some additional feature, you can almost certainly upgrade a component or two.

You can mix and match, swap in and swap out, until you've got your system exactly the way you want it—today. If your needs change tomorrow, you can reconfigure things again. And so on.

I've given you all the tools you need to be a smart shopper, but ultimately, buying a personal computer system today should not be viewed as a big deal.

6

Speeds and feeds

A buyer's guide
to add-on equipment

COMPUTERS ARE ADDICTIVE. AND THEY CAN BE SO MUCH FUN THAT THEY should probably be illegal. Once you have a basic system, you can add joysticks and trackballs (upside-down mice) for game playing. You can install sound boards capable of digitizing and manipulating music, voice, and just plain noise. You can feed your system images captured by your VCR or camcorder, and either play with them or turn them into ten-second snippets of "live action" or animation.

With the right add-on equipment, your computer can read bar codes or recognize and respond to your voice commands. The blind or visually impaired can make their computers read aloud any text that appears on the screen. I have a number of blind friends with whom I correspond electronically. One of them is a university professor actively involved in securing books like this one on floppy disk so blind people can "listen" to them via computer.

The most important add-on equipment

Earlier, I compared a computer system to a component stereo system. The comparison still stands. The difference is that you can add so much more to a computer, should you desire and should your bank account allow. Truly, the possibilities are limitless. Both for work and for play.

However, since outlawing computers on Puritanical grounds is clearly out of the question, the very least the government should do is find a way to apply a tax to the enjoyment computers offer. Someday, they just might. And we will fall even further behind our international competitors, since "playing" with computers is an essential part of learning to *work* with them. The reason our kids take to computers so readily is that they have already learned to "think system," courtesy of Nintendo and the many other video games.

Six important items

This chapter, however, has nothing to do with fun and everything to do with add-on equipment that is either essential or potentially important to your business. The two essential items are a tape backup system for your hard drive, and a surge suppressor to make sure your data doesn't get zapped by an electrical "transient" or voltage spike.

The three items I think you'll find either important or exceptionally useful are a fax modem to let you send and receive faxes via your computer, a hand scanner to scan in images, and a hands-free telephone headset. It also seems likely that you will be buying a CD-ROM drive in the not-too-distant future.

Those are the six pieces of add-on equipment we will consider here. We'll tell you what they do, how they work, what to look for when setting out to purchase them, and, most important of all, what they can mean to your daily work. There is no need to buy any of this equipment right away. It's not terribly expensive, and I definitely think you should get to know your computer first. But keep these items in mind, particularly the tape drive and the surge suppressor, and put them on your list of "What to Buy Next."

Buying a tape backup system

Your hard disk drive is probably the most important component in your entire system. As I've said before, you *live* on your hard drive. It holds all of your programs, all of your reports, all of your spreadsheets, customer lists, billing records, inventory, contact addresses, and everything else. Having a hard drive die is almost like having your house burn down. You stand to lose everything. And the thing of it is, all hard drives die eventually.

If you knew that there was an absolute certainty that your house would burn down some time in the future, you definitely would take out insurance. That's what backing up your hard drive is all about.

Now, I should tell you that if your hard drive buys the farm and you don't have backups, all is not lost. Necessarily. There are companies that specialize in bringing hard drive data back to the land of the living. Some of them are so sophisticated that, as one of them told me, they can often recover data that has been wiped from the disk by a software program and recorded over several times. Interestingly, my source said that the IRS was particularly intrigued by this technology as an aid in retrieving evidence to convict white collar criminals.

However, restoring precious data is expensive, and there are certainly no guarantees. When backing up a drive can be so easy, it simply doesn't make sense to "go bare." The problem is that just as we know we should exercise several times a week, few of us take the time and trouble to do so. I don't need any exhaustive market research to be certain that the vast majority of hard drives installed in computers today have *never* been backed up.

The floppy disk shuffle

You know it too, since most of the time backing up a drive is a royal, time-consuming pain. Software companies have rushed in to help. A program like Fast-Back, for example, can dump the contents of your hard drive to a stack of floppy disks in far less time than you could copy them yourself. Even DOS includes a rather feeble program for this purpose called BACKUP.EXE.

But, friends, floppy disks are not the answer. Not if you're in business. Not if you place any kind of value at all on your time. (No matter how fast the software, *someone's* got to sit at the machine feeding in blank floppy disks.) You will need about 56 high-density floppy disks to back up 80M of hard disk data.

Nor, in my opinion, does it make sense to get a second hard drive and use it as a backup (unless you are operating a local area network and want to use a "disk mirroring" approach). Nor do WORM (Write-Once, Read Many) drives offer a cost-effective alternative.

To my mind, there is only one way to back up a hard drive, and that is to install a "streaming tape drive" backup system. The hardware is relatively inexpensive. And the system is easy to use. All you have to do is insert a tape cartridge, run the supplied tape backup program, and go home or out to lunch. You can use the tapes to transfer files to a similarly equipped computer, if need be. But the real advantage is ease of use. Since tape backup is easy, you are likely to do it more often.

DC2000 and DC6000 tapes

You can buy a tape system by mail for as little as $250. Figure a backup cost of $16 for 40M of tape; $20 for 120M. That's not too expensive as it is, but it is even less expensive than it seems, since you will use the same tape cartridges over and over again.

All the leading tape backup systems are based on cartridges that use quarter-inch tape. The two main sizes of these quarter-inch cartridges are DC6000 and DC2000.

DC6000-style cartridges are about the size of a paperback book. Cartridges of this size used to be called "DC600" but have been renamed to achieve consistency with other cartridge styles. DC2000-style cartridges measure about 2.5"×3.25". A variety of factors determine how much data can be packed onto a single DC6000 or DC2000 cartridge. These factors include the number of feet of tape in the cartridge and the recording format used by the tape drive.

It is important to note, as well, that the software supplied with most cartridge systems has the ability to *compress* the data it stores. This can reduce the required tape capacity to about half of what would be required without using compression.

In most cases, you will find that a DC2000 system is the best choice for backing up a single-user PC equipped with a 120M hard drive. But, to be safe, make sure you tell the vendor how large a drive you have, and ask about the capacity of the DC2000 cartridge-using tape unit he sells. Ask about the capacity of the tape when the data is not being compressed and the capacity when data compression has been invoked.

It may be that you can fit more data on your hard drive than can be stored on a single DC2000 tape. That isn't a huge problem, and it won't begin to affect you until your hard disk starts to get full. The key thing is to make sure that the tape drive software can split a backup over two or more cartridges. Most can, but you should definitely ask.

DC6000 cartridges are better for multi-user systems and PCs with larger (up to 600M or more) hard drives. The most important feature of DC6000 systems, however, is speed. These drives move information at rates nearly as fast as some hard drives. That means quicker backups and faster data restoration after disaster strikes.

DC6000 systems achieve this kind of performance by using a proprietary interface. That means you'll have to buy a special add-on card as part of the package. DC2000 systems, in contrast, typically plug into your hard drive/floppy drive controller card. (If you already have both an A and B drive, ''Y-coupling'' cables are available from the drive maker to let the cartridge system share the card with your installed drives.)

In general, a DC2000 system can transfer data at the rate of about 1M per minute, while a DC6000 system can operate at between 3M and 6M per minute. Personally, I don't think this is a severe disadvantage for DC2000 systems. Normally, you will start your backup and go do something else for a half hour or more. Unless you're using your system every minute of the day, there is always the ''downtime'' you need to do a backup in the normal course of things.

Size considerations

It is also worth noting that virtually all DC2000 drives are designed to fit into the same size bay used for 3.5-inch floppy disk drives. They will fit anywhere a 3.5″ floppy disk drive will, including a 5.25″ drive bay with the appropriate adapters. Most of today's DC6000 tape drives, in contrast, are the same size as half-height 5.25″ disk drives. They will fit easily into a full-size desktop or tower computer, but you may have problems squeezing one into a ''slimline'' machine.

External units are also available. The main advantage of an external unit is that it is completely portable. You can move it to one system, do a backup, and move it to a second computer and repeat the process. Personally, however, I prefer a built-in system.

QIC standards

The ''DC'' standard determines the physical size of the tape cartridge. But there is another standard to look for. These are the standards promulgated by the Quarter-Inch Cartridge (QIC) committee, an organization made up of leading manufacturers. This standard refers to the format used to record the data. All of these standards are identified by the name ''QIC,'' like QIC-100. If the tape drive follows one or more of the industry standards, you have a better chance that third-party software is available for the drive.

The two most popular QIC numbers you'll see are QIC-40 and QIC-80. Both apply to DC2000 tape systems, and both require the tape drive to work in essentially the same way (connected through your hard drive/floppy drive controller). QIC-80 adds extra capacity through data compression.

The number following the "QIC" designation indicates the nominal, non-compressed storage capacity of a cartridge. However, some cartridges are filled with more tape, so some QIC-40 drives may be able to store 60M with the right cartridge.

Tape backup software

Most tape drives come with the special software you will need to activate the unit and set it to automatically back up your hard drive. However, it is wise to check when you order your tape drive to make sure the system includes its own backup program. If it does not, you'll have to factor in the cost of backup software.

Also, be sure to ask about the availability of adapter cables to let you install a tape unit and still have two floppy drives. Worst case, you can add an extra floppy drive controller. In short, ask your vendor how you can install an internal DC2000 system and still have the use of Drives A and B.

Also, make sure you know the proper software installation settings to integrate your new tape system with your computer. In general, even if a tape drive is attached to your floppy drive's "B" position, you should not tell your system about it when preparing your CMOS setup. Again, ask the vendor for specific instructions.

In closing this topic, we should tell you that all magnetic media, be it floppy drive or hard drive or magnetic tape, must be formatted before you can record data on it. Formatting a tape cartridge is easy, but time consuming. Therefore, you may want to consider paying a dollar or so more to get "pre-formatted" tapes when buying cartridges for your system. Just make sure that the formatted tapes you buy are indeed compatible with your particular tape unit.

Backup procedures

We should also say just a word about the importance of establishing a *regular* backup procedure. I'm sorry to say that I'm not impressed by the elaborate backup routines outlined in many magazine articles. If you are a small business-person or professional, there are just a few simple points to keep in mind.

First, the most important items on your disk are those you have created. If some kind of glitch wipes out your hard disk copy of DOS or some other program, you can always restore it from your original floppies (or your backups of those floppies). But if a glitch hits the spreadsheet you were working on or your receivables database, and you don't have a backup, the data is either gone forever, or gone until you can painstakingly recreate it.

Second, you should always back up your most important files and put them in a safe place. I keep copies of all of my books on disks stored "off-site" in our barn. I keep another copy in a fireproof safe in the attic. And I keep a third copy on 3.5″ disks at my workstation in case I need to refer to them. This may sound a bit obsessive, but three copies is not at all a bad idea for archival storage.

I make a complete tape backup of my various hard drives about twice a month. Only one cartridge is required per drive, but three cartridges are associated with each of them. I simply erase and re-use the oldest cartridge each time. That seems to work well for me, but you may want to use five or seven cartridges, one for each day of the week. Everything depends on how much new information is added to your system each day or how extensively currently recorded information changes. If you add large quantities of irreplaceable information every day, then you'd better make a backup every day.

I should make clear that I also make daily backups, but not of an entire disk. For example, I write a book chapter or an article using the hard disk. But before I power down for the night, I copy what I have written that day to a 3.5″ floppy.

That's *my* system, and over the years I have found that it works quite well. Your situation may be different. The key thing is to develop the backup habit, whether to tape or to floppy, and to establish a regular procedure for backing up the entire system. Figure out how often you think your tape drive should be used, and just put "BACK UP SYSTEM" on your calendar at each appropriate date.

You really don't have to make a big deal out of backing up your hard disk. But you *do* have to do it.

Surge suppressors and UPSs

I feel that a tape backup system is the single most important piece of equipment any user can add to his or her computer system. But a close second is some kind of power-line protection. Computers, unlike almost any other electrical item in your office or your home, are quite sensitive to power-line irregularities. It is true that most systems have some degree of protection built in. And it is also true that you may not need this particular category of add-on at all.

In *my* area of the country, however, the electrical power coming out of a wall jack can fluctuate wildly. In my office, whenever I turn on my photocopier, a unit that draws a lot of power to heat its fuser rollers, my screen can start to wobble. The office has 200-amp service, and the copier is plugged into its own line. But that doesn't solve the problem. A "line conditioner" capable of smoothing out power flow to my computer equipment, however, did.

My area of the country also receives its share of thunderstorms in the summer. I don't know why it is, but even the weakest of thunderstorms inevitably manages to put the cable TV system out of commission. They keep raising subscription rates, but they never seem to spend the extra money on better, more lightning-resistant equipment.

A slightly stronger storm will usually cause the power to completely fail, either momentarily or for minutes at a time. If you are in the midst of creating deathless prose for a computer book—which is to say, if you are in the oxymoron business—this is not good.

Finally, on two separate occasions over the past ten years, lightning has hit some distant telephone pole and managed to zap first an answering machine and then a modem board. The modem board got fried even though the computer that held it was turned off. It was plugged into the phone line, and that was its undoing.

I'm not fatalistic enough to believe that the gods have singled me out for special treatment. "Dirty" electrical power and lightning can be real problems, although their seriousness will undoubtedly depend on your geographical location.

Therefore, it only makes good sense to take arms against this sea of troubles, and, by opposing them with the proper equipment, end the threat they pose to your system and your data. The technology is available. And it's not all that expensive, particularly when you consider what it can cost in time and money should disaster strike.

Line conditioners and UPSs

To solve the electrical power problem, there are two main solutions. In my case, a "line conditioner" did the trick. This unit plugs into the wall socket and offers some six outlets. Its job is to smooth out and filter the flow of power to the components plugged into those outlets. I got mine from Black Box, Inc., (412) 746-5530, in Pittsburgh. Prices range from $190 to $500. Call Black Box for a free catalogue.

If complete power failures are the problem you want to protect against, you need a UPS (Uninterruptible Power Supply). These units are most often employed in network installations—where several computers are linked to a single "file server" PC. All of them operate by keeping a large battery charged up and ready to go. High-performance circuits enable UPSs to switch to battery power so fast that your PC won't notice the difference. Most units will alert you to a power interruption and be able to supply enough power for you to save your files to disk and shut off your computer.

How to buy a surge suppressor

You may not need a UPS. You may not need a line conditioner. But you are almost certain to benefit from, and possibly really need, a genuine "surge suppressor." Electrical current is neither constant nor clean. I once had a computer technician plug a special power reading device into a wall outlet, and you would be amazed at how the needle on the readout jumped around. PC power supplies are designed to take most fluctuations in stride. But every now and then, a real tidal wave comes through that is so large no ordinary power supply can deal with it. That's a spike or a surge.

This happens everywhere. So I believe that a really good surge suppressor, for both your electrical and your phone lines, is essential. The phone line protection will prevent lightning-strike damage to your modem or serial card. In most cases, you will need a special surge protector unit. So forget about those multi-outlet power strips that claim to offer "surge protection." Most of them are simply junk.

Here's what to look for. Don't worry about what the specifications mean. The three crucial points are:

- A "first-stage peak clamping voltage" of 200 volts, plus or minus five percent. This is the voltage at which the unit responds. The lower the figure, the better.

- A response time of five picoseconds. A picosecond is a trillionth of a second, or 1000 times faster than a nanosecond or billionth of a second. The faster the response, the better.

- Identical protection for *both* the electrical and the phone line.

If you live in an area prone to frequent electrical brownouts, you should also consider a unit offering "voltage dropout" protection. Such units should automatically shut everything off if the power falls to 80 volts, plus or minus five percent. At the very least, this will prevent damage to your hard drive during a voltage dropout incident.

Two of the leading manufacturers of really good surge suppressors are Dynatech and Panamax. Both offer a variety of power and phone protection units that meet the above specifications. Models and prices differ with the number of electrical receptacles. Expect to pay between $75 and $150 for a quality unit. Contact:

Dynatech Computer Power, Inc.   Panamax
5800 Butler Ln.   150 Mitchell Blvd.
Scotts Valley, CA 95066   San Rafael, CA 94903
(800) 638-9098   (800) 472-5555
(800) 443-2391, from Canada   (800) 472-6262, in California
(408) 438-5760   (415) 499-3900

Add-on fax boards

Fax or facsimile communications is a very old technology, but, it is all the rage today. Indeed, it is nearly impossible to be in business today without some kind of fax capability.

I bring this up because I want you to know that you may not have to buy a dedicated, separate fax machine. For under $200, you can add a board to your computer that will let it both send and receive faxes. The board fits into one of your expansion slots, and you simply plug your phone line in at the exposed socket at the back of your computer and load the fax software.

This lets you receive any fax from anywhere in the world and print it out on your laser or dot-matrix printer. It, in effect, gives you a "plain paper" fax. (No need to fool with rolls of fax paper.) It also lets you preview a received fax on your screen, so you can decide whether to delete it or print it.

You can run the fax software in the background. That way, if a fax is coming in while you are working on a report, the software will pop up a window indicating that a fax is being received and put your word processing or other program on hold. It will then return control of the system to you when the reception is finished.

It also lets you send any computer file—text or graphics—as a fax to somebody else's machine. Indeed, you can tell the system *when* you would like it to begin dialing the distant fax machine's number, and it will do so on schedule. It is also easy to arrange "broadcast" faxes, when you want to send copies to several people.

Personally, I use a fax board made by Frecom, (415) 438-5000, and it works like a charm. At today's prices, you can expect to pay between $135 and $200, considerably less than most fax machines and far less than any plain paper fax. And for that amount of money, you may be able to get a unit that not only does faxes—at 9600 bps (bits per second)—but also connects you to distant database systems via a built-in 2400-bps modem. (Fax modems and data communications modems are two separate animals.) Many other excellent fax boards are available, so be sure to check current computer magazines for reviews.

Only one problem

Unfortunately, my fax board, like all others, suffers from one major drawback. It does, indeed, employ the power of the computer to handle sophisticated send and receive operations. And it works beautifully with my HP laser printer. But, of course, it doesn't include a scanner.

This isn't a huge problem for me, since most of my outgoing faxes are almost always text files I have created on my computer. Text files are no problem at all to a fax board. Indeed, they tend to produce crisper text on the receiving end, since no resolution has been lost through scanning.

But there is no getting around the fact that if I want to send a copy of a *New York Times* or *Wall Street Journal* article to someone, I can't do it—unless I can get the article scanned into the machine as a graphics file.

The problem is more or less solved by adding a hand-held scanner to the system. This allows you to scan an article, photograph, or other hard copy into your system as a graphics file to be sent via fax. A hand-held scanner has many other uses besides. You can scan in your corporate letterhead, for example, and size it down to produce the master mechanical for a business card.

Scanners

There are two main categories of scanners: hand-held and flat-bed. A *flat-bed* scanner is about the size of a desktop photocopier, and it handles paper originals in much the same automated way. A *hand-held* scanner is roughly the size of two mice, and you provide the power by pulling it across the paper by hand. Flat-bed scanners cost $1200 or more and are capable of scanning in an entire page at a time. Hand-held scanners sell for $100 to $150 or so and can scan an image about four inches wide by about ten inches long in a single swathe.

Both types of scanners turn paper-based images into computer graphics files. As with a photocopier, light is aimed at one narrow strip of the paper at a time. A sensing mechanism picks up the light as a series of dots.

Each dot has a specific location, and each may be either "on" or "off," "dark" or "light." This information on the dots and their status is fed to the computer, where it is used to reproduce the image by turning dots on and off on the screen. The information may also be saved to disk as a graphics file.

OCR conversions

I can see no reason for most users to invest in a flat-bed scanner, at least not when just starting out. The main exception might be if you had a great deal of printed or typewritten information that you wanted to get into your computer to edit and modify with your word processor. A flat-bed scanner with an automatic paper feed is nearly essential for this.

So, too, is "OCR" (Optical Character Recognition) software. Many flat-bed scanners come with OCR packages, and many other programs are available to work with the output of leading scanners. Remember, when scanning, everything appears to the computer as a graphics file. The on-screen image may look like text to you, but to the computer, it might as well be the Mona Lisa.

You can alter and edit graphic images with a paint program, but you cannot edit and adjust it the way you would text created by a word processor. It is the role of OCR software to translate the graphic images of letters and words into genuine text that can indeed be manipulated with word processing software.

Again, this is a specialized application that most users shouldn't even think about until they have worked with their machines for six months to a year. In fact, even if you have a pile of documents you really need to get into your machine, you may be better off hiring an independent firm to take care of the scanning and OCR translation for you.

Ask at computer dealers in your area, or check the "Services" section of the classified ads at the back of computer magazines. Check the "Typesetting," "Desktop Publishing," and "Typing Services" categories in your Yellow Pages. Or call your local print shop.

Buying a hand-held scanner

A hand-held scanner does not eliminate the possibility of using OCR software, but it's really not practical. Hand-held units are great, however, for scanning parts of documents so you can send them with a fax board. If the document is too large to scan in a single pass, consider making a photocopy of it using your photocopier's reduction feature and then scanning the copy. Or simply make more than one pass and send the fax as more than one graphics file.

As noted earlier, you can also use a hand-held unit to scan in logos and special letterheads. Once the image is saved to disk in your computer, you can use a graphics or paint program to modify it or size it up or down. You can insert it into brochures or use it to create camera-ready mechanicals for business cards and other pieces.

There are three main categories of hand-held scanners: black and white, gray scale, and color. Black-and-white (one-bit) scanners are sometimes called *binary scanners*. They work best with line art or simple, high-contrast charts and graphics that have limited detail. The results are okay for in-house publications, fliers, or simple drawings within documents, but not for professional newsletters, advertisements, or brochures.

Gray-scale scanners, in contrast, are designed to handle continuous-tone images such as detailed drawings. Some models are even good enough to do an acceptable job scanning photographs. This is probably the type of unit you will want. Color hand-held scanners are nifty, but likely to be of little use to you unless you also have a color printer.

Be sure to ask how much memory you need in your system for efficient operation. And ask if the scanner board that goes into an expansion slot can hold any memory itself, and, if so, how much. Some scanner boards, for example, come with as much as 700K of RAM.

Assuming you are using DOS and will be using the scanner software under that operating system, make sure that said software supports either EMS or XMS memory, or both. Also, it is usually a good idea to preview a scanner at your local computer dealer, even if you opt to buy through the mail. Take some sample materials with you (a plain black-and-white line drawing, a color photo, a newspaper clipping, etc.). Ask the dealer to show you the scan on the screen and on a printer like the one you use.

The unit you choose should let you vary your scanning resolution from 100 dpi to 400 dpi. The higher the dpi resolution, the more detail you'll get in your image. But you may find that at 400 dpi, you can't scan as much in a pass. Also, look for a scanner that lets you switch gray-scale levels—whether through software or a switch on the scanner. The scanner software should also let you print directly from its screen, instead of having to save the image and load a paint program or other piece of software.

A telephone headset

A telephone headset is like a pair of headphones for a Sony Walkman or other sound device. The difference is that most headsets cover only one ear and all of them have an arm curved to stop in front of your mouth. The tip of the arm contains a small microphone. Anyone old enough to have watched a NASA space launch or otherwise seen people working in Mission Control knows what a headset is.

Whether you need one or not depends completely on the nature of your work. If you spend most of your time seeing patients, consulting with clients, or walking the shop floor, you probably don't need one. On the other hand, if you are a consultant, a writer, or someone else who spends most of the day in front of a computer screen, a telephone headset is simply essential.

I have used one for many years and cannot imagine conducting business without one. That's because many of my business-related calls require me to use information that takes two free hands to retrieve. The information might be in a book on my shelf, in a nearby file drawer, or in a file on my hard disk. Or, I may be in the midst of an online session with a distant database when the phone rings, and want to be able to continue the session while taking the call.

I've been preaching the headset gospel for years, but only recently have they become widely available. You used to have to really hunt for a manufacturer, but now you can find them in AT&T phone stores, discount stationery stores, and many other places.

Costs range from about $60 for a basic unit, to about $370 for a battery-powered, cordless model. If you can't find a unit you like locally, consider requesting a free catalogue from Hello Direct in San Jose, California. The company specializes in phone gear and can be reached at (800) 444-3556.

The promise of CD-ROM

Finally, we should say a word or two about CD-ROM drives. The term stands for "Compact Disk—Read Only Memory." As with most add-on equipment, I don't recommend buying a CD-ROM drive until you have used your basic computer for a while, or unless you already have a specific application in mind. But this is a technology full of possibilities, and you cannot afford to completely ignore it.

We'll touch briefly on the technology in a moment. Right now what you need to know is that the main feature CD-ROMs bring to the party is mind-boggling capacity. For example, a single CD—identical to the ones you purchase to play music—can accommodate 100 history books or all 13 volumes of the Oxford English Dictionary. It can contain a residential phone directory for the entire United States (more than 90 *million* residential phone listings and addresses) or a national Yellow Pages directory containing more than 9.2 million businesses.

Or, as is the case with Microsoft Bookshelf, a single disk can contain the full text of the following reference works: *American Heritage Dictionary*, *World Almanac*, *U.S. Zip Code Directory*, *Bartlett's Familiar Quotations*, *Chicago Manual of Style*, *Roget's Thesaurus*—and more!

Now here's the real kicker. CD-ROM disks are stamped out like vinyl records of old. Once the master has been prepared, the unit cost on each copy is about $2. With the right software, it is even possible for a company to prepare and produce its own CDs at a very low cost. In fact, the vast majority of CDs produced today are created for internal corporate use.

What's in it for you?

CD-ROMs may or may not have an application in your business today. But you should definitely know that they exist, and you should know that most come with software designed to make their contents useful. For example, the phone databases on CD-ROM typically have software that lets you bring a phone number to your screen and then have your modem dial it at the press of a single key. Microsoft Bookshelf includes software to let you search *Bartlett's Quotations* for quotes on the subject of interest. No need to flip back and forth between the index and cited references. All relevant quotes are pulled together and presented on your screen.

There are lots of other applications for businesspeople and professionals, and even more are on the way. The massive storage capacity of CD-ROMs makes them ideal for the new "multi-media" software that will add sound, full-motion graphics, television images, and all kinds of other goodies to your system.

Imagine being able to load a CD-ROM multi-media disk containing an entire encyclopedia. You search for "Beethoven" and, in addition to seeing the traditional text and pictures of a printed book, you also have the option of listening to famous passages from Beethoven's work.

Or imagine you call up an article on space exploration. You get the text and still pictures as usual. But in a window on your screen, you see a video tape snippet of a rocket blasting off and hear the roar through your speakers. The possibilities are all but limitless. They will take some time to be realized, though, due to the complexity of the software and the need for really powerful hardware.

A word about CD-ROM technology

Since you now know about bits and bytes and "on" and "off," it is only fair to tell you how CD-ROMs can hold such a tremendous amount of information. The answer is the laser. Laser beams can be focused with incredible precision, and they can be turned on and off very quickly. These two facts are at the heart of CD-ROM technology. When an inscribing laser beam is focused on a spinning CD and turned on, it makes a very, very tiny pit in the CD's surface. When it is turned off, there is no pit.

Thus, as a reading laser beam traverses the CD's surface, at any given second it is focusing on an area that either is a pit or a solid place on the disk. If it is over a pit, the laser light reflected back from the disk looks one way. If it is over a solid area, the reflected light looks another way. In computer-talk, these two, and only two, possible conditions constitute binary information. The readings of the laser can be transformed into on/off pulses, magnetized/non-magnetized spots on a hard disk, or any other form of digital information.

What sets a CD-ROM apart is the terrifically fine precision of that laser. The pits and non-pits are much, much smaller than the magnetized or non-magnetized areas used to represent 1's and 0's on a floppy or hard disk. Indeed, it has been estimated that if you were to stretch out the spiral data track of a 4.7″ CD-ROM, the track would extend to three miles or more.

The image of a three-mile long track of data is certainly striking. But let's put it into more conventional terms. Because of the fineness of lasers, a single side of a single CD-ROM can hold 650 to 700 *megabytes* of data. That is the equivalent of more than 1850 5.25″ 360K floppy disks. A disk of 650M is also equivalent to 325,000 double-spaced typewritten pages or 650 reams of paper. Or a stack of pages 135 feet high. If you were to transmit all the data on a CD-ROM using a 2400-bps modem, working around the clock, the process would take 23 days.

Buying a CD-ROM drive

Like all computer hardware, CD-ROM drives have evolved and improved over the years. They are bound to improve still further, which is another good reason for waiting until you really need one.

Most CD-ROM drives come with an add-on interface card designed to plug into one of your computer's expansion slots. Some can use the SCSI interface used by some hard disk drives. Drives today also tend to be faster than those of just a few years ago. At this writing, the top access time is about 300 ms to 350 ms, or 20 times slower than a 15-ms hard disk drive. Older drives, some of which you will see offered at deep discounts, come in at around 450 ms to 1000 ms (one second). Disk format is not much of an issue any more: ISO-9660 and High Sierra formats are different terms for the same thing.

Finally, when you decide that it's time to buy a drive, consult recent issues of computer magazines for the latest details. One feature you may want is a headphone jack and music-playing software. As I said at the beginning, the technology for an audio CD and a CD-ROM is identical. With the right machine and software, you can use the same drive to retrieve data, then load a different disk and listen to an entire Beethoven symphony instead of just a sound bite.

If you would like to get a better idea of what CD-ROM titles are available, your local library may be able to help. Ask if the library has *CD-ROMs in Print* from Meckler Publishing, (203) 226-6967. This book is published each October, and the cost is $50. You might also look for the *Directory of Portable Databases* from Gale Research. Published twice a year (April and October), a subscription to this directory costs $99. To order, call (800) 877-4253. For more information, call Gale Research, Inc. at (313) 961-2242.

Conclusion

Yes, it's true. Just as you suspected—buying a basic system is only the beginning. Once you've got this essential unit, there are all kinds of things you can add. That's very much the main point of this chapter: not that you *should* add peripheral equipment, but that you *can* do so if you have a genuine need. In other words, it is important to be aware of what's possible, even if it is not appropriate for you.

The only two add-ons that are sine qua nons in my book are a tape backup system for your hard drive and some kind of electrical power protection or conditioning unit. Please place these at the top of your list. Everything else is essentially optional.

7

Support sources

Where to get help when you need it

AT ONE TIME OR ANOTHER, EVERY COMPUTER USER, NO MATTER HOW sophisticated and knowledgeable, needs "support." That's computer-talk for help, assistance, information, hand-holding, explanations, and any other commodity that can either solve a problem you are having or help you accomplish a particular task. "Support" sounds like a good thing. And it is—when you can get it.

The trouble with "support"

It is one of the great paradoxes of our current computer age that the need for support services has never been greater, yet their availability has never been more problematical. Oddly enough, the reason, in a nutshell, is you and me. We all want the best deal possible on any hardware or software we buy. We want the lowest price. Yet, having gotten the lowest price, we also expect to be able to pick up the phone and call the vendor, the manufacturer, or the software publisher and receive expert answers to our questions and unlimited help in using the high-tech items we have bought.

Now, as a businessperson or professional, you know that there's no way this can be. If a software company is going to offer toll-free, round-the-clock support, provided by legions of superbly trained men and women, someone is going to have to pay for it. Prices will have to be higher.

On the other hand, software companies often have extraordinary margins to work with. After all, the manuals and disks supplied to you when you buy a $500 commercial package cost the software company about $15 to produce. If you assume that they sell a $500 package to a distributor for $250, their gross profit is $235 per package.

Of course, there are expenses to deduct. A single full-page ad in *PC Magazine* can cost $15,000 to $20,000 or more. And to have a chance at success, a software company must place lots of ads in lots of magazines. There are development expenses to work off, stockholders to pay, and there's always the next version of the package to prepare.

It isn't all gravy. Yet, as with a blockbuster book or movie, when you hit it big, you hit it BIG! One movie might make $100 million at the box office, while another film might make only $20 million. Yet both films might have cost roughly the same to make and to advertise. The same phenomenon occurs with commercial computer software.

Somewhere in among all the expenses, there is also a line item for customer support. Any software house that wants to be taken seriously by the computer press *must* offer telephone support. It doesn't have to make a toll-free number available. It can even get away with asking customers to pay for support services by dialing a "900" number, though software reviewers are sure to grumble about it. But it has to offer something.

"It doesn't sell software!"

There are as yet no objective standards for judging and evaluating the customer support services offered by competing packages, however. A reviewer might offer anecdotal evidence—noting that he got right through when he called or that he was put on hold and had to wait 20 minutes for a customer service rep to be free. But that's about it.

There is a reason for all this, of course. The hard fact is, a company's customer support service is virtually never a factor in selecting one program over another. People buy a program based on features and power and on whether it is the one used by business associates and colleagues. Customer support simply plays no role in most software purchase decisions. Not surprisingly, software firms tend to deploy their financial resources elsewhere.

You would think that things would be different. You would think that customers would *demand* top-quality support and refuse to buy products from companies that did not offer it. But that simply is not the case. Not that you and I don't want support. Just don't ask us to pay for it.

I have no idea how much longer computer hardware and software companies will be able to get away with supplying incomprehensible manuals and all but non-existent telephone support. But I don't see any change on the horizon.

Indeed, I'm afraid that I see a general lowering of standards. Poorly written manuals and interminable waits "on hold" for phone support provided by often poorly trained individuals is the norm. Therefore, these points are no longer given much consideration when product reviews are written. But the fact that "everybody is doing it" (or not doing it) doesn't make it right.

The net-net is that if you are a computer user today, you may have to use some imaginative strategies to get the support you're sure to need at one time or another. That's what this chapter is all about. And that's the bad-news portion of the lesson. The good news is that the kind of support, help, and assistance you need *is* available—often free of charge—if you know where to look for it.

We will touch briefly on the service warranty that may come with your machine and offer some advice for getting your equipment serviced locally. Then we'll help plug you in to the computer user group community, probably the best source of support (hardware and software) available anywhere, yet undoubtedly the least well known. Finally, we will tell you what you need to know to broaden support availability to include users and experts all over the world via online user groups you can reach with your modem.

Hardware service warranties

When you buy a computer, particularly an IBM-compatible clone, you should not expect much in the way of comprehensible, easy-to-use documentation. With luck, there may be a toll-free support number. But you may find that it is staffed only eight hours a day. If you buy from a dealer, he or she may indicate a willingness to answer your questions by phone, though such arrangements are almost always informal, unless you buy a service contract.

Service contracts typically cost about ten percent of the purchase price of your system—every year. They can be a real money-maker for the dealer since, if a system works for the first 90 days (a period often covered by the manufacturer's warranty), it will usually work forever. In general, I advise against service contracts for small business operators. At least wait until you're approaching the end of the warranty period before signing up for one.

Mail-order dealer service

As I have said before, as long as you stick to reputable companies—those whose machines tend to be reviewed by leading computer magazines—you need have no fear about buying a computer through the mail.

The good firms offer strong service warranties. Lesser firms may claim to do so as well, but, unfortunately, there are as many interpretations of how a warranty should be handled as there are software programs.

At the bottom of the mail-order offerings is the so-called "return to us" policy that says only that your vendor will fix the equipment after you mail it back. The next step up are the vendors who will ship parts so you can fix the computer yourself. And at the top of the list, of course, are the vendors who send a repairman for on-site service. Often leading firms include one year of on-site service as part of their computer system packages. The service is usually provided by companies like TRW or RCA, or some other organization with a national branch network.

As you know, I feel it is vital to seek out a really good computer dealer and establish a relationship. Such a dealer will have one or more "techies" on staff who can usually fix just about anything you bring them. Always give your local dealer first crack at your business. But if he can't come close to the mail-order price, buy through the mail. If you need service down the road, there is no need to be shy about asking your dealer to repair it. In fact, the dealer may be able to give you a faster turnaround than whatever arrangements the mail-order firm offers.

One quick tip before moving on: Whenever you buy a computer, be sure to save the boxes the components came in. You don't have to save them forever, but if you have the storage space, it wouldn't hurt to keep them. The best way to send a piece of equipment anywhere is in its original packing materials.

Tapping in to computer user groups

The best source of hardware and software support available to anyone is a local computer user group. User groups have existed since the dawn of the computer era. They undoubtedly began when the first computer user took one look at the manual supplied with his system, threw up his hands, and called out to a co-worker, "Say, Joe. Gotta minute? I've never seen such gibberish in my life. Maybe we could pool our knowledge and work on this together."

That's what user groups are all about—pooling knowledge, needs, and experience. But don't be surprised if you've never heard of them. These non-profit mutual aid societies are staffed and run by volunteers. The dues are very low—usually about $25 a year—and there is no money for advertising or promotion. Membership is open to everyone of every level of knowledge, but to find out about the groups in your area, you pretty much have to know someone who belongs. Either that, or you have got to know where to look. That's what we'll show you here.

User group structure

Computer user groups are very much a grassroots phenomenon. They can range from ten interested people who meet irregularly in some member's living room, to a group sponsored by a local firm, to a registered not-for-profit organization that regularly attracts a thousand people or more to its monthly meetings. Much depends on the group's location—groups in urban areas with a high density of computer users tend to be the largest and most active—and on the energy, imagination, and personality of the individuals involved. Consequently, it is impossible to present a definitive list of activities and services you can expect from each and every user group.

However, while there is no typical group, there are typical group activities, some of which you are sure to find whichever group you join. Virtually all groups, for example, hold a monthly meeting. Small organizations may meet in someone's home; large ones may take over the ballroom of a local hotel or an auditorium on a college campus. Meetings are usually held once a month on weekday evenings or on a Saturday, and after the treasurer's report, announcements, and other club business has been transacted, there will usually be a guest speaker.

Savvy hardware and software manufacturers are well aware of the word-of-mouth influence user group members wield. So at a large group's meeting it isn't uncommon for someone like Bill Gates (Microsoft), Philippe Kahn (Borland), John Sculley (Apple), Steve Jobs (Next), or other computer industry luminaries to appear. Computer columnists like John Dvorak, shareware authors like Jim Button, and computer book authors have also been featured speakers at such meetings.

Sometimes the monthly meeting will be preceded by "buying sessions." For example, I once had the honor of sharing the podium with Gordon Eubanks of Symantec Corporation (Norton Utilities, Q&A, etc.) at a meeting of the Houston Area League of PC Users or "HAL-PC." It is no accident that "Hal" was the name of the computer that ran amok in the film *2001: A Space Odyssey*. You'll find that many user groups adopt humorous names.

The buying session at the HAL-PC meeting begins an hour and a half before the main meeting. Local retailers and other vendors assemble to offer hardware, software, disks, disk boxes, printer ribbons, paper, and other supplies at discounted, user group prices. After one such session, Duane Hendricks, then president of what is now a 9600-member group, announced as the main meeting was getting under way that 35,000 blank floppy disks had been sold, down slightly from the previous month's total.

As I say, a user group can have considerable clout. Local businesses ignore them at their peril. And I'm sure that hardware and software executives view them as assemblies of every computer guru in a given area. If you can convince a company's in-house guru of the merits of your product, he or she might just recommend that the firm buy several dozen copies.

SIGs (Special Interest Groups)

I had the great good fortune to be one of the founding members of a group that was formed five months after the original IBM/PC was announced. It is easy to recall the early meetings. The PC was so new that the basic machine itself was the group's main focus. What adapter cards should you buy? Should you get one or two (single-sided!) disk drives? What is DOS (version 1.0) all about anyhow? Will CP/M become an important alternative operating system for the PC?

That was in early 1982. The field has expanded so far since then that no single group can address every interest or need. If you want to know about Clipper or FoxPro, you might find a session on local area networks a waste of time. If desktop publishing is a major interest, you don't want to sit through a session devoted to comparing Lotus and Excel. And so on.

The development of special interest groups (SIGs) within the user group structure was a natural response to this situation. For example, the Capital PC User Group based outside of Washington, D.C., has SIGs devoted to exploring APL, BASIC, CAD/CAM, educational software, and Lotus 1-2-3, as well as SIGs focusing on applications in accounting, law, and investing.

HAL-PC has a SIG devoted to PC applications for the oil and gas industry. As other areas of personal computing develop, other SIGs will be formed. All that is required is a number of user group members interested in learning more about a particular PC product or application, and someone willing to serve as chairman of the SIG. In the larger organizations, at least, most members belong both to the main group and to one or more SIGs. SIGs are typically headed by chairmen and hold regular meetings, often at someone's home one weekday evening a month. Or they may meet after the main group's monthly session. It all depends on the group.

As we'll see in Chapter 8, every user group maintains a library of shareware and public domain software. The software librarian is responsible for maintaining the collection, and, often, for selling disks at the main meeting. Sometimes, you can even bring in your own blank, formatted disks and have the librarian copy software to them for a small fee.

Newsletters and journals

User groups are by their very nature devoted to serving the needs of people who live in the area. But most do publish monthly newsletters. So, if you cannot make it to the meetings or if you live an inconvenient distance away, you can still keep in touch.

As you might imagine, the quality of user group newsletters runs the gamut in quantity of pages and quality of information. One small local group might produce four or five stapled, dot-matrix-printed pages a month. A group based in a large metropolitan area might produce a saddle-stitched journal that could rival many computer magazines (except for the ads).

The newsletter or journal is truly the focal point for all user group activities and services. If the group operates a computer bulletin board system (BBS), for example, the newsletter will give you the number to dial and tell you how to log on with your modem. In some cases, there will be a "best of the BBS" column in the newsletter containing the most interesting tips and information people have posted there during the previous month. Some groups maintain a 24-hour information line that provides recorded messages about meeting schedules and group activities. Those numbers too can be found in the newsletter.

The names and home phone numbers of the group's special interest group chairmen will be included. But you may also find lists of group members who have volunteered to answer questions on specific products or topics.

HAL-PC, for example, easily has over 1000 members on its Help Committee. The IBM PC Users' Group, operating under the umbrella of the Boston Computer Society (BCS), has nearly as many on its Dial Help list. Name a piece of hardware or a commercial or shareware package, and these two groups will almost certainly have anywhere from one to nearly a dozen members who have volunteered to answer member questions and provide free support. Topics include Lotus, accounting systems, batch files, communications, genealogy, hard disk management, PageMaker, Paradox, PC-Write, ProComm, Timeslips, Windows, WordPerfect, and Xtree.

The names, phone numbers, and the hours between which you may call these members are published in the journals, categorized by topic. Not every group has such an extensive help program. But that doesn't really matter.

The key point is that as a member of a user group, you have access to scores, if not hundreds, of people and the help and expertise they willingly provide. Surprising as it may seem in this day and age, there actually are people who really enjoy helping other people. And you'll find a lot of them in computer user groups.

Three of the biggest groups

There are many, many excellent computer user groups. However, at least judging from recent copies of their monthly journals, the Big Three of years past are still the Big Three today: Houston; Washington, D.C.; and Boston.

We'll look at how to find a group in your own area in a moment. But I strongly suggest you write for more information on each of the following three organizations. Due to postage, paper, and handling costs, I suggest you include two or three dollars with your request for a sample copy of their newsletter/journal. I think you'll find that the Big Three do a remarkable job, thanks to the unswerving dedication of their officers and members. Here are the addresses to contact:

Houston Area League of PC Users, Inc. (HAL-PC)
P.O. Box 299426
Houston, TX 77299-0426
(713) 623-4425

Capital PC User Group, Inc. (CPCUG)
51 Monroe Street, Plaza East Two
Rockville, MD 20850
(301) 762-9374

BCS IBM PC Users' Group
188 Needham Street, Suite 230
Netwon, MA 02164
(617) 964-2547

You might also want to contact the Boston Computer Society, the organization founded by Jonathan Rotenberg to serve as an umbrella group for machine-specific user groups (IBM PC, Macintosh, Atari,etc.) As a member of BCS, you receive the monthly magazine *BCS Update*, plus one additional publication, such as the *PC Report* magazine published by the BCS IBM PC Users' Group. (Publications of other BCS-affiliated groups are also available for a small additional fee.) Contact:

Boston Computer Society, Inc. (BCS)
One Kendall Square
Cambridge, MA 02139
(617) 252-0600

How to find a local users group

I want to emphasize again that there are many, many top-drawer user groups. But that still leaves the question: If user groups are such a great deal, how come more people don't know about them?

Part of the answer lies in what I said before: As volunteer organizations with very low dues, there is no money for advertising. Groups may operate booths at computer fairs, swap meets, and computer flea markets, but they usually don't have the budget to place ads in local newspapers. The other part of the answer is that there is no natural point of intersection between first-time computer buyers and the user groups that could make their lives so much easier.

If you're in the market for a computer, you check the mail-order ads or go to a computer store. You get some advice from the salesperson, and a visit or two later, you either walk out with a system or place your order with a mail-order firm. Unless you hear about a group from a computer-using friend or associate, read an article in a computer magazine, or are lucky enough to have a knowledgeable salesperson, the topic will simply never come up in the normal course of things.

Ask the right people

So here's a little trick. Start with the computer stores in your area. If possible, try to find a store that has its own on-site service and repair facility. Then call up and ask to speak to one of the technicians. Since technicians tend to have a more passionate interest in computers than salespeople, the chances are that if anyone in the store knows about computer user groups, they will.

If that approach isn't possible, stop in and simply ask the first salesperson you see whether there are any computer user groups in town. If that person doesn't know, ask if he or she would mind checking with the other store personnel, including the tech staff.

What you're looking for is a name and a phone number. You need some point of access to the user group world. Call the individual (at a reasonable hour), explain that you are interested in IBM/MS-DOS computers, and that you hope to be able to locate a user group. Could the person help you? Obviously, it would be best if the person is an IBM-compatible user. But many local groups embrace all makes and models. So if the guy or gal happens to be an Amiga or an Apple user, don't hesitate to call. In addition, people who are really into computers tend to know others with the same degree of interest. The person you call may not know of a group that suits your needs, but he or she may know of someone else you can call.

It's also a good idea to ask for suggestions from friends or business associates who own computers. You might also contact someone at your local school system to see if any groups use the school's facilities for meetings. If there is a college in your area, check with the secretary of the engineering or computer science department to see if the college hosts a user group of some sort. Attending a local computer fair or swap meet is another good way to make contact. Some groups also set up tables and booths as part of hobbyist and crafts exhibitions at local shopping malls.

Radio and electronics stores can also be good sources of computer contacts. Amateur and ham radio operators have been heavily involved in personal computers from the beginning. I've seen a local ham couple an interface box or two to a computer and use it to access radio-based computer bulletin boards halfway around the world. (Look Ma, no phone bill!) There is thus a good chance that a member of a local ham radio club will know of computer clubs in your area. It might be worth checking with an electronics store for the name of a local ham radio club.

Check computer magazines

Computer Shopper, the monthly tabloid-size magazine that you will want to check for the most comprehensive list of mail-order suppliers, also runs a regular multi-page list of computer user groups. The list includes not only groups in the United States but in Canada, Australia, Panama, Israel, Germany, France, and other countries as well. Only a small fraction of the world's user groups are included, but the addresses and groups on the list are typically quite up-to-date.

If you can't find a listing for a group within a reasonable driving distance from your home, contact the next nearest group and ask if they know of any group that's nearer that may not have been listed. Also, consider going to the library and checking the *Readers Guide to Periodical Literature* in the reference section for references to articles about user groups in leading computer magazines. I know they exist, because I've written some of them in years past. But you will want to get the most current information.

User groups online

At this point, it is my fondest hope that you are beginning to see what I see. And that is that computer support, help, and assistance is everywhere—once you know where to look. Truly, you are not alone.

You may be surprised, but that's an accurate statement, even if you live in a shack on the north range of a cattle ranch in the Big Sky country of Montana. As long as you've got a computer, a modem, and a telephone connection, you can tap the expertise of literally tens of thousands of computer users worldwide. Personally, I think this is a good idea even if you don't live out in the wilds, even if you have half a dozen user groups in your area.

The mechanism for literally plugging into the worldwide computer user group network is computer communications. Don't worry about how it works right now. We'll get to that in Chapter 12. All you need to know at this point is that by connecting your modem to your computer, loading a comm program like ProComm, and telling it to dial what is usually a local number, you can "sign on" to a system like CompuServe or GEnie or some privately owned and operated bulletin board system (BBS).

The modem will make a little noise, and the word CONNECT will appear on your screen. You will be asked for your account number and password (or just your name and location on a BBS). Key that in, and you will be through the front door and into the system. One could write a book (or two or three) on all that can happen next. Here, we'll limit ourselves to the online equivalent of a local computer user group.

SIGs online

We'll limit the discussion to commercial systems like GEnie and CompuServe. What I'm about to say applies to America Online, Delphi, and many smaller systems as well. But for the kind of support information described here, you really need to use a system with a very large subscribership, and CompuServe and GEnie are the main contenders in this arena. As you read this, CompuServe will probably have topped the 1 million mark, and GEnie will probably be over 350,000.

Both GEnie and CompuServe offer the equivalent of computer user groups or SIGs. On GEnie, they are called RoundTables or RTs. On CompuServe, they are officially called Forums, but everyone calls them SIGs. SIG is the term we will use for all such online offerings.

All SIGs have three main areas. There is the conference area where members can converse in real time as if they were using a CB radio. There are the file libraries with their collections of shareware and public domain software, text files, and other items of interest. (This is where downloading comes in.) And there are the message boards, where members may raise questions, either for discussion or to request help with specific problems.

There is no fee for joining a SIG, but you will probably be charged "connect time" while you are using one. Costs are $6 an hour on GEnie (after 6PM) and $12.80 an hour on CompuServe (all hours). But at 2400 bits per second ("baud"), you can get a lot done in just a few minutes. There are also special free or shareware programs like Aladdin (GEnie) and TAPCIS (CompuServe) to help you cut costs even further by letting you do your typing offline, before you sign on.

Please don't feel that you have to try to understand all of the details right now. The key thing is that, once you have a subscription to an online service, you can dial a local number (usually), sign on, and post a question or request for help on one of the SIG message boards. Someone, somewhere is almost certain to have had a similar problem and be eager to help. Thus, you may find that you can sign on to the system 24 hours later and one or more responses to your query will be waiting for you.

You should also know that many software and hardware companies operate online support services, usually as a so-called "vendor" Forum or RoundTable on CompuServe or GEnie, and possibly other systems as well. This lets you ask questions and download files, drivers, and updated information directly from the company that made the product you are using. A number of shareware authors offer online support this way as well. Indeed, shareware authors originated the process.

It is possible that one response will recommend you download a file in the SIG library. So you enter a command to move to that section and enter another command (or pick an item from a menu) to tell CompuServe or GEnie that you want to download the recommended file. Your computer and the distant computer mate, thanks to your software; the transmission proceeds; and you enter a command to hang up. Once you are offline, you will have a program or a text file on your disk that's ready to run, or view, or print, or otherwise solve your problem.

More important, you will have plugged yourself and your system into a "computer user group" that spans the globe. In addition to more or less blanketing the United States, for example, both GEnie and CompuServe have a substantial number of subscribers in Japan, Germany, the Pacific Rim, and Western (and soon Eastern) Europe.

Conclusion

As with any user group, some of those hundreds of thousands of "members" are rank novices and seekers after help and support. Some are experts. And most fall somewhere in between. But whether it is an online, electronic user group or just a bunch of guys and gals who have gotten together in your kitchen for a beer and computer conversation, mutual assistance, knowledge sharing, and person-to-person help are the key characteristics.

As I said earlier, there really are people out there who enjoy helping others. And I'm betting that after you get your feet on the ground, after others have helped you to achieve a certain proficiency and level of knowledge, you will become one of them. You will want to help new users just as others helped you when you were inexperienced.

That's what makes computer user groups the great unknown resource. And it's why I urge you to tap in as soon as possible, even before you actually buy your system.

8

The shareware concept
High quality, low prices

IN THESE DAYS OF THE SO-CALLED DECLINE OF THE UNITED STATES, THE PHRASE "high quality at a low price" can only accurately be applied to products made in Japan or in Germany. Right? If it's inexpensive and it's made in America, it can only be junk. Right? And if you're talking about business software, it's got to be expensive to be good. Right?

Wrong. On all counts. Shareware and public domain software are among the most creative, top-quality, products of the computer age. Programs of this sort are available for a tiny fraction of the price of major, well-advertised packages. It may be heresy to say so, but at its best, shareware represents a return to the old-fashioned American principles of quality and value. And personal pride as well, for like the craftsmen of old, shareware authors sign their work and stand behind it—personally.

In this chapter, we're going to look at the shareware field in general. You'll learn how it is created, how it is distributed, how and where to look for the programs you need, and what you can expect when you get them. You will learn that, as with commercial software, not all shareware programs are of the highest quality, but the best shareware compares favorably with and sometimes surpasses equivalent commercial products. In short, this chapter will give you the knowledge and tools to save hundreds—and possibly thousands—of dollars on the software you need to make the most of your computer.

Defining terms

Let's start by defining terms. As you know by now, there are two main categories of freely available software: public domain and shareware. Public domain or "PD" programs have been placed in the public domain by their authors and are yours to do with as you please. Shareware is different. Shareware authors explicitly retain their copyrights, but they offer you the opportunity to use their programs free of charge. The assumption is that if you like what you see, you will send them the small registration fee they request. If you don't like and use the program, you owe them nothing. As noted at the beginning of this book, shareware is software on the honor system.

You wouldn't think it would work. But I know of at least nine shareware companies that are doing between $1,000,000 and $5,000,000 a year or more. Scores of other one-and two-person shareware-producing companies earn far less, but find that the amount is still large enough for a comfortable income.

On the downside, there are also many thousands of shareware authors who have never seen a dime for their labors. There are reasons for this, as we'll see in a moment. But not all of it has to do with "cheating" by users who fail to send in the fee. All of the really successful shareware programmers work hard at their business—supporting registered users, preparing updates to current products, and generally making it very worthwhile for a user to register the program in the first place.

Crippleware, bannerware, and freeware

No one has ever accused the computer industry of being particularly creative or inventive—or accurate—when it comes to coining words and phrases. In the little corner of the computer universe we're exploring here, there is an unshakeable addiction to the suffix "-ware." Thus, you will hear about "crippleware," "bannerware," and "freeware," to name but three popular terms.

Crippleware is software that has been deliberately crippled in some way by its author. It might be a database program that has been crippled so that it can only handle a dozen records, or a word processing program that lacks the ability to print. The idea is to offer enough functionality to show you what the program is like and to thus encourage you to register to get an uncrippled version. This is completely contrary to the shareware ideal, and the crippleware concept has generally come and gone, though you may hear references to it now and again.

Bannerware is a program specifically designed to show off the programmer's skills. It's a turn, a tour de force, an advertisement for the programmer. It might be a program that has no purpose other than displaying splendid, clever graphics on your screen. Or it might be a really cool game. There is absolutely nothing wrong with this. In fact, bannerware is often a delight, even if it doesn't really accomplish anything useful.

Finally, freeware is the original name for what we today think of as shareware. The term was coined by the late Andrew Fluegelman, editor of the first *Whole Earth Catalog*, editorial director of *PC World* and *MacWorld*, and author of PC-Talk, the first "freeware" program.

As Andrew told me in 1983, "I got my PC within about the first month after the machine was released. At the time I was working on a book with a co-author who had a NorthStar system (CP/M), and we had this vision that we'd be able to swap files—the great promise of computer communications, you know."

Unfortunately, Mr. Fluegelman discovered that there was no communications program available at the time that would allow a PC to transfer files to a non-IBM system. He spent an evening trying to modify the programs that were available, but after looking at the code, decided that this was not the right way to go.

"The next morning, I started writing a program for myself. Originally it was just for me, but once I saw that it was working, some of my friends used it and liked it and suggested that I should do something publicly with it. I think if I hadn't been in publishing for the last eight years, I would have gone ahead and taken the traditional publishing route, with advertising and marketing, and so forth.

"But somehow I was either very tired of all that or very inspired by the computer vista. The local PBS station was having one of its pledge drives, and suddenly, in one of those flashes, the word 'freeware' just popped into my mind. Along with the notion of sending programs out for free and encouraging people to copy them and requesting them to make donations if they liked the program. It really all kind of gelled, and from that point on, it was just too unusual an idea not to pursue."

A week after posting a notice of the program's availability on an online system, Andrew received his first order. "I just couldn't believe it. I was making contact with a world out there that I'd only imagined existed. And very quickly I had to get a bigger post office box and hire people and replace three disk drives. The thing really mushroomed."

Keeping it simple

Shareware is a term coined by Bob Wallace, author of PC-Write. Originally, the idea was to distinguish it from freeware. Bob's idea was to offer everyone who registered his or her copy of PC-Write a commission on registrations received due to the user's efforts.

The concept was and is simplicity itself. When you register your copy of PC-Write, you are given a registration number. With a few keystrokes, you can incorporate that number into your copy of the program. Then you pass it out to your friends. When your friends register, they will be asked for the registration number that appears on their copy of the program. That's your number, of course. The folks at PC-Write make a note of that fact and allocate a portion of the new user's fee to your account. The new user is issued a registration number of his own and encouraged to do exactly what you did with *his* friends and associates.

It sounds a little like a pyramid scheme, but it's not. Your involvement with each copy you distribute ends as soon as the recipient registers. Bob Wallace once told me that several bulletin board system operators were earning between $400 and $500 a quarter in PC-Write commissions, just from making the program available for download on their boards. (I should point out here that copies of PC-

Write available from Glossbrenner's Choice do not earn a shareware commission of any sort.)

To my knowledge, PC-Write is the only true "shareware" program, in the original sense of the word. No one else has such a well-developed program for turning satisfied users into salespeople. The reason "shareware" is now applied to the entire field is that, for reasons I've never understood, Andrew Fluegelman trademarked the term "freeware." Since no one else could use this term, the search was on for a substitute. For some years "user-supported software" filled in.

But that was always a clumsy phrase. When Bob Wallace specifically refused to trademark the term "shareware," it began to be applied to all freely available software. For the sake of simplicity, we will apply it universally as well. With the understanding that it covers many different subcategories and that the support, update, and fee policy of individual shareware authors can vary widely.

A dearth of information

I've taken us down this historical path for two reasons. First, words and word origins are always interesting. Second, and much more significant, it is important to realize that shareware is a well-established, well-developed phenomenon with roots as deep as the personal computer industry itself. This is not some flash-in-the-pan, fad-of-the-month phenomenon. It has existed and thrived all along, even though you may have never heard of it.

And just why have you never heard of it? More to the point: Why have huge numbers of experienced power users never heard of shareware? The answer is a simple question: Who's going to tell you?

I mean it. Your computer dealer or mail-order vendor isn't going to say, "I've got WordPerfect here for $500, but PC-Write will fill all of your needs—and your only cost is for the disks and the postage." Nor is a magazine that charges $20,000 or more for a full-page ad going to bang the drum for shareware and public domain software. They'll run an article now and then—indeed, I've written many of them—but only on special utilities and other programs that have no commercial equivalent. And few, if any, shareware programs are included in "roundup" reviews of the leading packages in a product category.

I don't blame magazines or computer vendors for any of this. If I were in their shoes, I would do the same thing. There is no point at all in biting the hand that feeds you. Yet, at the same time, there is a crying need for more information about shareware. New users need to be made aware that it exists, and experienced users need guidance on which of the tens of thousands of available programs are really worthwhile. At this writing, however, you won't find a regular shareware column in any commercial magazine.

So don't be surprised if you have never heard of shareware. Telling you about shareware is not in the best interests of those who have the means to tell you about it (assuming that they even know about it themselves), and shareware programmers generally don't have the money to advertise. To get the money, they would have to go commercial. And as we'll see, that is not in *their* best interests in most cases.

Are the programmers crazy?

Having sketched the territory and defined our terms, we're ready to get down to the real nitty-gritty. Namely, how in the world is it possible for anything of value to be available for free or for a modest registration fee? Are the people who are writing these programs crazy? Or is it just possible that the stuff simply isn't any good? The answer is a categorical "No" on both counts, but it requires a bit of explanation.

Fundamentally, the answer lies in the unique nature of computer software— any computer software—regardless of how it is marketed. One must never forget that a computer program is a creative work, every bit as much as the books you read or the movies you watch on your VCR. The cost of the ink and paper or the magnetic tape and plastic cassette are important, but they have almost no bearing on the product's worth or its price. As *Business Week* (10 August 1987) put it:

> Like perfume—and unlike hardware—software prices have relied more on the perceived value of programs than on production costs. This started with mainframe and minicomputer software and continued when the first popular business program, VisiCalc, appeared in 1979. VisiCalc's authors felt around for the right price, trying $99 before settling on $250 . . . Now the top companies are using more scientific approaches to pricing. Lotus spends about $1 million a year on studies by market researchers, who try to figure out what customers will pay . . . While the actual cost of the materials that go into a program, including several disks, a manual, and packaging, generally comes in at under $15, marketing and R&D can eat up 30% of revenues. Moreover, software companies might spend up to $20 per program on a toll-free customer service line for advice. Still, the bottom line is that with enough volume, programs selling at $400 to $700 can bring pretax margins of 20% to 40%.

Programming talent is the key

When you strip away the expensive office space, the marketing staff expense accounts, and the $20,000+, four-color, full-page ads in leading computer magazines, personal computer software almost always comes down to one thing—a single individual sitting alone in front of a computer screen, laboring to turn his or her ideas into a useful product.

Until the program itself is written, nothing else can happen. The results may be awkward and ill-conceived, or they may be elegant and thoughtfully designed. Either way, the penumbra of marketers, packaging consultants, market researchers, distributors, and retailers that surrounds a commercial program has little to do with the quality of the product.

There is nothing magical about commercial software. You can just as easily pay top dollar for a program that turns out to be a real stinker as you can for one that will perform as advertised. Nor is purchasing a commercial product any guarantee that the company supplying it will still be around when you need its services. Commercial software publishers go out of business all the time.

Production and reproduction

The second factor that makes computer software unique is that the means of producing it are both cheap and widely available. As we've seen in previous chapters, fully-equipped computer systems are cheap. So cheap, that virtually anyone can easily acquire the means to produce a program that 60 million or more IBM-compatible owners can use.

And that software can be quickly, easily, and inexpensively reproduced. A software author doesn't need printing presses and carloads of paper or hundreds of VCRs and cartons of blank cassettes to reproduce and publish his or her work. All that's required is a magnetic disk. The same machine used to create the product can reproduce it an infinite number of times.

Distribution is another matter. Indeed, distribution is the key element in the shareware equation, for along with advertising, it's the only thing that costs any serious money. The world's most talented programmer may be able to set up shop for less than a thousand dollars, and the costs of publishing a program may be insignificant, but without distribution, it is all for naught.

What to do? Well, put yourself in the programmer's running shoes. Here you've got a great idea for a program, you've got the talent to execute it, and you've got the personal computer. Working nights and weekends, you'll eventually have a finished program. Now what? What are your options?

Cracking the distribution nut

One alternative would be to form your own software company to market the product commercially. But these days it takes a million dollars or more just to get into the game. Unless you've got that kind of money lying around someplace, you're going to have to raise it from venture capitalists, banks, relatives, and friends. That's going to take a lot of time and energy, and may mean re-mortgaging your house and putting all of your assets at risk. And what's your family going to live on before you hit it big—if you hit it big?

Perhaps you could sell rights to the program to a commercial company instead? Many a freelance programmer has followed that route and had a lot of success. But it usually means settling for a royalty of five to ten percent on sales and surrendering all control over the product. In addition, you've got to find the right company, sell them on the idea, and hope they really can give you the distribution you need. More time. More energy. More effort put against activities you'd really rather not have to deal with. Besides, you've got your daytime job to think of.

As you can see, there's a lot more to selling a program than most people think. It is not simply a matter of building a better mousetrap, particularly not today with so many programs on the market. Whichever path you choose, there will be risks and rewards.

It is for this reason that many programmers have chosen the shareware alternative. Not because they're crazy, or because their work can't hold its own against commercially sold software, but because they find the risks and rewards of shareware marketing and distribution not only acceptable but eminently appealing.

By not following the commercial route, shareware authors probably give up the opportunity to have a mega-hit—like Lotus or dBASE—that will earn them tens of millions of dollars. But a programmer can do quite well asking, say, $30 for his package. Surprisingly, perhaps, that figure is very close to the gross profit some commercial companies earn on their products.

Shareware economics

Of course, the $30 or so that you send a shareware author does not represent the gross profit. The printed manuals many authors provide to registered users must be paid for, and time spent providing customer support and improving the product must be accounted for. The really successful shareware authors also issue press releases, attend computer fairs, and publish newsletters for their registered users. But promotional expenses like these are tiny compared to an advertising schedule in a major computer magazine.

Thus, with a very good program and a firm commitment to providing user support and continual product improvements, someone with programming talent can do quite well. He or she may not make millions of dollars, but at least the programmer has the chance to be paid at a decent rate.

The risks are minimal. There is no need to take a second on your house or put all your assets on the line. There is no need to quit your daytime job, at least not until you see how things go. If things don't work out, all you really have to lose is the time you have spent writing and perfecting the program. The shareware route, in short, can make a lot of sense if you are a talented programmer.

Where to get shareware and PD software

All of this sounds great, but it still doesn't address the problem of distribution. How can a programmer get the product into the hands of people who are likely to register? Or to look at it another way, where can you go to obtain shareware and public domain programs? The answers to both questions are the same.

In general, there are four main distribution channels for shareware and PD software. All were established long ago by personal computing hobbyists and enthusiasts. They include:

- computer user groups.
- mail-order sources.
- commercial online systems.
- free public bulletin boards.

You were introduced to some of these terms in the previous chapter when we looked at sources of help and support. Now let's look at them from the shareware distribution perspective.

User groups and shareware

As you know, a computer user group is a non-profit organization staffed by volunteers who are dedicated to facilitating the sharing of computer knowledge. Whether you are an experienced user or someone who is merely thinking about buying a computer, there's a place for you in your local user group.

Virtually all user groups have a shareware collection that is tended and presided over by a software librarian. Local members contribute programs; group librarians exchange programs among themselves; and, mindful of how important user groups are, many aspiring shareware programmers send their work to the librarians of leading groups.

Policies and procedures vary, but it is not unusual to find that shareware plays a central role in group activities. For example, there may be a regular column in the group's monthly newsletter discussing the latest additions to the shareware library. Some groups prepare a "disk of the month" containing the latest and greatest stuff and make it available to members for a small fee.

For many groups, shareware distribution is a major fund-raising activity. I've been at meetings where club business is conducted from the platform, while the group's shareware librarian, clutching fists full of dollars, conducts business at the back of the room. Group librarians offer copies of library disks for two to eight dollars, for example.

The librarian and assistant librarians typically donate the time needed to maintain the collection and copy the disks, though some part of the fee members pay per disk may be allocated to cover wear and tear on the librarian's disk drives and other expenses. But most of the profits go into the treasury to fund club activities and out-reach programs.

Mail-order sources

Shareware is also available through the mail from companies that specialize in its distribution. As you might expect, some of these firms do an excellent job, and some are in it merely because they think they can make a quick buck. Fortunately, the quick-buck artists don't last very long. They may take a few full-page ads in computer magazines offering disks at some ridiculously low price. But when customers find out that many of the disks these firms offer are nearly empty—when they discover that they can get three or four times more software per disk from a reputable vendor—the firms lose business and quickly pass from the scene.

Maintaining a mail-order shareware collection takes a lot of work. If you're going to do it and do it right, you've got to be in it for the long haul. You've got to keep an eye on the new stuff coming out and on updates of existing programs. Then you've got to reconfigure your master disks to add the new material. If your masters are already filled to the gills, that can be a time-consuming challenge.

Fortunately, there are many top-quality shareware vendors staffed by people who take their jobs seriously. Indeed, I know of at least three firms that are especially good. These are PC-SIG, Public (software) Library, and Public Brand Software. Each charges $5 or $6 per disk, plus $4 or $5 per order for shipping and handling. And each takes a slightly different perspective.

PC-SIG, PsL, and PBS

The PC-SIG collection grew out of the collection of the Silicon Valley Computer Society's library. PC-SIG is probably the most commercial of the three. Policies change, but in the past, PC-SIG catalogues have been quite lavish, even "glitzy." PC-SIG also makes its entire collection (over 3000 disks) available on a single CD-ROM, and it publishes the slick monthly magazine *Shareware*.

The main downside is that PC-SIG appears to accept nearly every program it receives and in the past, at any rate, it has been less than vigorous about updating its disks. Polices can change, of course, so this may not be the case when you contact them today.

The Public (software) Library or PsL, on the other hand, is a much smaller operation run by Nelson and Kay Ford and several assistants. It grew out of the collection of the Houston Area League of PC Users (HAL-PC), possibly the largest user group of all. A CPA by training, Nelson was the group's software librarian. The company was originally called The Public Library, after a shareware column Mr. Ford used to do for one of the early computer magazines. The Fords had to insert "(software)" in the name shortly after they opened because the local public library was getting all their mail.

PsL is tireless in making sure that the programs and disks stay up-to-date and that junk programs don't get into the library. A programmer himself, Nelson was the catalyst and guiding light behind the formation of the Association of Shareware Professionals (ASP), a group designed to set quality standards for shareware software.

The main downside of PsL is that its combination newsletter and catalogue is probably the least user-friendly of all. The 4000 disks it offers are all neatly categorized and numbered, but only four or five words of description are given for each one, making it very difficult for a novice to know what to order. PsL is absolutely excellent, but its approach is generally directed at the shareware aficionado.

Public Brand Software (PBS) grew out of the Indianapolis PC User Group's collection. In fact, it grew so well that in 1991, Ziff-Davis, publisher of *PC*, *PC Computing*, *PC Week*, *Computer Shopper*, and many other magazines, bought the company. The full impact of that acquisition has yet to be felt at this writing, though Ziff-Davis has made the entire PBS collection available online via Compu-Serve.

The PBS catalogue format, developed before the acquisition, is excellent. Its pages are filled with illustrations and screen shots of various programs. And each program gets at least one paragraph and sometimes several paragraphs of explanation and description. PBS even attaches a rating to each program, ranging from "tremendous" to "probably worth five bucks."

The main downside is that the amount of information provided is very nearly overwhelming. What do you do when faced with a single 8.5″×11″ page containing accurate and detailed descriptions of four "relational" database programs, all of which get the highest or next to highest rating? And those are just the programs PBS chose to include. As Nelson Ford's PsL catalogue reveals, there are many others to be considered in the same category.

All three of these mail-order firms have a lot to offer. Their approaches differ, and one may quibble with this or that, but I think you'll like them all. And I know that there is no better way to plunge into the mainstream of the shareware world than to send for their free catalogues. Here are the addresses and phone numbers to use:

PC-SIG
1030 D East Duane Avenue
Sunnyvale, CA 94086
(800) 245-6717

Public (software) Library
P. O. Box 35705
Houston, TX 77235-5705
(800) 242-4775

Public Brand Software
P.O. Box 51315
Indianapolis, IN 46251
(800) 426-3475

Glossbrenner's Choice

I should say a word here about Glossbrenner's Choice as well. This is a special collection designed to remove what I feel is one of the main obstacles to wide-spread shareware use—the problem of over-choice. The Public (software) Library, for instance, offers over 30 disks under its "Word Processing" category.

PC-SIG lists over 60 disks under "Wordprocessor and Text Utilities" and 30 more under "Wordprocessors, Text Editors, and Outliners." No explanation is given for these two apparently identical categories, and, on close examination, it is clear that not all of the disks listed really belong under these classifications.

Public Brand Software lists five "Text Editors," three of which receive its highest rating, and five "Word Processors." But many of the programs listed by PC-SIG and PsL show up in different categories in the PBS catalogue. So things aren't as narrowly defined as they seem.

My point here is not to criticize these and other sources for offering so much. Indeed, I am glad for their comprehensive approach. But I am also aware that if I were a businessperson interested in word processing software, I would take one look at the vast array of shareware choices available and conclude that it would be easier and cheaper to buy a well-reviewed commercial product, even if it cost $300 or more.

The reason is time. Assume you could somehow narrow the field to, say, 15 disks. At $5 per disk, your cost to obtain the software would be $75. But even if money were no object, imagine how many hours you would have to spend print-ing out and reading the documentation and running and testing all these programs to find the one that's right for you.

And that's just for one application. You will face a similarly daunting task selecting a shareware database, spreadsheet, or communications program. To say nothing of the many other important business applications.

Glossbrenner's Choice is founded on the conviction that it does not make good sense for each individual to personally re-invent the wheel. Instead of offer-ing multiple programs in each category, it offers just one—the one I personally feel is the best in its class, based on my testing and comparing of everything else in the field. Glossbrenner's Choice grew out of a book I wrote about CompuServe some years ago and was sparked by the need to supply readers with inexpensive communications software to enable them to use that online service.

I ran and tested countless programs and selected ProComm. I offered to send it to readers for a small fee if they couldn't find it elsewhere. The response was gratifying. "At last, someone is offering some guidance!" one reader wrote. "No one else will speak out and take a stand," wrote another. "Thank you for your insights and definitive recommendations. You've made shareware usable at last."

Other books followed, and the collection gradually grew to just under 100 disks holding what I feel are the best programs for every major PC application, plus a clutch of wonderful utilities guaranteed to make your computer easier to use.

I want to emphasize that all of the programs discussed in this book are widely available from user groups, mail-order, and online sources. Indeed, there is probably something wrong with any shareware source that does *not* offer them. But, since I've got the software anyway, if you find it convenient, they are also available from Glossbrenner's Choice. The cost is $5 for 5.25" disks, $6 for 3.5", and $3 per order for shipping and handling. You'll find an order form covering the programs discussed in this book in Appendix B. For a free catalogue of these and other programs, contact:

Glossbrenner's Choice
699 River Road
Yardley, PA 19067-1965

Distribution fees and registration

Please remember that the fees cited by any mail-order vendor cover only the costs of distributing these disks. The public domain programs are yours to do with what you wish. But if you like and regularly use a shareware program, you are expected to register it by sending its author the requested registration fee.

Believe me, this is something you will really want to do. Once you see how good this software is and how much time, money, and frustration it can save you, you will be happy to pay for it. Fees, terms, and benefits differ with the program. But in general, shareware authors offer things like a printed manual (to supplement or expand the instructions offered on disk), one or more free updates when new versions are released, and telephone support, often directly from the programmer.

The online process

The third and fourth channels of distribution are both "online." That means that you will need a modem and communications software to tap into them. We'll go into more specific detail in Chapter 12 when we show you how to use ProComm. However, here is a quick sketch of the process.

Let's suppose you're interested in a program to help you keep track of your genealogy research. You will find numerous shareware programs of this sort listed in comprehensive mail-order catalogues. But let's suppose that you don't have such a catalogue or that you do but you want the program right *now*.

What's involved is a three-step process. First, you've got to sign on to an online system. That means you must go into your communications program and issue commands telling it to tell your modem to dial the phone. The modem will do so, and in a moment you will be connected to a distant computer. You will be asked to key in your account number and secret password (or information to that effect). At that point, you are "online" with the remote computer.

Step two is to search for the programs available on the system that are most likely to meet your needs. All online systems offer some kind of search facility or procedure that involves typing in a key search word or phrase. In this case, the keyword would be "genealogy." You type that in and hit Enter and the system searches through its files for a match.

Depending on the particular online system, the number of matches could be as few as one or two or as many as 25 or more. You will probably see a list of filenames, but often a paragraph or two of additional information is available for each of them. You look at this information and use it to decide which file or files you want to get.

Then you take step three—downloading the file or files you have chosen. During the download process, your computer and the remote system strive for perfect harmony. Your software talks to the remote system's software, and together they effect a flawless transfer. When the download is complete, you will have an exact copy of the requested program stored on your hard disk.

At that point, you may sign off by keying in "bye" or some other word. The connection will be broken, and you will be free to run the program and see if it does, indeed, live up to your expectations. If it doesn't, you can sign back on and download another program to see if it is the one you want to use.

Online cost considerations

The costs involved vary considerably. Commercial online systems like Compu-Serve, GEnie, and America Online charge you by the minute for the time you are connected to them. At least during the download. Depending on the system, your other activities when you are online may be covered by a flat monthly fee of $5 to $8.

If you opt to use a privately owned and operated bulletin board system (BBS), your only cost will be whatever long distance charges apply to the call. The process is essentially the same: sign on, search, and download. The difference is that a BBS typically consists of a personal computer like yours, while a commercial system is typically housed in a mainframe system with gigantic disk drives and sophisticated system software.

As a result, commercial systems almost always offer many more programs than a typical BBS. They are also very stringent about making sure that all software is tested for viruses before being made available to users. Many bulletin board system operators do this as well, but many don't. Consequently, while I love BBSs, in general you're probably better off using them to exchange messages with electronic friends than as a source of shareware software.

The online world is so vast that a complete discussion of even this small segment is well beyond the scope of this book. Fortunately, the essential information regarding online shareware software can be reduced to a few key points. Online systems are best used as a source for utilities, games, and smaller applications programs. In general, it is not really cost-effective to obtain major programs by downloading them from an online system—at least not at today's standard speed of 2400 bits per second (bps).

For example, a major program like PC-Write occupies nearly a megabyte (three 5.25", 360K floppies) of space. At a speed of 2400 bps, you would need to spend nearly 75 minutes online to download three floppies' worth of files. If your connect time cost for the download was about 22 cents per minute (CompuServe's lowest 2400 bps rate), the download would cost you at least $16.50.

That isn't too bad if you don't mind tying your system up for over an hour. But it does not factor in the time you must spend moving to the place on the system where you can do your download, and it assumes that the transfer will take place at an average speed of 2400 bits per second. When you allow for unavoidable delays and what we can simply call "error-checking overhead," the download could actually take ten to 15 minutes more, for a total of close to 90 minutes and a cost of nearly $20.

A rule of thumb

We could explore the technicalities forever, but let's get to the bottom line. The fact is that there is no way to know precisely how much any given download will cost. There are simply too many variables. However, as a rule of thumb, assume that in the best of all possible worlds you can download the equivalent of a 360K floppy at 2400 bps in 25 minutes. Multiply the number of minutes by the connect time cost, and add ten to 15 percent to the dollar figure to allow for error-checking overhead and other delays.

If you are technically inclined, here is what you need to know to figure things out for yourself. Because of the way computers communicate, ten bits are required to transmit a single eight-bit byte. Therefore, a speed of 2400 bits per second is equivalent to 2400 divided by ten, or 240 bytes per second. Dividing the number of bytes you want to download by 240 will give you the number of seconds. And dividing the seconds by 60 gives you the minutes.

When to go online

In general, if you have a 2400 bps modem, you'll be best off getting major shareware applications on disk from user groups or mail-order firms. The cost differential may or may not be significant to you. The fact is that at 2400 bps, a major program just takes too long to download. Small utilities, games, and "little" programs are a different matter. Here is where the online channel comes into its own for most users.

The reason is the online search option. Suppose you wanted a program to turn off your computer's speaker so you could play games at night without waking your spouse who is sleeping in the next room. You could spend literally hours combing mail-order catalogues for such a thing and come up empty—even if the mail-order firm had the program. This is because there are so many small, single-function utility programs that most are never specifically cited in the catalogues. Instead, small utilities are placed on a disk with scores of other useful little programs, only a few of which are likely to be mentioned in the printed catalogue.

When you are online, in contrast, you can do the equivalent of searching every disk in a mail-order catalogue for what you want. And you can do it in seconds. The system will come back with one or more matches, and you can take your pick. If you don't feel like trying to choose among them at the moment, download them all. They are generally so small that you'll spend only a minute or two downloading each program.

All bets are off at 9600 bps

There is one final point to be made regarding getting shareware from online sources. As I have tried to make clear, everything discussed above regarding download times and costs assumes you are using a 2400 bps modem. If you are lucky enough to have a 9600 bps unit, possibly with built-in "data compression," all bets are off. Modems of this sort currently sell through the mail for about $400. Those capable of data compression can produce an effective throughput of a blistering 38,400 bits per second when connected to a distant modem that also supports compression. At that speed, downloading the complete PC-Write package (over a megabyte of software) would take about five minutes, not the 75 minutes required at 2400 bps.

At speeds of 9600 bps and above, downloading megabytes of software suddenly makes a lot of sense. Best of all, more and more online systems, like CompuServe and GEnie, are offering 9600 bps connections. Sometimes the systems charge a premium for these connections, sometimes they don't. Also, at this writing, 9600 bps "nodes" are available only in major cities. But the trend is growing.

Should you buy a 9600 bps modem now? Not if you are a brand-new computer user. There are too many other things to learn without adding the complications of advanced data communications. Instead, do this. Get a copy of ProComm, either from Glossbrenner's Choice or some other source, and use the 2400 bps modem that was probably included as part of your computer package to call Exec-PC, the "world's largest BBS."

Try Exec-PC for free

This system was created by Bob and Tracey Mahoney, and at last count, it had over 250 phone lines supporting every kind and speed of modem, over 300,000 programs and files, and had received over 4 million calls. It is, in my opinion, what every online system should be. But try it for yourself. Their voice line is (414) 789-4200.

To access Exec-PC's data line, load ProComm. Key in Alt-D to get to the dialing directory. Select an empty slot on the table that will appear. Key in R to "revise" the entry, and answer the prompts ProComm will give you. The number to tell ProComm to dial is 1-414-789-4210. Respond to the succeeding prompts so that settings of eight data bits, no parity, and one stop bit are entered. Then just keep hitting your Enter key until ProComm returns you to the plain dialing directory screen. Hit Enter once again to tell ProComm to dial Exec-PC, and the adventure will begin.

The system will connect, and you will be prompted for your name. Then you will be free to explore. Your only cost will be whatever the phone company charges you to call Elm Grove, Wisconsin, where Exec-PC is located. If you like what you see, you will be able to subscribe at a cost of $20 per quarter or $60 per year. That gives you complete access to all files and virtually unlimited usage.

With a system like Exec-PC to access, a 9600 bps modem with data compression makes an awful lot of sense. If you were impressed with what you saw, you may want to speed up your 9600 bps modem acquisition schedule. Or you may choose to wait until hardware prices drop still further.

Again, everything depends on your own needs and your own current level of experience. The key thing is to be aware that if you are really interested in public domain and shareware software, it can be located and transmitted quickly and inexpensively from a system like Exec-PC using a high-speed modem. You may want to wait a while before taking on this challenge, but you should definitely tuck it away in the back of your mind for future reference.

Also, I would be remiss if I didn't note that Exec-PC is not the only system in its class. It may be the largest in terms of phone lines and gigabytes of storage, but there are dozens of others, including Canada Remote Systems, U.S. One, Aquila BBS, etc. The best source of information about these and other super BBSs is Jack Rickard's *Boardwatch Magazine*. For a voice connection, call Boardwatch at (303) 973-6038 or (800) 933-6038. To sign on to the Boardwatch BBS, have ProComm dial (303) 973-4222.

What to expect

In the chapters that follow, you will learn many details about specific shareware programs. Here, I'd like to take just a moment to tell you the kinds of things you can expect from shareware packages in general.

First, whether you obtain the program through the mail or over the phone lines, you can generally expect it to be delivered as some kind of compressed or archived file. Utility programs like LHA or LHARC, PKZIP, ARC, and others are used to assemble a group of files and squeeze them down into a single, archive file. This has two advantages. First, it means that a program and its associated files take up less space on disk and require less time to transmit over the phone. Second, it means that a program and its files can be distributed as a *single* archived file.

Dealing with archived files

The disadvantage is that if you end up with an archived file on your disk, you won't be able to use the program it contains until you un-archive the file's contents. For those of us "in the biz," as it were, this is routine. But it can throw new users. Generally, however, software distributed on disk will contain a GO.BAT or INSTALL.BAT file that will present you with the necessary instructions when you key in GO or INSTALL. The instructions will tell you how to use a program supplied on the disk to un-archive any compressed files.

Since it is possible to create an archive and make it self-extracting, you may be told to simply copy one of the large files on the disk onto your hard disk and key in a command to start the de-archiving process. Or you may be told to put the floppy disk in Drive A and key in something like QFILER-Z C:\QFILER to get the program QFILER-Z.EXE to unpack itself onto Drive C in a subdirectory called \QFILER.

If you obtain the software from an online system, it may be on your disk as a self-extracting archive file (ending in .EXE), or it may be a plain archive file ending in .ZIP, .ARC, .LZH, or some other extension. In this case, you will need a utility program like PKUNZIP.EXE, ARC-E.COM, or LHA.EXE to perform the extraction.

I realize that all this is likely to be quite confusing to many new users. Unfortunately, space does not permit a complete explanation. For that, you will have to see Glossbrenner's *Master Guide to FREE Software for IBMs and Compatible Computers*. The key point to take away from this discussion is that shareware is often distributed as compressed files and that these files can either be self-extracting (ending in .EXE) or can require the use of an un-arcing utility program.

Fortunately, there is plenty of help available. If you can't get a program un-arced, call the shareware vendor you bought the disk from. His or her on-disk instructions may have been less than clear. If you have the same trouble with something you have downloaded from an online system, leave a message for the ''sysop'' (system operator) asking what to do.

Find and review the manual

Let us assume that you now have a shareware program on your hard disk in its own subdirectory. All the files have been un-archived, if necessary, and you are ready to begin exploring. The first thing to do is to look for files ending in .ME, .1ST, .DOC, .MAN, and .TXT. These are the files shareware authors use to talk to their users. Thus, you should look for READ.ME, README.1ST, or the program name followed by .TXT (text), .DOC (documentation), or .MAN (manual).

A program like LIST, discussed in Chapter 16, makes it easy to view files like these on the screen. You can key in LIST READ.ME and hit Enter and you will be able to scroll through the READ.ME file on your screen. You can also use PC-Write or some other word processor or text editor to look at and print such files. Or you can simply key in a command like COPY READ.ME PRN to produce a hard copy printout of the file.

These files will tell you about the program. They will tell you how to get started, how to use the program, how to register, what you will receive as a registered user, and so on. Often they contain the programmer's address and phone number or electronic mail (CompuServe, MCI Mail, GEnie, etc.) address. In short, most shareware authors make it easy for their users to get in touch.

You might want to give the manual or .DOC file a quick once over. But don't fight your instinct to ''play.'' Look for any file ending in .COM, .EXE, or .BAT and key in the filename to the left of the file extension. (You can use the commands DIR *.COM, DIR *.EXE, or DIR *.BAT to locate these files.) Don't worry about learning how to use the program at this stage. Plunge in and take a look around. Try hitting your function keys (F1-F12) to see what happens. See if your Esc key lets you exit immediately or back up through succeeding menus.

The key word really is *play!* The more you play with programs, the sooner you will develop a sense of how they work and of the conventions most programs follow. Usually, for example, the F1 key will act as a call for help. Often the Esc key will let you exit immediately. The PageUp and PageDown keys will often take you to the top and bottom of something, or perhaps the Home and End keys will be used. And so on.

When you have some sense of the program and how it works, then, and only then, print out and read the manual. You will find that the manual or documentation makes a lot more sense when you have some real experience with the software to use as a reference point.

Why one should support shareware

The next step is to begin using the program for small tasks. Again, you are interested merely in getting your feet wet at this point. If all goes well and if you genuinely *like* what you see, you can feel good about moving on to more complicated tasks and about making a larger time investment in the software. Believe me, at some point you will be able to tell very quickly whether a given shareware programmer is any good or not. To reach that point, you have got to experience a lot of software (good and bad), and you have got to "think system."

But that's not as difficult as it sounds. If a program seems inherently difficult to use, if it makes you go through contortions to accomplish simple tasks, if the manual isn't clear, if the look and feel isn't professional, you'll quickly conclude that it is substandard. On the other hand, when you encounter a really good program written by a talented, inspired programmer, you will sense it immediately.

To put it even more simply, think of the books you have read or started in the past year. In most cases, you know after reading the first chapter whether the book is any good or not and whether you will stick with it. It is exactly the same with shareware or, for that matter, commercial software.

If you do indeed like a particular program, you owe it to yourself and to the program author to send in the registration fee. Andrew Fluegelman once told me that he calculated that only one in ten users of his PC-TALK program sent in the fee. Over the years, other shareware authors have reported generally the same phenomenon.

That's too bad, but it is also understandable. Every group of people has "takers," men and women who make a point of taking advantage of others and never give anything back. Every society also has its share of "louts," men and women who never give a thought for anything or anyone but themselves. But I simply do not believe that these characters make up 90 percent of the shareware-using population.

It seems much more likely that most shareware users are simply busy people who obtain, install, examine, and decide to use a program but never get around to sending in the registration fee. I honestly don't think it's the money. Most registration fees are so low, the dollar amount is almost insignificant, particularly if the program is being used for business. We simply forget. The program works as advertised, and time goes on, and before you know it, a year or more has passed and you still haven't sent in the requested fee. Hopefully, enough of your brothers and sisters will have done so to make it possible for the shareware author to keep programming, updating, and improving the product. But without your support and my support, these men and women cannot continue turning out top-quality software. After all, they've got mortgages to pay and kids to feed as well.

I don't want to be a Dutch Uncle about this. But, by golly, talent should be rewarded. If you like a shareware program and if you use it on a regular basis, you should make yourself take time out from your busy schedule to write a check and send the person who created it the small fee he or she requests.

Direct contact with the author

If you and I don't support shareware, it will cease to exist. But it is important to point out that an inner sense of moral satisfaction is not the only benefit that accrues to those who take the time to register shareware programs.

Shareware offers something you will never find in the commercial software world—the opportunity for direct contact with the person who wrote the program. I do not want to leave the impression that this is a universal phenomenon. But the first time I had a question about PC-Write, I called Quicksoft, the company that publishes the product. And, Bob Wallace, the man who wrote the program, answered the phone.

I don't mind telling you that I was more than a little taken aback. "Overawed" might be more like it. Imagine being able to talk personally to the man or woman who wrote the program you are using. Imagine trying something like that with WordPerfect, Lotus 1-2-3, or dBASE. It would never happen. Indeed, Quicksoft has grown so and hired so many customer support people that it is not likely to happen with PC-Write today.

But it could. If you had some question that the Quicksoft customer service people could not answer on their own, they would ask the man who wrote the program and get back to you. Or Bob Wallace himself might call. That's the kind of personal attention you can expect as a registered user of PC-Write and many other shareware products.

Again, I do not want to leave you with the impression that all shareware companies operate this way. But many do. Indeed, shareware authors prize customer feedback. Most are keenly interested to know which features you like and which new features and capabilities you would like to see in future versions. Tom Smith, co-author of ProComm, attributes much of that program's amazing success to simply listening to his customers. Consequently, when Smith and partner Bruce Barkelew sat down to add improvements, they didn't have to guess what people would want—they already knew.

Sometimes a shareware author will even add a feature to a program to serve the needs of a single user. David Schulz, author of the Lotus-compatible spreadsheet program As-Easy-As (Chapter 11), told me of correspondence he had with a professor at a large midwestern university. "The professor was thinking of using As-Easy-As to directly query his lab instruments," Schulz said. "But to do that, he needed somehow to be able to import data from the PC's serial port. So I added two macro commands to the program for his use and testing.

"We decided to call them IOLABEL and IOVALUE. They allow you to send a command to the testing equipment and place the text string or numerical value it returns in any cell on the spreadsheet. I didn't document the feature because I had no way of testing it myself. But the professor reports that it works beautifully and it is in the program."

If you are new to personal computing, you can't fully appreciate this kind of user-to-programmer interaction. You will simply have to take our word for it that it is common in the shareware world and all but non-existent in the commercial software world.

Conclusion

Shareware and public domain software is a world all by itself. Its roots are deep, and over the years it has developed its own traditions, assumptions, and conventions. But it is a wonderful world, populated by bright, interesting, talented people. In the space available here we have shown you how to plug in and begin participating and benefiting from all that shareware in general has to offer.

In the chapters that follow, we're going to move in even closer. You have learned about computer hardware and how to buy a system. You have learned about operating system software and about shareware application programs and utilities in general. Now you're ready to learn how to get started with word processing, database management, spreadsheet, and communications software—the "Big Four" computer applications.

All of the specific programs cited in the chapters that follow are available from the sources cited in this chapter. In fact, since the chapters that follow offer hands-on instructions on how to use specific programs, you may want to take time out at this point to actually obtain the software. As this chapter has shown, there are many sources you can tap.

Part III

Shareware in your business: The ''Big Four'' applications

9

Word processing

WORD PROCESSING IS UNDOUBTEDLY THE MOST POPULAR OF ALL COMPUTER software applications. Not everyone needs an electronic spreadsheet, a database management system, or other specialized programs, but everyone needs to write letters and reports, invoices, memos, and to-do lists. That's why selling typewriters used to be such a good business.

Today, word processing software has virtually replaced the typewriter. You'll still need your trusty IBM Selectric or similar machine for filling out multi-part forms, express delivery air bills, or typing up a quick address label. But you'll find that a good word processing program and printer can handle everything else.

In this chapter, we'll introduce you to the general concepts behind any word processor. You'll learn about the important features and what they can mean to you and your business. Then you'll learn about Quicksoft's PC-Write, the program I feel is not only the best shareware word processor, but one of the best such programs available anywhere at any price.

We'll show you how to install and immediately start using Quicksoft's flagship product, PC-Write Standard Level. By helping you zero in on the program's key features and operating modes, this part of the chapter will considerably flatten the learning curve. We'll have you producing letters and memos with PC-Write in minutes.

Word processing: The big idea

These days, nearly everyone has at least a vague notion of what a word processing program is and does. They may not know the term, but, with the possible excep-

149

tion of my mother, virtually everyone is aware that you can type text into a computer and produce a hard copy on the computer's printer. The term "word processing" is derived from "data processing." The thought was that computers are always processing something, and since most people assume "data" means numbers, dealing with text must mean "processing words."

As you delve deeper into the world of public domain and shareware software, you will also hear the term "text editor." A *text editor* is generally a small, fast, program that lacks the advanced features of most word processors. The truth is, however, that for many people, a simple text editor offers all the features they will ever need or use.

My favorite text editor is Sammy Mitchell's QEDIT. It is widely available in shareware collections, including my own, so you may want to take a look at it. There are two reasons why it is not covered here. The first is space—it is necessary to draw the line somewhere.

The second is the conviction that one should learn as few programs as possible. If memory and disk space, screen and processor speed were still the problems they were several years ago, it would make sense to learn to use both a full-featured word processor and a small, fast text editor. As it is, I think it makes more sense to invest your time and effort in a word processing program that gives you everything, even if you don't use all the features. PC-Write is just such a program.

The captured keystroke

I'm going to tell you all about PC-Write in a moment. But first it is important for you to understand some basic points about the way computers view and handle text. Once you understand this, you will see how your word processing program can be the fountainhead for all kinds of applications. Indeed, you may well discover that word processing is the most important application of all.

When you tap a key, your keyboard sends a code number into the computer. The code numbers for every key or keypress combination are unique. Thus A and Shift-A and Alt-A and Ctrl-A, and so on, are all different. If you check your DOS 5 manual under ANSI.SYS (in the Device Drivers chapter), you will see that these keyboard "scan codes" seem to go on forever.

Now, what happens when a keycode arrives at the computer? The computer examines the code closely and checks it against an internal lookup table. If the code corresponds to a displayable character, that character will be displayed on your screen. If you have opened a file, as is the case when you run a word processing program, the character will be displayed on the screen, and the numerical code for the character will be saved in the file. When you leave the program and close the file, the entire file and all the code numbers it contains will be written to disk.

Tomorrow morning, you may want to add some information to that file, or you may wish to change some things. No problem. Just start your word processor and tell it to get the file you were working on last night. In a few seconds, the file will be on the screen again, just as it was the last time you saw it.

As far as the computer is concerned, the file is nothing but one long sequential player-piano roll of numbers, each of which corresponds to a displayable character. Using your PgDn key to look at the text is like turning a crank to reel more of the piano roll paper onto the top cylinder. The PgUp key reverses the process. Ditto for your various arrow keys.

Capturing your keystrokes and saving them in a computer file is the central concept upon which word processing is based. For, once your keystrokes have been captured, they can easily be manipulated.

Block moves and boilerplate

For example, suppose you have created a document consisting of over a dozen paragraphs. You review it and decide that the second paragraph really should follow what is now the fourth paragraph. There's no need to retype anything. Just use the word processor's commands to mark off the block of text that is the second paragraph, cursor down to the new location, and hit a single key to effect the move.

Let's carry this idea a step further. Many small businesses are frequently called upon to submit bids on jobs. The specific details of every bid are different, but there are sure to be two or three paragraphs setting forth your terms that are the same in every letter. As you probably know, those kinds of paragraphs are often called *boilerplate*.

If you don't have a computer, you've basically got two choices. Either you type up a fill-in-the-blanks form and make a bunch of photocopies, or you type each letter from scratch every time you submit a bid. In either case, a word processing program makes things easier and lets you turn out a much more impressive result.

All you've got to do is create a file containing your boilerplate text. From then on, you can load your word processor, prepare the customer-specific portion as you used to do on the typewriter, and then tap a few keys to insert the boilerplate text file into the letter. In seconds, you will have accomplished what would have taken you or your assistant several minutes to type by hand. That's a real productivity increase.

And not only that, the printed results *look* a lot better than either a typewritten letter or a photocopied form. To my mind, that's a genuine down-to-earth example of what Tom Peters and all the other management pundits mean when they talk about "working smarter"—higher quality results produced with less time and effort.

Mail merge and mass mailings

Continuing with this theme, let's take things even further. Let's suppose that business is down and that you'd really like to remind your customers about your services. Perhaps you would like to make a special offer to encourage them to call you. Or perhaps you have a retail establishment and want to contact your best customers about a special sale. Whatever. The key point is that you feel you could build your business if only you could find a way to put certain information into the hands of your customers. Let's assume there are 500 of them, though any number will do.

What are your alternatives? The cheapest alternative is probably to have a copy shop print up a bunch of postcards and have your secretary type up 500 labels. Not bad, but not impressive, either. The next alternative might be to have the copy shop print a batch of flyers and fold and staple them to mailable size. You would then have to apply the labels and stamps. Not terrible, but on balance, probably less impressive than a postcard, and probably as expensive to mail as a first class letter.

Okay, what about a first-class letter? In these days of more junk mail than real mail, that might get your customers' attention. Particularly if it were done with good quality stationery. But you know what would really get their attention? Suppose they opened the letter and it began, "Dear Mr. Jones," or "Dear Frank" if Mr. Jones is a friend. Suppose it said, "I hope you're enjoying the slacks you bought last September," and then continued with your gentle sales pitch or special offer.

Suppose, in short, that every first class letter you sent out to your customers was similarly personalized with the customer's name and most recently purchased item. It would look as though you had sat down and written a personal letter to each customer—all 500 of them.

It sounds like a Herculean task. But once you know how to do it, you can pump out 500 personalized letters and addressed envelopes with only a few minutes of work. The one thing that will slow you down is your printer, since it is likely to require an hour or more to complete the job.

Two things are required. First, you've got to have a database containing your customers's names and addresses, the item they last purchased, and the date of that purchase. Presumably this is the kind of information you have been collecting all along. Indeed, you might use this identical database to send out invoices to your customers. (More on that in Chapter 10.)

Note that I've picked these pieces of information solely for demonstration. The key point is that whatever personalized information you want to use in your letters must be saved in a database file like the ones created by File Express.

Second, you need to prepare a letter your word processing program can use as a template. The inside address in such a file might look like this:

```
{title} {fname} {lname}
{company}
{address}
{city}, {state} {zip}

Dear {title} {lname},

I hope you're enjoying the {product} you bought from us
   last {purch-date}. As you know, we do our best to . . .
   {purch-date}. As you know, we do our best to . . .
```

The next step is to tell your database software to create a text file containing the customer information you need in "mail merge" format. Then you simply bring the template into your word processor and activate that program's mail merge feature. The program will read the customer information from the mail merge file and insert it in the proper places in the template to produce a customized letter.

There are lots of ways to do the envelopes. But assuming you have a plain laser printer without a special envelope cassette, your best bet is to use your database program to produce the labels. File Express, for example, has a built-in label printing feature. Or you might use your database program to produce an address file that you can feed to a program like Avery LabelPro (commercial) or Mail Machine (shareware; see Chapter 14). All of these programs let you feed sheets of pressure-sensitive labels through your laser printer, or drive a dot-matrix printer loaded with pin-fed continuous form labels.

I do not mean to minimize the time and effort and general fiddling required to get everything set up. Nor would I recommend that a brand-new user attempt this task right away.

But I haven't pulled any punches, either. The general procedure for producing highly personalized mailings is exactly as outlined here, and clearly it isn't brain surgery. With a little effort, anyone can do it. Best of all, once you get things set up, you can do it again and again with truly minimal effort.

ASCII text and graphics

Word processing software offers lots of other productivity-and quality-enhancing features as well. But before discussing them, it is important for you to know the difference between ASCII text files, graphics files, and binary or machine language files. I know this sounds like a major assignment, but it is much simpler than it seems.

As you may recall, computers deal in eight-bit units called *bytes*. Each byte is a number, expressed in the on/off, 1s-and-0s form that is the only thing computers can understand. There is no need here to explore the mysteries of the binary numbering system. All you need to know is that it is possible to represent any number using only two symbols (on/off, 1/0, etc.).

Because you've only got two symbols to work with, however, a larger collection of symbols is required to represent the same number we humans can write with our ten symbols (0–9). And with a maximum of eight bits ("symbols") in a byte, you can represent only the numbers from 0 through 255, for a total of 256 numbers.

When you consider all the things a computer has to do—all the numbers it needs—that just isn't enough. You need 128 numbers to symbolize all the capital and lowercase letters, the main punctuation signs, and the digits from 0 through 9. If you want to use special non-text graphics characters, like the ones used to draw boxes or supply non-English accented characters, you will need another 128. That's 256 numbers right there, and we haven't even gotten to the numbers needed to convey commands to the microprocessor.

Computers solve this number shortage with what you might think of as two pairs of glasses. When they've got one pair of glasses on, they see and treat the 256 numbers as characters and text. When they're wearing the other pair, they treat those same 256 numbers as machine language—binary instructions to the

CPU. That's what the file extensions .COM and .EXE are all about. When the computer sees them, it knows to put on its "binary" glasses and treat the file's contents as machine language programming instructions.

Most of the time, however, computers are wearing their "text" glasses. They look at the codes you send from your keyboard or in your word processing file and assume that they are meant to symbolize text characters. This text code is so important that it has a special name: the American Standard Code for Information Interchange or *ASCII* ("as-key"). This code assigns a number to each and every text character, punctuation mark, and digit. Virtually all computers in the world follow this practice and thus "speak ASCII." By definition, an ASCII file is a text file.

Consequently, when your system sees an ASCII 65 in a file, it knows to display a capital A. When it sees an ASCII 97, it knows that you mean a lowercase a. And so on. But how does it know which pixels (picture elements) to turn on and off on your screen to display a given character? The answer is that it has a built-in table with preprogrammed instructions for each ASCII code. When it sees an ASCII code, it looks for it on the table and instantly learns which pixels to turn on and off to make the character appear on your screen.

Graphics files, in contrast, are quite different. There are no ASCII codes in a graphic image file. There is simply an image—in 1s and 0s—of which screen pixels should be on or off, or set to a certain color or intensity. In technical terms, graphics files are "bit-mapped images," though there is more to it than this, depending on the file format.

Graphics files are created whenever an image is scanned into the computer with a hand or flatbed scanner. They are created by paint programs like PC Paintbrush, PC-Key-Draw, and similar programs. They can be created by programs like HiJaak that take graphic snapshots of screens. The key point is that the only way to alter or display a graphics file is with a program specifically designed to do so. Such programs work by giving you the tools you need to effectively change individual pixels.

Is this trip necessary?

I know this sounds esoteric, and I'm sure you're wondering why and whether you have to know these things. You will simply have to trust me when I say that an understanding of the differences among ASCII, binary, and graphics files is bedrock, essential information that you will draw upon again and again.

For example, any laser or 24-pin dot-matrix printer you buy today is sure to come equipped with a collection of "fonts." In the simplest terms, a font is basically a lookup table that tells a printer how to form a particular ASCII character. When one font table is in effect, the printer produces a capital A in the Times Roman typeface. When another is in effect, the printer might use the italic or boldface version of Times Roman or some other typeface.

The ASCII code the printer receives is the same in all cases. (An ASCII 65 for a capital A.) What's different is that before it gets the code, you or your program have told it to "put on a different pair of glasses" by switching to a different font table.

Similarly, you will find that graphics files take up a lot of disk space and require a long time to print. Why do you suppose that is? You have all of the information needed to answer that question. Because graphics files are bit-mapped images, there are no lookup table shortcuts. Each pixel must be recorded in the file. And each pixel must be processed by the chips inside the printer and printed individually.

Other nifty word processor features

Now that you have this background, you are in a position to understand many of the other powerful features word processing software places at your disposal. Consider what is called "desktop publishing" or "DTP." This is the feature that lets you create brochures, flyers, manuals, reports, and many other pieces of a look, feel, and quality one would expect from a professional printer.

The key is really your printer, since the quality of your output can be no better than the quality of your output device. But word processing software can make printer features easily available to you as you create your documents. For example, when you install PC-Write, you will be asked to choose your printer make and model from a menu. The installation program will then create a printer definition file for your equipment (PR.DEF). That file will contain the instructions necessary for your printer to access many of the fonts it is equipped with.

When you are creating a document with PC-Write, you can turn on bold printing by keying in Alt-B at the point you want boldface to start and Alt-B again where you want it to stop. Alt-I will toggle on italics, and Alt-O will toggle on "overstrike." The color of the text on the screen will change to indicate that it has been "enhanced." When it comes time to print the document, PC-Write will look in the PR.DEF file for the specific instructions it must send to the printer to switch bold or italic printing on and off.

The text you create will thus no longer be limited to pica or elite or whatever your collection of IBM Selectric "golf balls" can supply. You will have an entire "print shop" at your disposal, limited only by the capabilities of your particular printer.

As in many books, you can have your documents printed with a running header that includes the title of the book or the chapter. Or, if you are producing a report, the running head may include the title and the date. You can select a footer line if you choose. The program can make it easy to create an index listing the major topics and the page numbers where they are discussed. All of these features are built-in. You have only to key in a few commands to activate them.

When you have finished preparing your document, you can activate the built-in spell checker. In the case of PC-Write, this causes the program to read through the file, comparing every word to its built-in 50,000-word list. When it encounters a word not on the list, it will highlight the word and give you the opportunity to make a manual correction, add the word to the master list, or let PC-Write guess at the correct spelling.

If there is a word, phrase, or topic you want to find in a long file, you can tell PC-Write to search for it and take you there immediately. If you have made a mistake, perhaps calling someone "John" who spells his name "Jon," you can tell PC-Write to locate every instance of "John" and replace it with "Jon." The program will adjust the text to account for the difference in the number of characters in the two names.

There is plenty of online, pop-up help (just hit F1). And unlike most equivalent top-of-the-line word processors, by default PC-Write creates pure, clean ASCII text files. That means that anyone with any word processing program (IBM, Mac, or whatever) can read them. No "funny characters" or machine language garbage will appear on their screens, as is the case with the native files produced by many other programs.

The mother of all applications

I said earlier that a word processor is in many ways every computer user's core application. Let me tell you what I mean. You will certainly use PC-Write (or a text editor, or some other word processing software) to do virtually everything you now do with a typewriter. Reports, memos, letters, short notes, any kind of text.

But you will also use it to prepare letters you wish to send via electronic mail. For example, I'm currently working on a book with a co-author in Colorado. I live in Pennsylvania, and there is thus a two-hour difference between us. But a few moments ago I sent him an electronic letter regarding the chapters we are working on right now. I prepared the letter in PC-Write and then transmitted it to his mailbox on CompuServe.

When he checks his mail on CompuServe later this evening, he will receive the letter, prepare a reply with his word processor, and upload it to my mailbox on CompuServe, where I will find it later this evening or tomorrow morning. I will save the letter as a disk file and then bring it into PC-Write for reading and printing.

Or consider facsimile transmission. If I need to send somebody a fax, I prepare the text in PC-Write. If I had a regular fax machine, I would print it out and feed the paper into its hopper. Since I use a fax board inside my computer instead, I prepare the letter as a text file, call up the fax software, and tell it to send the file as a fax to its destination. The software converts the text file into a graphics file and handles the transmission.

We'll cover communications options in much more detail in Chapter 12. The point I want to emphasize here is how central word processing is, and how it intersects with virtually all of your other applications programs.

PC-Write Standard Level—An overview

Now let's look at PC-Write and Quicksoft, the company that publishes it. We can start with a simple question: Why do you buy a particular novel or audio CD? Why do you rent a particular movie? The answers are complex, but in the end, they all boil down to talent. Much of the time, you are, in effect, buying the work of a particular individual—an entertaining author, a great rock band, or a favorite film star. Other people may be essential to the production, but the talent of the "artist" is always the motivating, creative force.

That, in a word, is why you will find PC-Write such a super program. Word-Perfect, Microsoft Word, and PFS:Write are all fine products, but do you have any idea who wrote them? Would you ever in a million years dream of being able to contact their authors and saying, "I wish you would consider adding this particular feature?" Users of PC-Write do that all the time. In fact, the program's author encourages it.

Not that easy access to the programmer is the determining factor. If PC-Write weren't absolutely superb, I would not recommend it. But its excellence, the talent of Bob Wallace (its creator), and the philosophy of the $3 million company he has built on this product (27 employees and 1 cat), make it irresistible.

Not for nothing does it get boffo reviews in *InfoWorld*, *BYTE*, and the *New York Times*. Nor is it any accident that corporations as diverse as Airborne, DuPont, Honeywell, Martin Marietta, and Whirlpool Corporation have licensed the product, or that colleges like Clemson, Indiana University, Iowa State, Rutgers, and the U.S. Naval Academy have done so as well. Nor is it an accident that it is available in Spanish, Danish, Finnish, French, German, Icelandic, Dutch, Swedish, Greek, and Russian.

Versions and features

At this writing, PC-Write (PCW) is available in three versions. There is the original program (v3.02, at this writing), the "lite" version, and PC-Write Standard Level. These versions can be confusing, and I wouldn't mention them if all three were not available through most shareware sources. Since PCW Standard Level is the company's new flagship product, it is the one you should get. It is the one we will discuss here. Thus, if you are ordering disks from a mail-order firm or downloading files from an online system, make sure that the program description notes that it is the "standard level" of PC-Write.

If you are a longtime PCW user, you should know that Standard Level operates in essentially the same way that the PC-Write you are now using does. The guts of the program are the same. The difference is that Standard Level incorporates some really nifty, user-friendly features like "mousable" pull-down menus and pop-up hyper-text help. The installation program is a joy, and while PC-Write does not yet offer WYSIWYG ("wissy-wig," short for "What You See Is What You Get") displays when enhanced fonts are used, it does offer a "preview" feature to give you an idea of what the printed pages will look like.

Customize and "Add-a-Feature"

Standard Level also offers an "adapt" feature that lets you customize the selection of features available. You can opt for the Core, Basic, or Standard collection of features. For example, if you set the print function to Core, when you click on the PRINT selection at the top of the screen, you will be given just one option ("print all pages"). If you set the function to Basic, you will be given the options of looking at a preview of what the printed page will look like, printing all pages, or print-ing a range of pages. If you ratchet things up to the highest level, Standard, you will have the additional option of controlling the printer setup. The available items on the pull-down menus, in other words, change with the level you select for each operation.

That's an interesting feature in and of itself. But what's really interesting is what Bob Wallace told me in 1987 when I was writing *Alfred Glossbrenner's Master Guide to FREE Software*. I asked him how he felt about criticisms that his program was too complex and offered too many features.

He said, "I agree with your suggestion of the 'use what you need and forget the rest' approach. But people are funny. On an emotional basis, they just don't like to have all of those features there. They don't like seeing them on the menus and help screens, and they worry that they will accidentally hit a key combination that will do something unexpected.

"So after going to a lot of computer shows and listening to a lot of people, I've finally figured out that people really want something that at least looks sim-ple."

I noted at the time that "Mr. Wallace plans to do a version of the program that will mask all but the most basic features. He envisions such a version as being equipped with an 'add-a-feature feature.' You would start with a bare bones pro-gram and add features as needed by calling up the 'add-a-feature' menu. Once a feature was added, the appropriate selections would appear on the program menus and help screens, and the keys to activate it would be enabled."

It is now clear that PC-Write Standard Level is what Bob Wallace had in mind. The reason it has taken so long is that Bob was overburdened with management responsibilities and had no time to program. So he hired a capable chief executive named Leo Nikora and got back to the keyboard. PC-Write Standard Level appeared a few months later.

A programming genius

I could list the features of PC-Write until the cows come home, but that would put most people to sleep. When you boil it all down, the essential reason for recom-mending PC-Write is Bob Wallace himself. Mr. Wallace began designing text proc-essors in 1969 while a student at Brown University. He holds a master's degree in computer science, and, in 1978, he was one of the first dozen people to join a little Bellevue, Washington, firm called Microsoft.

While at Microsoft, Wallace designed the language and architecture, wrote the compiler front end, and wrote much of the runtime module for Microsoft's MS-Pascal. Mr. Wallace's commitment to his product is obvious for, as with all suc-cessful shareware authors, he is constantly updating and improving it.

His firm, Quicksoft, has a very flexible registration policy. If you want the full package, the cost is $129. This brings you the disks, the Getting Started booklet, the 130-page Reference Manual, and technical support (phone, mail, and fax) for one year. The two manuals are well written, cleanly designed, and professionally produced. They are definitely non-threatening.

Registered users also receive a year's subscription to the quarterly *Quick Notes* newsletter with its tech comments, user tips, and advice. For power PCW users, Quicksoft offers the *PC-Write Wizard's Book* (sold separately). This contains customization information and appendices not everybody uses.

If you don't want to register but just want the disks, the cost is $24, including shipping charges. If you merely want the newsletter, the cost is $15 a year. If you want an additional year of tech support, the cost is $60. Site licenses, rush and C.O.D. orders are available, as is shipment to overseas locations. Plus, there's a full 90-day warranty. If you don't like a Quicksoft product, you may return it to them in good condition with proof of purchase for replacement or full refund. Try that with WordPerfect, Microsoft Word, or some other commercial product!

How to install PC-Write Standard Level

Now let's really get into the product. We are going to assume that you have obtained PC-Write Standard Level from a disk vendor or by downloading the program from an online service. You will have four files with names like PCWSTD-1.ZIP, PCWSTD2.ZIP, etc. If you don't know how to unzip a file, see Chapter 12 for instructions. If you do know the technique, uncompress each file onto its own disk and label the disks "1 of 4," "2 of 4," etc.

To install PC-Write Standard Level on your hard disk, put Disk 1 in the drive and key in **INSTALL**. You will be greeted with a screen like the one in Fig. 9-1.

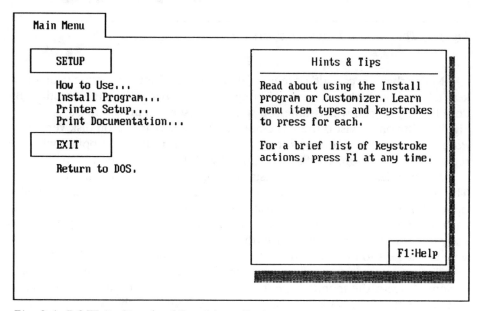

Fig. 9-1. PC-Write Standard Level installation.

Making the most of the INSTALL program

Notice that the installation screen is divided into three main areas: Setup, Exit, and Hints & Tips. The Hints & Tips screen will always tell you what the Setup selection means. If you would like instructions on installing the program, hit your Enter key when the "How to Use . . ." selection is highlighted. Otherwise, use your arrow keys to move the highlight bar down to "Install Program . . ." This will take you to a screen like the one shown in Fig. 9-2.

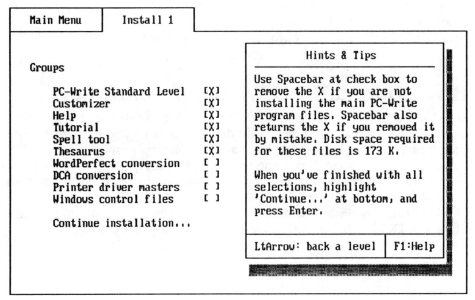

```
 ┌─────────────┬──────────────┐
 │ Main Menu   │  Install 1   │
 ├─────────────┴──────────────┴──────────────────────────────┐
 │                                                            │
 │                               ┌────────────────────────────┤
 │   Groups                      │          Hints & Tips      │
 │                               ├────────────────────────────┤
 │     PC-Write Standard Level [X]│ Use Spacebar at check box  │
 │     Customizer              [X]│ to remove the X if you are │
 │     Help                    [X]│ not installing the main    │
 │     Tutorial                [X]│ PC-Write program files.    │
 │     Spell tool              [X]│ Spacebar also returns the  │
 │     Thesaurus               [X]│ X if you removed it by     │
 │     WordPerfect conversion  [ ]│ mistake. Disk space        │
 │     DCA conversion          [ ]│ required for these files   │
 │     Printer driver masters  [ ]│ is 173 K.                  │
 │     Windows control files   [ ]│                            │
 │                                │ When you've finished with  │
 │     Continue installation...   │ all selections, highlight  │
 │                                │ 'Continue...' at bottom,   │
 │                                │ and press Enter.           │
 │                                ├──────────────────┬─────────┤
 │                                │ LtArrow: back a  │ F1:Help │
 │                                │ level            │         │
 └────────────────────────────────┴──────────────────┴─────────┘
```

Fig. 9-2. The "Install Program..." screen.

Notice that you can add or remove an installation feature by using your arrow keys to move the highlight bar and hitting your spacebar at the target location. By default, the program will assume you want the first six items on the list shown in Fig. 9-2. The only twist is the "Thesaurus." This refers to the on-disk version of *Roget's II: The New Thesaurus* from Houghton-Mifflin that is supplied with the registered user version. This is not supplied with the shareware version.

You may leave the thesaurus installation enabled (X) or not at your option. The other files ("WordPerfect Conversion," "DCA Conversion," etc.) are also optional. If you have lots of hard disk space, use your spacebar to put an "X" at each of these selections. Otherwise, you may leave them on the floppy disk and copy them over to your hard disk in the future should you ever need them. Use your arrow keys to move down to "Continue installation . . ." and hit Enter.

The next screen you will see is shown in Fig. 9-3. Notice that your main options concern the monitor, the feature profile, the screen display, and document formatting. The monitor selection is a no-brainer. Either you have a color

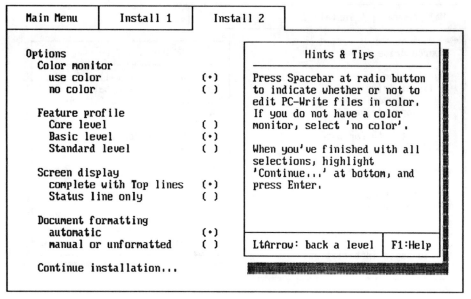

Fig. 9-3. Installation options.

monitor or you don't. The feature profile gives you a choice among Core, Basic, and Standard. By default, the program is set for Basic, but I think you may want to cursor down to "Standard level" and hit your spacebar to opt for the full-powered profile. Personally, I'm not bothered by seeing items on a menu that I rarely use. But if you want a reduced selection, choose Basic or Core level. (You can always change things later.)

As for the screen display, leave it set at "Complete with Top lines." The last selection, "Document formatting," is also up to you. Personally, I prefer to see the text enhancement codes and other formatting codes, so I have my program set for "manual or unformatted." If you have never used PC-Write before, however, you should probably leave the default setting of "automatic" as is and move on to "Continue installation . . ."

The next installation screen lets you tell the program where you want it to put the PC-Write files (Fig. 9-4). Notice that you can select a floppy drive or leave the default setting of a hard drive in place. By cursoring down to the "Target path" line, you can tell the program the letter of the hard drive volume, as well as the subdirectory "path" you want to use. The default is "C:\PCW," which is fine, but you may prefer something even simpler like "C:\ED" (for "editor").

Make your choices and press F9 as instructed on the screen. The program will start copying files from the disk in Drive A and prompt you to insert disks. Notice that if you have left "Thesaurus" enabled as discussed above, the installation program will prompt you for "Disk 5," but tell you to press F10 if the thesaurus is not included in your edition.

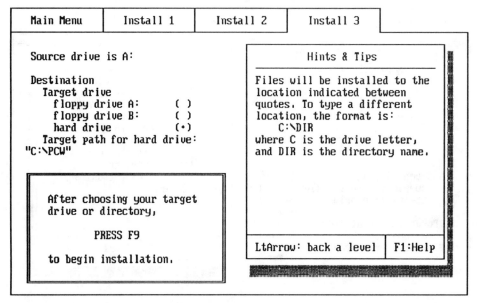

Fig. 9-4. Where to install the files.

Printer installation

Now, the next step is very important. What you have just done is to install the program itself. But the process is not complete. Now you will be returned to the screen shown in Fig. 9-1, and the highlight bar will be on the "Printer Setup" selection. If you do not follow through with this step, PC-Write will not know how to print your documents. So your next move is to hit Enter.

That takes you to a screen where you can tell the program whether you have a non-laser or laser printer. You will also be able to tell the program to use something other than the default printer port of LPT1. The Hints & Tips screen will guide you. When you move the cursor to "Continue with printer . . ." and hit Enter, you will be prompted for the printer definition file name and path. If you have installed the program itself into a directory other than C:\PCW, it is a good idea to make sure that you use that same path when installing the printer definition file on this screen.

There is no need to change the name of the printer definition file from the default of PR.DEF. But you will be offered the option to "Print test files when done." That's not a bad idea, since it will show you the fonts that PR.DEF has activated. So use your spacebar to toggle on an X at that prompt. Note that you can activate the printer test at anytime later as well.

Since the printer picker is on Disk 4, you will probably be prompted to insert that disk in the drive. You will then see a screen like the one in Fig. 9-5. Note that you will first be prompted to enter a letter corresponding to the manufacturer of your printer (HP, Kyocera, Panasonic, etc.). Then, when you press the letter selection, a list of models will appear in the lower half of the screen. Figure 9-5, in other words, contains both the maker selections and the model selections.

```
1. Adobe PostScript       D. IQ Engineering       P. Roland
2. AST                    E. Kyocera              Q. UDP Data Products
3. Blazer                 F. Mannesmann-Tally     R. Xerox
4. Brother                G. NEC
5. Canon                  H. Okidata
6. Corona                 I. Olympia
7. Digital (DEC)          J. Pacific Data Products
8. Epson                  K. Panasonic
9. Fujitsu                L. QMS
A. HP (Old carts)         M. Quadram
B. HP (Resident,New carts) N. Radio Shack (Tandy)
C. IBM                    O. Ricoh
Printer Picker.  Press letter or digit for your printer model:
1. LaserJet/LaserJet Plus  D. LJ IIIsi, Times,Uni-2
2. LJ Series II            E. LJ IIIsi, Courier
3. LJ IID                  F. GlobalText
4. LJ IIP                  G. Great Start
5. LJ III,IIIP,IIID {New}  H. Persuasive Presentations
6. LJ III,IIIP Times,Uni-1 I. Polished Worksheet
7. LJ III,IIIP Times,Uni-2 J. ProCollection {New}
8. LJ III,IIIP Courier     K. ProCollection, Times,Helv
9. LJ IIID, Times,Uni-1    L. ProCollection, Pres,Goth
A. LJ IIID, Times,Uni-2    M. TextEquations
B. LJ IIID, Courier
C. LJ IIIsi, Times,Uni-1
```

Fig. 9-5. The Printer Picker.

As soon as you pick a printer model, the program will flash through some screens and start printing the PC-Write printer test page (assuming you have enabled that option). The page is headed "Font Demonstration," and each font is preceded by a letter. There is **B** for "bold," **C** for "compressed," **I** for "italic," etc. These are the font letters you will use to switch on enhanced text as you create a document.

For example, if you want to put some word in bold, you hold down your Alt key and hit your **B** key (the Alt-B sequence). Then type the word. Finish up by toggling the font off with a second Alt-B combination. The text on the screen will change color to indicate that it will print in an enhanced font of some sort.

If your Font Demonstration sheet does not reproduce all the fonts you know your printer is capable of, don't worry. It is possible that you have selected the wrong model of printer and will have to go through the printer installation again. Or you may have to alter your PR.DEF file to change the fonts Quicksoft has chosen for each letter. Once you register the product, the company will be able to tell you how to do this.

Don't let yourself get hung up on the PR.DEF file. Proceed with the installation and try out the word processor. However, for an excellent explanation of how PR.DEF and its font definitions work, see the file PRDEF.DOC on the disk supplied with this book. Written by Don Phillip Gibson, this essay will tell you everything you need to customize PR.DEF to your liking.

After the font demonstration has been printed, you will be returned once again to the screen shown in Fig. 9-1. Only this time, the highlight bar will be over

"Print Documentation . . ." By all means do so. You will have the opportunity to "Print Manual Addenda" and to "Print Tutorial."

The addenda is only about 3 pages, while the tutorial is about 40 pages. I suggest that you print them both.

With the printing finished, you will again be returned to the main screen (Fig. 9-1), and at this point, you should opt to "Exit to DOS."

Getting started with PC-Write

The first thing to do after you have installed PC-Write, or any other program, is to go to the target directory and call for a list of files with the DIR command. You will see something like the file list shown here. The distribution disks contain many more files, but this is probably what your working copy of PCW will contain:

PR.DEF   Printer definition file; tells PCW how to implement the various fonts supported by your make and model of printer. As you gain more experience, you may want to have several printer definition files (under different names) and tell PCW to switch among them.

ED.DEF   The file PCW looks at to load your "profile." Both ED.DEF and PR.DEF are text files that you can edit and modify with PCW if you like.

ED.EXE   The main PCW program. Just key in **ED filename.ext** to create or edit "filename.ext."

ED.HNT   When you turn the PCW "hints" feature on, one or more hint lines appear below most top-line menus and prompts. This is where they come from. The hint feature is activated by keying in Alt, followed by **V**, followed by **T**. You will see a line on the menus that will now be on your screen reading "Hints line."

ED.PIF   The PCW program information file for users of Microsoft Windows. If you are a Windows user, you will find that PCW's built-in speed is a real asset in Windows. Also, look for the file WINREAD.ME on the distribution disks. It will tell you everything you need to know to quickly install PCW for Windows.

PRINT.TST   This is a file that lets you check the current fonts implemented by PR.DEF. You can print it out at any time by keying in ED PRINT.TST and printing the file from within PCW (F1, F7, and follow the prompts).

OLDPCW.DOC   A text file for users of previous PCW versions. Skip it if you are a brand-new PCW user. However, if you are a user of 3.x or previous versions, you will definitely want to review it.

ADDENDUM.DOC   Information that did not make it into the printed manual you receive as a registered user.

REGISTER.NOW   An easy-to-print registration form. Key in **ED REGISTER.NOW** and print it. Or key in **COPY REGISTER.NOW PRN** to dump the file directly to the printer.

INSTALL.EXE   This is the PCW installation program we have just stepped through.

CUSTOM.EXE   CUSTOM is activated whenever you want to change your PCW settings or profile. It is called by the installation program or by PCW itself, should you want to change things while you are editing a file. Or you can key in **CUSTOM** at the DOS command line to activate it directly.

CUSTOM.OVL   An overlay file used by CUSTOM.EXE.

CUSTOM.HLP   Help file for CUSTOM.EXE.

ED.HLP   The main help file for PCW. It contains the information that pops up on your screen when you call for help as you are using the program. It is a text file and can thus be customized to your liking, should the need arise.

ED.TUT   This help file is specifically designed to be used with the PCW Standard Level tutorial. (More on this later.)

TUTORIAL.DOC   When you want to start working on the PCW tutorial, load this file (ED TUTORIAL.DOC) and print it out. Then activate the HELP feature and select "tutorial" from the pull-down menu that will appear.

WORDS.MAS   The master word list used by the spelling checker feature.

WORDS.NUL   Used by WORDS.EXE.

WORDS.EXE   This program is used to add more words to the master word list. The spelling checker saves the words you want to add in a file called WORDS.USE. That file gets loaded along with the master word list. WORDS.EXE, however, lets you incorporate the words in your user file into the master word list itself. WORDS.USE is then erased.

WORDS.TOV   Used by WORDS.EXE

Preparing a document with PCW

We are going to show you how to use the PCW tutorial in a moment. First, however, let's create a simple letter or text document. To do so, get into the PCW directory and key in **ED LETTER.TXT**.

The program will give you a prompt reading: File not found: Esc to retype, or F9 to create "letter.txt". Hit your F9 key to tell the program to create the file. That will take you to the editing screen. Whether you are creating a new file or editing an old one, you must hit either F9 or Esc as prompted.

When editing a previously created file, PC-Write will actually show you the first page as it asks you whether you want to make a backup copy (F9) or not (Esc). As a new user, it is generally a good idea to let PCW make a backup of the file. It only takes a second, and you can always delete it later. PCW's backup copies are easy to spot—an ampersand (&), dollar sign ($), or percent symbol (%) is used as the first character of the file extension (LETTER.&TX, for example).

You can also easily customize PCW Standard Level to automatically make a backup without prompting you when you are starting the program. But one word of advice: If the version of the file you want to edit contains any information you think you might want to use in the future, copy the file to a floppy disk or give it a different name. Since whenever PC-Write makes a backup, it overwrites the previous version of the backup file, this is the only way to be sure of preserving all of the information in the "original" file.

If your mouse is active, PCW will sense the fact and give you a mouse cursor at the top of the screen. (If you are a new computer user, the quickest way to activate your mouse is to check the disks that came with your system for a program like MOUSE.COM and run it.) The mouse cursor will remain visible for only about five seconds. Then it will wink off. To bring it back, simply move your mouse.

The main PCW editing screen is headed with a top line listing the following options: File, Edit, Search, Layout, Print, Tool, Adapt, View, and Help. If you have a mouse, you can cursor over to any of these and click on it with your left mouse button. If you do not have a mouse, hit your Alt key to gain access to the top-line menu. Once that menu appears, you will be able to select an item by cursoring over to it and hitting Enter, by pressing the key corresponding to the first letter in the item, or by using your mouse. You can toggle the menu off by hitting Alt again.

However you activate them, the result will be pull-down menus like the ones shown in Fig. 9-6. As you click or hit Enter on the pull-down selections, you will be taken to additional menus or to a menu that lets you control a setting or start a process (like printing).

You can leave the menus until later. Right now, we're going to assume you

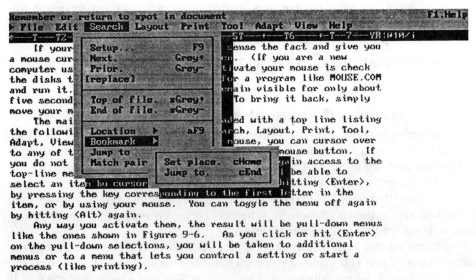

Fig. 9-6. Example of PCW Standard Level pull-down menus.

have a letter to key in. So start typing. If you don't have a letter to type, pick a paragraph from a magazine or book. The main idea is to get some text on the screen. When you have entered five or six lines or more, use your cursor keys to move up to a particular word and hold down your Alt key while you hit your **B** key (the Alt-B combination). That will activate boldface printing. Move to the place you want bold printing to stop and enter another Alt-B. Try the same thing on a different word with Alt-I for italics. Consult your Font Demonstration print-out for more ideas.

Now, assuming that you have keyed in several lines of text, let's print it out. If you are a speed demon, hit F1 and then hit F7 and then F10 to print "all pages." If you want to take a more leisurely approach, use your Alt key to activate the top menu or use your mouse to click on the Print option. Tell the program that you want to print all pages by mousing or cursoring down to the "All pages" selection on the Print sub-menu and clicking or hitting Enter. Your printer will come to life, and the text you have entered will be printed.

When you are finished and want to leave the program, hit Alt to bring up the menu, **F** for File, and **E** for exit. Or simply key in F1 followed by F3 to exit without saving. If you are a longtime PCW user, you will notice that all the function key commands work as usual. You don't have to use the menus. But if you have a new employee to train or if you are new to PCW yourself, the menus are there for you. And they certainly make things easy.

Running the tutorial

You now have a pretty good idea of how to create and print text in PC-Write. (Yes, that really is all there is to it.) But, of course, there are all kinds of other things you can do. Chief among them is working through the tutorial supplied with all PCW Standard Level distribution packages.

If you have not opted to print the tutorial during the installation process, do so now. Key in **ED TUTORIAL.DOC**. Notice that PCW will show you the file at first and prompt you to hit F9 or Esc, unless you've already customized the program to do automatic backups on startup. Hit Esc to get into the program.

Next use the skills you have just learned to print out a copy of the file. When the printing is finished, activate the Help function on the top-line menu. This will produce a sub-menu of Index, Context, and Tutorial. Select Tutorial. That will load the special help file (ED.TUT) designed to guide you through TUTO-RIAL.DOC. Notice that when using a PCW menu option, the Esc or the left arrow key will almost always allow you to back up to the previous menu, and that the Enter key will almost always select an option. If you activate Help, for example, hitting the Esc key will make the Help window go away.

We are going to assume that you have keyed in **ED TUTORIAL.DOC**, that you have printed the file, and that you have opted for the "tutorial" version of help as discussed. Your screen should look like the one shown in Fig. 9-7. The top half of the screen will contain the file TUTORIAL.DOC. The lower half will display a window of tutorial help information. The two windows scroll independently, depending on which window you are "in" at the time.

```
+---+---T1----+-T--2----T----3-I-+----4T---+---T5----+-T--6---YC----7--T-+--r
                    AVANTI LIVERY LINES, INC.
                    219 First Ave.N #200
                    Seattle, WA 98105
            (206) 658-0000   1-800-324-1021


July 16, 1991

Marcia Winslow
Special Events Coordinator
KLEIN FASHIONS
300 Stone Avenue Way
┌Home:contents   Arrow:select-topic   Enter:to-topic   cF1:to-edit   Esc:done┐
│              Welcome to the PC-Write Tutorial!                              │
│ Use the Arrow keys to highlight a lesson or exercise. Then press the Enter  │
│ key to jump to it. To exit the Tutorial and return to editing, press Esc.  │
│ Or, press Ctl-F1 to return to editing and leave the tutorial window up for │
│ your reference. You can scroll pages in the Tutorial while editing.         │
│                       TABLE OF CONTENTS                                     │
│ LESSONS                              EXERCISES                              │
│ 1:Creating a New Document            Exercise 1 (on-screen tutorial)        │
│ 1:Creating a New Document            Exercise 1 (printed tutorial)          │
└PgUp/PgDn:scroll───────────────────────────────────cPgUp/cPgDn:by pages─────┘
```

Fig. 9-7. The PCW Tutorial.

Now here's the trick. Notice the command "cF1:to-edit" located at about the middle of the screen on the right. This is the command—Ctrl-F1—you will use to switch between the editing window and the tutorial help window. Let us assume that you are in the tutorial window. Use your cursor keys to scroll through the text. Notice that some items are highlighted—in bright white on a color screen. Move to one of these and hit Enter. You will immediately be transported to the relevant section of the tutorial. That's the "hypertext" feature of PCW's help system. To return to the top of the help file, hit your Home key.

Now switch to the editing screen by keying in Ctrl-F1. Use your cursor to scroll. To return to the top of the text file, hold your Shift key and hit +. To go instantly to the bottom, press Shift and hit −.

The tutorial is quite extensive, and you will want to take your time working through the lessons and exercises. The tutorial help exercises contain a great deal of hands-on instruction on which keys to hit to accomplish a particular task. I urge you to work through them.

If you need help with the tutorial, Quicksoft will provide it—even if you have not registered the program or otherwise sent them any money. (What a company!) You may call (206) 282-0452.

Tech support is available on the following schedule. All times are Pacific Time:

Monday	7AM—5PM
Tuesday	7AM—5PM
Wednesday	7AM—12:45PM and 3PM—5PM
Thursday	7AM—12:45PM and 3PM—5PM
Friday	7AM—5PM

PC-Write hints and helps

The best way to learn any program is to simply play with it. Set aside some time, load PC-Write, and start trying things. Try to develop a feel for the way it does things, and don't worry about messing up. Worst case, you can always re-install the program from floppy disk. Also, it is never a good idea to try to master any program in one session. Not only is it impossible to do, it also affects your attitude and how much you remember. It is much better to play for a while, try a few things, then put it aside and go do something else.

Concentrate on the basics. Wait until you actually need a feature before trying to master it. In other words, wait until you find yourself saying, "I wonder if there's a way to do thus-and-so?" PCW is such a powerful, well-written program that there is probably a way to do just about anything you want. But there is no point in learning about it until you need that feature.

Making the most of HELP

We've covered the most basic tasks of getting into the program, entering text, printing it out, and leaving. The next most important feature to try is the Help function accessed from the top-line menu (mouse or Alt key). The help window that pops up at your command lets you scroll through a text file called ED.HLP. The help window will pop up in the top half or the bottom half of the screen, depending on where your cursor is when you activate Help. (See Fig. 9-8.)

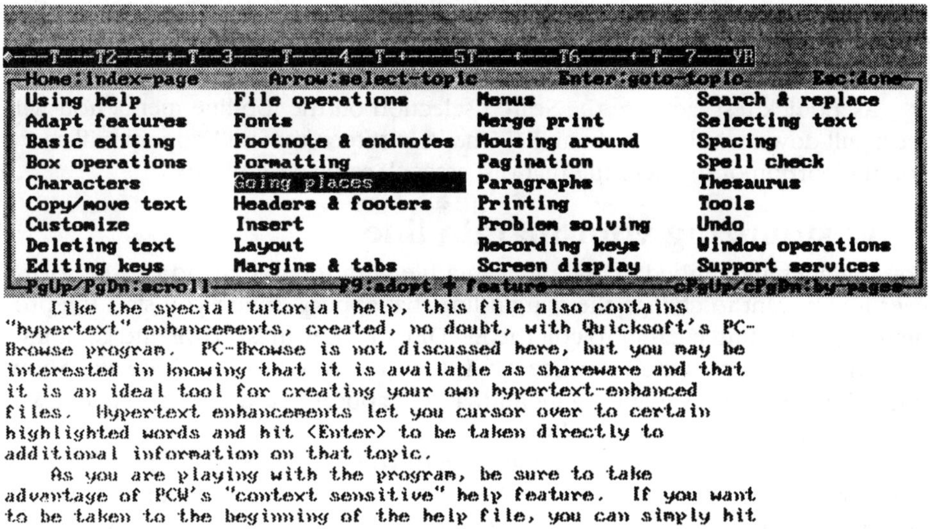

Fig. 9-8. The topic index of the Help screen.

Like the special tutorial help, this file also contains "hypertext" enhancements, created, no doubt, with Quicksoft's PC-Browse program. PC-Browse is not discussed here, but you may be interested in knowing that it is available as shareware and that it is an ideal tool for creating your own hypertext-enhanced files. Hypertext enhancements let you cursor over to certain highlighted words and hit Enter to be taken directly to additional information on that topic.

The Help feature is fairly self-explanatory—use your Home, End, and arrow keys to scroll through. The combination Ctrl-PgUp moves up a page at a time; Ctrl-PgDn moves down a page. Use the Esc key to return to your editing.

Notice the prompt "F9:adopt = feature" at the center of the bottom border of the help screen. This refers to the current setting of your profile (Core, Basic, or Standard). As you will recall, the profile setting for each feature controls the number of choices you will see when using the menus.

If you have used the highest setting (Standard), all features will be adopted (made part of your profile). But if you have chosen one of the lesser settings, those features you have *not* enabled will be tagged with an equals sign at the far left of the help screen. The Help function is smart enough to know what you have enabled in each case.

This is designed to keep you from getting confused. Tagging un-adopted features this way says, "This particular feature does not apply to you at this time." If you want to *make* it apply, cursor to it and hit F9 to adopt it. The relevant equals signs will disappear from the help window, and your PC-Write profile will be changed and written to disk.

Context-sensitive help

As you are playing with the program, be sure to take advantage of PCW's "context-sensitive" help feature. If you want to be taken to the beginning of the help file, you can simply hit F1 twice in a row. But if you are using the top-line menus, you can hit F1 and the program will display the help information relevant to whatever main menu function you have selected.

As a quick test, activate the Search selection on the top-line menu. You will see a pull-down window. Now hit F1. The help screen that will pop up will show you the portion of the help file that discusses "Search & Replace."

Customizing your margin line

You can alter and embed margin lines in a file with the command Ctrl-F2. However if you want to change the margin line that appears when you start the program, you may find it easier to edit the ED.DEF file. Key in **ED.DEF** and get it into PC-Write. Then enter the sequence Alt-A, then **W**. Look for the "Hide and Show codes" line on the overlapping menu that will appear. Hit **S** and the system will be set to show codes. Then hit Enter.

This setting will reveal the margin line to you in your ED.DEF file. Edit it as you would a line of text. Enter a **T** where you want a tab stop. Enter an **R** where you want the right margin to end. Save the file to disk, and the margin line you have edited will become your new default.

Zipping around a file

PC-Write offers a wide range of ways to move around a file, through a sentence, or through a paragraph. But there is no real need to learn all of these commands.

Listed here are the ones you will use most of the time. Note that the gray keys are on your numeric keypad:

Go to bottom of file: Shift-Gray Minus
Go to top of file: Shift-Gray Plus
Move a screen at a time: Shift-PgUp/PgDn
To mark your place: Ctrl-Home
To return to the place you have marked: Ctrl-End
Go to a specified word or phrase: F9, specify the phrase, hit Enter, and then hit the Gray Plus key to search forward or the Gray Minus key to search backward.

Editing tips

PC-Write can be in one of two modes when entering text: push-right and over-write. Its default setting is push-right, meaning that the program makes room for each new letter you type by pushing existing characters to the right. (Some programs call this "Insert" mode.) In overwrite mode, each new letter overwrites any text already beneath the cursor. You can toggle between the two modes with your Scroll Lock key.

Personally, I prefer to make overwrite mode my default. If I need to insert something, I will toggle push-right on, key in the text, and toggle it off. You will want to try it both ways and set your profile to match your preference.

The F7 key will adjust a paragraph to match your current margins (if automatic formatting is not enabled). The Ctrl-Enter combination will delete any text to the right of the cursor. (A great way to get rid of an entire line quickly.) See the pull-down Edit menu activated from the menu line across the top of the screen for help in marking, moving, copying, and deleting blocks of text. You can also use PCW to mark and move columns of text with its "boxing" feature, also accessible from the Edit pull-down.

Introduction to the macro function

A "macro" in computer talk is short for "macro-expansion." The idea is that by hitting a single key combination, you can set off a whole series of actions that have been "programmed" into the key combination. A single keystroke, in other words, effectively expands into many keystrokes.

The macroing or "record" function of PC-Write is quite powerful and guaranteed to save you loads of time. To use it, you toggle on the record mode, enter the keystrokes you wish to save, and toggle record mode off. Then you simply hit the Gray * key on your keypad to tell the system to repeat all of those keystrokes automatically.

If you'd like to give it a try right now, here's what to do. Hold down your Alt key and hit F3. That will bring up a top-line menu. Notice that the menu says to strike F4 to turn record mode on. Do it. Type your name. Use the Alt-F3 combination again to bring up the top-line record menu. Select F4 to turn record mode off. Now each time you hit the Gray * key, PC-Write will type your name, starting from the cursor's current location.

This is just a basic introduction to using macros in PCW. As you explore further, you will find that you can cause the macro to repeat continuously until the end of the file is reached. You can also assign those keystrokes to a keypress combination of your own choosing. And you can tell PC-Write to record your macros and key assignments in ED.DEF so they will be in force automatically from then on.

Be sure to check the disk supplied with this book for Writer's Heaven, a package of clever PCW macro definitions prepared by Mark Shepard. Mr. Shepard is a professional storyteller. Writing under the name Aaron Shepard, his latest children's book is *Savitri: A Tale of Ancient India*. Written for grades two through seven, and beautifully illustrated by Vera Rosenberry, *Savitri* is the story of a princess who finds her true love and then must use all her wit and strength to win him back from Death. The book is published by Albert Whitman & Company ($15.95) and can be ordered from any bookstore.

Mr. Shepard is a longtime user of PC-Write, and, at our request, he revised and updated his Writer's Heaven package for PC-Write Standard Level. If you are a brand-new user, you're not in a position just yet to appreciate what Mr. Shepard has done and the time his macros can save you. If you are an experienced user, you will particularly admire the pop-up notepad, address grabber, and envelope printer built into Writer's Heaven. There are many other features as well.

For experienced users only

Once you have had some experience using PCW, you will definitely want to spend some time experimenting with its macro functions. You can use Writer's Heaven as a complete package, or you can pull out just the macros you want to use, for example. Or you can create your own macros.

For example, suppose you wanted to assign a macro to the Alt-Tab combination. We'll keep things simple and assume that you want to assign the normal functions of the F1 key to Alt-Tab.

Key in **ED ED.DEF**. Move the cursor to the end of the file. Then toggle on PCW's numeric keycode mode with Ctrl-6. In this mode, each key or key combination you strike produces a keycode on the screen instead of a character or an action of some sort. Hold down your Ctrl key and hit your Tab key, and the number 649 will appear. That's your activation keycode. Then hit your F1 key, and a colon followed by the number 315—the keycode for F1—will appear. You will have a line on your screen that looks like this: **649:315**.

Now, enter a Ctrl-6 again to toggle numeric keycode mode off. Hit F1 and F3 to save your work. Then hit F1 and F2 to exit PCW. Now activate PCW again and start to edit a file. Enter a Ctrl-Tab to activate your macro. You will see the same results produced by the F1 key.

This is just a simple example. There are many kinds of things you can do with PC-Write macros. You can create a macro that inserts the current date, for example. Or you can create one that will automatically key in your name and address. (For more information on advanced functions like macros, you will want to order *The Wizard's Book* from Quicksoft.) In the meantime, I strongly recommend that you add a word or two of explanation to each macro. Simply enclose your comment in parentheses. That way, you will always be able to quickly tell what each macro does and what key combination activates it.

Activating the spelling checker

To take advantage of PC-Write's built-in 50,000 word spelling checker, hold down Alt and hit F2. That will produce a top-line menu. There are a number of selections, including one for "F5 Thesaurus." As mentioned, the thesaurus is supplied only with the registered user package. A brief line of text appears directly below the top line as you move from selection to selection. Also, you may hit F1 to bring up context-sensitive help.

The way I like to use the spelling checker is to go to the top of the document I have finished writing, hit Alt-F2 to bring up the spelling checker, and then hit Esc to return to the edit screen. To start the spelling checker, I then hit the Gray Plus key. The system will examine each word in my file and check it against its master word list.

When it encounters a word it thinks is misspelled, it gives you the opportunity to let it guess at the correct spelling, make an editing correction, add it to its word list, or add it to a "skip" file so it will ignore the word from that point forward. To make an editing correction, hit Esc to leave the spell checker. Resume checking by hitting the Gray Plus key again.

When you are finished checking the file and you want to return to DOS, PC-Write will prompt you before you exit to either save or discard the list of skip words and the list of words you have told it to add to its master word list. That way, you won't have to waste time on the next file you check telling the spell checker how to respond to the identical words.

Two crucial DOS tips

There are two final tips I'd like to pass along. First, when creating files, always give the file both a filename and an extension: MONDAY.TXT, MARCH.DOC, CHAP 2.REV, and so on. File extensions make it very easy to copy, move, or back up files. Thus, to copy all of the revised chapters (Chapters 1 through 32) to a floppy in Drive A, you need only key in a command like **COPY *.REV A:**.

Second, to make PC-Write available from any location on your disk, be sure to take advantage of DOS's PATH command. Check your current path by keying in **PATH**. Then look at your AUTOEXEC.BAT file for a line beginning with the word "PATH." Use PCW to look at and edit the file by keying in **ED C:\AUTOEXEC .BAT**. If there is no PATH line in AUTOEXEC.BAT, enter the following line: **PATH C:\;C:\PCW**. If there is already a PATH line, simply add **;C:\PCW** to the end of it. (Path locations are separated by a semicolon.) Then reboot the computer to make the new path take effect.

From now on, you won't have to go into the PCW subdirectory to use PC-Write. Whenever you want to edit or create a text file, just key in **ED** followed by the filename. The PATH command tells DOS to look in C:\PCW for the ED.EXE program. Whatever files you create will be recorded at your current disk and sub-directory location.

Conclusion

There is simply no doubt about it—word processors are special. Not for nothing is word processing the most popular of all computer applications. And while one could say, "Well, of course. Typewriters were equally popular in their day, too," I believe there's more to it than that. The speed and ease with which you can create, alter, and edit text with word processing software puts it on a totally different plane.

To my mind, a computer equipped with word processing software is nothing less than a superconductor of thought. Admittedly, you must be able to type comfortably to gain the full benefit. But once you've got that skill, you need only think a thought to have it appear on the screen. If you don't like it or want to change it, only a few keystrokes are required. The word processor thus gives you a liberating sense of power that not even the most advanced typewriter can approach.

All of which is by way of saying that any really good word processing package will repay you handsomely for the time and effort you expend mastering its mysteries. Indeed, once you've learned a particular package, you will not want to change. That's why I think it is so important to get started with a truly splendid program from a company that will take good care of you, as it has hundreds of thousands of other registered users for the last decade. That's why I recommend PC-Write so highly.

10

Database

The term "database management system" or "DBMS" sounds like it's straight out of *The Forbin Project*, a book and movie in which two computers take over the world. You can almost hear H.A.L., the supercomputer of *2001: A Space Odyssey* saying, "What are you doing in the pod, Dave?"

There's a kernel of truth in this, since the concepts underlying personal computer database software really are taken directly from the mainframe domain. In many ways, they represent quintessential "computerness." But that's part of the excitement of having these types of programs available on a micro—instead of a mainframe—computer. There is probably no other type of software that so firmly places mainframe-like power in your hands. And, next to word processing, there is probably no application more important to a small business.

Small business applications

Why? Because database software puts you in *control*. Its power to store, sort, locate, print out, and otherwise manipulate information can dramatically reduce the time you spend fiddling with paperwork, while simultaneously improving your access to customer and business information. For example, suppose you run a car dealership. A couple comes in to buy a car. You keep their names, address, phone number, the purchase date, and the model they bought on a 3×5 card.

You put the card in a file box, alphabetized by last name or some other single criterion. Twice a year, or whenever business is slow, you and your sales manager thumb through the cards looking for past customers who should now be in the market for a new automobile. The qualifying customer cards get pulled and divvied up among the sales staff for personal phone calls.

That's not necessarily a bad way to do things. But it sure is labor-intensive. At best, you're managing your data with Stone Age tools. And don't forget, someone's going to have to refile the cards after each customer has been called.

Now shift the scene and imagine that you have all of your customer information in a database on your personal computer. All of a sudden, *you're* in control. You can tell your database program to locate and print out the names and phone numbers of every past customer who made a purchase three years ago or more. You can use the same database to send every customer you have ever served a greeting during the Christmas holidays.

Knowing what you know about the car business, you can send every customer who is likely to have put 30,000 miles on his or her car a special offer (free state inspection, free lube job, free tire tread analysis, whatever). If there is a recall on 1993 Ferrets, you can instantly identify everyone who bought a Ferret from you who is affected by the recall and contact them personally.

Let's shift the scene again. Let's suppose that instead of cars, you operate a television repair shop. You've got a lot of different parts to stock, and keeping track of them has always been a problem. Not only is it a paperwork nightmare, you have the sneaking suspicion that you have far too much of your working capital tied up in inventory.

A database program can put you back in control: instead of logging each parts shipment on paper, key it into your computer. It doesn't require any more time and effort than making a paper record, but the benefits can be enormous. If you keep track of the parts you use, at a glance you will be able to tell how closely your inventory matches your actual needs and adjust things accordingly.

Getting a handle on your data

The small business applications for database management software are simply endless. In fact, this kind of software is so important that, my two examples notwithstanding, it is hard to believe any automobile dealership or television repair shop exists that does not already use a database program in one guise or another.

This brings up another important point about database management software. If you have a hankering to spend your money, you will find that there are literally thousands of software companies that will be happy to help you do so. There are specialized programs aimed at doctors, attorneys, traffic managers, dispatchers, convenience store owners, and nearly every other "vertical" market you can think of.

At their core, however, most of them are essentially just database programs that have been created or customized for a particular market. If you've got a good database program to work with, you can do the same thing yourself—without spending a lot of money on a shelf-full of specialized applications.

This approach lets you "have it your way," as well. The problem with most vertical market software is that it is written for everyone's business, not your own. That means you may have to put up with some things you don't like about a given program. You may even find that you have to change the way you operate to conform to the program's requirements.

Not so when you are working with your own database program. We are about to discuss how database software gives you control over your data. Well, using such a program in the first place gives you control over the software. You can set things up just about any way you want. Please see Fig. 10-1 for a quick list of the kinds of things a database program can do. Then think of the applications you'd like to use this kind of software for as you read the rest of this chapter.

The tasks one can accomplish with database software are all but endless. Here are just a few of the ways this kind of software is used for both business and for personal needs:

Business Uses
Keep track of customer names, addresses, and purchase information.
Generate mailing labels and personalized correspondence.
Maintain inventory of business supplies, parts, and equipment.
Enter customer orders; produce pick tickets, invoices, and sales reports.
Print personalized telephone directories.
Create and maintain a product catalog.
Keep records on buildings, individual units, and tenants.
Generate price quotes and job estimates.
Maintain personnel records.
Dispatch and track service people.

Personal Applications
Track magazine subscriptions (what they cost and when they expire).
Organize information on CD/record/tape/VCR collections (and "wish lists").
Collect data on high school or college alumni for class reunions.
Prepare household inventory (for insurance purposes).
Maintain Christmas card and gift lists.
Record birthdays, anniversaries, and other special events.
Assemble "vital records" information (in case you unexpectedly expire).
Organize bank and credit card information (to simplify loan applications).
Track auto maintenance and repairs.
Plan a wedding (guest lists, gifts received and acknowledged).

Fig. 10-1. How to use a database: Let us count the ways.

In this chapter, you will learn the basics of database software and what it can mean to your business. You will see that the essence of database management software is the ability to *find* information, and find it quickly. Once found, the information you are seeking can be sorted, formatted, exported, or printed a thousand different ways.

Or mathematical functions can be applied. That means that the same program and database you use to send brochures or fliers to your customers can also be used to produce invoices, track sales, ride herd on inventory and orders from suppliers, generate telemarketing lists, organize a service dispatching operation, and do hundreds of other things besides.

Best of all, database software is probably the easiest of all computer applications to understand and use. Even easier, in some respects, than word processing. The key concept is what is known technically as "database design," or what might be called the "atomization of information."

Pattern matching

There really isn't anything mysterious about database software. You start by building an empty shell or template designed to accommodate the data you want to
store. The template contains a separate slot for each important piece of information.

Then you enter data, filling the slots. When you want to find, say, all customers who have spent $500 with you in the past six months, you simply tell the
program to scan through all the data templates you have filled, focusing on just a
few slots.

The program works on the concept of pattern matching. Just as a word processing program's "search" feature looks for the ASCII codes that match the letters you have specified in a text file, a database program looks for similar matches
in the slots you have told it to examine. It thus might look first in a slot called
"Total Purchases" for a number equal to or greater than $500. The results would
form a preliminary selection.

Then it might zero in on this preliminary selection and look in a slot called
"Date" for a date greater than or equal to some date occurring six months ago.
That would produce its final selection of all your customers who meet the criteria
you have specified. By entering a few commands, you could tell the program to
produce mailing labels for just those select customers.

Atomizing your data

My friends, this is child's play. Even the worst, most poorly programmed database
program available today can perform this trick with one hand tied behind its back.
Yet for a businessperson, even this routine capability can make a major impact and
produce significant time savings.

A database program can have a major impact on your business. But at heart,
none of them is all that complicated. The key thing is the number of "slots" you
allow for when building your template. That's what I mean by the "atomization
of data."

For example, suppose you created a database template with one slot for
NAME (first and last), one for ADDRESS (number and street) and one for LOCA-
TION (city, state, and zip code). You might add a fourth slot for AMOUNT to
accommodate the total amount of money a person had spent with you. With a
database like this, you could easily produce a mailing list of all of your customers.
You could even produce a list of just those customers who had spent a certain
amount of money with you.

But that's about it. You could not prepare a mailing list containing only those
customers in, say, Kansas City, who had spent $100 with you in the last month.
You could not tell which state produces the largest number of customers. You
couldn't even alphabetize your customer list by last name.

Why? Because with only the NAME, ADDRESS, LOCATION, and AMOUNT
slots to deal with, there is no way for the software to sharpen the resolution to just
the *last* name or just the *state*. The information has not been "atomized" finely
enough. To prevent the problem, you need to design a template with separate

slots for the first name, the last name, the street address, the city, the state, the zip code, and the total amount the customer has spent.

You need at least seven slots, not just four. That way, the database software can narrow the focus of its pattern matching. It can look in just the LAST NAME slot if you want to sort (alphabetize) the file by customer last name. It can easily tell you how many customers you have in Kentucky by zeroing in on the STATE slot. It can easily produce a list of everyone in Ohio who has spent $300 with you by looking at the STATE and the AMOUNT slots.

The lesson is that the more finely atomized your data, due to the greater number of slots in the template, the more useful information your database can deliver. Of course, it is possible to go overboard. There is not usually a reason for a slot containing a person's middle name or initial, for example. It may or may not be important to track the actual items a person bought instead of just the total amount spent. There is always the danger of collecting far more information than you will ever use or need. But the principle idea of breaking information down into small components is quite sound.

File, record, and field

As you would expect, "templates" and "slots" make too much intuitive sense to be part of the standard database management vocabulary. The preferred terms— the ones you will hear again and again—are "file," "record," and "field." Fortunately, there is an easy way to get an unshakeable mental grip on these terms and what they mean. All you have to do is imagine a collection of last year's canceled checks.

The collection taken as a whole is the *file*. Each individual check is a *record*. And each piece of information on the check—the name of the payee, the date, the amount, the signature, etc.—is a *field*. Or consider your Rolodex address collection: the entire pack of Rolodex cards is the file, each individual card is a record, and each piece of information on the card (name, address, phone, etc.) is a field.

This is exactly how database programs see and handle information. Therefore, if you are going to keep information in a database, you must start by creating a template—excuse me, you must start by "defining the database structure." That means you've got to tell the program about the fields—"slots"—you want to have in each record.

Defining the database structure

The first step in using any database program, whether it is dBASE IV or File Express, the program recommended here, is to define the structure of the database you wish to create. All this really means is telling the program about the fields you want to include in every record. You would think this would be simple—and it is—but "simple-minded" is more to the point. If you haven't caught on by now, let me be the first to tell you—computers are dumb! You've got to tell them *everything*.

Thus, when defining a database, you must start by telling the machine what you want to call a field. Each field has got to have a unique name; otherwise you won't be able to focus the program's attention later, when you want it to find specific records. If you were creating a database to track your customers, for example, you would probably want the following fields: FNAME, LNAME, ADDRESS1, ADDRESS2, CITY, STATE, ZIP, AREA-CODE, and PHONE.

There are any number of additional fields you would want to have as well, but let's keep things simple for the time being.

The FNAME field would be for a customer's first name and middle initial; LNAME is for his or her last name. (With an LNAME field, you'll be able to look up customers by their last names.) The two ADDRESS fields are to allow for customers with more than just a simple number and street address. The other fields are self-explanatory.

Thinking ahead

Simply giving each field a unique name is not enough, however. You must also tell the program how much space to allot for each field. Remember, what you're building here is a template—a pattern for storing your data. You don't want a customer named "GLOSSBRENNER" to get mail addressed to Mr. "GLOSSBR," but that is exactly what would happen if the LNAME field is too short.

We'll give you some suggested field lengths for address information in a moment. The point to be emphasized here is how important it is to think ahead when laying out a database structure. The ZIP field offers a perfect example. As you may know, there are five-digit zip codes and there are "Zip+4" or nine-digit zip codes. At this writing, the nine-digit zip code is not really important for most people. But if you ever plan to do a mass mailing to hundreds of customers, using the nine-digit code can significantly reduce your mailing costs.

Therefore, it just makes good sense to allow for the possibility that you will want to use nine-digit zip codes in the future. So how many characters' worth of space do you tell your database program to allocate for the ZIP field? Nine? Nope. The correct answer is ten. And the reason is the little dash that is used to separate the first five digits from the last four (19067-1965, for example).

I'm not trying to trip you up. I merely want to get you thinking ahead and trying to anticipate the fields and the space you will need for each one. That is the artistry of database design.

Changing database specifications

And what if you make a mistake? What if you discover that the database you first defined needs more or longer fields to be truly effective? There you are with over 1000 customer records painstakingly entered over the last few months—into a database that does not do all that you want. Does this mean that you will have to create a new template and type in all of that information all over again? Not at all!

The solution is to "change the specs" of your current database. File Express and most other modern database programs make this very easy to do. You can add or delete a field, make it longer or shorter, specify a different format, and change its order within the database. Once you've specified the changes, File Express will "rebuild" the original database according to your new specifications, or create a brand-new one and leave the original unchanged.

Thanks to this feature, you're not likely to get seriously stuck if your first attempt at database design does not result in the "perfect" database for you. Indeed, you should expect to have to fine-tune things as you go along. No one can anticipate everything. Nonetheless, it is good practice to try to think ahead when defining a database structure template. At the very least, this will save you time and effort in making modifications.

Now, here are the field names and field lengths you may want to specify when creating a simple name, address, and phone database:

Field Name	Field Length	Field Type
Mr./Ms.	5	character
Fname	30	character
Lname	45	character
Company	45	character
Address1	30	character
Address2	30	character
City	30	character
State	2	character
Zip	10	character
Area	3	character
Phone	7	character

Field "type"

Yes, we've thrown you a breaking ball. We have listed not only suggested field names and lengths, but also "types." File Express and other database programs not only need to know how many characters to allow room for in each record, they also need to be told how to view that information. In general, there are three "types" one can specify: character, numeric, and calculated.

A character field is treated as ASCII text. If you make a given field "numeric," the database software treats its contents as numbers, which can be processed mathematically. So why aren't the ZIP, AREA, and PHONE fields on the above list "numeric" instead of "character" fields? They're numbers, after all, aren't they?

They certainly are. But you are never going to do any calculating with them. You are never going to add up the sum of the zip codes and multiply the result by the area code for Bangor, Maine. So there is no benefit in making them "numeric." In fact, there are at least two drawbacks to doing so.

First, if you have defined a field as "numeric," the database program will not let you put anything but numbers into it. So if the ZIP field is numeric, you will not be able to enter Canadian postal codes, all of which are a combination of text and numbers. Second, there is the matter of sorting. If you made your zip code field numeric and entered 02057, the database software would ignore the leading zero when sorting by zip code. Indeed, numeric fields are not sorted alphabetically but by the size of the number. That's why zip code and phone number fields are almost always of the "character" type.

The third major field type is "calculated" or "formula." This kind of field is not filled in by you at all. Instead, its contents are inserted by the program on the basis of the information you have entered in other fields and on the formula you have told it to apply.

A good example of a formula field would be SALESTX (sales tax). You might tell the database that this should be a formula field and that the formula should multiply a TOTAL-PURCH (total purchase) field by a specified percentage.

For example, imagine that a customer buys an item priced at $44.95. He or she decides to charge it on a Visa card. You key in the person's name and address and $44.95 in the TOTAL-PURCH field. As soon as you have done this, the database program *automatically* fills in the SALESTX blank.

I know this is a new concept, and I don't want to lose you here. But calculated fields are important. Indeed, they are the secret to some of the truly wonderful things a database program can do for your business.

If you don't yet feel that you understand the general concept of formula fields, read the above section again. It is worth the time because the concept is so crucial. If you do understand it, you're ready for the next step—the formulas themselves.

"Smart" databases

Let's assume that you have a retail store in Pennsylvania. You get walk-in trade and both in-state and out-of-state phone orders. You want to use File Express or some other database program to automate the calculation of customer bills.

For all of your in-state customers, you must charge sales tax. But, at this writing at least, out-of-state customers who order by mail or by phone are exempt. Therefore, you attach a formula to your SALESTX field that says, "If the STATE field equals PA, then make this field contain 6% of the amount in the TOTAL-PURCH field; otherwise, leave the SALESTX field blank." But why stop there? Why not create a field called AMOUNT DUE and attach a formula that says "The contents of this field equal TOTAL-PURCH + SALESTX." Let the software do the work for you!

This is just a simple example, of course. As you go deeper into using a database management program, you will find that you can create some very sophisticated structures indeed. Suppose you wanted to offer a trade discount to special customers. There are lots of ways to do this.

One of the easiest is to include a one-character field in your database called, say, TD. If you want to give someone trade discount status, call up the person's record and put an X or some other character in that field. You could then define a field called DISCOUNT with a formula that said, "If TD is not empty, then multiply TOTAL-PURCH by 15 percent." A second new field called SUB-TOTAL would operate on the formula "TOTAL-PURCH minus DISCOUNT."

You will want to take it slowly. Start with a simple database definition and wait until you find yourself saying, "I wonder if there's a way to do thus-and-so," before plunging into formulas. The capability is there to do just about anything you want to do, but there is no point in pursuing it until you really need it.

Searching

Once you have defined your database and entered your data, you can find any record on the basis of the contents of any field. If you wanted to find a customer named Johnson, for example, you could tell the program to find all records where "Last Name is Johnson." In a database of 1000 records, there might be ten people with that last name, and the database will show you each of their records in turn.

But suppose you want to be more specific. Suppose you want to find a customer named Robert Johnson. In that case you could tell the program to bring you all records where "Last Name is Johnson AND First Name is Robert." That'll get you all the Robert Johnsons.

But what if you think you may have entered the customer's name as "Bob Johnson?" If so, *that* record will not be found by the above search logic. To be sure of finding such a record, you would tell the program to find "`Last Name is Johnson AND First Name is Robert OR First Name is Bob.`"

Sorting

You can search a database this way on any field the moment you have finished entering data. But you will find that even a simple `LNAME=JOHNSON` search will take some time. The amount of time required depends on the speed of your CPU and the speed of your hard disk. But the major factor is the number of records in your database. In a database of 100 records, you might not notice the delay. But you would quickly get tired of waiting if the database held 1000 records or more.

The reason for the delay is that the software must read in each record, look for a match in the specified field, and then read in the next record. That's like telling it to read every page of a book looking for every reference to France. The program can do it, but you'll have to wait for your answer.

The solution to this problem was developed long ago in the mainframe computer world. The trick is to sort the database on the basis of the contents of one of the fields. Like the pages of a book, every record has a number. When a database is sorted, the records are not physically re-arranged or renumbered. Instead, a little index file is created to hold all of the record numbers and the contents of just the field you sorted on in each case.

The index file is like the index of a book. It contains the search word ("France") and the pages ("records") on which that word can be found. And it lets you locate specific information just as quickly. Sorting a large database does take time, but once the index files have been built, you can zip to any target record like lightning the next time you search the database. (File Express can be set to automatically sort records as you enter them. So once you've done a sort, you may never have to spend the time doing another.)

Most of the time, you will sort your database on just the fields that are most important to you and your type of business. But you may wish to create several index files, each of which uses a different sort method. For example, at times you may wish to search for records on the basis of a person's last name, so you would activate the last name sort index. But if you were preparing a mass mailing, you might want to sort by zip code, and so you would activate the zip code sort index.

I don't want to confuse you, but you can also do sorts within sorts. You might want to tell the system to sort your data alphabetically by the contents of the STATE field, but within each state group to also sort by Last Name. In this case, "State" is the primary sort and "Last Name" is the secondary sort. Once again, if you need the capability, it is almost certain to be available from the software. But wait until you need it before exploring further.

Printing reports

In computer-speak, a database "report" is any printed output. It could be a batch of mailing labels, invoices, inventory lists, a phone directory, or anything else. The term "reports" covers it all. The reporting function of a database uses all of the other features we've talked about, but it adds formatting, layout, and printing to the mix.

The fundamental concept behind printing reports is quite simple. Imagine that you have a blank sheet of paper and a pack of Post-It notes containing one note for each field in your database. Designing a report is essentially a matter of applying the Post-It notes to the desired locations on the page. The process lets you tell the program which fields you want it to print and where the information should be placed on the page.

File Express and other programs also give you a toolbox of techniques to really dress up a printout. You can add titles, column headers, ruler lines, and text. You can incorporate printer codes to select different typestyles and fonts.

But everything still boils down to the data. And here, you can do some fancy things indeed, thanks to the use of formulas.

Remember the SALESTX formula we discussed a moment ago? Remember the trade discount (TD) field and the way it triggered a special discount if it was not empty? You can use the same techniques in defining your report formats.

For example, suppose you are using your customer database to print monthly invoices. The database has all the fields we have discussed before, plus one for PURCH-DATE (purchase date). You could include a special formula as part of your report definition. The formula might say, in effect, "If the difference between the purchase date and today is greater than 30 days, print the message 'Your account is Past Due. Please send payment.'"

"Functions"

To make it even easier to specify a formula like this, many database programs have built-in "functions." File Express, for example, has an AGE function that is like a prepackaged formula for calculating the number of days between two dates. You might thus define a field on your report called PAST-DUE and attach to it the following File Express formula: If AGE(PURCH-DATE) is greater than 30, then print "Your account is Past Due. Please send payment." By default, the AGE function compares the first date to today's date, but you can direct it to use some other date as well.

Similarly, there is a File Express (FE) function called BEFORE that lets you search for dates that come before a certain date. TIMEDIFF will calculate the number of minutes between two times. The CENTER function tells FE to print the contents of a field centered on the page or label. And so on.

There are also the standard math operators to add, multiply, subtract, divide, calculate a percentage, or raise a number to a particular power. And there are higher level math functions like absolute value, arctangent, cosine, natural log, square root, etc.

As with everything else beyond the basics, there is no need to explore functions until you feel you need them. But it is nice to know that the power is there. In fact, that's one of the really nice things about database software. Many of its features are discrete, so you don't have to deal with them until and if you want to. In the meantime, as we have seen here, even the most basic database operations can give you undreamed of power over your business (and personal) data.

About File Express

The program I feel can give you the greatest amount of power for the least amount of effort is David Berdan's File Express.

I'm pleased to report that I'm not the only who feels this way. In its August 1991 issue, *PC Sources* noted that "File Express has features that make other programs in its price range seem sickly by comparison . . . you have all the functionality required by typical small businesses . . . With superior reporting capabilities and an easy, affordable way to convert to it, File Express is perfect for most small businesses and home-office applications."

But wait a minute. Aren't we supposed to be talking about shareware here? We are. And File Express 5.1 *is* shareware. But like many leading shareware products, it is also available through retail channels. The retail price and shareware registration fee are the same: $99, plus $5 for shipping and handling. If you'd like to try before you buy, you can order File Express from Glossbrenner's Choice, user groups, online services, and all the usual shareware channels. To order directly from the company, consult Fig. 10-2 for contact information.

Expressware Phone Numbers and Contact Points

Toll-free Order Line: (800) 753-FILE [i.e.,(800) 753-3453]
  Orders only (no technical support available on this line).
  Available 24 hours a day, seven days a week.

Technical support number: (206) 788-0932
  8AM to 4PM Pacific Time, Monday through Friday

Fax line: (206) 788-4493
  Available 24 hours a day for technical support and orders.

BBS: (206) 788-4008
  24 hours a day, seven days a week. Available for technical
  support, tips, orders, and downloading

Fig. 10-2. File Express/Expressware contact information.

Now that you have a basic understanding of what database software is and does and how it does it, you're in a position to appreciate the specific details that make FE such a super program. We will start with a brief summary of its most outstanding features and then show you how to get started quickly using the PHONES database you will find on the disk accompanying this book.

Capacity: How many and how long?

The first thing to ask about any database program is "How many and how long?" How many records can the program accommodate? And how long can each record be? How many fields may you have per record, and how many characters can you put into each field?

Though database capacity is no longer the issue it was when personal computers were new, it still offers a quick way to compare the relative power of different programs. Here are the relevant capacity figures for File Express 5.1:

Maximum number of . . .

Records per database	2 billion
Characters per record	4000
Fields per record	200
Characters per field	1000
Indexes per database	5
Fields per index	10

Naturally, comparisons of this sort don't tell the whole story. Realistically, you'll probably never need anything close to 2 billion records per database. But it is worth considering whether 20 or 30 thousand will be enough in your particular case, since that's all some commercial DBMS programs offer.

If you figure an average of seven characters per word, a limit of 4000 characters per record gives you the equivalent of about 570 words to work with. That's a bit more than the equivalent of two double-spaced typewritten pages (62 lines of text at 65 characters per line). That is plenty of room for most applications. The other specifications are equally capacious.

Formulas, functions, and natural language

We have already touched on FE's use of formulas and functions in defining a database structure or a report format. There is much more one could say, but rather than burden you with too much detail, we can simply note that File Express offers more power in this department than most users are ever likely to need.

But, while other programs are also quite powerful, few are as easy to use. For example, File Express is specifically designed to work with "natural language" commands. That's computer-talk for "conversational English." You don't have to use symbols like =, +, or >. You can use words like "is," "plus," and "greater than" instead.

The program also includes a "soundex" feature that lets you search for names and other information when you are not certain of the correct spelling.

You might tell FE to find all records where "Last Name sounds like 'Smith'." That would get you Smith, Smyth, Smithe, and so on.

Automatic sort

As you can tell from the previous capacity listing, you can create up to five separate indexes (sorts) per database with up to ten different fields each. That means you can do a primary sort on, say, State and do secondary sorts on, say, Purchase Amount and Last Name. Or you might do a sort on Last Name and another sort on City, thus creating two separate indexes. If you want to see a list of people by Last Name, you switch to the Last Name index. If you want to see a list organized by City, you switch to that one. Only a few keystrokes are required to make the switch.

Best of all, once you have established your indexes, you can tell FE to automatically update them as you enter new records. With many programs, including earlier versions of FE, you must resort the database every time you add or change something.

Context-sensitive help and printer support

FE 5.1 includes over 500 help screens offering information on everything from how to insert new lines on a page when you are defining a report format to how to use its various formulas. The help is context-sensitive, which means that whenever you press Alt-H, the help information you are shown is directly related to whatever you are trying to accomplish.

In addition, FE supports over 280 printers—everything from dot-matrix, to ink-jets, to laser printers. The printer installation program presents a list of makes and models for you to choose from and then copies the proper software driver for you.

Import/Export functions

Since there are typically many things one may want to do with the same data, I have long been a strong advocate of robust "import/export" functions. One of the reasons I like PC-Write is the ease with which you can use the files it creates with other word processors. I feel the same way about FE's ability to output data in file formats usable by other programs.

File Express can export your data to standard mail-merge, WordPerfect mail merge, DIF, fixed-length, text editor, Lotus 1-2-3, and dBASE files. It can import from the same types of files, plus from another FE database.

This means that regardless of the word processor you use, FE can generate a file of names, addresses, and other information that can be "merged" into a word processor template to create customized form letters. It means that if an associate has a database prepared with Borland's dBASE program, you can bring the information directly into File Express. If you want to apply the "what if" and graphing capabilities of Lotus 1-2-3 or any spreadsheet that can read Lotus 1-2-3 files (like the As-Easy-As program described in Chapter 11), you can do so.

In other words, with PC-Write, File Express, and As-Easy-As, you can print, publish, view, review, and analyze your business data in just about every imaginable way. Once you get the information keyed into FE, you can export it for additional processing without ever having to retype a record.

Incidentally, if you need to see your data graphically, you might consider Expressware's ExpressGraph program. It offers line graphs, bar charts (regular, overlapped, stacked, percentage, and 3-D), and pie charts (uncut, exploded, separated). It too has a powerful data import/export function. It is available as shareware from the usual sources.

Relational database features

In technical terms, File Express is a "flat-file" database, as opposed to a "relational" database like dBASE. A full explanation of these two terms is beyond the scope of this book. However, in brief, a relational database program creates a master file containing all of your information. You are then free to create subsidiary "databases" that contain fields from the master file.

You might thus have a database of customers and one for invoices. The two databases would contain some of the same information (name, address, etc.), but they would appear to exist separately. However, you would find that if you updated a customer address in your invoice database, that address would also be updated in the customer database the next time you looked at it. That's because there is really only one copy of the customer's address (in the master database).

With a flat file database, in contrast, you would have to update the address in the invoice database and then load the customer database and update it there as well. The two databases are not "related," and they physically consist of two complete sets of data.

File Express does not claim to be a fully relational database, but version 5.1 includes some important relational features. Basically, you can tell FE to look into another FE database and extract the information you need for the one you are working on at the moment.

If you had an FE database called INVENTORY and one called PRICES, you might want to have the current price of each product in both files. With FE's relational LOOKUP function, however, there is no need to manually update each database. You can keep all of your current prices in the PRICES database. Then load INVENTORY and tell File Express to go get the current prices for each item from the FE PRICES database.

This is kind of like driving a relational database with a manual (as opposed to an automatic) transmission. It is a little more work, but either way, you will arrive at your destination.

A host of other friendly features

There is always a trade-off between power and ease of use, but well-designed, thoughtfully programmed software can make the transaction a real bargain. That's why you will appreciate a feature like FE's "increment field." If you designate a field as "auto-increment," the program will automatically boost the contents by one each time you add a new record. You might use this with a field called INVOICE NUMBER to make sure that each new invoice was numbered one more than the last one entered.

FE also offers 36 user-definable macro keys. As we learned when we discussed PC-Write, a macro function lets you load multiple keystrokes into a single keypress combination. This is a real time-saver when you are entering data. Since producing mailing labels is among the most popular of database functions, FE includes a built-in label printing program. There is no need to prepare a special report format for labels in most cases—just use the built-in function. FE even includes a built-in letter writer for those who do not want to fiddle with mail merge files.

Installing File Express 5.1

Let me tell you one of the reasons I like shareware in general—and File Express in particular—so much. When FE 5.1 was introduced, David Berdan, Expressware's founder, president, and chief programmer, sent a letter to all registered users. The letter summarized 5.1's new features and made a generous offer for those who wanted to upgrade.

Then, under the heading "And One Thing We Brought Back," Mr. Berdan cited a feature and said, "You wouldn't believe how many calls and letters we got about that one . . . [The feature] was in Version 4. For reasons I won't go into, it wasn't in Version 5.0. But it's back in 5.1, and we will keep it in from now on."

This is precisely what I mean when I speak of the special relationship registered shareware users have with the programmers who write the software they use. When you register a shareware program, you're not buying a product—you're entering into a personal relationship with the programmer and your fellow users.

In our highly mechanized, computerized, mass-market world, this kind of thing is very unusual. But before the Industrial Revolution, it was the norm. When you wanted a piece of furniture made or when you needed an iron farm implement, you walked over to the local cabinetmaker or blacksmith and discussed the job. You had a personal relationship, and you knew that the resulting hand-crafted item would fit your needs exactly.

I do not wish for a moment to suggest that most shareware programmers would welcome users calling simply to pass the time of day. Like you and me, they're busy. But if there is a feature you want or need, or something you would like to see in the next version of the program, I promise you, they will be all ears. They may or may not be able to deliver everything you want, but they will definitely listen.

It's curious, but the very thing that makes modern high-tech, processed, pre-packed society possible—the computer—also makes it possible to return to a kind of craftsman/customer relationship that hasn't existed since George Elliot flossed her teeth by the mill—or whatever that pastoral novel was called.

All the more reason to get going with File Express 5.1 as soon as you can. I really think you're going to like it. At Glossbrenner's Choice, it virtually runs the business.

Taking the first step

As supplied by Glossbrenner's Choice, FE 5.1 comes on four disks. The first three—Program, Supplemental, and Supplemental 2—are available from many other vendors. But for some reason, at this writing, no one else seems to include the fourth disk containing the documentation. That very well may have changed as you read this, so you may want to check around. The Documentation disk should include both the file FE5.DOC (the complete 400-page manual for 5.0) and 5POINT1.DOC, the 30-page supplement explaining the new features in 5.1).

I mention the disks because Expressware's installation will ask you to insert a given disk in turn. There is a little file on each disk that identifies it to the installation program. If you are a brand-new user, begin by looking at your CONFIG.SYS file. Get onto Drive C and key in CD\, followed by **TYPE CONFIG.SYS**. Look for a line reading **FILES=**, and note the number.

Then begin the installation process by putting the Program disk in your floppy drive and keying in INSTALL. You will be cautioned that FE requires a hard drive or a high-density floppy with at least 720K of disk space. Parenthetically, in my opinion, you have no business trying to run any database software on anything other than a hard drive (unless you like to take long naps while working at the computer).

Hit a key, and you will be presented with two installation options. You can install the program, or you can install printer definition files. Don't let these choices confuse you. FE 5.1 supports over 280 makes and models of printers. The "Install Printer Definition Files (PDF's)" option is there to make it easy to install additional printer driver files at some time in the future. Should the need arise, there will be no need to step through the entire installation process—you can opt to go straight to printer installation.

Select the option to install FE (The option will be in reverse highlighting and will be flashing), and you will next be given a chance to select your target disk drive (Drives A through F). Drive C is the default. Select a drive, and you will be asked to specify a subdirectory. The default is \FE5, but you can change it to something else. The program will then report your system configuration and the input and output drives and directory you have selected.

Next, you will be given a choice of letting the program modify your CONFIG.SYS file and your AUTOEXEC.BAT file. The installation software wants to make sure that you have set FILES= to at least 22 in CONFIG.SYS, and it will offer to set your PATH to C:\FE5 (or whatever) in your AUTOEXEC.BAT.

If your CONFIG.SYS is set for less than **FILES=22**, go ahead and let the program modify your CONFIG.SYS. If your setting is 22 or greater, hit your down arrow key and opt for "No, show modifications on the screen only." Incidentally, a setting of **FILES=30** is about right for most users. For more information on the FILES= command, see Glossbrenner's *DOS 5*.

The next choice is whether to let the program modify your AUTOEXEC.BAT PATH statement. I advise against this. If you want to add FE5 to your path at a later date, you can always do so by editing your AUTOEXEC.BAT file. So hit your down arrow to move the blinking bar to "No, show modifications on the screen only."

Installing the printer driver(s)

Next, you will be shown a window containing lists of printer makes and models. Use your arrow or paging keys to scroll through the list until you find your own printer. Then—and this is *very* important—hit your spacebar. You will see the "No" in the far right column change to a "Yes."

Since most people have only one printer, the natural inclination is to move the flashing bar to a printer name and hit Enter. But the FE installation is set up to allow you to install drivers for multiple printers. That's why you must "tag" the ones you want first by hitting the spacebar. Then you can hit Enter to move to the next step.

Running FE5SETUP

That next step lets you tell the program what to do immediately after it has finished installing the software. For most users, the correct choice is the default: "Run Setup Program." However, you can opt to run FE instead, or simply return to DOS. Once you have made your selection, the program will take over and begin unpacking files onto your target directory or disk drive. At one point, you will be prompted to insert the "Supplemental Disk." Do so, and hit Enter.

Still more files will be decompressed. Then you will be asked to insert "Supplemental Disk 2." Hit Enter, and still more files will be placed on your target drive, including all of the ones associated with FE's built-in tutorial. Some screens will appear announcing the lines that should be added to your CONFIG.SYS and AUTOEXEC.BAT files, and then you will be asked to insert the Program Disk again. Do so and hit Enter.

If you have opted to run Setup, the Setup greeting screen will appear. Hit a key and you will be taken to the first of six screens that will let you customize FE 5.1 to your needs. You will be able to set the colors FE uses, the way it talks to your modem when dialing numbers in your files, how it should format labels with its built-in label program, and the spacing defaults it should use for its report printer and form-letter writer.

A window of context-sensitive help information appears at the bottom of the screen as you move your cursor from one setting to another. You will be told what the setting means and what options you have for changing it. My advice is that you not change anything. I've taken you this route to emphasize that this feature exists. You can run the Setup program at any time by keying in **FE5SETUP**. For now, I suggest you hit Esc to leave the program and exit without saving anything.

Loading File Express

When you leave the Setup program, you will see the DOS prompt on your screen. Now what? Now you run File Express by keying in **FE**. You will see a greeting screen and be advised to press any key to continue. Before you do, however, note the line at the very bottom of the screen. This line informs you that you may press Alt-H at any time for context-sensitive help. So don't forget to do so. Whenever you are puzzled or stumped, give FE an Alt-H.

When you hit a key to continue, you may be surprised to find a pop-up window notifying you that no printer has been set as the default. Do an Alt-H for more information. Read the two screens of help, and hit a key. (We'll deal with this in a moment.)

You will be asked to indicate the drive and path to be used for data. Go with the defaults. Next you will see a list of available databases. Right now, there will be only one: Tutorial. Select that by hitting Enter, and the Main menu will appear. (See Fig. 10-3.)

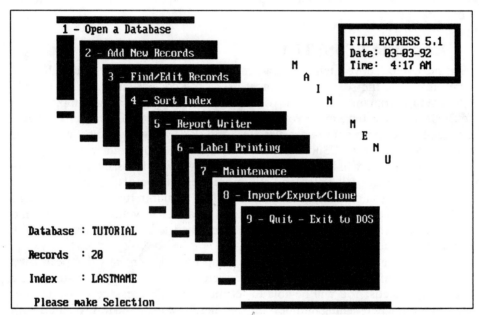

Fig. 10-3. The File Express Main menu.

"Playing" with File Express

Now it's time to have some fun—or at least get your feet wet. There is no way you can harm anything—the only data you are dealing with is the tutorial database, and you've got a copy of that on the distribution disk. As you will see, the database contains 20 records. So why not take a look at them?

The way to do that is to select "3—Find/Edit Records" from the Main menu. That will take you to the Find Menu, where one of the choices will be "1—Find/ Edit a record." Hit Enter on that choice, and you will see the Record Selection screen. This is the screen you will use to look for specific records on the basis of the contents of specific fields. Notice that there is a box listing the first ten fields in the database to the left of the screen. To look at fields 11 through 15, use your paging keys.

Notice that the cursor is located near the bottom of the screen on a line beginning "Find all records where: ALL." Just for fun, you might try an Alt-H here. Glance briefly at the screens. Then hit your spacebar to exit, and hit Enter to accept "ALL" as your search criterion. A record will quickly appear on the screen for one Larry Anderson, attorney-at-law.

Hit your N key to see the next record.

Notice the line of key commands at the bottom of the screen. Hit E to edit a record. Notice how the cursor appears at the first field (date). Try the other keys at your pleasure. Then key in E for Edit on a record of your choice and notice how the commands at the bottom of the screen change. Opt for Alt-V for an alternate view of the record. This will bring up a Select View screen giving you a choice of the default (which you have just seen) or FOLDER or FOLDER2. Move the cursor to FOLDER and hit Enter.

There will be a slight pause, and FE will show you the identical record as an index card. (See Fig. 10-4.) It may not be immediately obvious, but all of the information you saw when looking at the record in the default view (fields down the side of the screen) is on this view as well. But the "Folder" view is more user-friendly because it looks more like the kinds of materials most people are accustomed to using when entering information.

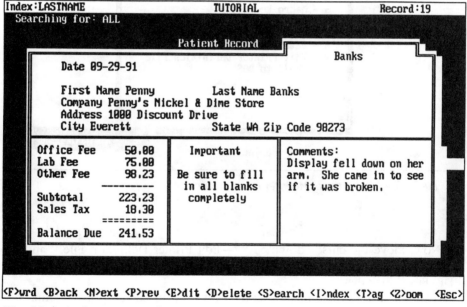

Fig. 10-4. A view to your data.

These "views" are created using the File Express "screen painting" function. You begin by defining a database as discussed earlier in this chapter. Then you tell the program how you would like records to appear and where you want each field to be on the screen. Now hit your Esc key and then your N key to look at the next record. Since you have set your "view" to FOLDER, it too will appear on a screen like the one shown in Fig. 10-4.

Setting your printer definition

Okay, back to work. Hit Esc again until you reach the Main menu. Now select "7—Maintenance." That will take you to a screen like the one shown in Fig. 10-5. Linger over this menu for just a moment. Notice that the first selection lets you change your database specifications. That means you can add fields or lengthen fields. The program is set up to allow you to modify the "template" into which you pour your data at any time. Also notice the "Paint a View" selection. This is the option you will use when you want to create data views like FOLDER.

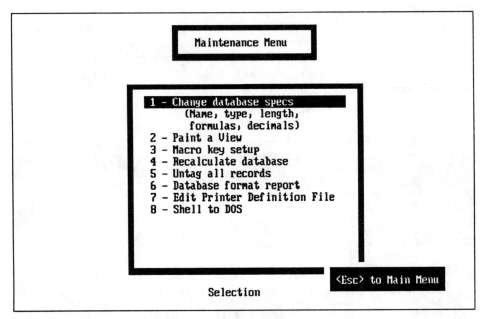

Fig. 10-5. The File Express Maintenance menu.

Now, move the cursor down to "7—Edit Printer Definition File," and hit Enter. That will lead to a menu, the last selection of which is "4—Set Default 'PDF' File." Pick that.

This will take you to a menu that lets you set your default printer definition. More than likely you will have at least three selections: ASCII, DEFAULT, and something like HP-3. The last selection is the printer driver copied over to your disk during the installation process, when you picked your printer(s).

That's almost certainly the one you want, so cursor down to it and hit Enter. You will find yourself back at the menu from which you came. The next thing to do is to hit Esc (Just like the on-screen prompt advises) and return to the Main menu. You will have to hit Esc twice to accomplish this. (As you gain experience, you will use FE's hot keys to zip around the program in an instant.)

Viewing and printing the documentation

You can exit FE from the Main menu by selecting the "Quit" option. Probably, you should do so now, since there's more work to do outside of File Express. That work consists of printing out the manuals. As noted earlier, Glossbrenner's Choice puts the manuals on a documentation disk (Disk 4 of 4). To get started, put that disk in the drive and key in **GO**. You will see some text explaining self-extracting archives. Hit Esc to exit the text display and do the following.

First, log onto the floppy drive and key in **COPY FEDOX-Z.EXE C:\FE**. (I'm assuming that you have opted to place File Express on Drive C, in a directory called FE. If not, amend the command accordingly.)

Second, key in **COPY LIST.COM C:\FE**. That will copy Vernon Buerg's LIST.COM into your \FE directory. Third, log onto C:\FE by keying in **C:** and **CD\FE**. Then key in **FEDOX-Z**. You will see the doc files for File Express unpack before your very eyes. Preserve your hard disk space by keying in **DEL FEDOX-Z.EXE**, since you no longer need the archive file.

Now do a **DIR *.DOC** to get a directory of the two documentation files. They are FE5.DOC and 5POINT1.DOC. To view them on the screen, key in **LIST FE5.DOC** (hit Esc to exit) and **LIST 5POINT1.DOC** (hit Esc to exit). That will give you a preview.

Since these are plain ASCII text files, you can easily bring them into your word processor for printing, if you like. But the files include form feeds (special control commands all printers recognize), so you can simply key in **COPY FE5.DOC PRN** and **COPY 5POINT1.DOC PRN** to produce an immediate, paginated printout. Just make sure your printer is on and loaded with plenty of paper. As noted, FE5.DOC runs to more than 400 pages, and 5POINT1.DOC tops out at around 30 pages.

Take the Tutorial

The documentation supplied on the fourth disk is identical to the printed File Express 5.0 manual and 5.1 supplement all registered users receive, except that FE5.DOC does not include any screen shots. This is due to the fact that there is no single graphics format supported by all printers. However, since you will have the program and will have installed it at this point, you can easily follow along.

The first part of FE5.DOC concerns the tutorial supplied with the FE 5.1 package. If you are a brand-new user, and if you have no previous experience with database software, we strongly urge you to take the time to work through it. As you know by now, the TUTORIAL database is already on the disk, and you have only to follow the supplied instructions to bring it up and get started.

Glossbrenner Tutorial—report formulas

We've created two File Express databases and included them on the disk supplied with this book. The first is the PHONES database. You will find that this offers an ideal way to create your own customized phone book. Enter the names, companies, addresses, and phone and electronic mail numbers of your friends and associates.

Then use the supplied PHONES File Express report format to print the database on letter-size pages. Punch the pages and put them into a three-ring notebook, and you're all set. The report format includes a formula called Alpha Check that makes sure that each section from A through Z starts with a new page.

Emily and I created this database and report format because we find that Rolodex cards are hard to thumb through and because the cards do not offer enough room for notes and updates. A letter-size page, in contrast, can hold about six addresses and still leave plenty of room for notes. We add those notes and changes to our "phone book" as necessary, and every few months use them to update the database. With the updates entered, printing a fresh, current phone book takes only a few minutes, and even fewer keystrokes.

You will enjoy exploring the PHONES database on your own. Here, we will focus on the second database on the accompanying disk, MAGS. This database is designed to help you keep track of your magazine subscriptions. As everyone knows, most magazines send you dire warnings that your subscription is about to expire six months or so before the actual date. We subscribe to so many publications that more than once Emily and I have taken the bait and ended up renewing or extending a subscription when we had no plans to do so.

Emily came up with the ideal solution. Using File Express, within about ten minutes she had created a database listing all of our magazines, the number of issues per subscription, the cost of a subscription, and the date each expires. Now whenever one of those annoying subscription renewal notices arrives, we merely load FE and check to see when the publication really expires.

This not only lets us avoid unwanted renewals, it also lets us hold onto our money longer. I can see no point in making an interest-free loan to a magazine publisher. The actual amounts are trivial, so it's as much a matter of principle as anything else. But if the items being tracked were your stocks of expensive components or raw materials, the money saved this way and the effect on your cash flow wouldn't be trivial at all.

You can modify the supplied MAGS database to suit your own needs, of course. And we encourage you to do so. You may even want to use it to track your *own* subscriptions. (Just use FE to delete all the records in the supplied database and add your own information.) The main purpose of including this database, however, is to help you get a better grasp of FE's report writer.

Note that we are going to assume that you have already worked your way through the TUTORIAL supplied with the FE 5.1 package and explained in the manual (FE5.DOC).

Load and look

Start by putting the disk accompanying this book in a drive and keying in **DIR**. Look for the file MAGS-Z.EXE. This is a self-extracting archive containing all the files you will need for the MAGS database. Go over to your hard drive (where we assume File Express is installed in C: \ FE) and key in **CD** to get to the root directory. Then key in **MD MAGS** to make C: \ MAGS. Next copy MAGS-Z.EXE to C: \ MAGS and key in **MAGS-Z**. Or log on to your floppy drive and key in **MAGS-Z C:\MAGS** to extract the files directly into the target directory of your hard drive.

Now, let's load the database. Go to C:\FE with the command **CD C:\FE** entered from Drive C. Key in **FE** to bring up the program. Step through the opening, and when you are asked to "Indicate path to data," key in **C:\MAGS**. Follow the prompts to load the database. When finished, you will be at the FE Main Menu screen as illustrated in Fig. 10-3.

The first thing to do is to look at the records. Using either your mouse or your cursor keys, select "3—Find/Edit Records." Use what you learned in the File Express Tutorial to look at a few records. Then hot-key back to the Main Menu by entering Ctrl-F10. This keypress combination will take you instantly back to the Main Menu from just about any location in the program. No need to keep hitting your Esc key to back up.

Now we want to look at the database structure—the field names, types, etc. So go to the Maintenance menu and cursor down to "6—Database format report." You will be allowed to view the format on the screen, send it to the printer, or record it in a disk file. The structure you will see is shown in Fig. 10-6.

File Express Database Format report

```
-----------------------------------
Database......:C:\MAGS\MAGS
Date..........:03/03/92
Time..........:3:39 PM
-----------------------------------
```

#	Field name	type	length	decimals
1	Pubname	C	25	0
2	Issues	N	3	0
3	Cost	N	6	2
4	Expiration	D	8	0
5	Payment	C	15	0
6	Date Paid	D	8	0
7	Comment	C	50	0

Total field lengths	115
Overhead per record	1
Total record length	116

Fig. 10-6. Format of the MAGS database.

Check the report format

As you can see, the information required is really quite simple. It is all that is necessary to accomplish the purpose for which the database was created. However, there is more you can do with the facts recorded here. For example, it might be interesting to know the total amount of money we're paying for magazine subscriptions. And we might want to know what each issue costs, if only to make us feel that we really are getting a deal compared to the newsstand price.

The way you develop information like this in File Express or any other database program is through the report writer. Here's the concept. When producing reports, you can obviously cause each field or only a selection of fields to be printed. That's basic. The key point is that you can also perform calculations and apply formulas to your data at the same time.

The report format for the MAGS database includes a field that is not in the database itself—cost per issue. The field is filled in at print time on the basis of a formula that divides the COST by the ISSUES field for each publication. (The formula is simple: **COST/ISSUES WITH $**.) The report also includes a field for totalling the COST fields of every record. (This formula is simple too: **COST.TOTAL WITH $**.).

Clearly, the report format is different than the database format. To check and/or edit it, select "5—Report Writer" from the Main menu. Choose an existing report from the menu that will then appear. (There is only one.) You will then see the Report submenu shown in Fig. 10-7.

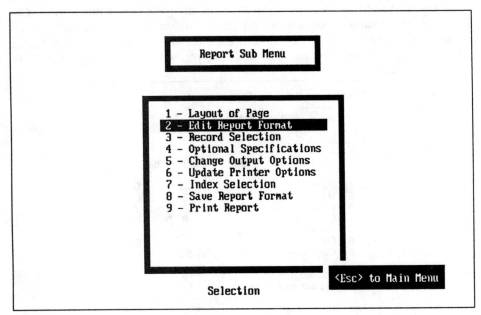

```
          ┌──────────────────────────┐
          │     Report Sub Menu      │
          └──────────────────────────┘


          ┌──────────────────────────────┐
          │  1 - Layout of Page          │
          │  2 - Edit Report Format      │
          │  3 - Record Selection        │
          │  4 - Optional Specifications │
          │  5 - Change Output Options   │
          │  6 - Update Printer Options  │
          │  7 - Index Selection         │
          │  8 - Save Report Format      │
          │  9 - Print Report            │
          └──────────────────────────────┘

                                  ┌──────────────────┐
                                  │ <Esc> to Main Menu│
            Selection             └──────────────────┘
```

Fig. 10-7. The FE Report submenu.

Now select "2—Edit Report Format." That will take you to an editing window containing the template of the report. Here is where you tell FE where to place each field you want to print on the report. Here, too, is where you create special report format fields. The two fields we're most interested in are COST-PERISS and MAGTOTALS. The first is visible about a third of the way down the screen to the right. To see the second, use your arrow keys to scroll down.

Important tip about formulas

We're going to look at the formula for COSTPERISS here and let you look at the formula for MAGTOTALS on your own. The process is the same in both cases. Move the cursor to COSTPERISS, and you will see commands available at the bottom of the screen change. Hit Alt-E to edit the field and keep hitting Enter until you see a screen like the one shown in Fig. 10-8.

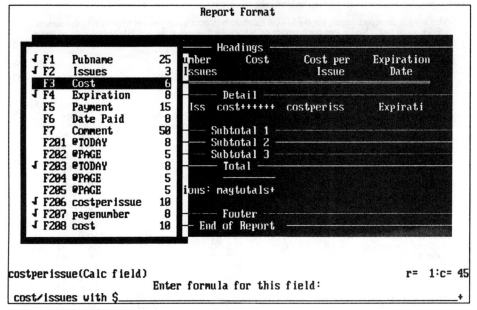

Fig. 10-8. Editing formulas.

Notice the line at the center and bottom of the screen advising you to "Enter formula for this field." Notice the formula reading COST/ISSUE with $ at the bottom left of the screen. Finally, notice the list of available fields that pops up to show you what you have to work with. (The checkmarks signify that the field has been placed in the report.)

We've brought you here for at least two reasons. First, we want you to see how simple and easy formulas can be. What could be simpler than using a slash mark to divide one field by another. Second, we want to convey a really crucial tip about preparing report formats.

That tip concerns how you refer to the fields you want FE to work with. As the manual states, you can enter formulas using only field numbers (F3/F2 with $) if you want to. We strongly advise against this, however. The reason is simple— If you ever want to add fields to your database structure, all the field numbers will change. You will then have to go through and re-do all of your report format formulas. You can avoid this if you use field *names* instead, since the field names are likely to remain the same, regardless of what you do to the database structure. That's why the formula here is COST/ISSUE—COST and ISSUE are the actual names of the relevant fields.

As noted, the formula for the MAGTOTALS field is also simple: COST.TOTAL WITH $. The dot here is part of the .TOTAL function offered by FE. (See the manual or FE5.DOC for other functions using dots.) The "with $" simply tells FE to treat the total it calculates as money.

For an example of the printout generated by this particular report format, please see Fig. 10-9.

This is what the report format for the MAGS database produces when you opt to print it to the screen, printer, or to disk. Notice that the program calculates the Cost per Issue and fills in that field as the re printed, and that it finishes up with a total calculated as the report finishes.

Magazine Subscriptions

03-03-92   Page 1

Publication	Number of Issues	Cost	Cost per Issue	Expiration Date
Antiques	12	$38.00	$3.17	06-01-92
Bucks County Courier	312	$128.70	$0.41	10-01-92
Business Week	52	$39.95	$0.77	09-01-92
Colonial Homes	12	$27.97	$2.33	08-01-93
Computer Shopper	12	$19.97	$1.66	03-01-91
Consumer Reports	24	$30.00	$1.25	07-01-93
Database Magazine	12	$53.40	$4.45	12-01-91
Highlights for Children	12	$24.97	$2.08	02-12-93
Information Today	52	$34.95	$0.67	08-01-92
InfoWorld	52	$110.00	$2.12	10-28-92
Link-Up	6	$25.00	$4.17	10-01-92
National Gardening	6	$15.00	$2.50	05-01-92
New Yorker	52	$32.00	$0.62	05-01-92
Old House Journal	12	$21.00	$1.75	07-01-91
Online Magazine	12	$53.40	$4.45	12-01-91
PC Computing	12	$14.97	$1.25	11-01-91
PC Magazine	22	$34.97	$1.59	08-01-92
Travel and Leisure	12	$32.00	$2.67	08-01-92
TV Guide	52	$37.88	$0.73	09-01-92
Wall Street Journal	260	$139.00	$0.53	01-01-93
Yardley News	52	$18.50	$0.36	08-01-92
Total for all subscriptions:		$931.63		

Fig. 10-9. The printed report.

Conclusion

It is no accident that this chapter immediately follows the chapter on word processing software. Next to word processing, database-centered applications are the most important of all to most small (and large) businesses. This chapter is designed to alert you to the many ways you can use database management software. It is also designed to make you think twice about buying a dedicated, single-application, vertical market package. More than likely, you will be able to do the same job, better and more in tune with the way you work, using a database program.

Now, there's no free lunch here. One of the reasons vertical market packages exist and continue to sell is that they are pretty much ready to go right out of the box. You won't have to define fields or prepare report formats. This is an ideal solution for many people, particularly those who do not have the time or the inclination to really master a database program.

However, if you are willing to spend that time and effort, I think you'll be way ahead of the game in the end. Don't forget, those who go the vertical application route are limited to the programs the software companies have chosen to offer. But someone who knows how to use a database has infinite possibilities.

If this advice resonates with you and your business, if you decide to invest the time and effort, then it just makes good sense to invest in a really good program. Personally, I think File Express is unmatched in its power, its ease of use, its thoughtfully designed features, and the control it gives you over your business. In my opinion, you just can't go wrong by making this the database you choose to master.

11

Spreadsheet

NO OTHER SINGLE TYPE OF SOFTWARE HAS HAD SUCH FAR-REACHING EFFECTS AS the electronic spreadsheet. Certainly it has been responsible for literally millions of better business decisions. But that's not the kind of effect I'm talking about here. I am referring to the fact that the electronic spreadsheet is principally responsible for today's personal computer industry.

It all began on St. Martin's Eve, November 10, 1619, when the French mathematician and philosopher Rene Descartes (1596-1650) had a dream. That dream revolutionized mathematics for centuries to come and led directly to the spreadsheet software of today.

Never blessed with robust health, Descartes had, from an early age, developed the habit of spending much of his time in bed. That's something all of us over the age of 35 can identify with. (Works for me!) But Descartes did not spend his time between the sheets sleeping or engaging in other bed-related pursuits.

Like a typical genius, he spent most of his time simply thinking. The previous day, as he lay there speculating on the nature of Man, the World, the existence of God, and the answer to life, the universe, and everything, he had idly watched a fly flitting from one place to another on the ceiling of his rented room in Neuberg, Germany.

As he went to sleep that night, his subconscious went to work, and he suddenly realized that if lines were drawn along two perpendicular sides of the ceiling and if numbers were equally spaced along the lines, then the location of the fly at any given point could be expressed as two numbers—one for its "horizontal" coordinate and one for its "vertical" coordinate. This was the beginning of analytical geometry and a host of other innovations, the most familiar of which are the X/Y axes and graphs we all encountered in high school.

The "invention" of personal computing

Nearly 360 years later, another young man had another dream. Only this time it was a waking dream designed to solve a particular problem. As it happened, the solution to this problem essentially created the personal computer industry.

The year was 1978, and Dan Bricklin, an M.I.T. graduate who had enrolled in the Harvard Business School, was spending the spring days inside, laboring at the mind-crunching task of working through the spreadsheets required by the "case studies" the Harvard B-School is famous for. He had only two alternatives—either do the work with paper, pencil, and pocket calculator, or do it on one of the time-sharing mainframe systems at the school.

The disadvantages and error potential of working through multiple calculations by hand are obvious. But in terms of total time, convenience, and ease of use, the mainframe alternative wasn't much more attractive. It is difficult to imagine a world before there were personal computers, but that's exactly the world Mr. Bricklin lived in, in 1978.

Mainframes and minicomputers were all that existed, and usually there were long delays between submitting a program to be run and getting its results. Indeed, with a heavily-loaded mainframe system of the era, it was necessary for students to transfer their programs to punched cards, drop the stack of cards off at the computing center, and come back later for the results.

If the program bombed, you had to make corrections and get in line again. With the classic words, "There's got to be a better way," Bricklin invented one. What he invented was the electronic, microcomputer-based spreadsheet. His metaphor was not a fly on the ceiling, it was "an electronic blackboard and electronic chalk in a classroom."

By the summer of 1978, Bricklin had programmed the first working version of his concept. It consisted of five columns and 20 rows. Being close to Boston's Route 128 complex, Bricklin thought he might be able to peddle the program door-to-door to the high-tech firms concentrated there.

User friendliness?

At about the same time, however, Dan Bricklin realized that his work was less than user-friendly. Indeed, his program required more than a passing knowledge of computer programming and thus had a limited audience. To punch it up a bit and give it a more human face, Bricklin enlisted the aid of Bob Frankston, a fellow M.I.T. alumnus. Frankston took to the idea and was eventually able to expand the program and pack the code into a mere 20K of machine memory, making it both powerful enough and practical enough to be run on a microcomputer of the day.

At about that time, another M.I.T./Harvard Business School graduate, Daniel Flystra, entered the picture. Flystra was looking for products to offer through a small software publishing company he had founded, and he suggested that if the

Bricklin/Frankston program could be run on the Apple, the three of them might really have something. The young men formed a company called Software Arts in January of 1979. And in April of that year, Flystra christened the program "Visi-Calc"—a compression of the words "visible calculator" and a reference to the fact that, unlike doing spreadsheets on a mainframe, all the elements of a VisiCalc spreadsheet were visible. Software Arts was eventually renamed "VisiCorp."

Impact and outcomes

The rest, as they say, is history. VisiCalc simply set the business world on its ear. Corporate planners, who were accustomed to preparing a maximum of two spreadsheets based on differing assumptions before making their decisions, could now change assumptions and produce spreadsheets in minutes instead of hours or days.

Executives who were reluctant to use corporate mainframes because of the inevitable delays could now get the answers they sought instantly—in the privacy of their offices where there was no DP professional to smirk if they made a mistake. And, by corporate standards, the Apple computers the program ran on were cheap enough to be buried in research, expense, and advertising budgets—much to the consternation of said DP professionals. Indeed, for a while, Apple computers were known as "VisiCalc machines."

It may well be that personal computers were inevitable. But there is absolutely no question that the invention of VisiCalc rocketed things forward. One might even say that the program "made" the Apple Computer company. Prior to the introduction of the electronic spreadsheet, "personal computers" were little more than a joke. No one took them seriously since, as far as anyone knew, they could do little more than play crude games.

The reverberations of VisiCalc were widespread indeed. Among other things, for example, a former teacher of transcendental meditation named Mitch Kapor was hired by VisiCorp to write a graphing program. The program was a big success, and Kapor retired on his royalties. He then founded Lotus Development and, with Jonathan Sachs, created Lotus 1-2-3.

Of course, the rise in sales of the Apple II did not go unnoticed in Armonk, New York, headquarters of IBM. Accordingly a team was created and assigned the mission of coming up with a "Big Blue" alternative in just one year, an unheard of schedule in the mainframe world. The result was the original IBM/PC, manufactured with off-the-shelf parts (only the keyboard was made by IBM) and equipped with an operating system from a tiny company called Microsoft.

What *is* a spreadsheet?

All this from a "spreadsheet" program? Pretty much, yes. That should give you some idea of how powerful the idea of an electronic spreadsheet really is. But what if you've never used one? What if you have only the vaguest notions of what even a paper spreadsheet really is? Well, as a rather wimpy chief executive we all know says repeatedly, "Stay tuned."

You may not think you've ever used a spreadsheet before, but I'm betting you're wrong. I'm betting that at least once in your life, back before you were so successful you could hire an accountant, you have had to fill out the IRS's "long form." A more perfect paradigm for a spreadsheet there never was.

Like a tax return, spreadsheets are designed to take all the relevant factors into account and come up with bottom line answers. That answer might be "Total tax due," but it might also be your projected profit on a given project, the difference between your year-to-date revenue and expenses, or even the proper dimensions of a custom-made machine tool.

The possibilities are endless, because the situations in which one must consider a wide range of data and calculate an answer are endless. In fact, one could fairly say that anytime you must deal with two or more numbers, one of which is the product of some other calculation, you are using a spreadsheet.

A hearth and home example

For example, let's say you're planning a wedding. You estimate that you will have 100 guests and that each guest will consume two cocktails before dinner. The catering service will bill you so much a drink. If your assumptions are correct, you will have to pay for about 200 cocktails and glasses of beer. That gives you a handle on your bottom line for that component of the party.

But what if the weather turns hot? What if, instead of two drinks apiece, your thirsty guests down an average of 3.2 drinks? How will that affect your bottom line? What if you shorten the cocktail hour so that each guest has time for only 1.2 drinks? What will the effect of that be? Suppose you forget about the open bar and opt for punch instead? Will that produce enough savings to hire a band for live entertainment?

This may sound a little silly. But it is an example everyone can identify with, and, frankly, the "what if" questions involved aren't all that different from the questions businesspeople must ask every day. What if taxes go up? What if the costs of five key items rise by 0.7 percent? What if Deal A falls through but Deal B turns into a real winner?

Until someone invents a fool-proof way to know with certainty what will happen in the future, the best any of us can do is to consider the possibilities. Most of the time we don't do so in a terribly organized fashion. Most of the time we operate by instinct and by the seats of our pants.

That's not necessarily bad. Instinct and experience count for a lot. But your instincts and experience-based judgments can be improved—if you've got the facts. You can get those facts if you can easily ask "what if?" That's what spreadsheet software lets you do—quickly and accurately—until the cows come home or the time to make a decision finally arrives.

Spreadsheets the easy way

Spreadsheets, like Lotus 1-2-3, Excel, and the lesser lights of the commercial software world, have evolved into incredibly powerful engines. After more than a decade of development, they have become over-muscled giants that really *can* leap tall buildings with a single bound. The trouble is, that doesn't do much for those of us who merely want to walk a few yards down the street.

So, while I have no data to back this up, I would not be surprised if researchers one day discovered that the main reason more small businesses didn't purchase spreadsheet software was that the products intimidated the daylights out of them. That and the fact that most commercial packages list for about $595.

Answering simple, basic needs

What I need is a simple way to project the year's income and expenses. In some months I know my income is going to be up or down, just as I know that expenses will vary considerably in different months as insurance premiums, taxes, and other bills fall due. So tell me, can I afford to buy a faster, larger hard drive for my computer this month? Or should I put it off until the month after next?

How much should be set aside for taxes, based on the year's projections? How much can I afford to contribute to a Keogh? Is an additional employee likely to add enough revenue to make him or her worth the salary I will have to pay?

This is not brain surgery, though after wrestling with questions like these with a pencil and pocket calculator, you're likely to want a little cranial relief. Most small business owners don't need the whistles and bells, the elaborate functions, and the "macroing" capability built into spreadsheet software today.

The four arithmetical functions, some graphs, and maybe one or two other things will do quite nicely, thank you. And by the way, don't expect me to pay for a Corvette when I have no intention of taking it over 45 miles per hour.

As-Easy-As . . .

It's ironic, but the spreadsheet I like best is anything but a bicycle with training wheels. It is, in fact, about as close to Lotus 1-2-3 as anyone is ever likely to get. Indeed, years ago when I asked its author about the lack of a manual with the then current version, he said, "Just get any book on Lotus, and you'll do just fine." The program I'm speaking of is As-Easy-As by David Schulz of Trius, Inc.

Though it is now available as a commercial product, like PC-Write and File Express, it remains true to its shareware roots. Version 5 of As-Easy-As (AEA) is available from most shareware sources, complete with an extensive on-disk manual documenting its many features. The registration fee is $69. A smaller, less feature-filled version called ALITE is available as well, with a registration fee of $20. For more information, contact

Trius, Inc.
P.O. Box 249
North Andover, MA 01845-0249
(508) 794-9377 *(Voice)*
(508) 794-0762 (1200/2400) *(BBS)*

As-Easy-As has more features than most small business owners are likely to use in a lifetime. Indeed, there are even undocumented features, added at the request of various users over the years. David Schulz once told me that the head of a laboratory wanted to use AEA for data collection, so David obligingly added the necessary functions to the program. Once again, this is the kind of thing that happens all the time in the shareware world.

You can opt for the company's ALITE, if you want fewer features or if hard disk space is tight (as may be the case when using a laptop computer). But I'm a great believer in using the full-strength version of any product and simply ignoring the features I don't want or need. After all, you can never know when you *will* need some feature in the years to come.

So use AEA, if you have the space, and zero in on just those features you really need. And how can you know which features to master? Well, I'm going to tell you.

I'm going to show you how to master the basic concepts and techniques, and how to set up your own revenue and expense reports for multiple locations of a mythical company Emily and I have created called Herbs and Flowers, Inc. We will be using a worksheet called TUTORIAL.WKS and one called HERBS.WKS, both of which can be found on the disk accompanying this book.

Basic concepts

Before we can get into the hands-on tutorial, however, there are some basic ideas you've got to master. First is the elegantly simple, yet extremely powerful concept behind an electronic spreadsheet—the cell. The program puts a line at the top of your screen and a line running down the left side. The top line is labelled with letters of the alphabet and the side line is designated with numbers, starting with 1 and stretching all the way down your screen. (Please see Fig. 11-1.)

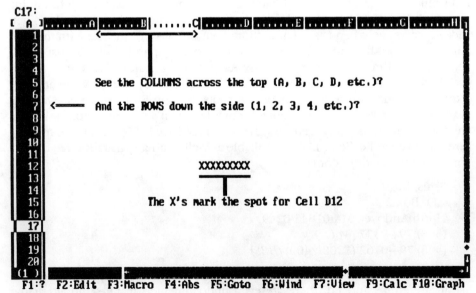

Fig. 11-1. The columns and rows of a spreadsheet.

As with the fly on Descartes's ceiling, this arrangement of columns and rows makes it possible to precisely locate any spot on the screen by referring to its coordinates. In effect, a spreadsheet program divides the screen up into easily identifiable intersections or *cells*. There is no need to worry about it now, but a cell can be anywhere from 0 characters wide (which makes it invisible) to 60 or more characters wide. The default in AEA is nine characters, but this can easily be changed.

A computer screen isn't big enough to display the whole spreadsheet at one time. In fact, the most you can look at is about eight columns and 20 rows. Remember, columns go up and down, like the columns supporting a Greek temple; rows go left to right.

When you move the cursor to the right, the screen will scroll horizontally. New column letters will appear as the A, B, C, etc., columns scroll out of sight. Moving the cursor down past row 20 causes the screen to scroll vertically, revealing more numbers while rows 1, 2, 3, etc. scroll off the top of your screen. The screen can thus be thought of as a window that you move around over an area that extends in both directions. In the case of As-Easy-As 5.0, you have 256 columns and 8,192 rows to work with.

The data of a cell

The cell is the basic element of all spreadsheet programs. Think of them as the boxes on a piece of graph paper. Each is a unique location, designated by its column and row (A2, C34, Z200, etc.) This design opens up lots of possibilities.

For one thing, you can cursor or mouse around the screen, moving from one cell to another. Or you can simply specify the coordinates of the cell you wish to move to and the program will take you there in an instant. Of course, you can also put information into any cell, whether it is *textual information*—as when you are laying out your sheet and labelling your columns—or *numerical information*—as when you are keying in relevant figures.

So what's the big deal? You could do much the same thing with a word processing program. The big deal is "formulas." If you have entered a chart with a heading of "Revenues" at the top and the months of the year listed down the side, you can easily tell how much income you expect to receive in the month of May. That's pure word processing.

But, let's move to a different cell, one directly beneath the last amount (December) in your Revenue column. And let's put a label nearby reading "Total." If this were a word processing program, you could pull out your pocket calculator and add up the figures to find out what should go in the Total cell. But with a spreadsheet, there is a golden difference.

With a spreadsheet, you tell the program, "This Total cell will always contain the sum of the figures in the cells directly above it." You do this by assigning a formula to the Total cell. That causes the program to work the formula and insert the proper results into the cell.

This is the essence of a spreadsheet program. Suppose the month is July. You have a figure in the July cell, but until August 1, it's only a projection. So now it's

August 1, and you are able to replace your projection with an actual figure. You do so—and the Total cell *automatically changes*. Each time you enter data, the program will automatically recalculate any formulas that focus on the cells containing that data.

That's why you can play "what if" games. If you get a spreadsheet set up with the appropriate formulas, you can change any figure, based on a "what if" query, and every number that depends on that figure will also change—automatically. Once you know this, it's easy to see why the early users of VisiCalc on Wall Street and elsewhere were wild about the program. It is easy to see why Lotus Development and its competitors have made hundreds of millions of dollars in the last decade. This is incredible power!

Taking it to a higher level

Now that you have the general concept of data cells and formula cells, let's move up to the next level. It will not always be convenient or appropriate for the Total cell to be located directly beneath the numbers it is totalling. In point of fact, what you really do when you create a formula for Total is to tell the program to add a series of specific cells.

In spreadsheet parlance, that series is called a *range*. As we will see in a moment, you can designate a range simply by moving your cursor. But let's stick with this idea that whatever information appears in Total consists of the sum of the numbers in a range of specific cells, designated as C10 through C22 or whatever.

This means that the Total cell can be located *anywhere* on the spreadsheet. It does not have to be directly beneath the cells whose sum it is reflecting. It can be the very first cell, A1, or it can be located someplace else. The program does not care. All that matters is that Total contains the sum of whatever numbers are in C10 through C22.

And you know what? You can have more than one "Total" cell. You might have one Total cell located directly beneath the column of numbers. But you might attach the same formula to a cell located on the equivalent of "Page 10" of your chart, where you present the summary. Change a number in cell C10, and *both* "Total" cells will be automatically updated.

To take things one step further, should you later decide to move the cells C10 through C22, possibly to locations E10 through E22, the program will *automatically* update your "Total" formula to include the cell names of the new location. (This option can be turned on or off, as you like.)

Emily and Alfred's As-Easy-As tutorial

At this point, it's time to roll up your sleeves and load the program. You will grasp the next batch of concepts faster and with far less effort if you can follow along with us at your keyboard. So get a copy of As-Easy-As 5.0. Make a directory on your hard drive called C:\EASY, and copy the program files into it. Next, copy all of the .WKS files supplied with this book into the same directory. Then log onto C:\EASY and key in **ASEASY**.

The greeting screen will come up, and if you have a mouse installed, you'll see a little white arrow appear momentarily in the top left corner of the screen. Hit any key to go into the spreadsheet. What you see will look almost exactly like the screen shown in Fig. 11-1, except that there won't be any text about columns and rows and X marking the spot.

Your author is now in the position of the counterman at an electrical or plumbing supply house. I've got hundreds of things I can show you, but there are only a few of them that you really need. Emily, our in-house spreadsheet expert, suggested the Father Guido Sarducci approach. Recalling Father Sarducci's famous "Five Minute University" sketch from *Saturday Night Live*, we've decided to boil things down to the bare essence.

At the "Five Minute University," you are taught only those key points most college students remember about major subjects five years after graduation. For example, the economics course at FMU consists of three words: Supply and Demand. Physics consists of a single formula: E equals MC squared. In Theology, you learn that the key question is "Where is God?"—and the answer is "God is everywhere." On to the next course.

Thanks to the Five Minute University, everyone is saved a great deal of time, trouble, and money. And the results are the same. (Tuition is only $20, including cap and gown rental, snack, and Polaroid graduation photo.)

With Father Sarducci's philosophy in mind, here are the five key concepts you need to get started with As-Easy-As:

- Forward slash (/) brings up the menu.
- The escape key (Esc) allows you to exit any menu function and return to the spreadsheet. Whenever you want to get out of something, hit Esc.
- The F2 key lets you edit the contents of a cell.
- In large measure, those intimidating cell references (C18, K34, etc.) are for the program's use only. You can do most of your work visually, specifying individual cells or ranges of cells by moving your cursor over the target cells.
- When you want to perform some action on a range of cells (for example, add a column of numbers or move several rows of numbers), use the period key to anchor the cursor at the starting point. Then move the cursor down or across the screen to highlight whatever area you choose and hit Enter.

That's it. With these little levers you can move the world. Or at least the As-Easy-As world. So let's get started.

Installing your printer

The As-Easy-As shareware package comes with a 100-page manual on the disk. It is called ASEASY.DOC, and it contains form feeds, so all you have to do is key in **COPY ASEASY.DOC PRN** to produce a hard copy. Alternatively, you can bring it into your word processing program and print it from there. You will definitely want to print the manual when you are finished here. But it is not necessary at this time.

We are going to assume that you are seated in front of your machine with the main, empty spreadsheet on the screen. The first thing to do is to tell the program what kind of printer you have. Hit your slash key (/) to bring up the menu. The first selection on the menu is Sheet; the last, Exit. Notice that the first letters of each selection are highlighted. You can make a selection by moving the cursor highlight bar to the item and pressing Enter, or by merely keying in the highlighted first letter of the desired selection.

As we list the command you should enter, we are going to refer to these first letters. Thus, from the Main menu, hit U (for User), then I (for Install), and then P (for Printers). Notice that as each menu appears, some text appears at the very top of the screen to tell you what a particular selection leads to. Move the cursor down to a different selection, and the text will change.

At this point, you will see a list of printer makes and models on the screen. The first item is Epson FX-80. The last is HP QuietJet. Select your printer or the printer with which your machine is compatible and hit Enter. Now hit Esc once to back out to the User Install menu, and notice the last selection, "Save Config." This lets you record your configuration so you do not have to go through all this each time you use the program. So hit S to save. You should now be back at the blank spreadsheet.

As you might imagine, spreadsheets can become quite large. They can contain many more columns than can be printed in regular-size type across a letter-size sheet of paper. The solution is often to print the worksheet in "landscape" (as opposed to "portrait") mode. Landscape means rotating the sheet 90 degrees at print time so that it prints on its side.

All laser printers have a code to enable landscape mode. But dot-matrix printers present a special problem. David Schulz, author of As-Easy-As, has solved that problem with Pivot!, a shareware program specifically designed to work with AEA and dot-matrix printers. Pivot! can be run independently or installed as an "add-in" to AEA itself. If you have a dot-matrix printer, you will also want to get Pivot! when you get As-Easy-As.

Bringing in the spreadsheets

The next task is to load the TUTORIAL.WKS spreadsheet supplied with this book. Bring up the menu. (Hit your forward slash key.) Choose F for File, then R for Retrieve. You will be presented with a list of all the .WKS files in C:\ASEASY. Cursor down to the Tutorial worksheet and hit Enter. Within seconds, columns of numbers and labels will appear on your screen. Use your up-arrow key to get to the top. You will see a screen like the one shown in Fig. 11-2.

This spreadsheet presents the business volumes for the Herbs and Flowers, Inc., store at the Barnsley location. Take a moment or two to absorb it. The sheet presents that store's revenue by month, with the October through December figures as estimates. The YTD (Year-to-Date) Revenue column offers a running total. Also listed are the number of orders, the YTD orders, and the average order.

Starting at location A19, you will find the totals, and below that row, the monthly averages. Now cursor down until you see the "What If?" box on your

```
F1:
[  A  ].........A.........B.......C.........D.......E.......F.......G.........H
   1            Herbs and Flowers, Inc. - 1992 Business Volumes
   2                          Barnsley Store
   3
   4 Month      Revenue   YTD Revenue       # Orders YTD Orders      Avg Order
   5 =====      =======   ===========       ======== =========       =========
   6 Jan         $3,643      $3,643            179       179            $20
   7 Feb         $5,134      $8,777            255       434            $20
   8 Mar         $7,893     $16,670            425       859            $19
   9 Apr         $7,587     $24,257            365      1224            $21
  10 May         $7,686     $31,943            342      1566            $22
  11 Jun         $6,222     $38,165            293      1859            $21
  12 Jul         $5,433     $43,598            256      2115            $21
  13 Aug         $5,000     $48,598            225      2340            $22
  14 Sep         $5,698     $54,296            243      2583            $23
  15 Oct*        $4,800     $59,096            220      2803            $22
  16 Nov*        $4,700     $63,796            230      3033            $20
  17 Dec*        $3,700     $67,496            175      3208            $21
  18
  19 TOTALS      $67,496                      3208                    $21.04
  20 AVG MONTH   $5,625                        267
(1 )   TUTORIAL.WKS
  F1:?  F2:Edit  F3:Macro  F4:Abs  F5:Goto  F6:Wind  F7:View  F9:Calc F10:Graph
```

Fig. 11-2. The Barnsley Store spreadsheet.

screen. This is your play area. It is designed to let you ask questions like, "What if this store can get its average order up to $25? How will that affect total revenue?"

Well, let's see. Move your cursor to cell F26, the number opposite the "Avg Order" label. It currently reads $21.04. Revenue is currently $73,640. Now ask yourself, suppose we could boost the average order by $2. We might produce little booklets about "Cooking with Herbs" and place them at the checkout counter to attract impulse purchases. We might offer customers a ten percent discount on their next purchase of $30 or more. But would it be worth it? How would it affect revenue?

To find out, use the spreadsheet. With your cursor over $21.04, key in 23.04. Notice that your keystrokes appear at the top left corner of the screen. Hit Enter, and the amount in the cell will instantly change. Now what's the total revenue? (The answer is $80,640.)

Printing a spreadsheet

Next, let's call for a printout of the spreadsheet. Call up the Main menu. Hit **P** for PrintTo and **P** again for Printer. This produces the PrintTo Printer menu. Now you've got to specify a range of cells to be printed. Spreadsheets default to this option because some sheets can be quite large, and you may not want to print everything every time. So here we go with our first range specification. Hit **R** for Range.

That returns you to the sheet, but notice the text at the very top of the screen. As-Easy-As is waiting for you to specify a range. Do so by either cursoring up to A1 or simply hitting your Home key. Then use a period to anchor the cursor and begin moving it down the screen. Notice how it leaves a swathe of highlighting in its path. Take it down to the end of the "What If?" box, and then use your right arrow to move to location H30. The highlighting will now cover the entire sheet. Press Enter to lock it in.

The menu will pop up again, and this time Range will show A1..H30. Cursor down to Go Print or hit **G**, and printing will begin. Since this spreadsheet occupies only about 26 lines, your printer will probably not automatically eject the paper. So hit **P** for Page Advance to get it to disgorge the printout.

The Help function

You've accomplished a lot already. You are getting a feel for moving around the sheet and working your way through the menus. You have already had some hands-on experience in playing "what if" games. And I hope you are beginning to imagine how a spreadsheet can be helpful in your own business.

So let's take a break for a moment. Let's go look at As-Easy-As's built-in Help function. As the on-disk manual notes, the help provided is context-sensitive. You always call for help by hitting the F1 key, but the information that appears may vary depending on when you make the call.

For example, As-Easy-As offers assistance when you are entering a macro, entering an equation, entering a function, or entering a printer setup code. Try this little experiment. Move the cursor to an empty cell and hit your left curly brace key ({). This is a signal to As-Easy-As that what follows could be a macro. So hit your F1 key at this point and watch as a list labelled "Select Macro" appears.

Toggle the list off with F1, get rid of the curly brace, and enter an "at" sign (@). As we're about to see, the "at" sign is the signal for the start of a "function." Once you have entered the "at" sign, hit F1 again and notice that you are now presented with a list of available functions. You can scroll through the list until you find the one you want and hit Enter to automatically include it in what you are typing. See the on-disk manual topic "Function Keys" for more information on using context-sensitive help.

Most of the time, however, hitting F1 will bring up a screen like the one shown in Fig. 11-3. This is the program's master help feature. Notice that the screen consists of a list of topics running down the left side, and text explaining each topic in a Help window occupying the right third of the screen.

The legend at the bottom of the screen informs you that you may use Home or End to rocket to the top or bottom of the Topic list. Or you may press the first letter of a topic for a quick search. Most important is the "LT/RT Window" item. It isn't very informative, but it is there to remind you that you can move from the topic list to the explanation screen and back using your left and right arrows.

This is important because there is often much more to a topic than can be shown in a single explanation screen. When you move to the Help screen, you will find that it scrolls independently of the Topic list. If you need a quick copy of the help information, simply hit your Print Screen key to dump it to the printer.

The topic shown in Fig. 11-3 is "@FINANCE." The "at" sign (@) introduces an important concept. All spreadsheets have certain built-in formulas or *func-*

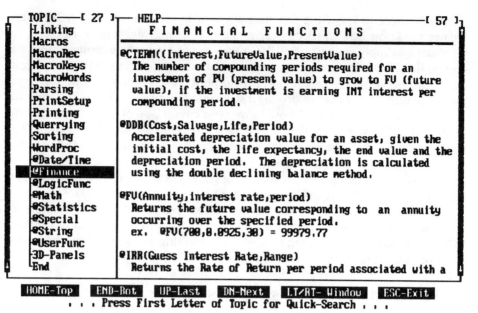

Fig. 11-3. As-Easy-As online help.

tions. There are a *lot* of available functions, each of them beginning with an "at" sign, so the subject can be quite confusing.

However, all you really have to remember is that functions are operations. Thus, if you want the program to calculate the average of a column of numbers, you would designate the cell where you want to present the average number and then key in @AVG, followed by the range of cells you want to average. If you want to add up a column or row of numbers, you would use the @SUM function and specify the range.

Entering formulas

Let's take a look at how this works. Hit your Esc key to return from the Help feature to the spreadsheet. Move your cursor to cell B19. This is the cell totalling the store's revenues. It currently contains the figure $67,496. Notice that when you move to this cell, the following line appears at the top of the screen: B19 [C0]: @SUM(B6..B17). That's telling you what formula has been attached to cell B19. As you can surmise, it calls for the addition of all of the numbers in column B, starting with January's figures and running through December's estimates.

To test the formula, cursor up to one of the monthly figures in column B and change it to something else. Notice how the amount in B19 changes as the program runs the formula again. As we've said before, this is the essence of a spreadsheet. And it is really easy to accomplish.

For example, move the cursor up to cell B18, right above the $67,496. Let's see if we can attach the same formula to that cell as is used in B19. We need two things. We need to know the function we want to use—in this case @SUM—and we need to know how to specify the range of cells we want it to work on.

Start by simply keying in @SUM(. (You do not have to use capital letters, but you do need the left parentheses.) Now move the cursor up to the January figure in cell B6 ($3,643) and—here it is—hit your period key. Hitting your period key at this point is the equivalent of driving a stake into the ground. It says, "Here is the cell I want you to start with." Now move your cursor down to the December figure in cell B17. You will see that your cursor leaves highlighting in its wake. Then hit Enter. That says, "The range stops here." Finish your formula by adding a closing parentheses and hitting Enter.

In an instant, the figure $67,496 will appear in cell B18, right above the same figure in cell B19. You've just entered your first spreadsheet formula.

Notice that there was no need to laboriously figure out precisely which cell addresses to specify when entering your range. You did it all visually. You said, "Okay, I'm going to enter a range now. Start marking as soon as I hit the period and stop when I next hit my Enter key."

Formulas in seven simple steps

We've been working with columns, but you can do exactly the same thing with rows. And as noted, @SUM is only one of scores of available functions. Just remember these seven steps:

1. Go to the cell you want to contain the results.
2. Key in the start of your formula; usually this means beginning with the "at" sign (@) that signifies a function.
3. Key in a left parentheses to signify the start of a range.
4. Move to the first cell in the range and drive a stake into the ground by hitting your period key.
5. Cursor down or across to the last cell in the range. The area you cover with the cursor will be highlighted.
6. Hit Enter to end the range specification.
7. Finish the formula with a right parentheses and hit Enter to activate it.

Entering text and editing cells

Putting the formula in cell B18 was a good exercise, but let's assume that you don't want to leave it there. Let's assume that you want to delete the formula. This, too, is quite easy. Move to the cell and hit your F2 key. Now focus your attention on the line at the very top of the screen. Notice the cursor up there at the end of the information you have entered in the cell.

You will find that you can edit cell contents just as if you were using a word processor. Hit your Home key and the cursor jumps to the beginning of the line. The Ins and Del keys work as you would expect. Indeed, by default, you will be in "insert" mode. Hitting your Ins key toggles the mode off and makes your space-bar "destructive" of the characters in its path. When you have removed the formula or text or numbers, hit Enter and the cell on the sheet will reflect your changes.

Looking at "labels"

As you can see from the TUTORIAL spreadsheet, cells can accommodate numbers, formulas, and text. Let's spend just a moment here talking about text. In spreadsheet parlance, text is generally referred to as a "label."

Labels are entered by moving to a cell and simply typing. The width of the column makes no difference. As long as the columns to the right are empty, the text you type will appear as if it is contained by several columns. We're not going to discuss it here, but if you need to change the width of a column, or insert a column or row at some location, see the Sheet submenus branching off the Main menu.

There are two things Father Guido Sarducci would tell you about labels. The first is that text and labels usually begin with a single quote mark and are displayed left justified within the column. Note that if you want to center a label, use a carat (^); if you want it to be right-justified, use a double quote mark (").

Most of the time, there is no need to enter the label character manually. The program assumes that you will be entering text, until it sees you enter a number, at which point, the single quote it has supplied will disappear. The exception is when you want to begin a label with a number, like "1992 Sales." To tell the program to treat the initial number 1 as text and left justify the label, you will have to first key in a single quote (').

The second essential point about labels is that they can be turned into "borders." A border is a label that doesn't move when you scroll the sheet beneath it. Imagine, for example, that the columns in the TUTORIAL sheet covered 48 months instead of just 12. The numbers would extend below the bottom of the screen window. As you cursored down to them, though, the header information (Revenue, YTD Revenue, etc.) would scroll up and out of sight. You can solve this problem by making the relevant rows into "borders."

Start by moving the cursor to the row *beneath* the row of labels you wish to turn into a border. In this case, move the cursor to cell A6, the one containing "Jan." Then call up the Main menu and hit **S**, followed by **B** to get to the Sheet Border menu. The "Horizon" option lets you fix rows above the cursor.

Hit Enter to confirm. You will be returned to the sheet. Now cursor down the sheet and watch as the row beginning with "Month" remains constant, as the columns scroll beneath it. If you had wanted to fix a vertical border, you could have done so as well from the Sheet Border menu.

Currency or numbers

In a moment, we're going to move on to an advanced tutorial involving As-Easy-As's many graphing functions. But first, we need to pause a moment and take stock. With the TUTORIAL worksheet as your guide, you now have all of the basic information you need to begin building useful spreadsheets of your own. You've got some exploring to do, and you will want to do a lot of experimenting. But we are confident that with just the information provided here, you can have a simple spreadsheet prepared and functioning in less than an hour.

There is only one further piece of information you need, and that concerns how to tell the program to use dollars-and-cents or to use plain numbers. As you might suspect by now, the technique is to specify the range of cells you wish to appear formatted in a particular way.

Start by calling up the Main menu and hitting **R** for Range. The resulting Range menu will contain a selection called Format. Select that option, and you will see a screen like the one shown in Fig. 11-4.

```
$xx.xx (See INSTALL PUNCTUATE to change currency!)
             ......B|......C|......D|......E|......F|......G|......H|
RANGE        686  $31,943      342    1566             $22
FORMAT   *   222  $30,165      293    1859             $21
             433  $43,598      256    2115             $21
Fixed   +/-  000  $48,598      225    2340             $22
Science Text 698  $54,296      243    2583             $23
,       Hide 000  $59,096      220    2803             $22
Currency Reset 700 $63,796     230    3033             $20
General  Eng 700  $67,496      175    3200             $21
Date    Label
Percent  Box 496               3200              $21.04
             625               267
21 AVG ORDER $21.04
22
23
24 (*) Estimate only        ┌──────────────────────────┐
25                          │        What If?          │
26                          │  # Orders        3500    │
27                          │  Avg Order      $21.04   │
28                          │  Revenue        $73,640  │
29                          │                          │
(1 )  tutorial.WKS          └──────────────────────────┘
F1:?  F2:Edit  F3:Macro  F4:Abs  F5:Goto  F6:Wind  F7:View  F9:Calc F10:Graph
```

Fig. 11-4. Setting the format of a range.

By default, As-Easy-As assumes you want to use plain numbers in all cells. So if you want it to present some numbers as dollars and cents, you must tell it to do so. The Range Format menu shown in Fig. 11-4 offers many options. Let us assume, however, that you're interested in currency. Select that option, and you will see a prompt at the top of the screen asking you how many decimal places you wish to use. The default is two, so just hit Enter.

Now you've got to tell the program which range of cells to apply this format to. Let's assume for demonstration purposes that you want to turn the numbers in the "# Orders" column into dollars and cents. Move your cursor . . . but wait a minute, why is the cursor leaving a trail of highlighting? Turn off the highlighting by hitting Esc. Then move to cell E6, the top of the # Orders column. *Now* drive your stake into the ground by hitting your period key. That turns on the highlighting, as you will see as you move down to the end of the column at cell E17. Hit

Enter to end. All of the numbers in the column will now be sporting a dollar sign, a point, and two zeros.

As a final exercise, see if you can change the format back to plain numbers. Hint: Select "General" on the Range Format menu.

Build one of your own

At this point, you should take a swing at creating your own spreadsheet. If you are already using a spreadsheet based on ledger paper, consider creating an electronic equivalent. If spreadsheeting is new to you, think about how you might apply the concepts incorporated in the TUTORIAL worksheet in tracking your own business.

Keep it simple at first. Just a column or two of numbers and labels and some simple arithmetic functions. Then gradually add data and functions as you explore further. The built-in Help function will guide you in the right direction, as will the on-disk manual.

Manual trick: Use LIST.COM

In fact, let me tell you how I use the on-disk version of the manual. I've got a printout, of course, but I like to search the electronic copy on my computer. The program I use is Vernon Buerg's LIST.COM, discussed in Chapter 16. One need only key in **LIST ASEASY.DOC** to bring the manual to the screen. Then hit **F** for "Find" and key in the phrase you are looking for ("printing," "graphs," "functions," etc.). If the first occurrence does not present the text you want, hit **A** for Again, and keep doing so until you meet with success.

Save your work!

We'll have much more to say about LIST.COM in Chapter 16. It is truly one of the ten best programs ever written. But right now it is time for the final Dutch Uncle warning:

Save your worksheet!

Saving your work is an important step when using any program, but it is especially crucial when using a spreadsheet. The reason is that As-Easy-As and other spreadsheets are designed to let you modify inputs (assumptions) and check the results. Consequently, they do not save your most recent changes by default.

The idea is that, most of the time, you will bring in a sheet you have created, run some numbers, and exit without altering the disk file. That is, indeed, how most people use spreadsheets. But it puts a special responsibility on you to make sure that you do save what you *want* to save.

When you have prepared something you want to save, call up the Main menu. Hit **F** for File, then hit **S** for Store to save the file to disk. You will be given the opportunity to use the current filename or to key in something different. Then you can Exit the program, secure in the knowledge that your work has been saved. Normally, you will simply exit and no changes will be made to the disk file.

Advanced tutorial: Spreadsheet graphs

In this section, we are going to concentrate on As-Easy-As's built-in graphing functions. This is really one of the most exciting aspects of using a spreadsheet, and it really isn't difficult, once you've mastered a few basic concepts and techniques. By the time we're finished, you'll be able to produce a report like the one shown later. This report combines both text and graphics, and not only can As-Easy-As integrate the two in the printout, it can show you what the report will look like on the screen.

If you want to use AEA's graphics functions, you will obviously need a graphics adapter and monitor (Hercules, CGA, EGA, VGA, etc.). See the on-disk manual for more information.

Also, note that you can set the video resolution AEA uses by bringing up the Main menu and entering U, I, V, and picking a mode from the Select Display menu that will then appear.

A few words about graphs

Some people are graph-crazy. They've never seen a column of numbers they didn't want to turn into a pie chart, a stacked bar graph, or spiderweb of intersecting lines. Lottery tickets, universal product codes, phone numbers from the white pages—you name it—if a graph can be produced, they're the ones to do it. Never mind that it takes them half a day and the results, while pretty, are essentially useless.

Just as not every inter-office memo has to look as though it were typeset by a master printer, not every collection of figures has to be turned into a graph. On the other hand, there are times when looking at information graphically reveals trends and anomalies that are not immediately apparent when simply reviewing the numbers. The tutorial Emily and I have prepared for you involves just such a situation.

The monthly report

At this time, we'd like you to bring up As-Easy-As and load the worksheet HERBS.WKS. You will find the worksheet on the disk accompanying this book. If you have not copied it into C:\ASEASY, do so now. When the worksheet has been loaded, your screen will look like the one shown in Fig. 11-5.

The HERBS.WKS worksheet is from Herbs and Flowers, Inc., a mythical company dedicated to beautifying the home and enhancing the general quality of life. Begun in 1982, the firm has grown to include six stores in the metropolitan area: Arborlea, Barnsley, Edgewood, Glenmont, Poplar, and Riverside. A seventh store is planned in the Squire's Chase section, as soon as the developers can get the corn fields plowed under and paved. With only little stick trees to look at for the next 15 years, the people who move into that development are going to need a lot of beautifying and life enhancing.

```
A3:
[ A ]........A .......B .......C .......D .......E .......F .......G .......H
 1                    Herbs and Flowers, Inc.
 2                        September 1992
 3
 4  Store                                             Exp. as
 5  Location          Revenue         Expenses        % of Rev.
 6  ========          =======         ========        =========
 7  Arborlea          $7,856          $5,004          63.7%
 8  Barnsley          $5,698          $3,534          62.0%
 9  Edgewood          $11,004         $8,999          81.8%
10  Glenmont          $8,843          $5,687          64.3%
11  Poplar            $10,354         $6,986          67.5%
12  Riverside         $13,324         $8,957          67.2%
13
14         TOTAL      $57,079         $39,167         68.6%
15
16
17
18
19  HERBS:7,3
20
(1 )  herbs.WKS
F1:? F2:Edit F3:Macro F4:Abs F5:Goto F6:Wind F7:View F9:Calc F10:Graph
```

Fig. 11-5. September's figures.

But that's all in the future. The September figures for the six current stores are in, and they have been entered into the spreadsheet you are viewing now. The cells in the Revenue column and the Expenses column contain just the numbers you see. Nothing special here.

Surveying the sheet

However, the cells in the "Exp. as % of Rev." use formulas to present expenses as a percentage of revenue. So let's go take a look. Move your cursor over to one of the cells in column G. Look at the top left corner of the screen. You will see your current cell name and "[%1] +E8/C8." This looks pretty mysterious, but it is easily explained.

First, the "[%1]" indicates that the cell format has been set to "percentage with one digit after the decimal point." Remember how we set the range of numbers in the TUTORIAL worksheet to the currency ($) format? Well, percentage format is handled the same way. Pop up the Main menu and select Range. Then choose Format from the resulting Range menu. As you will see, you can opt for zero to seven decimal places.

The plus sign (+) tells the program that what follows is a cell location, not a label or a number. Thus, the expression "+E8/C8" says "divide the value in cell E8 by the value in cell C8." The result will be expressed as a percentage, thanks to the format we chose.

That is all you really need to know at this point about the column showing expenses as a percentage of revenue. You should thus feel free to skip to "The power of graphs" later in this chapter. However, if you are curious as to how to set up such a column yourself, we can tell you in a relatively few words.

Duplicating a formula

You've got to start by getting your Revenue and Expenses columns (or whatever tabular information you want to use) set up and entered. Then you move to the first cell in what we'll call the "calculated column." Define it with the format and formula you want to attach to that cell. Then copy the cell to the range of cells directly beneath it.

Let's use the HERBS.WKS worksheet as a scratchpad. Move the cursor to cell H7, right next to the "63.7%" that starts the expenses as percentage of revenue column. The cell will be empty. The top left corner of the screen will read H7: to indicate the cursor location.

Now key in +E7/C7 to tell the program you want it to divide the value in E7 by the value in C7. Hit Enter, and the number "0.636965" will appear in cell H7. The next step is to change the cell's format. Bring up the Main menu and enter **R, F, P.**

You will be prompted at the top of the screen for the number of decimal places you want to use. Select "1" and hit Enter. Now you will be asked to specify the range to which you want the percentage format to apply. Hit Enter to indicate a range of just one cell (H7). H7 will now contain exactly what G7 contains: 63.7%.

Now all we have to do is copy this cell to all the other cells in the column. As-Easy-As will automatically take care of adjusting the cell references in the formula. With your cursor still on H7, bring up the Main menu. Select **C** for "CopyCell." This command will let you copy a range of cells.

You will now be prompted at the top of the screen for the designation of the cell you want to copy. This can be a range or a single cell. Here we are dealing with just H7, so hit Enter to confirm your "range of one." Next you will see a prompt asking for the "TO:" or target location. Move your cursor down one to H8 and hit your period key to "drive a stake in the ground."

Keep moving the cursor down until you reach location H12, the end of the column. (Notice the highlighting the cursor leaves behind, now that you have driven a stake in the ground at H7.) Hit Enter, and watch as the cells are filled with the appropriate percentage figures. The figures will match the ones already on the spreadsheet in the expenses as percentage of revenue column.

As you can see, creating a formula and copying it to a range of cells really isn't all that difficult. Just keep the basic spreadsheet techniques discussed earlier in mind, and you'll be operating like a master in no time. In fact, why don't you see if you can now delete cells H7 through H12?

Hint: Start with the Range selection from the Main menu.

The power of graphs

The figures have all been entered, and boy do they look great. Not the numbers themselves, necessarily, but the way they are laid out and arranged. Talk about toning up your operation and becoming truly professional! Like you and like me, the Herbs and Flowers, Inc., people gave them a quick once-over. And they too were lulled into a false sense of security by the neatness of the columns.

But there's a problem on this report. To instantly see what it is, hit your F10 key to call up a bar graph plotting each store's expenses as a percentage of revenue. The problem leaps out at you immediately. Something is clearly wrong with one of the stores.

The Herbs and Flowers, Inc., people investigated and discovered that one of the expense numbers was misreported. Apparently the figure $8999 should really be $6999. When the correction was made, they hit F10 again and the graph showed that all stores were operating in about the same range.

Now, here's the point. As a businessperson, you could probably look at the neat columns of numbers alone and detect the problem. But it is *so* much easier to do so when those same columns are displayed as a graph. We are a visually oriented species, and visual information is grasped much more quickly than columns of related figures. That is the essential power of graphs, and it is easy to tap with As-Easy-As.

Creating a graph

As a brief exercise, let's create a different graph. Let's create a pie chart showing the relative "slices" each store's revenue contributes to the whole. That will give you a quick, graphic impression of which store managers are doing their jobs and which could do with some improvement.

The first task when preparing a graph is to tell the program what type of graph you want to use. AEA offers a full range of options. Then you've got to tell the program what ranges of data you want it to use in creating the graph. Finally, you've got to add some text (titles) to the graph to explain what is being presented.

To make sure we are all playing with the same deck, start by loading the HERBS.WKS spreadsheet again. Next, bring up the Main menu and select **G** for Graphics. Hit **T** for type, and select **P** for Pie on the menu that will then appear. You will be returned to the Graphics menu. The next step is to specify the range of data you want to graph. So select **R**.

The Graphics Range menu that will appear will indicate that the X range is A7 through A12. That range covers the store names, so leave it as it is. The A range will appear as G7 through G12. Those are the cells in the "Exp. as % of Rev" column. We don't want to use those cells for this graph, so you must specify a different range.

Start by hitting **A** for the A range. Column G will switch to highlighting. But since we don't want to use that range, hit Esc to free the cursor. Move the cursor over to C7, the cell containing the revenue from the Arborlea store. Drive your stake into the ground here by hitting your period key. Now cursor down to C12, the Riverside store. (Highlighting will follow.) Hit Enter to signify the end of the range.

The Graphics Range menu will appear again with "C7..C12" next to the A range. Hit **Q** to quit. Then **Q** to quit from the Graphics menu that will appear. Now for the magic. Hit F10 to generate the graph. You'll see a pie chart all right. But the titles will no longer apply.

So we've got to change the titles. Hit Esc to return to the sheet. Then key in /, G, O, T. This will take you to a screen like the one shown in Fig. 11-6. Notice that there is already information entered here. Since some of this information does not apply to our new pie chart, we must change or delete it.

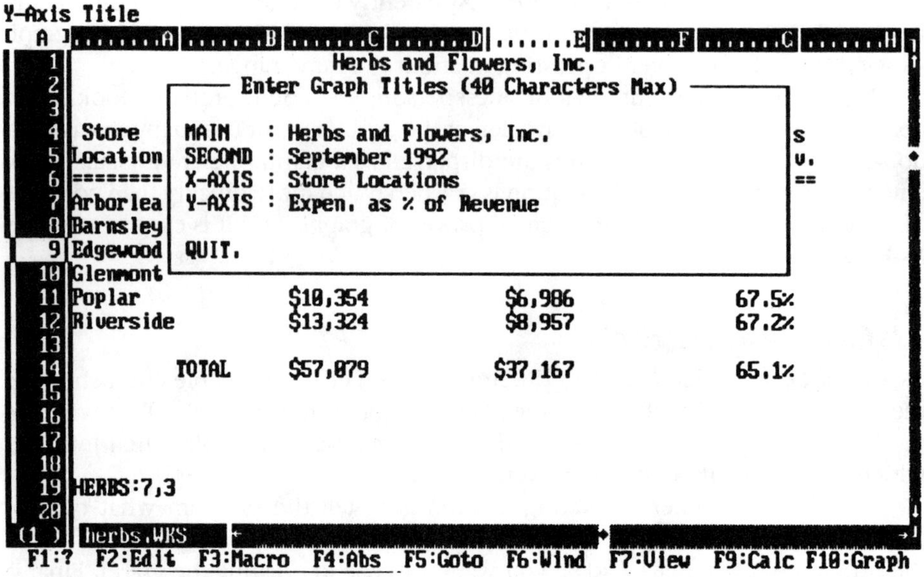

```
Y-Axis Title
[ A ].......A........B........C........D.......E........F........G........H ]
  1                        Herbs and Flowers, Inc.
  2              ┌── Enter Graph Titles (40 Characters Max) ──┐
  3              │                                            │
  4  Store       │ MAIN   : Herbs and Flowers, Inc.          │  s
  5  Location    │ SECOND : September 1992                   │  v.
  6  ========    │ X-AXIS : Store Locations                  │  ==
  7  Arborlea    │ Y-AXIS : Expen. as % of Revenue           │
  8  Barnsley    │                                            │
  9  Edgewood    │ QUIT.                                      │
 10  Glenmont    └────────────────────────────────────────────┘
 11  Poplar                $10,354          $6,986          67.5%
 12  Riverside             $13,324          $8,957          67.2%
 13
 14           TOTAL        $57,079          $37,167         65.1%
 15
 16
 17
 18
 19 HERBS:7,3
 20
(1 )   herbs.WKS
 F1:?  F2:Edit  F3:Macro  F4:Abs  F5:Goto  F6:Wind  F7:View  F9:Calc  F10:Graph
```

Fig. 11-6. Entering graph titles.

The Main title—Herbs and Flowers, Inc.—is okay. But let's change the secondary title to "Store Revenue—Sept. 1992." You can do this by hitting S to get into the Second title area and editing the text as if using a word processor. Hit Enter when you have finished. The X and Y axis titles no longer apply, so delete them in turn. (Hit X; delete the text; then hit Enter. Repeat with Y.) When finished, hit Q to quit. Hit Q again from the Graphics Options menu, and one more time to exit from the Graphics menu.

Now you're back at the sheet. Hit F10 to bring up the graph. Your screen should look like the screen in Fig. 11-7.

Previewing text and graphics

Spreadsheet graphics can be an engrossing and satisfying pursuit. There is no end to the kinds of graphs you can create or the various fill-in patterns, colors, and scaling techniques you can use. What you've seen so far is really just the briefest of introductions. There is much more one can do, given the need and the time.

The key thing is to learn the main techniques, as demonstrated with our pie chart above. Take your time experimenting with the various formats. Read the manual thoroughly. Then, when you have some real data, decide first whether it is

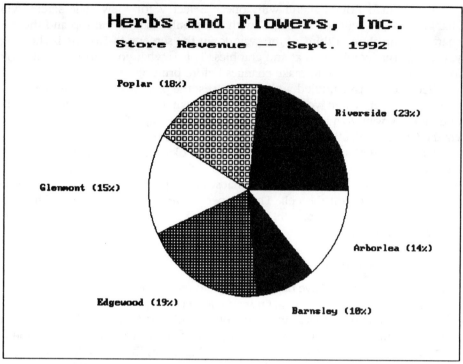

Fig. 11-7. Pie chart of store revenue.

worth graphing and second, what kind of graph will best display the information and relationships of interest.

We cannot leave the subject of As-Easy-As graphics without demonstrating one of the most powerful features of all—text and graphics previewing. This is something even some top-priced commercial spreadsheets have yet to offer. The feature lets you actually look at a page that mixes text and graphics before sending it to the printer. What you see really is what you get. It can save you tons of time, not to mention wasted paper, so it is well worth learning the technique.

A fresh start

Start by reloading HERBS.WKS. This will eliminate all the changes we made in creating the pie chart. When you are at the spreadsheet screen, hit F10. You should see a bar chart, not a pie chart. If you do not, copy HERBS.WKS from the disk that accompanies this book into C: \ ASEASY.

The first thing we are going to do is show you the results. Then we'll show you how they were achieved. As supplied, the HERBS.WKS worksheet is ready for you to preview. (That's what the line **MAIN:7,3** is all about in cell A19.) To do so, bring up the Main menu and select P for PrintTo. The PrintTo menu will then appear, with the cursor on Printer. Even though this does not seem like what you want to do, hit Enter to select that option.

The PrintTo Printer menu will appear. Select V for View. The screen will change, and you will see a "page" with the tabular data at the top and the bar chart, starting about a third of the way down the screen. As-Easy-As is showing you a page that combines text and graphics. This is what your printout will look like—unless you choose to make changes before printing.

Because we have fiddled with it ourselves, the page you see should be ready to go. However, when you are using your own tables and graphs, you will undoubtedly want to adjust margins and the positioning of things. You can do so via the Options selection on the PrintTo Printer menu.

Since the Herbs and Flowers report seems okay, hit your Esc key until you have returned to the sheet. As we discovered earlier, the Edgewood expense figure is off by $2000, due to a misreading of that store's report. So cursor over to E9 and hit your F2 key to edit the cell. The proper figure is 6999, not 8999. This will affect the graph, of course. (Hit F10 to check.) Now all store expenses will be within the normal range.

Order up the printout

The chart and the graph have been corrected to reflect the correct information. So let's do a printout. Call up the Main menu and enter P, P, V to preview the page with the new graph. At this point, you would think that you should simply select G for Go Print, but that option will only print the tabular data. The confusion is unfortunate, but there is a good reason for doing things this way. There must be a way to let users print just the tabular data without taking the time to print a graphic image.

So hit Esc to return to the PrintTo Printer menu. There you will see an option called Graphic. That's the one you want. As you move the cursor to Graphic, you will see the line at the top of the screen read "Print combined text and graphics." Selecting it brings up the PrintTo Graphic menu. Forget about the options for now and simply hit G for Go Print.

A window will appear at the top of the screen indicating the current status of the printout. Graphic or "plotted" images take a while to produce, even on a fast laser printer. Your printout will probably take two to three minutes on a laser printer. If you are using a dot-matrix machine, even more time will be required. When the printout is finished, you should have a page that looks like the one shown in Fig. 11-8.

Working the magic

Now that you have seen the end result, let's look at how we got there. I want you to start by deleting the area currently occupied by the MAIN graphic. The area occupied stretches from A19 down to A46 and across to H46. So move your cursor to A19 and select Range from the Main menu. Opt for Erase and move the cursor down to A46 and across to H46. Then hit Enter to erase this area. You will now have just the tabular data on the screen.

Let's assume that we now want to add a graph. Bring your cursor back to A19 and call up the Main menu. Enter G and N to go to the Graphics Name menu.

Store Location	Revenue	Expenses	Exp. as % of Rev.
Arborlea	$7,856	$5,004	63.7%
Barnsley	$5,698	$3,534	62.0%
Edgewood	$11,004	$6,999	63.6%
Glenmont	$8,843	$5,687	64.3%
Poplar	$10,354	$6,986	67.5%
Riverside	$13,324	$8,957	67.2%
TOTAL	$57,079	$37,167	65.1%

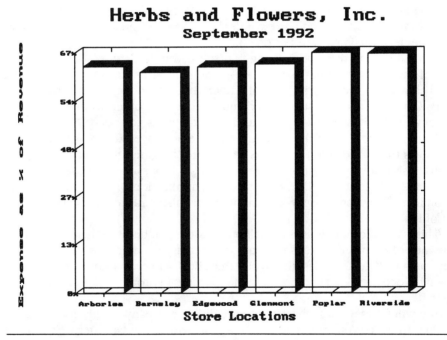

Fig. 11-8. Herbs and Flowers, Inc., report.

Select **I** for Insert, and a window will pop up at the top of the screen asking for the name of the graph you want to insert. If you hit Esc as prompted, you will find that there is only one, MAIN. Hit Enter when the cursor is on MAIN, and you will be taken back to the sheet, with a prompt reading "INSERT range is A19 . . A19."

Clearly we can't have a graph occupy only one cell. We've got to give it room to breath. Therefore, move your cursor across to column G, then down to G46. Hit Enter to lock everything in. The Graphics menu will appear, and you will be able to see that the area we have just marked off has changed color. Hit Esc to get back to the Main menu. Then select **P** for PrintTo.

Select **P** from the next menu, just as we did before. Then **V** for View from the following menu. Hit Esc to back out to the PrintTo menu, and select Graphic to actually print the combined text and graphic page.

Conclusion

By now you are probably tired of hearing that we have only scratched the surface of what a spreadsheet like As-Easy-As can do for you and your business. That happens to be the truth, but there is no reason to let it bother you. The best software in the world won't do you any good unless you feel or otherwise discover that you truly need it.

Personally, I believe that a spreadsheet's basic functions—the functions we've concentrated on here—can benefit any business, no matter how small. The game really *is* worth the candle, in other words. But that doesn't mean that you have to spend your entire life playing it. You don't have to do elaborate graphs and create complex models filled with wonderfully clever formulas—unless you have a genuine need or simply want to do so.

But I think you will risk cheating yourself if you don't at least look into the kinds of things a spreadsheet can do. Take the kind of minimalist approach that would earn you a professorial chair at Father Guido Sarducci's Five Minute University. Concentrate on what you need and forget all the other features. With this chapter and a copy of As-Easy-As, you have all the tools you need.

The one major spreadsheet feature we have not covered here is that feature that allows the program to be used as a software "engine" to drive other applications. Using advanced features, for example, it is possible to create a spreadsheet that looks and feels like a freestanding application program. In fact, the person using the program may have no idea that a spreadsheet package is at the root of it all.

This is significant to you as a small businessperson, because there are literally thousands of prepared spreadsheets out there that you can run with As-Easy-As. They contain all the formulas, the layout, the labels, and everything else you need. All you have to do is load them, respond to their menu prompts, and start entering data.

You will find several such sheets on the disk accompanying this book, including one to help you compare the cost of whole life and term insurance (INSURE.WKS) and one to help you decide whether to lease or purchase an automobile (LEASE.WKS). Many, many more are available through shareware and public domain channels. (According to David Schulz, 95 percent of the sheets designed to work with Lotus 1-2-3 will also work with As-Easy-As.)

You can even search for them via an online system and enter a command to have them transmitted directly to your machine. Literally, within minutes of thinking, "I wonder if there's a spreadsheet that will do thus-and-so," you can be sitting at your machine loading exactly such a program into As-Easy-As. That's the kind of exciting capability we'll look at in the next chapter, as we introduce you to the incredible world of online computer communications.

12

Communications

THERE IS NO COMPUTER APPLICATION LIKELY TO HAVE AS PROFOUND AN IMPACT on your life as online communications. When you plug your computer into a telephone line, an entire electronic universe suddenly materializes before your eyes, a universe that you probably never suspected was there. As you step into this universe, you will find that it is bristling with activity, full of fascinating people, and overflowing with possibilities you will never encounter any other way.

Now, with that kind of a buildup, you'd think that communications would be at the top of my list of the key applications everyone should learn first. But it's not. In fact, it is near the bottom.

The problem is that the online world isn't really ready for prime time. *Getting* online isn't all that difficult. (If you can follow the cookbook instructions presented later in this chapter, you shouldn't have any trouble.) But once you make a connection, you run into a welter of obscure commands—a different set for each online system—and highly technical procedures that are as idiosyncratic as they are essential.

This is not a place for a new computer user who has just learned to format floppies or move around a hard disk. If you are a small business owner who has only recently purchased a computer, I strongly advise you to spend your time learning DOS and learning to use your word processing, database management, and spreadsheet software. Though each is different, these knowledge areas are more or less connected. They are all of a piece.

Communications is an entirely different ball game, calling for an entirely different quantum of knowledge and skills. Unless you really need something the online world offers, you can afford to wait until you are more comfortable using your computer before starting up the online learning curve.

That's the real reason I urge new computer users to wait before trying to go online. I know the wonders that are waiting for you at the top of that curve. But I also know that if you start climbing before you are ready, you will get confused, become discouraged, and give up. You might decide never to go online again. And that would be a genuine pity.

The key thing at this point is to have some idea of what a modem and communications software can do for you when you *are* ready. That's what will be covered first. We will survey the electronic universe and alert you to the many possibilities it holds. If you are a brand-new user, that's about as far as you should take things for the time being.

Later, when you've had enough experience to become comfortable using your machine, return to this chapter and begin reading the technical section that follows the general survey. That section presents the basic knowledge everyone needs to understand the online world and the communications process. It is followed with a tutorial section that will show you how to use ProComm, a program I believe to be the best computer communications program ever written.

Surveying the electronic universe

If you're new to personal computing, it may come as a surprise to you to learn that all computers can talk to each other. Macintoshes, IBMs, clones, Amigas, and any other computer you would care to name can exchange information via computer communications.

What kind of information? Text files, mostly—although the development of certain standard file formats has made it possible to exchange graphics files as well. I can sign on to a system like GEnie or CompuServe, for example, and issue a command that will cause it to send me a text or graphics file that was created by a Macintosh user. I can display that file on my screen, edit it, print it out, and treat it just as if it had been created at my own keyboard. Any IBM-compatible or Mac user can do the same thing.

The reason this kind of interchange is possible is that all computers follow certain international standards when it comes to communications. They all use the ASCII code set to handle text, and most use a serial port that conforms to Recommended Standard 232 (RS-232). Of course there are variations. But at the most basic level, if a computer is equipped with a serial port and you've got the right kind of cable, you can connect your machine to it and exchange data, even if the machines are totally different internally.

The same thing applies to modems. Modems are needed to transform a computer's internal voltage-level-based signalling system into sound suitable for the phone lines, and vice versa. An external modem is a self-contained ''black box'' that can be cabled to any computer equipped with a serial (RS-232) port. Internal modems are machine-specific because they must be inserted into the computer's bus.

Don't worry if you do not yet understand these terms. All you need to know right now is that computers can communicate because they all follow the same set of internationally adopted standards.

For more information . . .

The goal of this tour is to give you a quick idea of what you can expect when you go online. It is thus rather like a travel brochure that gives you a few pictures and a few sentences of description to help you decide if the location is a place you might like to visit. In other words, we are really going to skim along the surface. The information not covered could fill a book in itself. In fact, it could fill several books—and has.

If you would like more information about the areas we are about to discuss, you might want to consult one or more of the following titles. They are probably available at your local library, but they can also be ordered from your favorite bookstore or from Glossbrenner's Choice:

The Complete Handbook of Personal Computer Communications—3rd Edition by Alfred Glossbrenner [St. Martin's Press]. Offers detailed coverage of everything you can do with a modem—and how to do it.

How to Look It Up Online by Alfred Glossbrenner [St. Martin's Press]. Designed for users interested in learning how to retrieve industrial-strength information from systems like DIALOG, BRS, ORBIT, NEXIS, etc. Intended as a companion to "The Complete Handbook"—for those who want to learn how to search and what to expect from major-league information systems.

The Information Broker's Handbook by Sue Rugge and Alfred Glossbrenner [Windcrest/McGraw-Hill]. Although it is aimed at people who want to become information brokers (professional information locators), the book may well alert you to resources and powers you never knew were at your disposal. For many people, it makes much more sense to hire an information broker than to learn online searching themselves.

The Master Guide to CompuServe by Alfred Glossbrenner [Brady Books/ Simon & Schuster]. How to make the most of this incredible system. Everybody subscribes to CompuServe. Includes detailed instructions for locating and downloading public domain and shareware software from CompuServe's forum libraries.

The Master Guide to GEnie by Alfred Glossbrenner [Osborne McGraw-Hill]. Produced by General Electric, GEnie began as a CompuServe clone but quickly established its own unique identity. It is among the most innovative of online systems, and, at $5 a month for unlimited non-prime-time usage, it is much cheaper. This book includes hands-on instructions for tapping the shareware libraries maintained by GEnie's many RoundTables.

What can you do "online?"

Machine-to-machine communication is the essence of the electronic universe. But it is the endless variations on this theme that make things so interesting. In 1982, for example, there were 600 databases (collections of computer-searchable information) offered by 93 online services. At this writing, there are over 4465 databases offered by nearly 650 online systems.

In addition, by some estimates, there are today more than 30,000 free computer bulletin board systems (BBS), each of which is a mini-online service consisting of someone's personal computer using special software and hardware that lets it automatically answer the phone and log callers onto the system.

There are information/communication utility services like CompuServe, GEnie, America Online, Delphi, and Prodigy. There are systems, like MCI Mail, that specialize in electronic mail, telex, TWX, and FAX systems. (Yes, you can send and receive faxes and cables with your computer using nothing but an ordinary modem.)

There are online shopping services; community information systems; telephone company "gateway" services; systems run by gigantic companies and systems offered by entrepreneurs. One commercial bulletin board (Exec-PC, discussed in Chapter 8) was started by a husband and wife team with a single phone line. At last count, the system had grown to 250 phone lines and untold gigabytes of storage.

RDP roots

Clearly, the field is alive with activity. That may be good for the general health of the online world, but the number and variety of activities taking place can make it difficult for a new user to get a handle on everything.

So let's first make clear exactly what we're dealing with. Today's online information industry evolved from the "remote data processing" (RDP) services that began in the 1960s as a low-cost alternative to buying or leasing a mainframe computer. In those pre-microchip years, few businesses could afford to have their own on-site mainframe. Yet they needed the power such machines could provide. RDP provided the answer. New companies sprang up with the sole purpose of acquiring and maintaining one or more large computers—and selling computer time to firms unable to afford machines of their own. The technique is called "time-sharing."

For a mainframe like those owned by CompuServe in Columbus, Ohio, to service a customer in Cleveland, some form of electronic communication obviously had to take place. Using a relatively inexpensive "terminal"—basically just a keyboard and a screen—the customer had to be able to send his payroll, billing, accounts payable, and other information to the mainframe for processing, and there had to be a way to get the computer's output back to him. This certainly wasn't the start of computer communications. But there can be no doubt that the needs of the RDP firms and their customers stimulated enormous growth and refinement in the techniques and technology of the field. The result was a delivery mechanism—a well-developed system of computers, specialized software, standards and protocols, electronic "packet switching" networks, and other components capable of reliably transmitting information from one computer to another.

Once the delivery mechanism was in place, it was only a matter of time before individuals and companies began to find ways to use it for something other than the transmission of the day's banking transactions to a remote mainframe computer. The only obstacle to further expansion was the cost of the equipment needed to use the delivery mechanism. The price simply prohibited widespread usage.

The development of affordable personal computers changed everything. The electronic information industry took off, and it has been tooling along adding features, systems, and services ever since.

Numbers games: A bit of perspective

But it has not been adding users, at least not in huge numbers. This is worth bringing up because it serves as an antidote to the hype about the online industry that has appeared in recent years.

Prodigy's expensive "You gotta get this thing" TV commercials notwithstanding, today—more than a decade after the personal computer revolution began—there are probably no more than about two million people who regularly use an online consumer-oriented service. I say "probably" because no one knows for sure how many users there really are.

Prodigy, for example, may report more than a million users. CompuServe, GEnie, and all the others may report figures in the high hundreds of thousands. But none of these figures should be taken at face value. And certainly, you shouldn't add them up and assume that the total represents the actual online population.

The problem is that a lot of people are counted multiple times since they have accounts on several systems. And each system has its own special way of calculating the number of its subscribers.

Prodigy, for example, multiplies each account by 1.8 or some similar figure on the assumption that everyone in the family is using the system on the same account number. (In the summer of 1991, when Prodigy trumpeted the fact that it had one million subscribers, it admitted that this represented only 600,000 households.) Other systems count everyone who has ever subscribed. Those who no longer use the service, even if they haven't signed on in years, are considered merely "inactive subscribers."

I am an unabashed online enthusiast, but it is important to put things into perspective. The December 1991 numbers collected by the highly respected Digital Information Group (DIG), the Stamford, Connecticut, firm that studies the information industry, can help us do just that. According to DIG, if you add everything up—all the subscriber figures reported by the consumer-oriented systems, the business and financial systems like Dow Jones News/Retrieval, the hard-core research services like LEXIS/NEXIS and DIALOG, plus all the newswires, credit reporting services, and airline reservation systems—the total is 5.2 million subscriptions.

Since we know that the number is grossly inflated due to the reporting policies of the online companies and due to existence of people like me with accounts on multiple systems, we can confidently reduce it by half to around 2.6 million. The real total is probably considerably less, but we'll give the industry the benefit of the doubt.

The point is that even if there really are 2.6 million individual online users, that number represents only a small fraction of the *100* million or more computers in existence, each of which, as you now know, has the ability to take their users online, if their users really wanted to go. I have no hard data to back this up, but I have a strong suspicion that there are an awful lot of modems gathering dust in people's closets.

Staying away in droves

The question is why? The technicalities and apparent complexities of getting connected can be overcome. In fact, I think you'll find that this chapter will help you solve most of those problems. And one can deal with the inconsistencies across various online systems, provided the prize is worth the struggle. Even the outrageous fees some online systems charge might be acceptable if what they delivered was guaranteed to be current and complete, and if you didn't have to have a masters degree in library science to get it.

The real reason online subscribership hasn't grown by leaps and bounds is that most people really have no idea what "online" (the adjective is rapidly becoming a noun) can do for them. The world undoubtedly felt the same way about radio, television, and even the typewriter when it was introduced: "The quill pen was good enough for granddad, and it's good enough for me!"

I don't think there is any question but that in the future, everyone will be online in one way or another, though they will probably use a television set instead of a computer. In the meantime, it's a bit wild and woolly out there, and it requires something of a pioneering spirit to take full advantage of all that "online" offers. Personally, I think the game is well worth the candle. But you be the judge as we take a whirlwind survey of the electronic universe.

A five-part matrix

This completes the "due diligence" part of this chapter. You have had fair warning that any media hype about the online world should be taken with a teaspoon of salt, and that getting the most out of an online system isn't always as easy as its advertising agency would have you believe. Now let's have some fun. Let's look at the many benefits the online world has to offer any small business owner willing to become an electronic pioneer. (Addresses and contact information for all online systems cited here are provided at the end of this section.)

The best way to get a handle on the many options at your disposal is to realize that everything in the online world falls into one of five categories: communication, information, services, special interest groups, and bulletin board systems. Of these, information and communication are the two major categories. Bulletin boards, services, and special interest groups or "SIGs" are really just combinations of the other two, as we'll see later. For now, though, if you keep this five-part matrix in mind, you'll have a much easier time figuring out where everything fits.

Communications services

As a small business owner, you are likely to benefit most from the various communications services that are available to you in the electronic universe. These include electronic mail, fax, and telex/TWX connections. No special equipment is required. All you need is a serial port, a modem, a communications ("comm") program, and a subscription to one or more online services. With these simple components, you can send a message to anyone, anywhere in the world.

"E-mail" communications

Think about this for just a minute. I said "anyone, anywhere," and I meant it. Imagine: Your son's an exchange student in Germany, and you want to send him a letter. You go online by dialing a local number, transmit the message to his mailbox on an online system, hang up, and go to bed. Hours later, your son awakens and, before he's had breakfast, he fires up his computer. He, too, dials a local number that connects him with the same online system.

As soon as he keys in his account number and password, the system responds "You have e-mail waiting." He enters a simple command and in seconds is reading the letter you sent only hours ago. The total cost? Less than $2, depending on the length of the message. The point here is that you could just as easily be corresponding with a business associate in Germany as well, provided you both used the same online system.

Or you could be corresponding with associates in the U.S. who are in a different time zone. There is no need to put up with "telephone tag" when you have electronic mail. Just transmit (upload) your message to your correspondent's mailbox when it is convenient to do so. Your correspondent will sign on and download it into his system when it is convenient for *him* to do so.

As long as both parties regularly check their e-mail mailboxes, this procedure can work like a charm. It is far faster and far cheaper than any overnight delivery service, and it lets you communicate information that cannot be easily conveyed on the phone (like the current version of your price list, bid specs, engineering data, etc.).

E-mail also facilitates joint projects. You can send your draft of a proposal to an associate. She can download it, make changes, and upload her version to your mailbox. And so on. Within hours you can have a final draft hammered out, even if the two of you are on opposite sides of the world.

And I'm not talking about just plain vanilla text, either. As long as both people use compatible word processing and graphics software, complete "desktop publishing" documents can be exchanged as well. In fact, using an inexpensive hand scanner, you can scan any image or article into your computer. It will be saved as a graphics file, and you can transmit that file to anyone with a modem or an e-mail account.

Facsimile communications

If your correspondent doesn't have a computer or does not subscribe to the same online system you use, you could opt to have your letter printed locally (in Europe, the Far East, or in the U.S.) and delivered by express mail the next day. This is more expensive than plain e-mail, but the stationery the letter is printed on could carry a black-and-white reproduction of your letterhead and your signature. And this approach would certainly be cheaper than using a conventional overnight delivery service.

More than likely your correspondents, whether abroad or stateside, will at least have a fax machine. There are a number of ways to communicate with fax machines via your computer as well. Often the easiest approach is to transmit your prepared text to an electronic mail system and simply specify the target fax machine's phone number as the "address." The online system will take care of the necessary conversion from ASCII text to the graphic images fax machines use. It will also dial the destination number repeatedly until it gets through.

Another method is to buy a "fax modem." Then you can load the fax software and send a file directly from your machine to the target fax. A fax modem or "fax board" cannot communicate with an online system. It is not a substitute for a real modem. But more and more standard modems are being manufactured with built-in fax modem capabilities. At this writing, for example, you can get a combination send/receive fax modem (9600 bps) and a 2400 bps regular modem on a single board for about $135.

And just why would you want to use a fax modem instead of a simple, easy-to-use, dedicated facsimile machine? The answer is in the quality of transmission and reception. Faxes that are sent directly from your computer do not have to be scanned in before transmission. As a result, they do not lose so much of their resolution, and they look much crisper on the receiving end.

Plain paper fax—Cheap!

Fax boards also give you what is, in effect, a "plain paper" fax machine. When your customers and associates send their faxes to your fax board, you can easily print them out using your computer's printer. You don't have to worry with curly, fade-prone fax paper rolls. Nor do you have to spend $1200 or more for a dedicated plain paper fax machine. For less than $140, you can add a fax board to your system that will give you all of these advantages.

In addition, once a fax file has been stored to disk, you can use your fax board to send it to someone else. You can use your fax software to "broadcast" this or any other message to a list of people at some pre-set time, if you choose. In other words, a fax board or fax modem and accompanying software can give you nearly everything that an expensive plain paper fax machine can offer—at a fraction of the price.

The one major drawback to computer-based faxing is that there is no scanner in the loop. If you can create it on your computer, you can fax it anywhere. But you cannot send newspaper articles and other pre-existing printed matter. The solution is to add a scanner. For about $160 you can get a hand scanner capable of scanning in a swathe four inches wide. A full-page, "flatbed" scanner, in contrast, goes for $1200 or more.

For many small businesses, the most cost-effective, high-quality middle road may be to get a simple, basic fax machine and a fax board or fax modem. Use the fax machine to fax pre-existing printed material, and use the fax board for everything else.

Telex, TWX, and cablegrams

Electronic mail undoubtedly offers the fastest, most cost-effective means of communicating, particularly if you need to transmit more than a few pages or so. After all, when using an e-mail system, you normally dial a local number to connect with a "node" that then patches you through to the main system. The system doesn't have to charge you a great deal because "data" calls are tariffed differently than "voice" calls. A direct call to a distant fax machine, in contrast, costs the same as a voice call.

The main drawback to e-mail, however, is that both communicators must subscribe to the same system and both must check their mailboxes every day. Plans are afoot to interconnect all e-mail systems, but relatively little progress has been made in recent years.

In the meantime, after a traditional phone call, fax has clearly become the business communications medium of choice. But, while it may seem that fax is all-pervasive in the United States, this is not necessarily the case in the rest of the world. Many parts of the world still rely on the telex system. Telex is old and it's slow, but its advantage is that most businesses have a telex machine and, like a fax machine, telex messages are delivered automatically. No need to fire up the computer and go check your e-mail mailboxes.

It does seem inevitable that telex machines and the network that connects them—both of which date to the early 1930s—will one day be replaced by electronic mail and fax networks. In the meantime, telex remains the single most efficient way to reach 1.8 million people in the world. In the far reaches of civilization, it is often the only way.

The key point to remember is that you do not have to have a telex machine to send and receive telexes, TWXs, cablegrams, or any of the other messages produced by the old radio-telegram network. All you need is a subscription to a service like MCI Mail. MCI Mail will take care of translating your ASCII text message into the form required by the telex network, and it will send it to any telex machine in the world. It will also work in reverse, translating incoming telexes addressed to your MCI Mail mailbox into ASCII text.

MCI is not the only system to offer such services. EasyLink, the system created by Western Union and later sold to AT&T, can do so as well. You can even use a system like CompuServe, GEnie, or Delphi. But, in my opinion, MCI Mail offers the best, easiest-to-use package of electronic communications features.

Remote access and cellular modems

We cannot leave the communications section without also mentioning the possibility of remote access and the topic of cellular modems. The best way to explain remote access is to tell you about a friend of mine who used to live in Alaska. He frequently had business in the lower 48, and when he was on the road he always carried a portable computer.

His employees back in Anchorage had instructions to leave his main desktop system turned on and loaded with a particular program. Then, whenever he had a spare moment and a spare telephone connection, he would dial up his office computer from his portable. He would check it for any messages left by his associates or employees, issue instructions, answer questions, and generally manage the office from afar.

That is the essence of remote access. If you'd like to try it yourself, the shareware program to get is Maxihost, a bulletin board system specifically designed for small business owners and professionals who want to have this kind of access.

In the commercial world, you can go even further. Today, thanks to packages like Close-Up, Remote, pcAnywhere, and others, you can not only check in from the field, you can use a portable machine to actually *run* the desktop system. If you're meeting with a prospective customer who asks some question you cannot answer immediately, you might use remote access to call up your desktop system and run some data stored on your hard disk through your spreadsheet.

To both you and the customer, the screen of your portable would make it appear that the program and data were coming from your portable's disk drive. But what you are really seeing is the same screen that you would see if you both were sitting at your desktop system. The portable is serving only as a terminal.

If you want to access your desktop system or any online system from your car, you will need a cellular modem. For example, you might have just finished with a customer and be sitting in your car. You use your car phone to call the office for messages, one of which turns out to be from a hot prospect.

You hang up and go online with your cellular modem to contact your desktop system. You need to retrieve a file that will be crucial to your presentation. As the file is being transmitted, you drive to the prospect's office. The cellular modem, unlike a standard modem, isn't bothered by the numerous hand-offs that occur in your phone connection as you travel. You arrive at the prospect's office, with the crucial file safely recorded on your laptop computer's hard disk, ready to make the sale.

Information services

Communications options are the most exciting portion of the electronic universe. The most interesting are the information options. Earlier I noted that there are some 4465 online electronic databases. If you have read Chapter 10 of this book, you already know a good deal about how they are set up. All follow the essential "file, record, and field" format used by File Express and every other database program.

But what's in those files? That is the question. The answer is, quite simply, just about every piece of information you can imagine. By now, so much information is available online that you can literally pick any subject, any person, any company or institution—anything at all you want to know about—and within seconds the answer can be scrolling up your screen. And, as we said when looking at communications options, it does not matter where you are on the face of the earth when you key in your request.

The quantity and coverage is simply staggering, even to someone who has been writing about the field for years. The full text (sans pictures and illustrations) of scores of thousands of newspapers, magazines, scholarly journals, and newswire archives is available to you at the touch of a few keys. There are transcripts of selected radio and television programs, including the McNeil/Lehrer Newshour and the BBC World Service.

You can access the Library of Congress to learn the title of any book or all the books in the collection on a given topic. You can tap into Who's Who to find information about people. You can search the files of the U.S. Government Printing Office for free or low-cost publications on your topic of choice. You can look for patents, chemical formulas, engineering data, or every doctoral dissertation submitted at an accredited college since 1870. And ladies and gentlemen, this is only the *beginning*.

But there's a catch

With this kind of power so easily accessible, you would think there'd be waiting lists to get subscriptions to the major-league online services that offer these databases. But as we've said, that is simply not the case. Part of the problem is poor-to-non-existent marketing by the online services. But even those who do know about such systems find that there's a catch.

To whom much is given, much is expected. As many new online users discover, the information you want won't pop out of the computer of its own accord. You've got to go in and get it, and that takes a certain amount of knowledge, skill, and practice.

The amount of information available is so vast that it is difficult to see how it could be otherwise. But there is another major problem as well: cost. Every database available on a system—and a system like Knight-Ridder's DIALOG has nearly 800 of them—has its own price.

Prices range from about $35 an hour to $300 an hour or more. You are charged for the minutes you spend connected to a database ("connect time"), but that is only the beginning. You will also be charged on the basis of how much information you retrieve. There are other nickel-and-dime charges as well. And here's the kicker: Each online service has its own pricing policies and procedures. There is no uniformity at all across the industry.

This means that it is nearly impossible to predict the cost of using a system in advance. A given online search may end up costing $75, or it may cost $175, or more. And, you can easily spend that $175 and end up with nothing you can use. Add to this the fact that DIALOG, LEXIS/NEXIS, Maxwell Online (BRS and

ORBIT), Dow Jones/News Retrieval, and all the others require you to use their own unique search languages and commands, and you can see why the online information industry is going nowhere fast.

Your best information options

If you'd like to get your feet wet searching a major-league system, I recommend subscribing to DIALOG's Knowledge Index (KI). KI lets you search about 100 of DIALOG's databases after hours (after 6:00 PM, your local time). It offers both a menu-driven and a command-driven interface, and it costs only $24 an hour. That's very cheap by information industry standards. If you find that you have a knack for online searching, you may then want to subscribe to DIALOG itself, or any of the other large online systems.

For financial information, and access to the full-text of the *Wall Street Journal*, I recommend Dow Jones News/Retrieval. You will especially like the system's DowQuest feature that lets you key in simple English sentences to tell the database what you want. Dow Jones uses a special computer that employs massively parallel processing to make DowQuest possible. It really is a remarkable feature that must be seen to be believed.

Hire an information broker

The best way for most small business owners to take advantage of online information, however, is not to go online themselves. Your best course is to hire a professional searcher, known in the trade as an "information broker." I should point out that information brokers are far from limited to online searching. From their perspective, electronic databases are but one of many tools. But many brokers have roots in the library profession, and many are skilled online searchers who are well able to cope with the quirks of the information industry.

An information broker is like your attorney or your accountant. You tell the person what you need, and he or she works with you to clearly define a solution. You might need to know what your chief competitors are up to: Have they filed for any patents or new trademarks recently? What articles have their engineers been publishing in scholarly journals? Are they in good shape financially?

You might want to know if any studies have been done focusing on the potential market for some new product you're thinking about making or selling. Or you may simply want information for personal use, such as a list of all colleges with courses in biomechanics or an authoritative report on the best state to retire to.

Whatever you want to know, an information broker can either find it for you or find out if the information even exists. Believe me, unless you have a continual need for a particular kind of information, there is no point in learning to search an electronic database. An information broker can offer a much more cost-effective solution.

The online service sector

The third division of the electronic universe consists of services. Services are essentially a variation on the communications theme, since they allow you to send and receive information from the service provider, usually some kind of retail store.

The process is easy to understand: You sign on to a system, enter an "electronic mall," and look into various stores to see what they are offering. If you select a product from the menus that will appear, a text description appears. If you want to order the item, you enter a command, and the product will be charged to your credit card and shipped. Or, in the case of travel services, you can order a brochure or book a cruise or a flight.

It doesn't sound very exciting. And it isn't. Nor is it very practical or cost-effective. After all, most retail establishments, travel agencies, and the like will happily send you a color catalogue and let you order via a toll-free number. (If you do not know the 800 number, dial 800-555-1212, the free, toll-free directory line.) Prodigy, which to my mind is little more than a selling service, has tried to counter these objections by dressing up its screen displays with medium-quality color graphics. And in case you miss the point, Prodigy takes it upon itself to fill your screen with unsolicited advertising.

I've focused on shopping services here because they are clearly the most dominant. Several years ago, the industry felt that electronic banking and bill-paying was the wave of the future. Many banks set up programs and tried to interest personal computer users in them. At this writing, most of them have either folded or become moribund.

Online stock trading is a service that has met with more success, thanks to aggressive marketing by companies like Charles Schwab, Fidelity, and Quick & Reilly. But this area is not exactly tearing up the track either. Much the same might be said of online education and the opportunity to earn college credits by taking courses by computer.

In my opinion, the most useful offering in the online services area is Comp-U-Store. This is an online system that grew out of a discount shopping service. It is accessible directly or via systems like CompuServe. The feature Comp-U-Store offers that is so worthwhile is the opportunity to search for products on the basis of the features you want and the price you are willing to pay.

The system will then show you descriptions of most of the leading products that meet your criteria. You can buy any listed product by keying in a command online, or you can simply use the information to do your own shopping locally. I've used the service to buy a number of items over the years and have always been very satisfied with the results.

Naturally, you will find much more information on Comp-U-Store, online stock trading, online banking, and earning college credit online in the third edition of my *Complete Handbook of Personal Computer Communications.*

Special Interest Groups (SIGs)

Although as a businessperson, you will find online communications options most useful, as a computer user, you will benefit most from online Special Interest Groups. A SIG is essentially an online club dedicated to the free-wheeling exchange of information on a particular topic. SIGs are such a popular feature that every general-interest system offers them. On CompuServe, for example, they are called forums. On GEnie, they are known as RoundTables. And so on.

As you would expect, there are far more computer-related or software-related SIGs than anything else. It is not too much of an exaggeration to say that there is a SIG somewhere for every brand of computer and for every leading software program. Sometimes the program-specific SIGs are organized and run by the company that produces the product. They thus serve as a form of online customer support.

Usually, however, a SIG is overseen by an independent entrepreneur called a *sysop* (system operator) who receives a percentage of the connect time dollars you spend using his or her feature. It is important to note that there is no additional cost for using a SIG. The sysop's royalty comes out of the standard connect-time fee charged by the system.

SIG Topics and design

As noted, the topics covered by SIGs appear to be all but limitless. A list of many of the SIGs accessible via CompuServe is presented in Fig. 12-1. As you review it, you will find that there are SIGs devoted to topics as diverse as astronomy, wine, coin and stamp collecting, cooking, genealogy, ham radio, religion, and rock

---

Listed here are the topics addressed by most of the Special Interest Groups (``forums'') accessible on CompuServe. To generate a current list, sign on to CompuServe and key in GO INDEX. Opt to search for a topic of interest, then search for FORUMS when prompted for a search word. The list that then appears will include the ``GO'' command words needed to reach each forum.

AI EXPERT Forum	Commodore Applications Forum
Adobe Forum	Computer Consulting Forum
Aldus Customer Service Forum	Computer Training Forum
Aldus/Silicon Beach Forum	Consumer Elect. Forum
Amiga Arts Forum	Cooks Online Forum
Apple II Users Forum	Crafts Forum
Aquaria / Fish Forum	DATASTORM Forum
Art Gallery Forum	DBMS Magazine Forum
Ashton-Tate dBASE Forum	DEC PC Forum
Ask3Com Forum	DECPCI Forum
Astronomy Forum	DTP Vendors Forum
Autodesk AutoCAD Forum	Desktop Publishing Forum
Automobile Forum	Diabetes Forum
Aviation Forum (AVSIG)	Digital Research Forum
Bacchus Wine Forum	Disabilities Forum
Banyan Forum	Dr. Dobb's Forum
Borland International	Education Forum
Broadcast Pro Forum	Engineering Automation Forum
CADD/CAM/CAE Vendor Forum	Epson Forum
CB Forum	Financial Forums
CDROM Forum	Flight Simulator Forum
CIM Support Forum(FREE)	Florida Forum
Cancer Forum	Foreign Language Forum
Canon Support Forum	Forum Conference Schedule
Central Point Forum	Forum Help Area(FREE)
Chess Forum	Fox Software Forum
Coin/Stamp Collect. Forum	Game Forums and News
Comics/Animation Forum	Game Publisher's Forum

Fig. 12-1. SIGs on CompuServe.

Gamers Forum
Gardening Forum
Genealogy Forum
Graphics Corner Forum
HP Peripherals Forum
HP Systems Forum
HSX Adult Forum
HSX Open Forum
Hamnet Forum
Hardware Forums
Hayes Forum
Health & Fitness Forum
IBM Applications Forum
IBM Bulletin Board Forum
IBM Communications Forum
IBM Desktop Soft. Forum
IBM European Users Forum
IBM Hardware Forum
IBM New Users Forum
IBM OS/2 Forum
IBM Programming Forum
IBM Special Needs Forum
IBM Systems/Util. Forum
IBM Users Network
Int'l Entrepreneurs Forum
Investors Forum
Issues Forum
Javelin/EXPRESS Forum
Journalism Forum
LAN Technology Forum
Legal Forum
Literary Forum
Logitech Forum
MECA Software Forum
MIDI Vendor Forum
MIDI/Music Forum
MS Applications Forum
MS DOS 5.0 Forum
MS Operating Sys/Dev Forum
MS Windows Advanced Forum
MS Windows SDK Forum
Mac Applications Forum
Mac Entertainment Forum
Mac New Users Help Forum
MacUser
MacWEEK
Macintosh Forums
Macintosh System 7.0 Forum
Markt & Technik Deutschland
MaryMac Industries, Inc.(FREE)
Medsig Forum
Mensa Forum
Microsoft BASIC Forum
Microsoft Central Europe Forum
Microsoft Connection
Microsoft Excel Forum
Microsoft Languages Forum
Microsoft WIN32 Forum
Military Forum
Model Aviation Forum
Modem Games Forum
Motor Sports Forum
Multi-Player Games Forum
Multimedia Forum
Multimedia Vendor Forum
NAIC Invest. Ed. Forum

Nantucket Forum
NeXT Forum
New Age Forum
Novell Library Forum
Novell NetWare 2.X Forum
Novell NetWare 3.X Forum
Oracle Forum
Outdoor Forum
PC Contact Forum
PC MagNet
PC Magazine(Subscribe)(FREE)
PC Plus Online
PC Vendor A Forum
PC Vendor B Forum
PC Vendor C Forum
PC Vendor D Forum
PC Vendor E Forum
PC Week Extra!
PDP-11 Forum
PR and Marketing Forum
Packard Bell Forum
Palmtop Forum
Pets/Animal Forum
Photography Forum
Play-By-Mail Games Forum
Portable Prog. Forum
Practical Periph. Forum
Practice Forum(FREE)
Quick Picture Forum
Religion Forum
Revelation Tech Forum
Rocknet Forum
Role-Playing Games Forum
SYM/Norton Utility Forum
Safetynet Forum
Sailing Forum
Science Fiction Forum
Science/Math Ed. Forum
SCUBA Forum
ShowBiz Forum
Soviet Crisis Forum
Space/Astronomy Forum
Spinnaker Software Forum
Sports Forum
Students' Forum
TAPCIS Forum
TBS Network Earth Forum
Tandy Professional Forum
Telecom Issues Forum
Texas Instruments Forum
Texas Instruments News
The Intel Forum
Toshiba Forum
TrainNet Forum
Travel Forum
UK Computing Forum
UNIX Forum
VAX Forum
Ventura Software Forum
Windows New Users Forum
Wolfram Research Forum
WordPerfect Supp. Group A
WordStar Forum
Working-From-Home Forum
Zenith Data Systems Forum

music. Notice, too, the many forums devoted to subjects of interest to IBM and compatible users. These are the places to go to ask questions, pick up tips, and download shareware programs.

There are business-related forums as well. Notice the International Entrepreneurs Forum and the PR and Marketing Forum. The Working-from-Home Forum operated by Paul and Sarah Edwards is also worthy of special mention. Its name is unfortunate since the forum actually serves as the main meeting place on CompuServe for smallbusiness people of every kind, whether you work from home or not.

A similarly business-oriented RoundTable exists on GEnie. It is called HOSB (Home Office/Small Business RoundTable). Operated by Janet Attard, the HOSB RoundTable is a great place to exchange information about business equipment, taxes, health insurance, and all the many other concerns we small business owners have to deal with.

Regardless of what they are called, all online SIGs follow the same general design. You might think of a SIG as a clubhouse, for example. You enter through the front door and to your right is a message board with various club announcements and bulletins. A little further on there is a board on which you can post questions you would like any club member to answer. If you know the answer to a question on the message board, or if you have some insight to offer, you can post it next to the original question as well.

Down the hall there are doors to a number of rooms members can use for conferences. You can enter any of them at any time to see what people are talking about. Conversations take place in real time, with people "typing" to each other or to the group using a CB-like facility. Sometimes the club manager (sysop) arranges for special guests to appear in the large common room on the first floor. All members are invited to attend and to ask questions of the guest.

Upstairs there is the club library. Here you will find transcripts of outstanding guest appearances, text files containing advice or opinions on various club issues, and files that present outstanding series of messages exchanged via the message board. In the library of a SIG for teachers, you might find essays on the significance of standardized test scores. In a SIG on culinary arts, you may find recipes for everything from blackened red fish to creme caramel. In a SIG for music lovers, you may find member-written reviews of the latest Solti or Serkin compact disk collection.

The SIG library is also where you will find the club's collection of public domain and shareware software. Members are encouraged to add to the collection whenever they can. Indeed, some online systems let you upload files to SIG libraries free of connect time charges. All SIGs offer a search facility to make it easier to find what you want.

Bulletin Board Systems (BBSs)

Bulletin boards are the fifth and final part of our five-part matrix of the electronic universe. A BBS is really nothing more than someone's computer attached to a modem and left on running special BBS software. When you call a board, the modem automatically answers the phone and connects the call. What happens next depends upon the particular BBS package the board is running, but most of the time you will be asked for your first and last name and your city and state.

The board software will then check to see if you have been on before, and if so, whether you have any mail waiting. If you are a new user, you will be asked to enter a password of your choosing. Key whatever you like, but be sure to remember it. You may be asked to key in your password a second time for verification. Then you will be welcomed to the board and presented with a menu.

From this point on, what appears on your screen could be coming from CompuServe or GEnie. Superficially, at any rate, there is no way to tell that you are actually logged onto an old XT with a 20M hard disk drive instead of a multi-million dollar mainframe array.

Though the offerings on some bulletin boards are quite sophisticated and even commercial, the best analog for the majority of boards is probably a very special Special Interest Group. As on a CompuServe or GEnie SIG, you can search for and download files, post and reply to messages, and send and receive private mail. You can even page the sysop, and if he or she is available, engage in typing a conversation back and forth.

The worst and the best

Bulletin boards are wonderful, but they have at least three drawbacks. First, much of the time, you'll have to dial a long distance number to reach them. Second, the best boards tend to be busy most of the time, so you will have to dial and redial to get on them. Third, downloading a file from a poorly run board is a good way to pick up a virus.

I want to be very clear about this last point. If the sysop of the board you dial is responsible, the chances of infecting your system with a virus from a file you download are about the same as if you were using CompuServe or some other commercial system—all but non-existent. On most commercial systems, the sysops are required by contract to check each file that gets uploaded for viral infection before making it available to the public.

A responsible BBS sysop will adopt a similar policy. In the absence of such a policy, a malicious individual could upload an infected program, and it would immediately be available for some unsuspecting user to download. With a vigilant sysop, however, uploaded files do not become available for download until they have been checked.

All of this is the bad news about bulletin boards. The good news is that there are tons of them, so if one is busy, simply try another. As we'll see later in this chapter, ProComm makes this easy to do. You can hand the program a dialing queue and it will cycle through it until it gets an answer. If there is one particular board you want to reach, ProComm's "attack dialing" feature will keep trying the board however many times you specify.

You will also find that BBSs are even more diverse than the SIGs on commercial systems. Most boards are definitely "general interest," but a large percentage are devoted to specific topics. A BBS sysop can do anything he wants to. If he wants to devote his board to fly fishing, swinging sex, or entomology, that's his privilege. It's his computer, after all.

The place to start

The other advantage BBSs have is that most of them are free. Once you make your connection, you may be limited to a 30-minute or 60-minute session, but there will be no charge, other than whatever you may have to pay in long distance costs. It is for this reason that BBSs make the ideal place to begin your online career. You don't have to worry about making a mistake or running up a huge bill. You don't have to worry about subscription fees and online charges. You can simply boot up your computer and have a ball.

You can download lists containing hundreds of BBS numbers from online systems like CompuServe and GEnie. And with a little software magic we'll tell you about later, you can import those lists directly into a ProComm dialing directory, so you won't even have to type in the phone numbers. Scroll through the list until you find a board that sounds interesting, and hit your Enter key to dial.

After you've had some experience "working the boards," making the transition to a commercial system will be a piece of cake. As we said at the beginning of this section, most BBSs look and feel like major-league online systems.

If you decide that you really want to get involved in BBS-ing, you may want to consider a shareware program like Wildcat! when setting up your own board. Or you may want to subscribe to the leading magazine on the subject, Jack Rickard's *Boardwatch*.

The cost is $36 for a one-year subscription. Contact

Mr. Jack Rickard
Boardwatch Magazine
5970 S. Vivian St.
Littleton, CO 80127
(800) 933-6038 (subscriptions only)
(303) 973-6038 (voice)
(303) 973-4222 (BBS)
MCI Mail: 418-7112
CompuServe: 71177,2310

Systems cited in the survey

Listed next are the telephone contact numbers for all of the online systems cited in this whirlwind survey of the electronic universe. While you are practicing with bulletin boards and building your skills, I suggest that you contact each of them and request a free information packet.

Although only nine systems out of more than 600 are listed, there is no better, quicker way to get an up-to-the minute overview of the commercial online world than to contact these particular systems:

America Online
(formerly Quantum Computer Services, Inc.)
(703) 448-8700
(703) 883-1585

CompuServe, Inc.
(800) 848-8188
(614) 457-8600

DELPHI (General Videotex, Corp.)
(800) 544-4005
(617) 491-3393

DIALOG/Knowledge Index
(800) 334-2564
(415) 858-3792

Dow Jones News/Retrieval
(800) 522-3567
(609) 452-1511

GEnie (General Electric Information Services)
(800) 433-3683
(301) 340-4000

LEXIS/NEXIS
(800) 227-4908
(513) 859-5398

MCI Communications Corp.
(800) 333-1000
(800) 333-4000 (Wash., D.C.)
(202) 872-1600

Prodigy Information Services
(800) 776-3449
(914) 993-8848

Part Two—Getting technical

If you are a brand-new computer user, this is probably where you should stop reading for now. Save the following material and the rest of this chapter for another time, a time when you are really ready to go online. You do not need to know or worry with the information that follows until that time arrives.

Bits, bytes, and the process

Regardless of what you plan to do once you get there, regardless of the kind of system you plan to call, the fundamental goal of going online is always the same: You want to establish a connection that will transport the characters and commands you type at your keyboard to a distant computer—and transport that computer's responses back to your screen. A variety of systems and components are needed to achieve this goal.

As you know from the first part of this book, when you strike a key on your keyboard, you send a signal into your system. The signal takes the form of a pattern of voltage pulses. Each pulse symbolizes either a 1 or a 0. The computer is designed to translate these patterns of 1s and 0s (bytes) into meaningful actions and information.

The computers you talk to when you go online operate the same way—internally. The problem is to get your pulse patterns into the distant machine, so it can translate them into action and information. If the computer you wanted to talk to were in the same room, you could simply cable the two machines together using a "null modem" cable. This is a special cable that is wired to fool both systems into thinking that they are talking to a modem.

You might well do this if you had a laptop and a desktop system with incompatible floppy disk formats. Or if you had a truly huge amount of information stored on your laptop's hard disk that you needed to transfer to your desktop system. You can get the necessary cable at any store selling computer equipment for about $10. Connect the systems and load ProComm or some other package on each one, and you're in business.

Serial ports and modems

But how do you accomplish the same thing with a system located in Rockville, Maryland, or Columbus, Ohio, or Paris, France? You have to use the telephone. This requires two steps at the physical level, neither of which you need worry about.

First, the parallel pulse pattern your system uses to communicate internally must be re-oriented so that the pulses travel one-at-a-time in serial fashion instead of eight abreast. This is necessary because the phone system typically offers only two wires for data (one for incoming and one for outgoing). This transformation is accomplished by the serial port in your machine.

Second, the voltage pulses inside your computer must be converted to a form suitable for transmission over the phone line. Broadly speaking, they must be converted into sound. That's what a modem or a "modulator/demodulator" does. Thus, to prepare your hardware to go online, you must cable your serial port to your modem, plug the modem into the phone line, and turn your modem on. If your modem did not come with a cable, ask your local computer store to sell you one. The cost will be around $10.

Modem considerations

I started life online with an acoustic coupler. This is a simple modem device consisting of two microphone-equipped cups designed to be placed over the mouth- and ear-pieces of a telephone handset. Today, in contrast, modems have evolved into little computers in their own right. In the process, they have come down with a case of "feature-itis" that would do a maker of microwave ovens or VCRs proud. Even the simplest modems today are packed with features that you will rarely, if ever, use.

Leaving all the features aside, however, there are a number of ways to make sense of modems. First is the matter of "form factor." Your modem can be an internal unit that plugs into your computer bus via an expansion slot. Or it can be a freestanding black box of some sort. Personally, I prefer the freestanding variety, since they often have lights that let me know what's going on. But I know that many users like the simplicity of internal models.

With an internal modem, you need only plug the phone line into the port it offers at the back of your computer, and you're ready to communicate. You don't need any cables or spare electrical outlets. On the other hand, if the modem fails, you must open up your computer to remove it for repair. And it does take up a slot.

In my opinion, if you have a choice, you should opt for the external model. But if an internal modem is included as part of the computer package you buy, fine. Unless you're going to be doing some really serious communicating, the modem's form factor is largely a matter of personal preference.

The other major dividing line among modems is speed. Modem speed is measured in bits per second or "bps." This is sometimes incorrectly referred to as "baud rate." The standard level speed today is 2400 bps. Indeed, 2400 bps modems are so cheap they are almost commodities. Do not under any circumstances settle for anything less than 2400 bps, and don't pay more than $100, if that. A 2400 bps modem can talk to any slower speed modem (1200 bps or 300 bps in most cases).

The next step up the speed ladder is 9600 bps. Modems of this caliber currently sell for about $480, less than half of the price charged only a couple of years ago. I have a U.S. Robotics HST Dual Standard modem that I absolutely adore. It operates at a nominal top speed of 9600 bps, but with built-in data compression, when talking to a compatible remote modem, it can deliver an effective throughput of a screaming 38,400 bits per second or 38.4 kilobits per second (Kbps). If it cannot make that optimal connection, it falls back to a mere 14.4 Kbps. Failing that, it tries for 9600 bps, and so on down the scale until a match is finally made.

The problem is, it's expensive, and there really aren't that many online systems that offer even 9600 bps connections. Many BBS sysops have installed 9600 bps or faster modems, and CompuServe and GEnie offer a limited number of 9600 bps connections. But that's about it in the general interest area at this writing.

Consequently, unless you do a lot of downloading or have an associate with whom you regularly exchange large files via modem, I cannot at this point recommend a 9600 bps modem to any new computer user. Over the years, I have watched 300 bps equipment be replaced by 1200 bps gear. And I've seen 2400 bps emerge as the new standard. It certainly seems as though the same thing is happening with 9600. But my advice is to wait until 9600 really does become the standard, since by then there will be many more 9600 bps connections available and modem prices will have fallen still further.

Qualitatively, it is important to point out that online text is a challenge to read at 1200 bps, and difficult at 2400. At 9600 it is impossible. That's why many online users find a utility like FANSI Console (Chapter 16) indispensable—since it makes it easy to re-call information that has scrolled off the screen. ProComm offers a similar feature, built into the program.

There is one final point to make regarding modem hardware, and that is

"Hayes" or "AT command set" compatibility. The Hayes modem company started the trend toward "smart modems"—modems equipped with microprocessors, memory, and built-in programming. As such, Hayes modems set the standard.

Part of that standard is the way one addresses the modem to give it some command. All Hayes-compatible modems respond with "OK" when you send them a capital AT. (This stands for "Attention, modem.") If you follow the AT with something else, like DT, this says "Attention, modem. Dial, using Touch-Tones, the following digits." Today, nearly every modem on the market follows the Hayes command standard. Still, it wouldn't hurt to ask the salesperson from whom you are buying the equipment if the modem is Hayes- or AT command-compatible, just to make sure.

Vee Dot what?

As should be obvious by now, communications can only take place if both systems obey the same set of standards. It doesn't much matter what happens between the time you strike a key and the signal it generates is delivered to the phone lines via your modem. But once that signal enters the "net" or what science fiction writers like William Gibson call "cyberspace," it had better play by the rules.

This is no problem, as long as hardware makers know what the rules are. And, fortunately, an international body has been created under the auspices of the United Nations to tell them. In reality, the standards are defined, set, and agreed to by the industry itself, acting through various committees. But the U.N. stamp of approval makes everything official.

The U.N. body is the Consultative Committee on International Telephony and Telegraphy, or CCITT. The standards it issues almost always begin with an X or a V, and often they incorporate the French word *bis*, which means "again" or "the same, but slightly different."

This leads to one of the most confusing and technical areas of computer communications. Here, however, we will simply nod in its direction and, cookbook-style, tell you what you need to know. Before the break-up of AT&T, the phone company set the standards. The Bell 103 standard assured that all 300 bps modems used the same modulation technique and thus could be assured of talking to each other. The Bell 212-A standard did the same thing for 1200 bps communications.

For a variety of reasons, after the AT&T breakup, the standard-setting power moved to the CCITT, which is where it resides today. This was probably a good thing, since prior to the AT&T breakup, international communications were not the major factor they have since become. Here are the CCITT standards you are likely to find most important when buying a high-speed modem:

- V.22—1200 bps
- V.22bis—2400 bps
- V.32—9600 bps

- V.32bis—14.4 Kbps
- V.42—error correction
- V.42bis—data compression

At this writing, the emerging standard for 9600 bps communications is a modem with V.32 modulation, V.42 error correction, and V.42bis data compression. These are the modems that, at this writing, go for a street price of $500 or less.

The *next* generation of modems, however, is already appearing. These offer V.32bis for a nominal 14.4 Kbps rate, but when combined with V.42bis data compression, the effective rate is 38.4 Kbps. That, according to many hardware experts, is about as fast as the serial port in many PCs will ever be able to go.

To summarize, then, if you are going to buy a 9600 bps modem, look for a model that offers V.32, V.42, and V.42bis. Then compare it with a modem offering V.32bis, V.42, and V.42bis. If the V.32bis modem is priced close to the V.32 unit, buy it. The extra throughput is likely to be worth the extra money at this level of performance.

It would be wonderful if the terminology were not so complicated. It would be nice if there were just three standards: fast, faster, and fastest. But that simply is not the way things are. Before leaving the topic, we need to toss in one other standard: MNP, short for Microcom Networking Protocol. The MNP protocol is available in flavors one through ten. It consists of a set of standards for modem operations, including error control (MNP-4), data compression (MNP-5), line organization, and data-rate negotiation.

The MNP protocol pre-dates V.42 and V.42bis and offers some of the same features, though it uses different techniques to implement them. To confuse matters even further, the V.42 error correction standard incorporates MNP error correction, as well as the less popular Link Access Procedure for Modems (LAPM).

The chief advantage of buying a modem with the MNP protocol (usually MNP-5) built in is that you will be able to talk to modems that support only MNP but do not support the more recent CCITT "V" standards. Everything depends on how you plan to use the unit and with whom you plan to communicate. But, at this writing, MNP support appears to be one of those nice-to-have, but non-essential, modem features.

Packet-switching, protocols, and data capture

Believe it or not, you are rapidly closing in on the final pieces in the puzzle. There are just a few more points to cover before you are ready to load ProComm or some other comm package and actually go online.

The first piece is the notion of packet-switching networks or "public data networks" (PDNs). You do not need to know anything about the technology. All you need to know is that it is packet-switching that makes it possible for you to dial a local number and connect with a distant mainframe computer. The number you dial connects you with a "node" on a packet-switching network and that network makes it appear as though you have dialed the target or "host" system directly. Any costs involved are normally included in the connect time charges assessed while you are using the host system.

The two leading PDNs are SprintNet and British Telecom's Tymnet. But many systems have created their own networks. GEnie can be accessed only via the General Electric Information Systems (GEIS) network. CompuServe can be reached via Telenet or Tymnet, but a connection via the firm's own network is much, much cheaper.

The materials you receive when you subscribe to any online system will tell you which network connections are available. If you live in or near a major city, the necessary node will almost certainly be located in your local dialing area. If you live out in the country, however, you may have to place a long distance call to the nearest city.

The next thing you need to know about is the subject of downloading protocols. Again, the technical details are not important. All you really need to know is that if you want to have a remote system send you a computer program, you will need to use a file transfer protocol of some sort. There are lots of reasons for this, but the main reason is that all binary transfer protocols involve some form of error-checking to make sure that the file is perfectly transmitted.

The best protocol is ZMODEM. The lowest common denominator, however, is a protocol called XMODEM. Nearly all online systems of every sort support XMODEM. In between are certain proprietary protocols, like CompuServe's B and B+ protocols. Until you find yourself doing a lot of downloading, however, you can leave the matter of protocol preference to the heavy users. The main thing you have to worry about is that your communications software must offer a protocol supported by the system you want to download from. You may not achieve the fastest transfers, but as long as the protocols match, you will indeed get a perfect copy of the downloaded file.

Finally, we must say a word or two about data capture. This is one concept that is easy to explain and to understand. Whenever you want to record incoming information on your disk, you "open your capture buffer." This requires a command to your comm program, and it means that whatever comes in the modem line will be both displayed on the screen and recorded to disk. When you are finished capturing, you issue a command to close your capture buffer and close the file. Later, when you have disconnected from the system, you can view, edit, and print the capture buffer file with your word processor.

A capture buffer is particularly handy when you are picking up your electronic mail. With ProComm, you merely key in Alt-F1 and respond to the resulting prompt with a filename (MAIL.TXT). Then you tell the system to send you your mail. It appears on the screen as it is recorded to disk. When all the letters have been displayed, key in Alt-F1 again to close the file and turn off data capture.

A ProComm 2.4.3 tutorial

There has always been a close link between computer communications and shareware. In fact, the main thing Ward Christensen and Randy Suess had in mind when they created the first bulletin board system (way back on February 16, 1978) was file exchange. That's why Christensen wrote his famous XMODEM file transfer protocol and made it a part of his board (CBBS #1).

As a result of this close connection, it is not surprising that there are scores of public domain and shareware communications programs. Many of them are excellent. But the one I like best, and the one I recommend, is ProComm from Datastorm Technologies, Inc.

Not only is it clean, fast, and imaginatively written, ProComm is backed up by a company that has grown to become one of the leading software firms in the country. The commercial version of ProComm, introduced several years ago, is consistently ranked among the top ten best-selling programs.

The version of ProComm we will be focusing on here is known as version 2.4.3. This is a slightly updated version of the program that built the company. It is a full-powered program that offers so many features that you may never feel the need to go any further. Those features that it does not offer, such as support for the ZMODEM file transfer protocol, can be added using shareware utilities and tools that enthusiastic ProComm 2.4.3 users have created. The registration fee is $50.

The commercial version, ProComm Plus 2.x, is even better. Among other things, ZMODEM support is built in. The list price for ProComm Plus 2.01, the version current at this writing, is $119. But the current street price is about $65. So here's what I suggest you do. Get a copy of ProComm 2.4.3 from a disk vendor and try it out. If you decide that you have no need for communications, the most you'll be in for is about five bucks.

If you find you like communications, however, call a company like Micro-Warehouse [(800) 367-7080] or Programmer's Connection [(800) 336-1166] and order a copy of ProComm Plus 2.01 for about $65. (I happen to have catalogues from these companies near at hand, but I'm sure other companies offer a similar price—so check the magazines.)

Getting started with 2.4.3

In this part of the chapter, we're going to assume that you have a copy of ProComm 2.4.3. Our goal here is to get you up and online as quickly as possible. (We'll even tell you about a free phone number you can dial to test your system and get your feet wet.) Start by making sure that your modem is properly connected to both the phone line and to the computer. See the manuals that came with your system and modem for instructions.

Make a directory on Drive C called PROCOMM by keying in **CD** (to make sure you are at the root directory) and then keying in **MD PROCOMM**. Next, key in **CD\PROCOMM** to change down to that directory. Then copy or unarchive the 2.4.3 files into that directory. If you got your disk from Glossbrenner's Choice, log onto Drive A and key in **PC-Z C:\PROCOMM**.

Now log on to C: \ PROCOMM and key in **PROCOMM** to activate the program. You will see a greeting screen attesting to the shareware status of the program. Hit any key to get to the main ProComm screen. Your cursor will be in the top left corner, and there will be a status line running across the very bottom of the screen. Notice that the first entry on the status line tells you to enter Alt-F10 for Help. Do so now. You will see the screen shown in Fig. 12-2.

```
╔══════════════════════════════════════════════════════════════╗
║                     P r o C o m m   H e l p                   ║
╠══════════════════════════════════════════════════════════════╣
║                                                              ║
║     MAJOR FUNCTIONS        UTILITY FUNCTIONS      FILE FUNCTIONS ║
║                                                              ║
║  Dialing Directory . Alt-D  Program Info ...... Alt-I   Send files ...... PgUp  ║
║  Automatic Redial... Alt-R  Setup Screen ...... Alt-S   Receive files ... PgDn  ║
║  Keyboard Macros ... Alt-M  Kermit Server Cmd . Alt-K   Directory ...... Alt-F  ║
║  Line Settings ..... Alt-P  Change Directory .. Alt-B   View a File .... Alt-V  ║
║  Translate Table ... Alt-W  Clear Screen ...... Alt-C   Screen Dump .... Alt-G  ║
║  Editor ............ Alt-A  Toggle Duplex ..... Alt-E   Log Toggle .... Alt-F1  ║
║  Exit .............. Alt-X  Hang Up Phone ..... Alt-H   Log Hold ...... Alt-F2  ║
║  Host Mode ......... Alt-Q  Elapsed Time ...... Alt-T                           ║
║  Chat Mode ......... Alt-O  Print On/Off ...... Alt-L                           ║
║  DOS Gateway ...... Alt-F4  Set Colors ........ Alt-Z                           ║
║  Command Files .... Alt-F5  Auto Answer ....... Alt-Y                           ║
║  Redisplay ........ Alt-F6  Toggle CR-CR/LF .. Alt-F3                           ║
║                             Break Key ........ Alt-F7                           ║
║                                                              ║
╚══════════════════════════════════════════════════════════════╝
              DATASTORM TECHNOLOGIES, INC.
```

Fig. 12-2. ProComm's Help screen.

The setup process

As you can see, you have a lot of commands at your disposal. Don't worry about any of them now. I'll tell you which ones are really important in a moment. Right now, the key thing is to get the program set up correctly. So hit Alt-S to bring up the ProComm Setup screen. You will see the screen shown in Fig. 12-3.

Notice that you have seven options: 1 through 6 and S for saving your setup. Fortunately, you will not have to change many of ProComm's setup specifications. In fact, there are really only two setup options you should review at this point: the Terminal Setup and the General Setup. The only reason you might need to select the first option, Modem Setup, is if you are using a non-standard modem. If your modem operates at a top speed of 2400 bps and is Hayes-compatible, you can probably pass over Modem Setup.

Start, then, by selecting 2 for Terminal Setup. You will see a screen like the one shown in Fig. 12-4.

The only settings you may want to change here are the settings for flow control (3) and the setting for enquiry (11). Start by keying in 3 and hitting Enter. Notice that the bottom of the screen contains a single line of explanation. You can toggle a setting to one or another setting by pressing your spacebar. When the item is set correctly, hit Enter.

Flow control is a technique supported by virtually all online systems. At the most basic level, when one of the two computers needs more time during a text

```
|======================| SETUP MENU |======================|


                        1) MODEM SETUP

                        2) TERMINAL SETUP

                        3) KERMIT SETUP

                        4) GENERAL SETUP

                        5) HOST MODE SETUP

                        6) ASCII TRANSFER SETUP

                        S) SAVE SETUP TO DISK



OPTION ➡                                          ESC▸ Exit
```

Fig. 12-3. The Setup menu.

```
|======================| TERMINAL SETUP |======================|

  1) Terminal emulation ... ANSI-BBS      18) Break Length (ms) .... 350

  2) Duplex .............., FULL          11) Enquiry (CTRL-E) ..... CIS B

  3) Flow control ........ XON/XOFF

  4) CR translation (in) .. CR

  5) CR translation (out) . CR

  6) BS translation ....... DEST

  7) BS key definition .... BS

  8) Line wrap ........... OFF

  9) Scroll .............. ON


OPTION ➡                                              ESC▸ Exit
```

Fig. 12-4. The ProComm Terminal Setup screen.

transfer, it sends an X-OFF signal to tell the other machine to hold up. It then takes care of whatever business was pending, like writing information to disk, and sends an X-ON signal to tell the other system to resume. The letter X in communications is short for "transfer," as in "X-fer."

You don't have to enable this setting, but I think it's a good idea. Your own system may be fast enough to keep up with incoming text, but even today, you can never know when the system you are talking to may need more time. If you do not enable this setting, the X-OFF signal sent by the other system will be ignored by ProComm, and the program will keep sending, even when the other system is not able to receive.

The Enquiry setting really applies only if you are a subscriber to Compu-Serve. Three settings are available: On, Off, and CIS B. ("CIS" is an abbreviation of CompuServe Information Service, the official name of that system.) Setting this entry to CIS B will make it easier to do downloads from CompuServe. If you are not a CIS subscriber, leave it OFF.

The general setup

Hit Esc to return to the screen shown in Fig. 12-3. You can safely skip all but item 4, General Setup, for the time being. Enter 4 now and you will see a screen like the one shown in Fig. 12-5. You can really leave everything set to its defaults. But there are two changes you may want to make.

```
━━━━━━━━━━━━━━━━━━━━┤ GENERAL  SETUP ┝━━━━━━━━━━━━━━━━━━━━

     1) Editor name .......... c:\pcw\ed
     2) Default d/l path ..... c:\procomm

     3) Default log file ..... PROCOMM.LOG      12) Xlat pause character . ~
     4) Screen dump file ..... PROCOMM.IMG      13) Xlat CR character .... !
                                                14) Xlat CTRL character .. ^
     5) Screen write method .. DIRECT           15) Xlat ESC character ... |
     6) Translate table ...... OFF
                                                16) Aborted downloads .... KEEP
     7) Sound effects ........ ON
     8) Alarm sound .......... ON               17) Transmit pacing (ms) . 25
     9) Alarm time (secs) .... 5
    10) Exploding windows .... YES

    11) XMODEM mode .......... NORMAL

━━━━━━━━━━━━━━━━━━━━━━━━━━━━━━━━━━━━━━━━━━━━━━━━━━━━━━━━━━
OPTION →                                              ESC Exit
```

Fig. 12-5. The ProComm General Setup screen.

Notice that the first line is "Editor name." We have changed this setting from its blank default to C:\PCW\ED to direct ProComm to PC-Write. Should you be online and wish to create a document, you can enter Alt-A to summon whatever word processing program or text editor you specify here. Second, notice that we have set the "Default d/l path" (default download path) to C:\PROCOMM. This means that the program will place any files it downloads into that subdirectory. As it happens, if you do not specify anything here, ProComm will save downloaded files in its own directory. But you may wish to specify a directory like C: \ TEMP or D: \ DNLOAD or something else.

The on-disk ProComm manual will explain the significance of the other settings. The only other thing you may wish to change here are sound effects (on or off) and exploding windows (yes or no). We'll leave this choice to you.

Hit Esc to return once again to the screen shown in Fig. 12-3. Then enter **S** to save your settings. The program will flash a line on the screen reading "Parm files updated." The word "parm" is computer talk for "parameters." Hit Esc to exit, and you will be returned to the main terminal screen.

Changing your line settings

By default, ProComm 2.4.3 comes set up to talk at 1200 bps. If you have a 2400 bps modem, however, you will want to change that. So key in Alt-P to bring up the Line Settings menu shown in Fig. 12-6.

```
                 LINE SETTINGS

     CURRENT SETTINGS:   2400,E,7,1,COM1

     1)    300,E,7,1     7)     300,N,8,1
     2)   1200,E,7,1     8)    1200,N,8,1
     3)   2400,E,7,1     9)    2400,N,8,1
     4)   4800,E,7,1    10)    4800,N,8,1
     5)   9600,E,7,1    11)    9600,N,8,1
     6)  19200,E,7,1    12)   19200,N,8,1

     Parity         Data Bits      Stop Bits
     13) ODD        16) 7 bits     18) 1 bit
     14) MARK       17) 8 bits     19) 2 bits
     15) SPACE

     20) COM1  21) COM2  22) COM3  23) COM4

     24) Save changes          YOUR CHOICE:
         | Press ESC to return |
                   LINE SETTINGS
```

Fig. 12-6. ProComm line settings.

If you think this looks like a lot of computer gobbledy-gook, you are absolutely correct. Fortunately, there are only two things you have to know. First, in order for communications to take place, both systems must be using the same settings. Second, only two settings really matter today. These are 7/E/1 and 8/N/1. Translated, this means seven data bits, even parity, and one stop bit; or eight data bits, no parity, and one stop bit. Virtually every online system on earth supports one of these two settings, and these days, most support both.

My advice is to set your system to 2400 bps and 7/E/1. That's setting number 3 on the Line Settings menu. This will keep "garbage" characters from appearing on your screen when you sign on. And, should a setting of 8/N/1 be necessary, as is the case when downloading a file with XMODEM or some other protocol, Pro-Comm and most remote systems will switch to it automatically. They will then switch back when the download is complete. In reality, either setting will do just fine on most systems. So feel free to select 9 for "2400, N, 8, 1."

The one setting to pay particular attention to here is the setting for your COM port. In almost every case, your modem will be connected to COM1. However, since the PC can support up to four COM (serial) ports, and since some mice are connected to COM1, you may have to come back here to change to COM2 if you find that your modem does not seem to be responding. It isn't very likely that you will need—or even be equipped for—COM3 or COM4.

Is everything "OK?"

Enter your Line Settings and hit Esc. You will be returned to the main terminal screen. Now let's test your work. Let's see if your commands are getting to the modem, and if its responses are coming back. Key in **AT** (use all capital letters) and hit Enter. If everything is working properly, you should see the letters "OK" on your screen. This comes from your Hayes-compatible modem.

If you do not see "OK," check your modem cable connections. Is everything properly plugged in? Is the modem turned on? If you have checked these points and still have no joy, return to the Line Settings screen (Alt-P) and switch to a different COM port (COM2). Then repeat the test. This *should* work.

As a final test, exit the program with Alt-X. Then key in **PROCOMM** again to go back into the program and re-initialize the COM port and the modem. If you have checked everything and you still don't get "OK" in response to your "AT," call your computer dealer or vendor for help.

The ProComm dialing directory

There are at least three ways to tell ProComm to instruct your modem to dial the phone. You can prepare a script file using the script file language that is explained in the documentation. You can key in **ATDT** followed by the phone number you wish to dial when at the main terminal screen. Or you can record a number in the program's "phone book" dialing directory and simply pick it off a menu.

To get to the ProComm dialing directory, key in Alt-D. You will then see a screen similar to the one shown in Fig. 12-7. We have added several numbers here to show you how things work. Your own dialing directory will be empty. To add a number, move the highlight bar down to the entry you want to use and hit **R** for "revise." You will then be prompted for the information you see displayed in the entries shown in Fig. 12-7.

Notice that you can enter a name; the target telephone number (including 1 and the area code); and settings for baud (bps) rate, parity, data bits, and stop bits. You can also set the "echo" on or off (Leave it off). The last column is headed "CMD Files." This stands for "command files," ProComm 2.4.3's name for a script file. Several script files are usually supplied with the 2.4.3 distribution disk. All you have to do is edit them to insert your own account numbers and

```
            D I A L I N G     D I R E C T O R Y

              Name              Number        Baud P D S  E    CMD File
  1- Darwin Systems BBS      1-301-251-9206   2400-N-8-1  N
  2- TRIUS As-Easy-As BBS    1-508-794-0762   2400-N-8-1  N
  3- Expressware BBS         1-206-788-4008   2400-E-7-1  N
  4- Extended Batch Language 1-407-738-1843   2400-E-7-1  N
  5- ....................    . ... ...-....   1200-N-8-1  N
  6- ....................    . ... ...-....   1200-N-8-1  N
  7- ....................    . ... ...-....   1200-N-8-1  N
  8- ....................    . ... ...-....   1200-N-8-1  N
  9- ....................    . ... ...-....   1200-N-8-1  N
 10- ....................    . ... ...-....   1200-N-8-1  N

 ==>          R Revise        M Manual Dialing      Entry to Dial
              P LD Codes      D Delete Entry        F Find
              PgUp/PgDn Page  L Print Entries       ↑/↓ Scroll
              Home Top Page   End Bottom Page       ESC Exit

 Modem Dial Cmd: ATDT                  LD Codes Active:
 Dial Cmd Suffix: !                    Com Port Active: COM1
                          AUTO DIALER
```

Fig. 12-7. The ProComm dialing directory.

passwords. You can then use them to automatically log on to the system of your choice. However, since you will not have any operative script files at this point, none should be attached to any numbers you enter.

The most important ProComm commands

Look again at the Help screen shown in Fig. 12-2, or key in Alt-F10 if you are sitting in front of the screen with ProComm loaded. The most important commands to know—the ones you will use in almost every online session—are as follows:

- Alt-D to bring up your dialing directory.
- Alt-X to exit the program.
- Alt-F4 to shell out to DOS. This is handy if you need to do a DIR, or if you need to delete or examine a file. To return to ProComm, key in **EXIT**.
- Alt-F6 to re-display text that has scrolled off the screen. Personally, I use FANSI Console (Chapter 16) to handle this function. But one way or another, being able to re-call previously displayed text is an essential feature when you are online.
- Alt-F7 to issue a BREAK signal that stops a remote system from continuing with something you want to get out of. If this does not work, send the system a Ctrl-C (Control-C).
- PgUp and PgDn. When you hit your PgUp key, you will be prompted to select a transfer protocol. If you are sending a text file, select ASCII. Otherwise, select the protocol the remote system supports. (XMODEM is the

least common denominator.) When you want to download a file, you will see the same protocol-related prompts. And you may be asked to enter the filename you want ProComm to use when storing the file to disk.

- Alt-F1 is probably the most important command of all. When you hit Alt-F1, you will be asked to provide the name of a "capture file." From then on, your "log" will be open. And all the text that is displayed—such as your e-mail letters—will be written to disk. You can toggle capture off by hitting Alt-F1 again. To append text to the file, hit Alt-F1 yet again and specify the same filename.

The filename I use most often is MAIL.TXT. When I'm offline, I use PC-Write to edit and print the file. Then I delete it so that tomorrow's letters don't get added to those received today.

Note that ProComm will automatically *append* data to an existing file (rather than writing over it) if you use that file's filename.

Printing the documentation and other items

The next step you should take is to print the ProComm 2.4.3 documentation. The file is paginated and contains form feed characters, so your best bet is probably to enter the command **COPY PROCOMM.DOC PRN**. It's a large file, so make sure you're loaded with plenty of paper.

At this point I feel like a parent sending his child (no offense) off to war or to the Big City. There is so much more to say, so many more details that can make your life easier. But the train/bus/plane is leaving, and time is short.

I would love to turn each and every reader of this book into a shareware master. I wish you could leap from online system to online system as effortlessly as the squirrels around our house travel from tree to tree. I would love to see you searching for files, downloading those of interest, and putting them to work solving problems.

But that's a book in itself. Here I can only tell you that you must be aware of compressed files. If you see a filename ending in .ARC, .ZIP, or .LZH, for example, you should know that it is a compressed, "archived" file. To extract the file's contents you must have the correct utility program. You will need PKXARC or ARC-E to deal with .ARC files; PKUNZIP to deal with .ZIP files; and LHA or LHARC to deal with .LZH files.

Almost all online systems and BBSs that offer compressed files for downloading also offer the utility program you will need to extract the contents of those files. If you cannot find them on the system, look for them in shareware catalogues. Glossbrenner's Choice offers a disk called COMM 10 that includes most major decompression programs, but many other vendors make them available as well.

Archiving does add an extra step to the process of obtaining and running shareware programs. But it also saves you money. Since compression programs often squeeze a collection of files to about half their normal size, less time is required to download them, and disk vendors can pack nearly twice as much software on a given disk.

I also wish there were space to tell you about the many nifty programs users have created to work with ProComm 2.4.3. Suffice it to say that you can add ZMODEM support, and you can download a leading BBS list like the one published by Darwin Systems, and bring it directly into your ProComm dialing directory. The best ProComm 2.4.3 utilities have been collected and are available on Glossbrenner's Choice Disk COMM 2—ProComm Utilities. The disk also includes the Darwin Systems BBS list, so you can get started BBS-ing right away.

Applying what you've learned

As I said earlier in the chapter, dialing a BBS is a great way for a new communicator to start. At best, there will be no charge at all, since you will be able to dial a board in your local calling area. Worst case, you will be charged for a long distance phone call, but you can minimize that cost by going online in the evening.

Once you've had some experience, you will definitely want to subscribe to CompuServe, GEnie, America Online, DELPHI, or some other general interest system. For information retrieval, try DIALOG's Knowledge Index.

Note that if you have the phone company's Call Waiting feature enabled on the line you use for your modem, it is a good idea to begin each call by keying in ATDT *70 or ATDT 1170. This will suspend Call Waiting signals for the duration of your call. If you fail to do this, and someone calls while you are online, the Call Waiting signal will break the modem connection. See the front of your phone book for more information on turning off Call Waiting for a given phone call. Look for the words "Tone Block."

Now, for a cost-free way to get your feet wet, let's tap SprintNet's free online phone directory. Go to your ProComm dialing directory and enter the following number: 1-800-546-1000. Label the entry SprintNet PHONES and opt for a setting of 2400 bps, 7/E/1. Then dial the number by moving the highlight bar over the entry and hitting Enter.

When your modem signals a connection, hit your "at sign" (Shift-2) and press Enter once. You will be asked to enter your area code and your exchange (the first three digits of your phone number). Enter them like this: 510,493.

An "at" sign (@) will then appear. At this point, key in MAIL. You will first be prompted for "User name?" Key in PHONES. At the "Password?" prompt that will then appear, key in PHONES again. You will then see information welcoming you to "Sprint's online directory of SprintNet local access telephone numbers." From here, you're on your own and free to explore. Remember, if you want to save your session to disk, hit Alt-F1 and give ProComm a filename.

Conclusion

If you'll forgive the informality, communications is the neatest of all computer applications. As we've seen in the other chapters in this part of the book, there are non-computer related ways to produce text, track information, or do spreadsheet projections. But there is no non-computer equivalent to going online.

Yet the online world, the electronic universe, as it exists right now is definitely not for everyone. It makes considerable demands on your patience and requires you to constantly pay attention. It's quirky, cranky, and inconsistent. Yet for those who are willing to put up with such problems, it offers immense rewards.

In my opinion, no one can ever be a ''complete'' computer user until he or she has at least tried ''online.'' It may very well be that the online world is not for you, that it does not offer you anything you value. On the other hand, you will never know until you take a look. So, wait until you are comfortable using your system without a modem. Then one day when the sun is bright and you're feeling terrific, give the electronic universe a try. You may run screaming from your keyboard. Or you may find that you never want to leave. The only way to know if ''online'' is for you is to take a chance. And as you step out into the great unknown, you can at least be certain that the information provided in this chapter and the software recommended will keep your risks to the absolute minimum.

Part IV

Shareware:
Beyond the basics

13

Accounting and money management

I DON'T KNOW ANYONE WHO'S NEUTRAL ABOUT ACCOUNTING. YOU EITHER love it or you hate it. Those who love it like the built-in orderliness of a general ledger. They like knowing exactly where the money is coming from and where it is going. Those who hate it are the ones who invented the term "bean counters" to refer to accountants. They would much rather spend their time making (and spending) money than drawing a map of where it comes from and where it goes.

Yet, love it or hate it, accounting is something all businesspeople have to deal with. The three packages discussed in this chapter can help. In fact, they can be an enormous help. Each is aimed at a different level of accounting and money management needs, and all of them are ideal for personal and small business use.

All successful businesspeople keep track of their money—of their current and projected income and expenses. Those who don't won't be successful for very long. But this doesn't mean that every businessperson has to put on the arm bands and green eyeshade once a month and dive into an endless lined sea of ledger paper. Nor does it mean that you have to hire someone to swim in these waters for you.

Avoiding accounting overkill

For many small businesses, the classic double-entry bookkeeping approach is overkill. If you are a consultant, for example, you are probably your firm's only employee. There is no reason why you can't keep a list of the fees you receive in a simple three-ring notebook. You can use a paper calendar to project your income.

If you use a single credit card for all of your business expenses, allocating those expenses each April as you prepare your Schedule C is a relatively simple, though time-consuming, matter of putting your charge slips in categorized piles. Do the same with your canceled checks, and you will have a very complete picture of how and where your money was spent.

The best thing a computer can do for you may be to automate your bill-paying. The shareware program Cash Control discussed later, for example, makes it easy to pump out checks on your laser or dot-matrix printer. As a side benefit, Cash Control and most other check-writing software will let you tag each check or disbursement with what it went for. It will do the same thing with credit card purchases. That can eliminate the need to paw through your paper charge slips and checks each April. The program will be able to give you a complete report.

Full-blown small business accounting

At the other end of the small business spectrum are those who really need a traditional accounting package. Most accounting packages are supplied as individual modules, such as General Ledger, Accounts Receivable, Accounts Payable, and Payroll. The general ledger is the key module that everyone works with. Your need for the other modules will depend on your business and the number of employees you have to pay.

The shareware program I recommend for this purpose is Jerry Medlin's five-module suite. In addition to the modules just mentioned, there is also an invoice-writing module. Though not as flashy as some of its shareware competitors, the Medlin package is exceptionally easy to use.

In addition, Mr. Medlin has continually updated the programs for more than six years. That's important, because the last thing you want is to have the maker of your accounting software disappear or otherwise stop supporting the package. After all, this isn't some ordinary computer application—this is *business*.

The middle way

In between automated check writing and double-entry bookkeeping is what we can call "financial management." A financial management package will automate the check-writing process. But it will also help you prepare budgets and cash flow projections. You can track loans and credit cards, accounts payable and receivable, and issue invoices. It will help you estimate your taxes, determine your insurance needs, and help you make financial decisions. Should you be fortunate enough to own a stock portfolio, it will track and help you manage that as well.

It is important to point out that each of these functions is available from other, separate programs. Both the shareware and the commercial worlds are filled with financial and investment-related programs. But Emily and I have looked long and hard, and we have not been able to find anything anywhere that remotely compares to Andrew Tobias's *Managing Your Money* (MYM) from MECA Software, Inc.

The first version was issued in 1984, and the program has been continually updated and upgraded since then. It has also continually garnered rave reviews. *Business Week* has called MYM the best personal finance software you can buy. *PC Magazine* has hailed it as "The king of finance software . . . THE finance manager for people who really want to track and manage their money—not just spend it."

MYM lists for $220, but it is routinely available at a street price of around $99. PC Connection [(800) 800-0004] sells MYM at that price. Knowing the program as we do, that's an incredible bargain. Again, this is *business* we're talking about here, not some optional or peripheral activity. And, truly, our business could not run without the control and convenience MYM provides. So it is with MYM that we will start.

Managing your money: An overview

Andrew Tobias has been writing about business and finance for the last 20 years. His most famous book is *The Only Investment Guide You'll Ever Need*, an audaciously thin volume packed with practical advice. Everything he says is basic common sense. But the intellectual rigor he brings to a topic, his Harvard M.B.A. credentials, and the delightfully irreverent way he presents his material gives it a resonance not present when most people say, "Buy low and sell high."

I've brought all this up for a reason. Contrary to what you might expect, Mr. Tobias has not merely lent his celebrity name to a software package. He was intimately involved in its design and its creation. Not only did he write the MYM manual in his usual witty, crystal-clear style, but he also wrote the prompts and the help information that appear as you use the program. MYM may be the only program dealing with such a serious topic as money that responds with phrases like "Presto!" or "Okay, you're the boss."

I do not mean to imply that the program is cloying or overly cute. It's just that every now and then you encounter a prompt or a response that takes you by surprise and makes you laugh out loud. MYM is simply a delight.

MYM extra feature summary

None of this would matter, of course, if the program did not perform as advertised. But it does. In addition to the program customization you would expect, the Desk feature lets you store the names, addresses, phone numbers, and comments for anyone you deal with on a regular basis. You can use this information and the built-in word processor to produce individual letters or mass mailings. You can enter appointments you have made, phone calls you want to return, and a to-do list, and the program will automatically remind you of them when the designated date arrives.

The Main menu features a top bar with drop-down submenus. There is an Analyze option on the Main menu that gives you access to features designed to calculate compound interest, yield to maturity, tuition planning, retirement planning—and to inflate or deflate figures to allow for inflation. There's even an option to analyze rental properties.

The Portfolio option on the Main menu takes you to a battery of portfolio management features (buy or sell assets, update prices, record income, split stocks, analyze, etc.). The portfolio you manage can be a real one or a fantasy portfolio created to see how you would have done if you'd had the money to buy low and sell high.

The Net Worth Main menu option will guide you in cataloguing and evaluating your assets and liabilities. It even includes a feature to produce a snazzy 3-D pie chart allocating assets. The Insurance Main menu option will guide you in determining how much and what kind of insurance you need.

It is important to point out that these Main menu options do not result in mere fill-in-the-blanks tables. It is rather as if Mr. Tobias and you were sitting across a desk, and he were asking you questions and explaining the significance of your answers. The various Main menu options are intelligently linked to share data. Thus the Net Worth option starts with what it knows about you from the other parts of the program.

You can print reports at any time. And, if you like, you can tell MYM to print them to disk in a format that will let you use the data with Lotus 1-2-3, As-Easy-As, or even Microsoft's EXCEL.

The meat of the matter

As important as these features are, however, the real action is to be found by selecting either the Money option or the Tax option from the Main menu. The Money option stores the core information about your cash flow and helps with bill paying. The Tax option estimates your taxes based on figures pulled in from elsewhere in the program.

Here's what the MYM manual says about the Money option: "MONEY is, for most of us, the heart of the program. If you write a check to the doctor here, your checkbook balance automatically knows, your budget automatically knows, your cash flow projection automatically knows, Schedule A of your taxes automatically knows, and so does your Net Worth."

In other words, once you get MYM set up, everything connects. You really do feel like the Puppet Master firmly grasping and controlling all the disparate strings of your financial situation. It would be misleading, however, to suggest that you won't have to make the commitment to spend the necessary time to get the program set up and to enter the data it needs. Then again, you don't have to set up those features you never plan to use.

From a small business perspective, the Money option handles accounts payable and receivable, with aging. It prints customized invoices and checks, and sums everything into tax categories in Schedule C. Its budgeting options let you prepare a budget and dynamically alter it as the year progresses. At the touch of a few keys, you can instantly forecast your cash position for any given month.

You can generate reports covering the dates you specify at any time. Thus it is a simple matter to tell MYM to prepare a report listing all the money you have spent with a given supplier or series of suppliers in the last six months. Or you can pull a report focused on specific budget categories. How much are you really spending on advertising? How much overtime are you paying your employees?

As for check writing, it is hard to see how it could be simpler. You can set up a series of payees whom you pay every month (mortgage, rent, electric company, etc.) And, of course you can add one-time-only checks. When you're ready, the checks will be printed, including payee addresses. Tear off the stub and slip each check into a windowed business envelope, and your bills are ready to mail.

The only step in the process we have not been able to automate is the need to actually sign each check. I asked a vice president at our bank about getting a rubber stamp with Emily's or my signature, and he indicated that this simply would not do. He's probably right—since with that stamp, anyone could theoretically write themselves a check on our account.

Check reconciliation is also a snap. MYM will sort your outstanding checks in any order you please (date, check number, etc.). You can then sit down with your canceled checks and run through the list, checking off each one that has cleared. The one thing you must remember is to always tell MYM about any in-flow or out-flow of funds from your account. Save your automatic teller slips (ATM machine) when you make a deposit or withdrawal and be sure to enter the transaction in MYM.

Preserving credit card billing details

There are many other features as well. But there is space to tell you about only one more. Let's assume you get a Visa bill for $500. Let's assume that that total is the result of several transactions, each of which properly belongs in a different budget category.

The problem is that if you pay $100 on the bill, next month none of the detail that went into the $500 total will appear. MYM solves this problem by letting you set up an account for each credit card and allocate expenditures against it. Thus, when you get that initial $500 bill, you enter the billing detail into MYM and pay your $100. Perhaps it is $50 for stationery; $100 for business entertainment; $200 for car repairs; etc. It may take you several months to pay off that $500. But come tax time, or anytime, really, you can easily pull a report with the expenditures arranged by budget category.

You've got to do something

As mentioned, Emily and I run our small business with MYM. We write all of our checks, do all of our budgeting, and all of our forecasting with it. We know what it was like without MYM and are convinced that we could not operate without it.

But that's us. The program suits *our* needs perfectly. It may not suit you. Many people, for example, are longtime Quicken users, and they are just as enthusiastic about their choice. The street price for Intuit's Quicken is $44. MYM thus costs about $55 more. In addition, if you become an MYM user, you will want the annual update, and that costs about $50.

There is also the fact that MYM demands a greater commitment on your part. In contrast, you will probably be able to start writing checks within minutes of loading Quicken.

Personally, neither the purchase price nor the required commitment is the issue. As I keep saying, this is your *business* we're talking about. Speaking as someone who has operated a business both with and without computers, in my opinion, you would be missing a bet if you do not use your machine to lighten your record-keeping and accounting chores.

Thus, it is not a question of whether you do something to minimize these burdens—it is only a matter of what you do. And only *you* can decide. So look around and ask around. Find out what the other businesspeople in your area are using. What do they like or dislike? What capabilities do they wish their software had? Then make your decision. If you need more information from MECA Software, Inc., you can reach them at (203) 222-9150 on weekdays from 8AM to 8PM, EST.

Automatic check writing with Cash Control

Now let's consider the simplest and easiest of the three alternatives. Let's consider plain automatic checkwriting.

Many people *like* making entries on ledgers and logs by hand. They say it gives them an almost tactile sensation of keeping their hands on their income and expenditures. I don't blame them a bit. If you've got a manual accounting system that you like, stick with it.

Few people, however, enjoy actually writing out checks, particularly for recurring expenditures like the rent, the mortgage, and utilities. When you add it all up, a lot of handwriting is involved, from the name of the payee to the check register to addressing the envelope. I get writer's cramp just thinking about it.

If all you really want or need to do is have your computer and printer produce your checks, there are lots of options. You could take the commercial route and buy a package like Intuit's Quicken or MECA's CheckWrite Plus at a cost of between $30 and $45. Or you could consider one of the many shareware options.

Emily and I have done just that. We've gone through all the leading shareware check-writing programs, and the one we like best is Cash Control from Ontario-based Adrian-Thomas Software. The registration fee is $29.95 ($34.95 in Canada).

The quality we like most about Cash Control is the way it combines powerful tracking features with simplicity and ease of use. We also liked the fact that it printed the first check we fed it almost perfectly. With a simple adjustment using the program's Options selection, the second check and all subsequent checks printed perfectly. Cash Control supports three standard DeLuxe check formats: dot-matrix pin fed without a stub, the same style check with a stub, and laser printer checks with a stub. The 31-page on-disk manual tells you which product numbers to order when sending for checks.

Cash Control operations

Cash Control's look and feel are quite modern, and the workflow is simple and straightforward. You begin by setting up one or more accounts and entering a starting balance. Select an account, and you are taken to the check register screen.

(The program comes with sample data files so you can see how it works.) From the check register screen, you may enter deposits and withdrawals, write checks, "void" checks or transactions, or switch to a different account. (See Fig. 13-1 for an example of the check register screen.)

Withdraw	Deposit	Checkwrt	Void	Row	File	Global	Autoentry	Year	Mode

	1 Withdraw	Cash Withdrawal		▮	140.00–
	Becker's	Food	food	▮	23.00–
	Withdraw	Cash Withdrawal	wd	▮	50.00–
	Simpson's	Clothes	clth	▮	67.00–
2411	1 Cash Withdrawal				100.00–
2411	1 Cash Withdrawal				100.00–
2412	1 Void			▮	0.00
*****	1 Standard Electric	Utilities	util		150.00–
2405	5 Dominion Food Stores	Food	food	▮	34.67–
2416	5 Withdrawal				50.00–
	Spending Money	Food	food		25.00–
	Groceries		food		25.00–
2406	10 K-Mart	Miscellaneous	misc	▮	54.96–
	14 International Transport	Joe's Pay	pay	▮	623.79

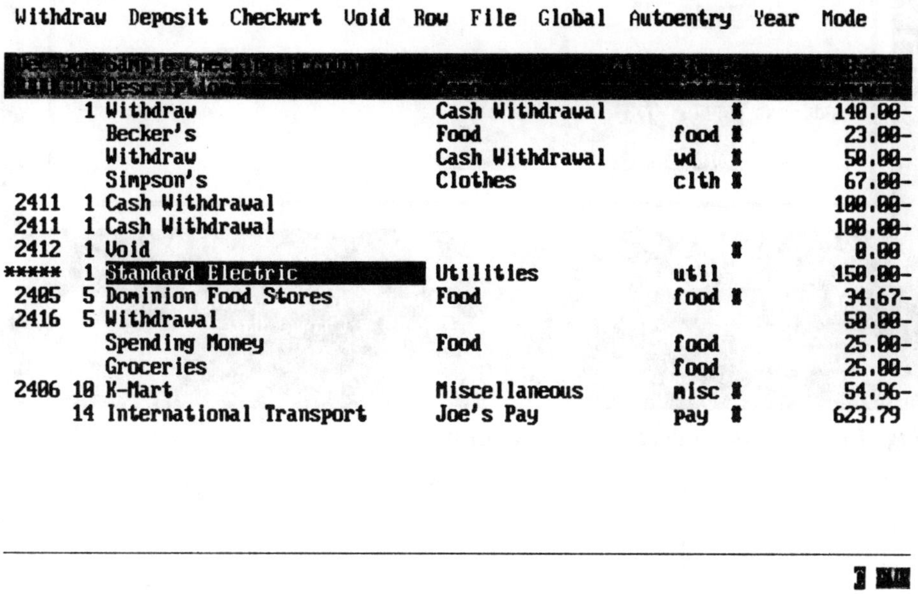

Fig. 13-1. The Cash Control Check Register screen.

Please take just a moment to look at the screen in Fig. 13-1. Your command options are listed across the top. Next is a bar showing you the date and name of the account; the current balance in the account; and headers for check number (####), day of the month (Dy), description of the transaction, a budget code, "CT," and amount. The "C" heads the one-character column that contains a symbol indicating that a check has cleared the bank, according to your statement. The "T" does the same thing if the transaction is taxable.

To write a check, you need only key in C for "Checkwrt." That will cause a screen similar to the one shown in Fig. 13-2 to appear. On this check-writing screen, you may enter all of the information you would enter on a hand-written check, and then some. Specifically, you may enter both a budget code and a memo field, and you may enter the payee's address.

When you hit Enter, you will be returned to the check register screen shown in Fig. 13-1. Notice that in Fig. 13-1, the check for Standard Electric that we wrote in Fig. 13-2 has four asterisks in the check number (####) column. This indicates that the check has been prepared but has not yet been printed.

Figure 13-3 illustrates the use of Cash Control's type, code, and memo fields. If you opt to enter a withdrawal from the check register screen, a window will

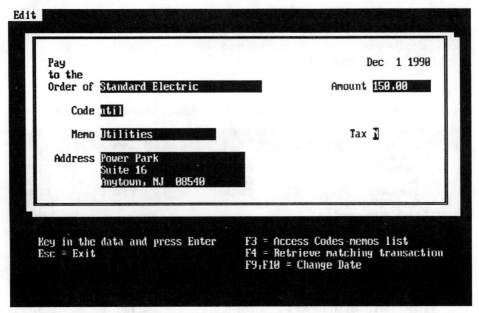

Fig. 13-2. Writing a check with Cash Control.

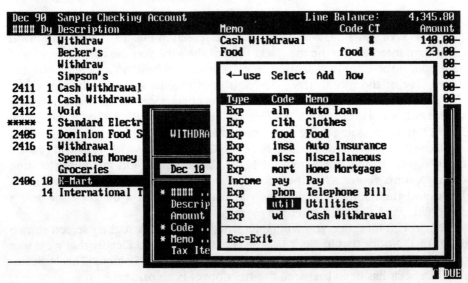

Fig. 13-3. Cash Control account codes and memory fields.

pop up to allow you to enter details (amount, description, code, memo, etc.) As you are working through this window, you may pop up your list of types, codes, and memos, and scroll through it. When you find the entry you want—like "Utilities"—you may hit Enter, and the fields in the Withdrawal window will be automatically filled with the correct information. (The same technique works when you are writing a check.)

Global operations and reports

Look once again at the check register field shown in Fig. 13-1. If you select Global from the top-line menu, you will be taken to a menu that lets you search for transactions, print reports, add or delete your code and memo information, review your balances, and print the checks you have prepared.

You can create accounts for your credit cards and break out the billing detail by code and memo. You can produce reports of just those transactions tagged with certain codes. All in all, you may have up to 15 accounts per DOS subdirectory, with a maximum of 3000 transactions per year in each account, and a maximum of 500 per month per account. And you can queue a maximum of 50 checks before printing.

As noted earlier, the check register entry for a transaction can be tagged as "cleared" when you get your canceled checks back. And, there is an "Autoentry" screen that resembles the check register screen. You use the Autoentry screen to set up recurring transactions. Enter all the setup data for, say, your mortgage company, and you can quickly authorize a check to that concern each month via the Autoentry screen.

What can you lose?

Cash Control does not attempt to provide a full-blown accounting function. (Some of the programs we looked at require you to make a credit and debit entry for each check.) It is designed to make check writing quick and easy, and to provide you with some fundamental data on where your money is coming from and going to via its code and memo fields and related reporting functions.

It is basically a very good, easy-to-use check-writing program that is also easy to understand. In my opinion, if your main financial management goal is to automate the chore of check writing, Cash Control is your program. It is also a classic example of the benefits of shareware. You can try it, play with it, and use it to pay your bills, all for about $5. If you decide that Cash Control and computerized check writing is not for you, the most you're out is five bucks. Just try that with Quicken or CheckWrite Plus!

Double-entry accounting

At the opposite end of the small business scale there is full-blown, double-entry bookkeeping. This technique was invented in Florence shortly before Columbus set sail for America. The approach requires that every item of income and every expenditure be credited or debited to an account category and that for each action there be an equal and opposite reaction. The goal is to make sure that when all credits and debits are added together, the result is always zero.

Double-entry bookkeeping is what most people think of when they think of accounting. But, as we've just seen, there are many ways to get and keep a grip on your income and expenses without mastering this arcane discipline.

Make no mistake: "Real" accounting of this sort is an art. The proper allocation of many items is not always obvious. So you can quickly get into deep yogurt if you don't know what you're doing. And the accounting software will not let you go back to fix a mistake since it must preserve a complete audit trail. The only way to fix a mistake is to enter a compensating transaction to zero out its effects.

The vast majority of small businesses and self-employed professionals do not need a double-entry bookkeeping system. If you think you do, get some advice first. Ask around for the names of professional accountants in your area. Then set up a consultation. A good accountant will be able to look at your business and advise you on the best approach. The accountant will not only be concerned about your need for financial control, he or she will also have Internal Revenue Service requirements in mind.

If a double-entry system appears to be advisable in your case, you might consider taking a course in accounting at your local community college. Then and only then are you likely to be ready to balance your own books.

Frankly, though, unless you have a knack for accounting, you have no business struggling to keep your own double-entry books. You should be spending your time doing what you do best—selling, managing, creating, and generally making more money. The best solution is often to hire a bookkeeper to come in for half a day a week to take this chore off your hands.

Obviously, you will want to make sure you understand how the books are kept. You don't want to lose control. But let someone with the proper training decide whether something is a debit or a credit and into which account it should be entered.

The Jerry Medlin accounting suite

If you already know accounting, or if you are new to the subject and would like to learn more, Jerry Medlin's shareware accounting package is just the ticket. The package consists of five modules: General Ledger (GL), Accounts Payable (AP), Accounts Receivable (AR), Payroll (PR), and Invoicing. All five modules are supplied, and each of the first four carries a registration fee of $35. The registration fee for the Inventory module is $25. (The Turbo Pascal source code for each module is available for $95, should you be interested in creating your own customized version.)

When you register, you receive a program that will let you customize the screen colors, the printer setting, the way the program handles certain elements, and the way certain reports are produced.

Clarity and simplicity

There are many good double-entry systems in the shareware world, many of them glitzier and more visually exciting than Jerry Medlin's programs. Emily and I ran and tested lots of them, but we kept coming back to the Medlin suite. The reason was simplicity. When you look at the main screen of the GL module, for example, you know exactly where you are and what options are at your disposal. (See Fig. 13-4.) There are no pull-down menus, no exploding windows, and no context-sensitive help. There is just simple, basic accounting.

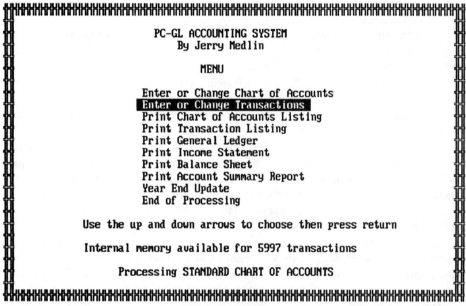

```
                PC-GL ACCOUNTING SYSTEM
                     By Jerry Medlin

                          MENU

            Enter or Change Chart of Accounts
            Enter or Change Transactions
            Print Chart of Accounts Listing
            Print Transaction Listing
            Print General Ledger
            Print Income Statement
            Print Balance Sheet
            Print Account Summary Report
            Year End Update
            End of Processing

       Use the up and down arrows to choose then press return

       Internal memory available for 5997 transactions

          Processing STANDARD CHART OF ACCOUNTS
```

Fig. 13-4. Medlin's General Ledger: Main menu.

There's also the fact that during the six or seven years they have been available, the Medlin programs have been updated on a regular basis, and Mr. Medlin has assembled enough enthusiastic users to be able to spend most of his time tweaking his programs and providing excellent customer support. The rest of his time is spent teaching accounting at a junior college and doing a bit of contract work for nearby firms. There is a steadiness and reliability there that is obviously very important when you're dealing with a company's books.

These programs are aimed squarely at small businesses and companies who want the benefits of commercial quality accounting software without being required to pay for modules they will never use. "The typical small business writes perhaps 100 to 150 checks per month," Mr. Medlin told me, "and most have many, many fewer General Ledger transactions than the 6000 that the PC-GL module allows per accounting period. Most of my registered users typically find that they need and use only one or two modules."

PC-GL: Double-Entry General Ledger program

Since General Ledger is the one accounting function almost everyone uses, we'll spend a bit more time with it than with the other modules. We should say at the beginning that none of Mr. Medlin's programs is designed to teach you double entry bookkeeping and accounting, though if you've had some experience in these areas you will know immediately how everything works. However, PC-GL does come with a file containing the standard Chart of Accounts commonly used by professional accountants. There are accounts for inventory, cash on hand, leasehold improvements, and so on. You can delete or modify these in any way, or you can simply start from scratch. In all, you may have a maximum of 800 items in the chart of accounts.

You can tell the program to use any length of accounting period you choose, and you can print reports to the printer, a file, or the screen at any time. The one exception is the General Ledger Report. This report must be printed on the printer before the program will save historical data and allow you to begin a new accounting period. This is in keeping with the Generally Accepted Accounting Principles (G.A.A.P.) published by the Accounting Standards Board, for it forces the creation of a paper audit trail.

The program will save up to 12 accounting periods, though you can change this to anything from 1 to 30 with the configuration program supplied to registered users. Account numbers can be three digits long (000-999) but, as noted, the maximum number of items on the Chart of Accounts is 800. This offers most people plenty of room to group similar or related accounts into the same subrange of account numbers.

When you are entering data you will be prompted for the account number, but should you forget which one you want to use, you can simply enter 999. This allows you to immediately scroll through all of the names you have assigned to your various accounts until you find the one you want. There is no need to leave the data entry screen.

Account codes are two-digit numbers, the first of which determines the account type (assets, income, net profit, etc.). The second digit specifies the totaling level (what totals and subtotals will appear on reports). You may enter up to five digits to serve as a check or reference number, and there is a feature to automatically increment the number when you are entering sequentially numbered checks.

The account description may be up to 27 alphanumeric characters long. The data entry field is ten digits, so the maximum transaction amount you can enter is $99,999,999.99—one penny less than $10 million—should the occasion ever arise. Every entry is verified instantly, and a maximum of 6000 transactions are permitted per accounting period (assuming you have 512K of memory or more).

The program can print the following reports: Chart of Accounts, Transactions, General Ledger, Income Statement, Balance Sheet (three-columns), and Account Summary. The Account Summary is a summary of the transactions in any one account, and you can request that the program give you a report for any or all prior accounting periods, up to a maximum of 12 periods.

There is much more, besides. But the information provided here will help you compare the Medlin General Ledger module to other accounting programs. Again, GL may be all you really need.

Selective integration

In the sections that follow, we will quickly summarize the vital statistics regarding the features offered by the four other Medlin modules. First, however, there's the matter of integration. Many accounting programs consist of modules that are connected in such a way that when you make a change in one, the change is recorded in the others as well.

I asked Jerry Medlin about that, and he said that he has deliberately avoided linking the modules. "Generally it takes far too much time for a PC to transfer all of the postings from one module into another. It really slows things down. Instead, I advise users to take, say, the sales total from AR and put it into GL as a single entry. This can usually be done in less than five minutes."

Mr. Medlin pointed out that there are two exceptions, however. The Accounts Payable module is integrated with the General Ledger module. Thus, as the documentation notes, "You must have PC-GL in order to use the Accounts Payable program." And the Invoicing program draws its data from the Accounts Receivable file. So you will need both Invoicing and AR. Thanks to the shareware concept, you have the chance to work with all five modules before deciding on the one or ones you want to register.

PC-AP: Accounts Payable

Now let's look at the Accounts Payable module. Here are the items that appear on the program's Main menu screen:

Enter or Change Vendors
Enter, Change or Select Invoices
Print Checks for Invoices Selected
Print Check Listing
Print Invoice Listing
Print Vendor Activity Report
Print Mailing Labels
Print Vendor Listing
Print Account Summary
Start a New Accounting Period
Export Vendor Data to ASCII File
Save Data and End

With AP, you may have a maximum of 2000 vendors and 2000 invoices per accounting period. Vendor names may be two lines of 31 characters each. A ten-character code is used to sort vendors and to post invoices and checks to the vendor's account. You will have 31 characters for the street address and 31 for the city, state, and zip code. Invoice amounts may be fixed monthly payments (like loan payments) or variable.

By default, PC-AP is set up to print checks using NEBS form 9020. However, the configuration program supplied to registered users lets you choose two other check styles, including the style used by the Payroll module. Also, your data can be exported to a Lotus 1-2-3 (or As-Easy-As) file.

PC-AR: Accounts Receivable

Next, let's consider Medlin's Accounts Receivable program. Here are the items that appear on the Main menu screen:

    Enter or Change Sales Codes
    Enter or Change Customers
    Enter or Change Charges & Payments
    Print Mailing Labels
    Print Charges & Payments Listing
    Print Accounts Receivable Ledger
    Print Statements
    Print Sales Summary
    Print Customer Activity Report
    Start a New Month
    Print Customer Listing
    Save Data and End

PC-AR allows a maximum of 2000 customers and 4000 charges and payments per month. Each time the menu is displayed, the number of charges and payments that can be added is printed at the bottom of the screen. The number may be limited by either disk space or memory available, and is subject to a maximum of 4000. The number of customers that can be added can be obtained by dividing the number by 6.

The field lengths permitted are the same as those for the AP module. But AR also has a field for "Late Charge." You enter this as a percentage. There is an "auto bill" function that posts the same amount to a customer's account each month. Under Balances Due, you may enter the current balance, the 30 day balance due, the 60 day balance due, and the 90 day balance due.

PC-PR: Payroll

PC-PR allows a maximum of 1000 employees and 1000 payroll checks per accounting period. Also, since federal and state tax tables are incorporated in the module, you will need an updated version each year. Here is what the module's Main menu looks like:

    Enter or Change Employee Data
    Enter or Change Payroll Checks
    Print Employee Listing
    Print Payroll Check Listing
    Print Payroll Ledger
    Print Quarterly Payroll List
    Federal Liability by Paydate

Start a New Quarter or Year
Enter or Change Employer Data
Export ASCII Data
End Processing

Payroll checks may be written on any cycle from daily to annually. After each batch of payroll checks, you may print the Payroll Check Listing report and the Payroll Ledger report. This provides a printed audit trail, so you will know where you got all those numbers on the employee's W-2s.

Payroll checks are printed as the payroll data is entered. When all of the payroll checks for the current payroll have been printed, you may begin printing reports. Reports may be printed in any order, and as often as desired.

You will need to enter a setup screen for each employee, including address, and federal and state identification numbers. You will also have to enter the number of paydays per year. Six payroll deductions are possible with PC-PR. The first two, federal withholding and Social Security and Medicare (FICA), are mandatory. The remaining four may be determined by you.

PCINV: Invoicing

PCINV is an invoice writing program for small and medium size businesses which works directly with PC-AR Accounts Receivable. Here is the menu that appears when you bring up the program:

Enter or Change Sales Codes
Enter or Change Customers
Enter or Change Charges & Payments
Enter & Print Invoices
Configure Program
Save Data and End

As the documentation points out, because the invoicing program works directly with the accounts receivable module, you should be familiar with PC-AR before attempting to use PCINV. Notice, for example, that the first three items on the menu are essentially identical to the first three choices in the PC-AR program. You may enter or change customers, sales codes and charges and payments entries just as you would with PC-AR. Anything entered using PCINV will also show up when you run PC-AR, and anything entered using PC-AR will be available to PCINV.

The fourth menu choice, Enter & Print Invoices, allows you to enter and print invoices one at a time. When the invoice is printed, the details of the invoice are immediately posted to PC-AR to be included in the next statement.

Conclusion

Whether you think of accounting as fun or as an onerous chore, there can be no doubt that it is necessary, at least for everyone but Congressmen and savings and loan executives. If your books don't balance, you'll soon be out of business.

Yet, as we have seen here, balancing the books does not always mean installing the traditional double-entry system used by large firms. For a small business owner, there are many other options. The key thing, in my opinion, is to *use* the technology.

Now that you've got a computer, let it do what it does best—crunch numbers. Unless yours is a very small business indeed, keeping track of income and expenses *without* a computer these days is as unthinkable as adding up a long column of numbers without a pocket calculator.

14

Printer productivity tools and techniques

IN THIS CHAPTER, WE'RE GOING TO SHOW YOU HOW TO REALLY USE THE POWER! Pushing numbers and words around a screen, or pumping them over the telephone lines is important, as we've seen. But, for businesspeople, where the pedal really meets the metal is in the printed results of all those applications programs.

Please don't misunderstand me. In my opinion, far too much time is wasted in corporate America every day wrestling with desktop publishing programs to get them to produce memos, notes, and inter-office correspondence that look like they came straight from the print shop. What the writers don't realize is that the artful use of a sans serif font, in three point sizes, can't make a stupid memo brilliant, no matter how much time and paper they waste trying to get it laid out "just right." A simple dot-matrix-printed message, or even a quick handwritten note, would often serve just as well.

But that's inside the "family." Outside, your public is waiting. And with the public and your customers, impressions count. Just ask yourself how many times you have discarded a letter or other material because it was messily printed on cheap paper and looked like it came from an office over someone's garage. The subtle message is "I'm not professional. I don't care how my business is perceived by others." To which you respond, "Well, then don't waste my time," and throw the letter or brochure away unread.

The key to looking good is a laser printer. Not that 24-pin dot-matrix printers and ink jets are not acceptable in some instances. If you are using multi-part forms to handle invoices, for example, an impact printer (dot-matrix) is essential. But you might consider printing multiple copies of the invoices on a laser printer rather than using multi-part forms. It's just as easy, and a lot quieter. (In the next chapter, we'll show you how to create invoices and other business forms using shareware programs like MORFORM.)

Focusing on lasers

As you know from Part II of this book, I believe that every small business owner should use a laser printer. Specifically, I think you should have a Hewlett-Packard LaserJet II-compatible printer or better. With prices so low, most small business owners probably will own such a unit someday. If a laser printer is not in your budget at the moment, however, there are ways to get more performance out of your dot-matrix unit. We will discuss several of them at the end of this chapter. For the time being, however, we are going to assume that you have or intend to buy a laser printer.

This chapter will show you how to improve a laser printer's performance. It will then offer a quick course in font and typeface terms before moving into a discussion of the best shareware "soft fonts" and font utilities. (The disk accompanying this book includes several stunning fonts from Elfring Soft Fonts that you can begin using right away.)

Next we'll show you how to produce your own stationery with a program called Laser Letterhead. Once you've got your letterhead, the next thing is to use fonts when producing your letters. We'll show you how to do it with PC-Write, but the same general techniques apply to all software.

The next logical step in the progression is envelopes and labels. Envelopes can be a nuisance, since addresses must be printed sideways in "landscape" mode. But a wonderful shareware program called Grab Plus makes short work of them. Grab Plus can be can be made to pop up and literally grab the address you want to use from your letter and print it on your envelope.

For volume mailings, however, there is Neil Taylor's terrific Mail Machine. Mail Machine will automate the production of labels for mass mailings or other purposes. If you'd like to produce special effects, or otherwise spiff up your labels, Mail Machine can be made to use just about any soft font.

And speaking of mass mailings, wait until you see what ZipKey and Pony Express can do. ZipKey is useful anytime you must enter an address. Instead of typing the city, state, and zip code, just pop up ZipKey, type only the zip code, and the program will automatically fill in the city and state. ZipKey is the ideal complement to File Express and any other program calling for the entering of addresses on a regular basis.

Pony Express offers an instant guide to U.S. postal rates and the rates charged by United Parcel Service and Federal Express. It can tell you what a mailing will cost and how long the piece will take to get to its destination. You can then easily compare prices and decide on the most cost-effective alternative.

We will also have a word or two to say about exporting name-and-address files from File Express for use by PC-Write, Mail Machine, Grab Plus and other programs. Finally, we will briefly discuss dot-matrix printers. In particular, we will show you how to get 24-pin output from an inexpensive 9-pin printer, how to take advantage of customized fonts, and how to print any file on its side (in landscape mode).

Improving printer performance

As you know from Chapter 3, the best way to save money operating a laser printer is to use toner cartridges, like the Super Cartridge, that are designed to be refilled. It goes without saying that the best deals on paper are to be found at "warehouse"-style stores like Staples that sell paper by the case (ten reams).

Once you've cut your costs, however, it is time to consider improving performance. There are at least four things you can do to improve the performance of any laser printer. You can add more memory, use cartridge fonts, use a print spooler program, and, if needed, use an inexpensive device to allow two machines to share the same printer.

Adding memory

The thing to remember about any printer is that it is really a specialized computer. It has a microprocessor or CPU, a data bus, ROM chips, and random access memory. (The Hewlett-Packard LaserJet series, for example, is powered by a Motorola 68000, the same chip used in Apple's Macintosh.) It just happens to take its commands through a cable connection instead of a keyboard, and to display output on paper instead of on a CRT screen.

Printers even have their own programming language consisting of the commands you or your software send them to get them to do particular things. When a printer is said to be "Epson-compatible" or "Hewlett-Packard LaserJet-compatible," what is meant is that it responds to printer programming commands in the same way as those printers do. Among laser printers, "HP" has set the standard. Its programming language is called PCL, short for "Printer Control Language."

I should note here that it is possible to purchase an add-on CPU for your printer to speed things up and give it even more power. But since these units tend to be very expensive, we can pretty much rule out add-on processors as an option. For most people, making sure the printer has enough memory is a much more practical and affordable step.

Just as your computer performs better when you give it more RAM to work with, your laser printer will often work better if you do it the same favor. In fact, there are some things a laser printer cannot do if it does not have enough memory. It may have to divide a single graphic image over two separate sheets, for example, since it does not have the capacity to hold the entire image in memory.

The amount of memory you add will be determined by your budget and the design capacity of the printer. Your printer may come with 512K (0.5M) of RAM. By adding two megabytes more, for a total of 2.5M, you should have the capacity you will need. You can print a full page of graphics at 300 dots per inch (dpi) with 1.5M, but it is a good idea to have some extra room for downloadable fonts (explained later), hence my 2.5M recommendation.

Whether you take the printer up to 4.5M (or more) depends on the kind of printing you do. Certainly one can never have too much memory. But unless you do a great deal of desktop publishing, with graphic images, 4.5M may be overkill. You might be better off spending the money above the 2.5M mark on more memory for your 386/486 computer. At this writing, a 2M memory upgrade for an HP Series II is about $250. For other models, the price is closer to $140.

In any case, wait until you have used your laser for a few months before deciding on any upgrade options. You may find that the amount of memory supplied in the basic system is plenty for your needs.

Cartridge fonts

A *typeface* is a particular design for creating alphanumeric characters, while a *font* is the actual implementation of a typeface in a given size. Most people don't make the distinction, so we won't be too picky. Instead we can say that we are surrounded by typefaces and fonts, even though we usually don't know their names. Newspapers, for example, are often printed in a Times Roman typeface. The typeface most often used in typewriters is called Courier, though Prestige Elite and Letter Gothic may also be available.

The key thing to remember here is that, from the laser printer's perspective, a font is a series of instructions that tell it how to draw a set of letters. Based on those instructions, the laser beam in your printer paints the letters on its drum.

All printers of every sort have a certain number of built-in fonts. These are nothing more than instructions frozen in ROM chips located on their main circuit boards. But, of course, like the computers they are, printers can be programmed to use a different set of drawing instructions.

There are two ways to do this and thus expand the number of typefaces and fonts your printer can produce. You can store a font file on your disk and send it to the printer whenever you want to use the font it represents. That's called a "downloadable font." The printer will keep the font in memory as long as it is turned on—or until you send it an instruction to dump the font you sent. That's one of the reasons why you may need 2.5 or more megabytes of printer memory. The amount of memory available limits the number of downloadable or "soft" fonts a printer can store at one time.

The other alternative is to, in effect, add a ROM chip to the printer that contains one or more fonts. Laser printers offer at least two slots into which you can plug "font cartridges." Using cartridge fonts can thus add flexibility while saving you time. Once a cartridge has been installed, the fonts in its ROM chips become available instantly. There is no need to wait while your computer transmits a font file to the printer. To avoid potential damage to your cartridge, always take the printer offline before inserting or removing a cartridge. That means pressing the "Online" button so that the Online light goes out.

HP offers a veritable alphabet soup of add-on font cartridges for its printers. The "P" cartridge, for example, gives you 10-point Times Roman fonts in normal, bold, and italic. The "V" cartridge gives you Helvetica ("Swiss") fonts ranging from 14 point down to 6 point, plus Letter Gothic at 9.5 point.

Don't worry about the terms. The point is that cartridges are available offering nearly every font you could wish. The best deal, however, is likely to be offered by a third party, not by HP.

Pacific Data Products, for example, sells the "25-in-One" cartridge that includes within it all of the fonts on 25 separate HP cartridges, and then some. In all, 172 fonts and 20 complete symbol sets are available—all in a single reasonably priced cartridge. Different versions exist for different HP printer models, but at this writing, you can expect to pay a street price of about $270 for a 25-in-One cartridge.

Sharing a printer

If yours is a very small business, you may never need to share your printer with another computer. But you can never know when it may be convenient or necessary to do so. That's why it is important to be aware of how easily and inexpensively it can be done. You don't need some elaborate local area network hookup. All you need is an electronic printer switch. In its simplest form, such a switch is no bigger than two packs of playing cards. It has three ports. You connect the printer to one port and your two computers to the others.

If you are the only one using the printer at the time, your job will print as if the switch were not there. But if the other computer is sending data to the printer when you issue your print command, the switch will put you on hold until that other job is finished. Believe me, this is much more convenient than having to go over to the printer and physically turn an A-B switch to manually open a channel. And the cost is only about $130.

The unit we use is made by Black Box Corporation, and it has the added ability to let a single computer use two different printers. You just change the cabling and tell the switch to select one printer or the other by sending it a command code. Thus, you could print your invoices on your dot-matrix printer and your correspondence on your laser, both of which would be connected to your computer's LPT1 port, thanks to the switch.

I'm sure other companies make similar units. But the one I've got works so well, I haven't had to look around. Black Box specializes in communications gear, and I've dealt with them for years. I have yet to find a cable they couldn't make or a connectivity problem they could not solve. For a free catalogue, contact:

Black Box Corp.
P.O. Box 12800
Pittsburgh, PA 15241
(412) 746-5530

Add a print spooler

Finally, the most important step you can take to improve your overall productivity vis a vis your printer is to use a print spooler program. You can't appreciate this until you have experienced it, but normally, when you create a document in PC-Write or some other program and send it to the printer, you cannot do anything else with your computer until the printout is finished. If you install a print spooler before you start the print job, however, you can be back at work using your machine in seconds—as the printing continues in the background.

A print spooler program works this magic by fooling the applications software into thinking that it is actually talking to a printer. PC-Write happily sends text to be printed as fast as the "printer" can accept it. When the last page has been transmitted, PC-Write and the spooler/printer exchange signals confirming the fact. Then, with its print assignment done, PC-Write is ready to go to work again—and you are free to exit the program or do something else. All the while, the text is being "spooled" to the printer by your special software.

It's almost like multi-tasking, that arcane art of getting a computer to do two or more things at once. But it isn't. The print spooler software simply takes advantage of the CPU's power during idle moments, like the eternity between the time you hit one key and another.

Of course, the text to be printed has to be stored somewhere as it is being paid out to the printer. Only two options are available: disk space or memory. The best spoolers can utilize all kinds of disk space (hard or floppy) and all kinds of memory (conventional, expanded, or extended).

The program DMP from DMP Software does exactly that. In fact, it is the best shareware print spooler ever. But you don't have to take my word for it—you'll find it on the disk accompanying this book, so you can see for yourself. In addition to being able to use any type of memory or disk as its storage space, DMP also includes an option to redirect output destined for the printer to a disk file.

That means you can enter a command like **DMP /MXT**, followed by **DMP / PFD:\TEMP\TEMP.TXT** to make sure that all "printed" matter ends up in TEMP.TXT in the \TEMP directory on drive D. This is a great way to capture the text that appears on a program's screen. Get DMP set up as suggested; load the applications software; and simply hit your Print Screen key. To turn off printer redirection, key in **DMP /PF-**. Note that /MXT tells DMP to use extended memory. If you prefer expanded memory instead, use the command **/MXP**. You may also enter a command to specify how much memory you wish to assign to the print spooler.

DMP has many other features besides. The key thing to emphasize here is that it works with *all* types of printers: lasers, ink jets, and dot matrix.

A quick course in fonts

The term *font* can mean many different things. Traditionally, among commercial printers, a font is considered to be a complete set of letters, numbers, symbols, and punctuation marks of a particular size in a specific typeface. A *typeface*, in contrast, is a particular type design, a particular way of making the letters. As noted earlier, you can think of a font as a specific implementation, in a specific point size, of a typeface design.

Things are a little more complex in the world of laser printers. Here, there are two basic kinds of fonts: bit-mapped and outline fonts. In a bit-mapped font, each character is made up of many tiny dots. The dot patterns for each character, in each font size, must exist before they are sent to the printer. For this reason, bit-mapped characters can take up a lot of room on disk and in a printer's memory. After all, the larger the font, the more bits will be in the file and thus, the larger the file.

Outline fonts, in contrast, store each character as an outline or a geometric description. This means you can produce different sizes and styles of characters from the same outline. In effect, the printer just multiplies each drawing instruction in the outline by the same factor to create a larger or smaller size. This is called *scaling* a font, and thus, outline fonts are also known as "scalable fonts."

The best known outline, scalable fonts are PostScript fonts from Adobe Systems. The PostScript approach offers ease of use and great flexibility. But PostScript printing is notoriously slow, due to all the processing that must take place as a font is scaled and as the bit-mapped images actually used in printing are created. Among the best known bit-mapped fonts are those created by Bitstream.

The HP LaserJet II, the least common denominator in the field, does not support scalable fonts. But the LJ-III (LaserJet Series III) does. And you can get a PostScript emulator cartridge for your LJ-II or other HP printer for about $370.

I'm sorry to say it, but there's even more to it than that. We won't discuss the following terms in detail, but you should have at least a general idea of what they mean, since they all apply to laser printer fonts:

Typeface	Times Roman, Courier, Helvetica, etc.
Point size	Maximum height of a character in $1/72$ of an inch.
Spacing	Fixed or proportional.
Pitch	Number of characters per inch with fixed spacing.
Width table	Width of each character with proportional spacing.
Stroke weight	Regular, medium, or bold.
Style	Upright or italics.
Symbol set	Non-text characters available.
Orientation	Portrait or landscape.

To elaborate just a bit, typefaces are fairly obvious, but it is hard to have any sense at all of what point size means. A size of 18 points, for example, is considered fairly large. But 18-point letters occupy only a quarter of an inch ($18/72$ inch). The size you will use most frequently for plain text will probably be 10- or 12-point type.

On a typewriter, every letter occupies the same amount of space, whether it's an I or a W. That's fixed spacing, often called *monospacing. Proportional* spacing means that the width of each letter determines how much horizontal space it gets. A related term is *kerning*, which is the process by which space is apportioned so that you don't have large, noticeable gaps between letters like A and W.

Finally, portrait orientation means that text or images are printed as if on a business letter, with the 8.5″ sides representing the top and the bottom of the page. Landscape orientation means "sideways," so that the 11″ sides of the page are the top and the bottom. Envelope addresses are typically printed in landscape orientation.

Font loading and selection

I said earlier that printers, particularly laser printers, are computers in their own right. If you have any lingering doubts about this, all you need to do is look at the manuals that came with your machine. It is difficult to avoid feeling that you could get your printer to sit up and speak, if only you knew which of the hundreds of available commands to send it. But try to get it to print a simple envelope or a page of labels, and you can waste an entire afternoon. "Escape" this and "left parens" that, plus some number in decimal or hexadecimal, plus upper- and lowercase characters—it is enough to drive you stark-raving mad.

Fortunately, as we will see in a moment, there is software to take care of these details. But there are, nonetheless, a few key points to tuck away for future reference. The first concerns the matter of producing the escape code that prefaces nearly all PCL commands. All you have to do is load PC-Write or some other word processor or text editor that produces clean ASCII files (no strange codes). Then hold down your Alt key while you tap in 2 and 7 on your numeric keypad.

An "escape" is the ASCII character 27 (decimal). And that is what you will have just entered. A little left-pointing arrow should appear on your screen. You can then key in the rest of the necessary command string and copy the file to the printer from DOS. Make sure you type very carefully, and make sure you use upper- and lowercase letters when told to do so. In the ASCII code set and HP printer control language, case counts.

A quick ESC trick

While you're at it, you might want to make yourself a little file called ESC. Go to your PC-Write directory and key in **ED ESC**. Enter an ASCII 27 as described and type some characters after it. Hit Home and enter Ctrl-F6 to begin marking. Move the cursor one space, so that the little left-pointing arrow is highlighted. Then enter Ctrl-F6 again. You will be asked for a filename. Key in **ESC** and hit Enter.

This will result in a little one-byte file, without the carriage return and line feed characters PC-Write puts at the end of every line. Typing in the extra characters after the escape arrow moved the carriage return and line feed out and away.

Once you know this simple trick and have your one-byte ESC file on disk, you really can control your printer completely from the keyboard. (For your convenience, you will find a one-byte ESC file on the disk accompanying this book.) I'll show you how in a moment.

Incidentally, there's one other tip that will help you tame your printer: If your printer maker offers a "technical reference" manual, as HP does, buy it. It will list all the codes you need to drive the beast.

Font ID numbers

The next thing you need to know concerns how to activate a printer font so that your text is printed in the typeface you expect. Two key concepts are "source" and "font ID number." Laser printers can take their font-making instructions from three sources: internal ROM-based fonts (I), external cartridges (either R for "right" or L for "left," depending on the slot into which the cartridge has been inserted), and soft fonts (S) downloaded on an ad hoc basis by you.

As your manual will explain, you may use the printer's front panel controls to select a source and a font number. The built-in "Print Fonts" test will generate several pages showing you each font's location and number, plus a sample of what it looks like. That way you can know exactly which font to select as the default.

Once selected, an internal or cartridge font will be remembered by the printer, even when you turn the power off.

Each font has a unique identifying escape sequence (a long series of characters that spell out its characteristics). Consequently, any font available to your printer may be selected and used for any print job by issuing commands from the keyboard. Your software normally takes care of this, though, so you don't have to worry with it.

Soft fonts

Soft fonts, on the other hand, require special consideration. As you will see when you load and print with the fonts supplied on the disk accompanying this book, several steps are required to activate a soft font. First, the printer must be alerted to the Font ID number you want to use. Then the font file must be downloaded (copied) to the printer. Finally, the font must be activated when you want to use it. Again, your applications software or font downloading software will usually take care of this for you.

It is important to note that soft font ID numbers are not the same as—and are not really related to—any ID numbers you see on the printer's front panel. The printer can tell you how many soft fonts you have loaded. But since it assigns its soft font numbers on the basis of the order in which it receives those files, its numbers may not correspond to the Font ID numbers you have chosen.

Rather than get confused, "consider the source." If a font comes from the printer (built-in or as a cartridge), you may use the printer's front panel to select and activate it. If a font comes from your computer (soft font), use your computer to select and activate it. That's the easiest way to keep things straight.

Soft Font ID numbers may range from 0 through 32,767—even though the printer can hold only about 32 soft fonts at a time. Also, the printer can be told whether to treat a given soft font as "permanent" or "temporary." When a font is tagged as permanent, the printer will hold onto it, even if it gets a soft reset signal (ESCAPE E) from some applications program. It will remain in the printer's memory until you either do a hard reset (by taking the printer offline and holding down the Continue/Reset button for about five seconds) or until you turn off the power.

Keyboard control

If need be, you can send the printer all the codes it needs, download fonts, activate them, and issue any other command directly from the keyboard. The key element is that little one-byte ESC file that contains an ASCII 27. You need this because it is impossible to issue an actual escape code directly from the keyboard.

As an example, suppose you want to download to the printer the Elfring font Black Chan, 14 point, and then activate it so that the next thing you print will use that font. The file is called BC140RPN.USP. A three-step process is required. First you must send the printer the Font ID; then you must copy the font file to the printer; and finally, you must activate the font by telling the printer to use the font associated with a given ID. We'll assume you want to use a Font ID of 15. Here's how to do it:

1. Key in **COPY ESC + CON PRN** and hit Enter.
2. Key in ***c15D** and hit Enter.
3. Then hit F6 or Ctrl-Z and hit Enter.
4. Key in **COPY /B BC140RPN.USP PRN** and hit Enter.
5. Key in **COPY ESC + CON PRN** and hit Enter.
6. Key in **(15X** and hit Enter.
7. Then hit F6 or Ctrl-Z and hit Enter.

The Ctrl-Z signifies the end of input. It can be generated by hitting F6, by holding down the Ctrl key and then hitting the Z key, or by entering the "hat" character (Shift 6) and Z.

When you hit Enter, the system will say "1 file(s) copied." Note the "/B" switch in the COPY command above. This tells DOS that you are copying a binary file, and that it is to ignore any codes in the file (like a Ctrl-Z) that might cause it to stop copying prematurely.

The final step is to print some sample text. Find a chunk of text that's 2K long or less (about one page) and key in the following command: **COPY filename .ext PRN**, where **filename.ext** is the name of your little text file. You can use PC-Write for this, but you must tell it *not* to use a printer definition file. Copying the file to the printer from the DOS command line is much simpler.

I realize that the Font ID command (**Esc*c#D**, where **#** is the number you want to use) and the font selection command are strange. But they are nothing compared to the long strings of codes needed to select a font or specify a printer's many other possible settings. It is important to know how to do things manually, but whenever you can, let software handle the chore for you. As it happens, font-related software is the subject we will turn to next.

Font-related shareware

When you get your laser printer, don't be surprised if you start seeing the world in a whole new light. Most of us pay no attention whatsoever to the fonts around us, but once you have a laser printer, you will suddenly realize that they are every-where. It really is amazing how many different ways there are to draw the letters of the alphabet. It is amazing how many typefaces we encounter every day.

Every one of those typefaces had to be designed by somebody. Some man or woman had to sit down somewhere and decide exactly how the letter A—and every other character in the typeface—will appear. It isn't stretching things at all to say that typefaces are works of art.

The Elfring soft font package

Fortunately for all of us, there are many typeface artists at work in the shareware field. There are hundreds of fonts one can obtain and use as shareware. Typically, the typeface designer will make a typeface available in one or two font sizes as a sample of his or her work. If you want additional fonts (sizes) of the same type-face, the designer will be happy to supply them for a modest fee.

One of the best typeface/font collections available anywhere is Gary Elfring's 23-font collection. The man is a true artist. But you don't have to take my word for it. You can view a sample of his work in Fig. 14-1. Or better yet, check the disk that accompanies this book for Elfring fonts you can print out and use yourself.

The Elfring shareware font collection may well supply all of your needs. The registration fee is only $25, and it brings with it full telephone support. The package includes a soft font downloader; a font information display program; a utility that examines soft fonts; printer drivers for WordPerfect 5.1 and 5.0, MS Word 5.0 and 5.5, MS Works; plus Windows, WordStar, PC-Write, Q&A, Ventura, and Pagemaker information. It also contains a tutorial that explains the basics of using soft fonts.

If you like what you see, you'll be interested to know that Elfring has nearly 50 other typefaces in font sizes ranging from 8-point through 30-point available. Each font package is priced between $35 and $50, and versions are available for Hewlett-Packard ink-jet printers as well, as are PostScript and LJ-III scalable fonts. The Elfring package is available on the Glossbrenner's Choice Laser 1 disk. For more information about Elfring products, contact:

Elfring Soft Fonts
P.O. Box 61
Wasco, IL 60183
(708) 377-3520

Notice the dingbats (yes, it's a real word) shown in Fig. 14-1. There are all kinds of neat symbols from those for copyright and registered trademark to arrows, currency symbols, and check boxes. It certainly would be nice to be able to use these, but to do so, you have to know which keys to enter. After all, there is no key on your keyboard with a little picture of a telephone or a pair of scissors.

You could operate by trial and error. But there is a much easier approach. There are at least two programs, CHART and KEYCHART, that will print out a page showing you which keys to enter to produce specific dingbat images after you have activated the dingbat font. Both programs can be found on the Laser 1 disk. CHART presents its information as an ASCII table. KEYCHART uses a keyboard-like display.

All you have to do is key in **KEYCHART**, followed by the font file name, and a page like the one shown in Fig. 14-2 will appear. As you can see, if you want the printer to produce a pair of scissors cutting to the left, the correct key is a lowercase z. If you want a little telephone symbol, use the question mark (?). Remember, the correct font must have been downloaded to the printer first, and you must tell the printer to use that font to print your dingbat symbol. As we'll see in a moment, this is very easy to do with PC-Write.

TSR Download and Jet Pilot

Soft fonts are inexpensive and flexible, but they do have a major drawback—you must download them to the printer before you can use them. Often this does not present a problem. You can incorporate font downloading instructions as part of

Black Chan 12 & 14 point

ABCDEFGHIJKLMNOPQRSTUVWXYZ
abcdefghijklmnopqrstuvwxyz
123456789!"$%&()?

Broadway 18 point

ABCDEFGHIJKLMNOPQRSTUVWXYZ
abcdefghijklmnopqrstuvwxyz
123456789!#$%&()?

Century Legal 12 point

ABCDEFGHIJKLMNOPQRSTUVWXYZ
abcdefghijklmnopqrstuvwxyz
123456789!#$%&()?

Flourish 12 point

ABCDEFGHIJKLMNOPQRSTUVWXYZ
abcdefghijklmnopqrstuvwxyz
123456789!#$%&()?

Helv 10 & 12 point

ABCDEFGHIJKLMNOPQRSTUVWXYZ
abcdefghijklmnopqrstuvwxyz
123456789!#$%&()?

Helv Bold 10, 12, & 18 pt

ABCDEFGHIJKLMNOPQRSTUVWXYZ
abcdefghijklmnopqrstuvwxyz
123456789!#$%&()?

Helv Italic 10 & 12 point

ABCDEFGHIJKLMNOPQRSTUVWXYZ
abcdefghijklmnopqrstuvwxyz
123456789!#$%&()?

Fig. 14-1. Elfring Soft Fonts font samples. These are just a few of the 23 fonts in the Elfring shareware font package..

Dingbats 18 point

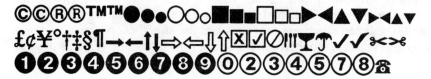

Roman 10 & 12 point

ABCDEFGHIJKLMNOPQRSTUVWXYZ
abcdefghijklmnopqrstuvwxyz
123456789!#$%&()?

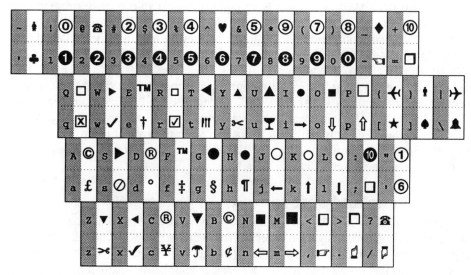

Fig. 14-2. KEYCHART reveals the font.

your AUTOEXEC.BAT file, so the fonts you normally use will be copied to the printer each time you turn on your machine.

But what do you do if you are in the midst of an application and you need to use a font that you know you have not yet downloaded to the printer? That's the problem that Elfring's TSR Download soft font manager was designed to solve. If you have loaded TSR Download before starting your application, you can simply pop it up, select the font or fonts you wish to use, and return to your application. There is no need to back out of a program, return to DOS, run a font downloader, and then load the application again and work your way back.

Elfring's TSR Download is widely available from shareware sources, and it can be found on Glossbrenner's Choice Laser 2 disk. It can work with either LaserJet or DeskJet printers, and any font file. But that only scratches the surface of its capabilities. It can compress font files and use them, decompressing them on the fly, to save you disk space. It can rotate or create landscape versions of your soft fonts from their portrait equivalents (important if you use a LaserJet Plus or LaserJet II).

The program can be used with a mouse or via the keyboard. And it can be popped up to do such mundane things as sending a form feed to the printer or changing the printer to a different lines-per-inch setting. The font list the program presents is not merely a column of obscure filenames. Fonts are identified in English as ''Roman 12 pt, bold ASCII portrait'' or ''Symbols, 18 pt, semi-bold Math7 portrait.'' To select fonts, you merely tag the ones you want and tell the program to send them to the printer. Then hit your Esc key, and you're back in your application. Gary Elfring's TSR Download is a very slick piece of work.

Jet Pilot from Morton Utilities is an equally remarkable control program. Jet Pilot can be installed as a pop-up TSR, or it can be run directly from the DOS command line. It gives complete control of virtually every feature of your LaserJet or compatible printer. Specifically, it supports Hewlett-Packard LaserJet models II, IID, IIP, III, IIID, IIISi, IIIP, and compatibles.

It can do everything from setting your top, bottom, left, and right margins, to rotating the printout by 0, 90, 180, or 270 degrees. Jet Pilot complements TSR Download because Jet Pilot deals with your printer's internal and cartridge fonts. TSR Download deals only with soft fonts. Between the two of them, you can do virtually anything you want with your laser printer, and you can do it *easily*. Jet Pilot is also on the Laser 2 disk.

PC-Write and soft fonts

The third package you will find on Laser 2 is Quicksoft's Font Selector for its PC-Write word processor. As you may recall from Chapter 9, PC-Write takes its printing instructions from a file called PR.DEF (printer definition). This is the file that is created when you install the program and select your printer from a menu. It contains the control codes your particular brand of printer needs to see to produce a particular font.

Thus, if you want to toggle on boldface printing, you might key in an Alt-B. A little funny face will appear at the cursor, signalling that bold printing has been enabled for the characters that follow. Those characters will appear in a highlighted color until you toggle bold printing off again with another Alt-B, or until you reach the end of a line.

Now, when it comes time to print the document, PC-Write loads the PR.DEF file and uses it as a reference. Whenever the program sees that little funny face (or some other font-activating character), it looks at PR.DEF to find out what commands to send to the printer to activate a particular font.

The main limitation is that there are only 26 letters in the alphabet, and there are hundreds of possible fonts. The solution is to create additional PR.DEF-like files and tell PC-Write to use a particular version when printing. The files can be given any names you please, though you will probably want to stick with something like PR-1.DEF, PR-3.DEF, and so on.

The Quicksoft Font Selector program on Laser 2 makes it easy to prepare the printer definition files you need. Key in **FONT** and respond to the prompt with the name of the printer definition file you wish to create. Let's use TEST.DEF for the time being. The program will come up, listing the letters B through Z and the default fonts activated by them when used with Alt in a PC-Write document. (Please see Fig. 14-3.)

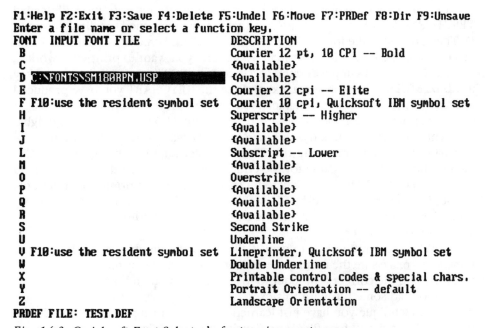

```
F1:Help F2:Exit F3:Save F4:Delete F5:Undel F6:Move F7:PRDef F8:Dir F9:Unsave
Enter a file name or select a function key.
FONT   INPUT FONT FILE                    DESCRIPTION
B                                         Courier 12 pt, 10 CPI -- Bold
C                                         {Available}
D   C:\FONTS\SM180RPN.USP                 {Available}
E                                         Courier 12 cpi -- Elite
F  F10:use the resident symbol set        Courier 10 cpi, Quicksoft IBM symbol set
H                                         Superscript -- Higher
I                                         {Available}
J                                         {Available}
L                                         Subscript -- Lower
M                                         {Available}
O                                         Overstrike
P                                         {Available}
Q                                         {Available}
R                                         {Available}
S                                         Second Strike
U                                         Underline
V  F10:use the resident symbol set        Lineprinter, Quicksoft IBM symbol set
W                                         Double Underline
X                                         Printable control codes & special chars.
Y                                         Portrait Orientation -- default
Z                                         Landscape Orientation
PRDEF FILE: TEST.DEF
```

Fig. 14-3. Quicksoft Font Selector's font assignment screen.

You can edit and move font assignments, but don't worry about that now. What we want to do is to assign the Elfring dingbat font to letter D. So move your cursor down to D, which is "available." Then hit F8 to tell the program where to look for the fonts you want to use. This appears as "F8: Dir" at the top of the screen in Fig. 14-3.

Respond with the pathname of the subdirectory containing your soft font files. You might thus enter: C:\FONTS*.*. That will cause the program to present you with a list of all the files in C: \ FONTS. You can then select the font file you want to associate with D by moving your cursor down the list and hitting Enter. In the example shown in Fig. 14-3, we have chosen the Elfring soft font file SM180RPN.USP because we know that that is the dingbat file, thanks to the KEY-CHART program mentioned earlier.

Next hit F3 to save the file. Notice that the Font Selector will create a file called SOFTDOWN.BAT in addition to TEST.DEF. This batch file will automatically download the font or fonts you have selected to the printer.

Steps to printing

Now you're ready to print. But let's take the entire process from the beginning so we don't miss a step. Start by creating a directory on Drive C called FONTS. Then use the KEYCHART program to produce a printout like the one shown in Fig. 14-2. Since we're dealing with dingbats here, I suggest you print up a chart for SM180RPN.USP.

Use the Quicksoft Font Selector to prepare a printer definition file called TEST.DEF as described. We will assume that you have assigned the dingbat font to D. Then download the font by keying in **SOFTDOWN**. Remember, there can be no magic unless the font is in the printer at the time you want to print your work.

Next, prepare a sample document. Go to your PC-Write subdirectory and key in **ED DING.TXT**. Type in some text and use the KEYCHART you have produced to learn which conventional characters to enter to produce dingbat symbols. To produce an image of a telephone, for example, hit Alt-D to turn on the dingbat font, enter a question mark (?), and then hit Alt-D again to turn off the font.

To print your work, using the TEST.DEF file, hit F1 to bring up the PCW menu. Then F7 to print. Now for the critical step. Notice that the printing menu includes ''F6 Def.'' This is the key to hit to tell PCW which printer definition file to use. Do so now and specify TEST.DEF. If TEST.DEF is located in a directory other than PCW, be sure to include the complete address path (D:\WORKING\TEST.DEF, or whatever).

Finish up by hitting F10 to print ''all''—and the dingbats should appear. If they don't, make sure the font has been downloaded to the printer, and make sure you are using the correct font letter to toggle the font on and off.

We've had some fun with this exercise. But, of course, it has a serious purpose. The technique you have just learned using the Elfring dingbat font file can be applied to *any* soft font file. With Quicksoft's Font Selector, you can create an unlimited number of PCW printer definition files containing any configuration of fonts you want. And the files work not only with PCW Standard Level, but with previous versions of the program as well.

There's just one thing missing: cartridge font support. You will be happy to know that Quicksoft has prepared a series of printer definition files to support most major cartridges, including Pacific Data's 25-in-One product. The software is not shareware, but it can be purchased for a very reasonable price from Quicksoft. (Prices vary with the files needed.)

Advanced font work

Since soft fonts are computer files, it stands to reason that they can be edited and altered to produce different results. This sounds like a lot of trouble, and it would be, were it not for programs like Kenn Flee's QFONT (Quick Font!) program. Mr.

Flee and his company, Jamestown Software, are responsible for QFILER, an absolutely essential utility program that we'll tell you about in Chapter 16. But if QFILER is brilliant, QFONT is dazzling.

I can't begin to tell you all of its features, so I will simply hit the high points. The program will work with Hercules, EGA, and VGA monitors. A mouse is not required, but is strongly recommended. HP LaserJets and compatibles are the supported printers.

You can use QFONT to design your own fonts or images, if you like. But you will probably use it most to *alter* existing soft fonts. Simply tell QFONT the name of the font file you want to start working on, and it will bring up the letter A as shown in Fig. 14-4. The letter will appear in the upper left corner as a reference, and on the main screen for editing and manipulation. To make any other letter appear, simply hit its key.

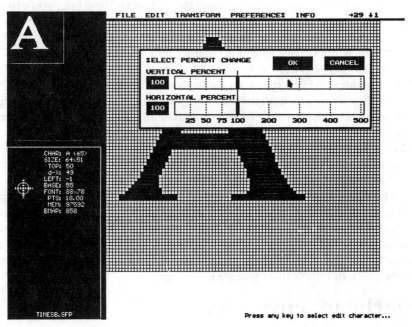

Fig. 14-4. QFONT puts you in control.

With the letter on the screen, you can physically change each and every bit individually. Just click on it with your mouse. Or you can use the program's drawing tools to add lines, curves, ellipses, boxes, etc. You can also cut and paste to create a unique design. But what you will find really exciting is the ability to change the size of the font. QFONT can increase the size of a font up to a maximum of about 144 points (two inches). Horizontal and vertical dimensions can be changed independently, in case you want to create squashed or elongated characters.

Similarly, you can cause the typeface to slant to the right or the left, and add shadowing or outlining. You can turn portrait fonts into landscape fonts. You can make the font bolder or lighter, or turn it into a reverse font (white characters on a black background).

When you select a change, the letter on the screen changes instantly to reflect it. That makes it easy to decide whether you like the effect or not. When you have made all the changes you want to make, you can tell the program to go through the font file and change all the rest of the characters, saving the font to a different filename on your disk. Then you can tell QFONT to download your new font to the printer and print a sample.

Kenn Flee brings years of professional programming experience to QFONT, and it shows. The registration fee is $80. QFONT can be found in many shareware collections and on Glossbrenner's Choice Laser 3 disk.

Also on Laser 3 is Will Temple's Fontloader. This program is more than a mere font downloader, however. Operating from the DOS command line, you can enter a single Fontloader command that will download the target font and re-size it to anything between eight and 24 points. You can rotate the font, turn it upside down, print as white on black, and do many other things.

Registered users ($25) receive a version with even more capabilities. Fontloader is intended as a quick way to produce font effects while saving your disk space. By altering a font on the fly, as it is sent to the printer, you eliminate the need to store each version of the font as a separate file. All you need is one version to serve as Fontloader's pattern.

Finally, Laser 3 also contains STP—the "Save a Tree text Printer." STP can print eight normal pages on a single sheet of paper. It does this by using very tiny, though still legible, type and by printing on both sides of the page.

During the first pass, the odd numbered pages are printed, and the even numbered pages are stored in memory. The program then prompts you to turn the pages over and put them back in the paper cassette. It will then print the even numbered pages. As I said, the type is very small. But STP can be ideal for printing documentation, since you can take in eight pages at a glance and thus more easily locate the piece of information you seek.

Letterhead, envelopes, and the Mail Machine

Now that you have a better idea how to produce different fonts on your laser printer, let's turn to practical applications. Let's look at how you can use your new skills and software to produce your own letterhead, how you can grab addresses off the screen in your word processor and use them to print envelopes, and how you can use your computer to automate your mailings to customers, prospects, and others.

Laser Letterhead Plus

Laser Letterhead Plus is an elaborate program with an extensive 64-page single-spaced manual. It is designed to let you prepare several different letterhead formats (personal, business, logo, etc.) and print them at the touch of a few keys. In my opinion, a few too many keys are required, and some of the program's setup screens are so busy they make a paisley scarf look restful.

Nonetheless, at this writing, Laser Letterhead Plus from CPI Software is hands-down the best shareware letterhead program. And it *does* perform—if you are willing to put up with a few rough edges in its user interface. Indeed, the features it offers and the letterheads it produces are so flexible and imaginative that it is clear an intelligence is at work. Consequently, it seems likely that the screens will be made more intuitive in future versions. (The version current at this writing is 3.0, release B.2.)

There are a number of things that I really like about Laser Letterhead Plus (LLP). First, I like the fact that one can use soft fonts, like Gary Elfring's package, in the text portions. The program has built-in support for both individual Hewlett-Packard cartridges and the Pacific Data 25-in-One cartridge, as well.

LLP also includes a feature to let you incorporate graphic images as letterhead logos. It uses the .PCX format established by PC Paintbrush. (For more information on the .PCX graphics format, see Chapter 15.) When you register the product, you not only receive the commercial edition of LLP and a printed manual, you also get a form for requesting a free customized logo letterhead image. You can even send the company artwork that you would like to have scanned and turned into a .PCX file specifically sized to work with the program. The registration fee is $25, far less than you would pay a commercial printer or copy shop.

The samples offered on the shareware disks are quite impressive. And I should point out that you do not need to use a logo. In an hour or so of working with the program, Emily produced a dozen different letterhead treatments using the Black Chan font from Elfring Software, boxes, shading, and shadows. There's even an option to use a "watermark" image. This is an image printed in a light gray screen that measures about 4" by 5" and is printed in the middle of the page.

Laser Letterhead Plus may not produce the on-screen images found in desktop publishing packages like Ventura, but it does get the job done. And CPI Software is clearly eager to help you make a good impression. Laser Letterhead Plus is widely available, but it can also be found on Glossbrenner's Choice disks Laser 4 and Laser 5.

"GRAB-ing" an envelope address

In this age of computerization, you would think that the typewriter would be a thing of the past. But there are at least two business tasks that are all but guaranteed to keep it alive. One is the need to fill out multi-part forms, like Federal Express air bills. The other is the fact that generating addressed envelopes on a laser printer can be a royal pain in the keyboard.

All HP LaserJets are designed to accept envelopes. In fact, some are designed to accept special envelope cassettes. But unless you are in the direct mail business or otherwise routinely send out a lot of mail, there is not much point in getting a special cassette. Most of us have the simple need of sending out a few letters a day, and it is often more trouble than it's worth to try to address an envelope with a laser printer.

That's what makes Grab Plus from ZPAY Payroll Systems so exciting. All you have to do is load Grab Plus into memory as a TSR and prepare your letter. When you are ready to generate an envelope for the letter, you press a hotkey combination and Grab will pop up onto your screen. You will see two windows. One offers a quick summary of available commands, while the other is a highlight box that you can move over the inside address in your letter.

Adjust the box with your function keys, hit another key to confirm your decision, and Grab will automatically send the text in the highlight box to the printer. All you have to do is place an envelope in the manual feed slot and Grab will print the address you have picked out, properly positioned in landscape mode, on the envelope. Depending on your preferences, Grab will automatically print your return address in the upper left corner as well.

Grab Plus is available on two disks—Grab 1, the main program disk, and Grab 2, a disk with two add-on modules. The add-on modules consist of an address database program and a program designed to produce labels. The database can accept input from most database programs, or you can use the data you enter yourself. The Laser Label program is designed to print labels on stock made by Avery/Dennison. It can take its data from the Grab database, utilize soft fonts, and produce postal bar codes.

You can use the main Grab program by itself. But the database and labelling add-ons can only be used with the main Grab module. To my mind, the main Grab program is essential, and the add-ons are nice to have, but not necessary considering the other options available.

Mail Machine

One of those options is a commercial program called Avery LabelPro, and another is Neil Taylor's Mail Machine. LabelPro lists for $99 and sells for about $45. The current registration fee for Mail Machine is $30. The one thing LabelPro has over Mail Machine is the ability to preview what a sheet of labels will actually look like when printed. But LabelPro will not let you use just any font, and it does not offer the flexibility found in Mail Machine. And LabelPro will not let you use a mouse.

Among other things, Mail Machine (MM) can print envelopes and labels of any size acceptable by your LaserJet up to 8.5″ by 14″. Support for most standard size envelopes and labels is built into the program, plus support for most Avery forms. (See Fig. 14-5.) In addition, MM lets you print both addresses and return addresses on envelopes. (You don't have to do just labels.) As with LabelPro, the addresses can be entered manually, or they can be imported from a file created by File Express, As-Easy-As, or some other database or spreadsheet (or word processor).

Mail Manager supports six lines of address information on each label. Label addresses are optional and can be entered manually, or they can be retrieved from text files, the same as with envelopes. MM also gives you the option of automatically printing the United States Postal Service "PostNet" barcode in the correct position on your envelopes and labels. That can speed mail delivery because it allows your mail addresses to be scanned and read by machines similar to those now used at grocery store checkout counters.

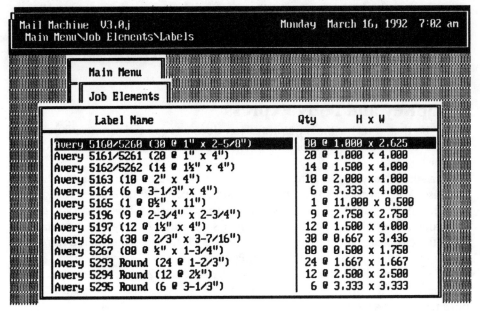

Fig. 14-5. Mail Machine does Avery labels.

In addition to printing addresses, you can optionally specify any number of original messages or comments. Such messages can be printed anywhere on the envelopes or labels, using any available fonts. For example, you might want to print messages like: DO NOT BEND, AIR MAIL, HAPPY HOLIDAYS, OPEN IMME-DIATELY, or HERE IS THE INFORMATION YOU REQUESTED.

Mail Machine lets you use any soft fonts, but it also supports the fonts built into your printer and cartridge fonts as well. You can print envelopes and labels with any combination of available fonts. And, as with LabelPro, you can use PCL and PC Paintbrush graphics files to add logos and artwork to your labels.

But enough about features. Let's talk about benefits. Let's imagine that you have been keeping your customer addresses in a File Express database. Now you want to send all of your best customers a letter announcing a special sale. You load File Express and tell it to search for all customers who have spent $100 or more with you during the last six months. Then you tell it to export their names, addresses, and zip codes to a "mail merge" or other file.

Now you load Mail Machine and define a label format, including a tagline like "Special Savings Inside." You tell Mail Machine to take its data from the file you just created with File Express, and you run a blank sheet through the printer to make sure everything is working. Satisfied, you load the printer's cassette with sheets of pressure-sensitive Avery labels, press a key or two, and in moments high-quality, professional-looking labels come trooping out of the printer.

As you know from Chapters 9 and 10, you could use the same "best cus-tomer" list to create a personalized letter with PC-Write. With your personalized letters printed via PC-Write, and your labels printed by Mail Machine, all that remains is the final assembly. Add a postage meter and don't be surprised if some-one someday says, "What are you? Some kind of mail machine?" The answer will be a proud "Yes, ma'am!"

Mail Machine can be found on the Glossbrenner's Choice disk of the same name.

ZipKey and Pony Express

It may be that your business or profession does not call for sending much mail. But if it does, you can't afford to be without programs like ZipKey and Pony Express.

Imagine that you are entering new customer names into your File Express database. You have fields for city, state, and zip code. With ZipKey loaded into memory, all you have to do when you reach the city field is hit a hotkey to pop up the program, and then type in the customer's zip code. ZipKey will automatically fill in the city, state, and zip. You can configure ZipKey to do the same thing with nearly any program you use, including PC-Write.

If you know the city and state but not the zip code, ZipKey will supply it. You may never need a printed zip code directory ever again. The program also sup-plies telephone area codes.

The benefits of using ZipKey are numerous. First, it saves keystrokes. A single hotkey keypress, followed by five keypresses to enter the zip code, add up to a total of six keystrokes, compared to the many more that may be required to enter the city, state, *and* zip code. There is also the benefit of error-checking. If you enter the zip code incorrectly, the city and state won't match your source mate-rial. If the source material is barely legible, the zip code may be the only address item you can clearly read.

The other program anyone who does even a moderate amount of mailing needs is Pony Express (PE). All you have to do is tell it where you want a package or letter to go and how much the item weighs. PE will then tell you how much it will cost to send via the post office, via Federal Express, and via United Parcel Ser-vice. Pony Express will also tell you how long it will take to get there, so you can easily determine whether any extra speed is worth the extra money.

Both ZipKey and Pony Express offer many other features, but those high-lighted here represent the essence of each program. On a personal note, we use both programs constantly as part of our Glossbrenner's Choice operations. And while Emily and I would not recommend them to someone who does not send much mail, they are nearly essential if you regularly send out even a few letters and packages a week. Both ZipKey and Pony Express are available from Glossbrenner's Choice.

For dot-matrix users

No two small businesses are alike, and not everyone needs the kind of quality that is produced by a laser printer. In fact, if your main interaction with customers is sending out invoices, you can probably get along quite nicely with a dot-matrix printer, particularly a 24-pin unit.

As you know from the first part of this book, a dot-matrix printer creates characters by pushing pins or "wires" forward in a particular pattern. When the print head is hit from behind with a "hammer," the pins are forced into a ribbon and make a series of dots on the page. Each character is thus formed of a "matrix" of dots.

The first dot-matrix printers to become widely available were "nine-pin" printers. These machines used nine pins to produce graphic images from the screen and eight pins to form characters. Now nine-pin printers are dirt cheap and 24-pin printers are the new entry level machines. A 24-pin dot-matrix printer cannot rival an inkjet or a laser, but its output is at least three times better than the nine-pin printers that came before.

However, should your budget only permit an inexpensive 9-pin printer, you should know that there is a program that can make it produce 24-pin output. The program is called LQ, and it works its magic by making three passes over each letter using eight pins during each pass. By causing the printhead and paper to shift ever so slightly, LQ can put enough dots on the page, close enough together to emulate what a 24-pin printer does in a single pass. The main drawback is time. When the shareware program LQ is active, printing takes three times as long on a 9-pin printer, but the results are worth the wait.

Many printers today also come with several built-in fonts. But few can hold a candle to the fonts offered by the shareware program ImagePrint. ImagePrint supports both 9- and 24-pin dot-matrix printers, and it offers fonts that include Courier, Cubic, Elite, Orator, Roman, Outline, OCR-A and OCR-B, Helvetica, Old English, and more. Both LQ and ImagePrint are available on the Glossbrenner's Choice PRINTER 2 disk.

Finally, there is the matter of landscape mode. If your printer does not have the ability to print text "sideways," then a program like OnSide may be just what you need. OnSide was written by the same folks who did File Express. It can take any kind of text—whether it is a large spreadsheet or a plain text file—and print it out at a 90-degree rotation on your dot-matrix machine. It performs this trick by converting the text characters in your file to bit-mapped graphics. That requires a little time, but, again, the results are usually worth the wait. OnSide is on the Glossbrenner's Choice PRINTER 4 disk.

Conclusion

In many ways the printing process represents the culmination of all your personal computing efforts. Printing is, ultimately, what it's all about. For what good does a well-written letter do anyone until it appears as text on a piece of paper? What good is your database of customer addresses if you can't pump out a mailing to them at the touch of a few keys? That's a slight exaggeration, I know. But the fact remains that for many small business owners, everything comes together on the printout.

The key thing is to get the most out of whatever printer you have—to *use* the technology you bought with your hard-earned dollars. Clearly, the shareware programs highlighted here can help you go a long way toward that goal as inexpensively as possible.

15

Business forms
and graphics

SHAREWARE AUTHORS HAVE ALWAYS PUSHED THE AVAILABLE HARDWARE TO ITS limits. They have created drawing and graphics programs that squeeze the utmost out of a CGA screen, and the performance that programs like LQ and ImagePrint manage to get out of a garden-variety dot-matrix printer is nothing short of remarkable. Still, software can be no more capable than the available hardware, and CGA or monochrome screens and dot-matrix printers have their limitations.

Today things are different. Today, a VGA screen and a laser printer or a 24-pin dot-matrix printer are the lowest common denominators. And that fact has opened the floodgates of graphics-related shareware. The things you can do today with a VGA/laser printer system and the right kind of software border on the astounding.

There's just one problem. If you plan to design and produce graphic images yourself, you've got a long row to hoe. Graphics, like communications, is an entirely separate area of personal computing, with its own considerable knowledge base. That's the bad news. The good news is that with the right shareware program, and a small investment of time, you can use your computer system to work wonders with your business materials.

It is precisely those programs that we're going to concentrate on here. But we're going to do more than discuss individual programs. We're going to show you how to assemble a *complete* graphics toolkit. Using nothing but shareware programs, we'll start off by discussing how to easily produce professional-looking business forms with the MORFORM package. Then we'll show you how to quickly create some really snazzy graphs with KDGraf—just the thing to impress your banker the next time you go in for a business loan.

Next, we'll discuss two programs that let you "clip out" graphic images—including the graphs created by KDGraf—and write them to a file. And just why would you want to do that? Well, once you've got an image off the screen and into a file, there are all *kinds* of things you can do with it. Provided you have the right software. The right software in this case is Steven William Rimmer's Graphic Workshop. This program will let you view almost any image, crop it, resize it, and convert it to a different image format. Its commercial equivalent is a program like HiJaak from Inset Systems.

Mr. Rimmer scores again with the next program, Desktop Paint. "DTP," as it is known, is a clone of programs like PC-Paintbrush. DTP supports Hercules, EGA, and VGA monitors and graphics cards. A second program, DTP256, supports Super VGA cards equipped with either 256K or 512K of memory. It can display and let you edit images containing as many as 256 colors.

In other words, you can generate a graph with KDGraf, tell the program to display it, clip it out and write it to a file, and then resize it or convert it with Graphic Workshop. Then you can bring it into DTP or DTP256 and paint, spray paint, edit, add text in several typefaces and point sizes, and print it or incorporate it in your other documents.

Graphic Workshop also supports scanners, so if you've got one, you can scan in any image you like—and do the same things with it that you might do with a KDGraf graph. Lots of people have access to scanners and paint programs, so shareware and public domain libraries are filled with "clip art"—images that you can clip out and modify for use in your business, using the tools presented here. As you can imagine, it is a vast (and rapidly expanding) category in the shareware field, and like everything else, some of it is super and some of it is pretty bad.

Finally, we will introduce you to an incredible CAD (computer-aided design) program called Draft Choice. Produced by the same folks who bring us the As-Easy-As spreadsheet, the drawings, floorplans, organization charts, and other line art you can produce with Draft Choice will knock your eyes out. All of the programs cited are available from the usual shareware sources, including Glossbrenner's Choice.

Create your own business forms

The easiest way to fill your business form needs is to go to a good stationery store and get a pad of preprinted forms. As you probably know, they are more than adequate for most purposes. But, of course, they do not bear your business name and address, and they force you to do things a certain way. If you'd like more control, and the possibility of infinite customization, the shareware package MORFORM is the one to get.

Unlike many other forms generators, MORFORM is as easy to use as a word processing program. It presents you with a blank page and lets you anchor and expand boxes, add text, insert fill patterns (shading), and draw lines at the touch of a few keys. You could do much the same thing in PC-Write, but considerably more effort would be required. Both PC-Write and MORFORM are "character-based." They use only the drawing characters available in the standard IBM extended ASCII code set.

But in PC-Write, if you want to draw a box, you must do so one character at a time by holding down your ALT key and tapping in an ASCII code number. (The box drawing codes run from 179 through 218.) In MORFORM, you can use these characters by hitting the appropriate function keys. If you want to draw a horizontal double line, for example, you merely position the cursor and hold down F2 until the line has extended as far as you want it to go. To add a right top corner at the end of your double line, hit F3. And so on.

The box drawing characters associated with each function key are shown at the bottom of the relevant MORFORM screen. Better still, you can cycle through *all* the box drawing, shading, musical note, happy face, arrow, and other symbols by pressing Alt-K. Each time you press Alt-K, a different set of characters is assigned to the function keys, and the bottom of the screen changes to show you which ones are involved.

Best of all, if you want to draw a box, you merely hit a key and are given a choice of ten different styles. Pick a style, and place the cursor at the upper left corner of the box you intend to draw. Then use your arrow keys to move left, right, up, and down as you size the box to your needs. It's not quite desktop publishing, but this function is close. A single MORFORM form can be up to 30 pages long.

MORFORM and fonts

As you would expect, there is a feature to replicate blocks of the form. That's handy, since most forms contain many identical rows and columns. You may enter any text you like, and you may specify any font your printer can produce. Fonts are specified in the setup portion of the program. You select your printer model, and MORFORM automatically generates the codes needed to activate the standard fonts.

If you want to use different fonts, like the Elfring soft fonts discussed in Chapter 14, you will have to do a little work. You must first download the fonts to the printer, making sure you remember each font's ID number. Then you must give MORFORM the proper escape sequence to activate that font ID. (See Chapter 14 for more detail on using soft fonts.)

That is not terribly convenient, even with Elfring's TSR pop-up font downloader. Fortunately, there is another solution. MORFORM includes an option to print a form to disk. Once you do so, you can edit it in PC-Write as a standard text file. And if you want to print it using soft fonts, you can use the Quicksoft Font Selector program to create a different PR.DEF file to do so.

Again, all of these terms and techniques are explained in Chapter 14.

MORFORM's "Form Fill"

MORFORM makes it very easy to create a master form that you can print and photocopy. And the package comes with many standard forms ready for you to modify and customize (invoice, packing list, daily log, telephone list, etc.). That's what I did with the form shown in Fig. 15-1. I thought the original "Inventory Report" heading looked a bit bare, so I framed it in a double-lined box. The process took about 15 seconds.

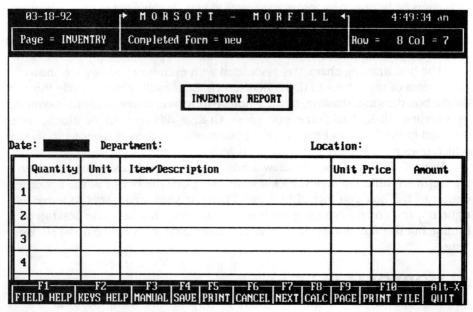

Fig. 15-1. One of many MORFORM forms.

If you don't want to photocopy and store a lot of forms, you can use MOR-FORM to print out copies on demand, or print the forms to disk and do the same thing with PC-Write.

But MORFORM does more than aid you in creating and modifying forms. You can also use the program to *fill in* the forms you have designed. That doesn't sound like much of a benefit. After all, what's involved but automatically tabbing from one field to another? Well, that is only half the story.

MORFORM has three modules. One will help you design and lay out your form. Another is called up when you want to fill in a form. The third is the forms definition module. And thereby hangs a tale. In the forms definition module, each blank is treated as a "field." You can define each field by specifying various characteristics (numeric, date, phone number, Social Security, etc.).

For example, if you define a field as "date-current," the current date will automatically appear in that field when you go into the "fill in" module. If you define a field as "multiple choice," a list of choices will appear on the screen, and you will be asked to select one. This feature has many potential applications. It might be helpful if you buy the same product from several vendors and need to record the source of a given item when taking inventory. Or you might use it if you or your employees are preparing an expense report and need to record the airline you used on a particular trip.

Most important of all, you can attach *formulas* to specific fields. MORFORM supports the basic arithmetic functions (add, multiply, subtract, and divide, as well as average), so if you want a field to be filled in automatically with, say, the sum of two or more other fields, you can easily attach the necessary formula. I say "easily" because MORFORM presents multiple prompt screens to guide you every step of the way.

MORFORM is a powerful, easy-to-use package that out-classes everything else in the field. It keeps things simple by limiting itself to character graphics, but the results you can produce with it are impressive indeed. If you've ever used a word processor, you already know the basics of operating MORFORM, and you will be able to turn out professional quality forms in minutes.

Impressive business graphs

Years ago, someone wrote a book called *How to Lie with Statistics*. Well, if you can lie with statistics, you can fool all of the people all of the time with graphs. Human beings are visually oriented creatures. We look at graphs and immediately grasp the point the graph-producer is trying to convey. But having gotten the "point," we are often reluctant to bear down on the numbers behind the graph to see if the image is a true reflection of the state of things.

If you look around, you may conclude that there are far too many graphs. Some of them are important and useful. But often, as is the case with computer magazines and some newspapers, graphs are done simply because it is so easy to produce them. That's my real point here. The information you choose to graph or not to graph is up to you. But whatever you do, it ought to be easy.

One of the easiest, most intuitive graphing programs going is KDGraf from David Befort at KD Ranch Enterprises. The shareware registration fee is $5, and it is optional. Thinking it might be a misprint, I called Mr. Befort and learned that he enjoys hearing from his users and feels that asking $5 gives them an excuse to write. When you see what KDGraf can do, I think you'll agree that it is worth many times more than $5.

KDGraf Features

The program offers over a dozen different graphing styles, and it comes with lots of sample graphs so you can quickly see what options are available without entering any data. The graph types available are as follows:

- Vertical bar
- Vertical stacked bar
- Vertical 3-D bar
- Vertical stacked 3-D bar
- Horizontal bar
- Horizontal stacked bar
- Horizontal 3-D bar

- Horizontal stacked 3-D bar o Pie
- Line
- 3-D line
- Stacked line
- Stacked 3-D line

KDGraf is designed for use on an EGA or VGA system, and it supports most Epson compatible printers (FX-80 and above), HP LaserJets and compatibles, and CalComp ColorMaster and PlotMaster thermal transfer printer/plotters. The CalComp printouts are in color. A maximum of six sets of values can be displayed over 60 occurrences. So a maximum of 360 values can be shown. The sample graphs provided track sales of six product categories over 12 months, for example.

In addition to values and names of data items, you can add up to three titles using varying fonts and colors. You can also incorporate up to nine notes and place them at any location you like on the graph. There's even a free-form line drawing capability.

There are lots of other features as well. But the one you will probably like best is the way you can easily look at your data as presented in each type of graph. Enter your data, select a chart type, and when you press Enter, the program takes you to "View." Press Enter again, and you will quickly see your graph on the screen. If you want to try a different chart style, it is easy to zip across the top-line menu and pull down the Chart menu again.

The only real drawbacks to KDGraf are the fact that it does not have any facility for importing data from, say, a spreadsheet or database program, and the fact that you have to tell the printer the orientation (portrait or landscape) you want to use the first time you print a graph during each session. But these are only small inconveniences, particularly when you consider that the program makes it so easy to produce results like those shown in Fig. 15-2.

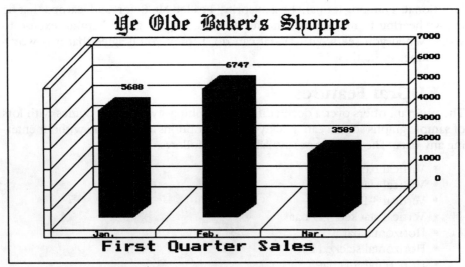

Fig. 15-2. A demonstration of KDGraf.

Capturing the screen

The images you see on your screen, whether text or graphics, exist in computer memory as bits and bytes. To capture and save those images to a file, you need a program capable of writing that area of memory to disk. That's what PCXDUMP and GRABBER do. Both programs operate as TSRs. You load them into memory before you display an image you want to capture, then call them up by pressing a hotkey combination.

Each program has its strengths and weaknesses. Gerald Monroe's GRABBER is by far the more professional of the two. But the images you capture with the shareware version of his product all contain a box of text urging you to register. Previous versions of GRABBER placed the box smack dab in the middle of the image, making it completely unusable. In the current version, the advertising is more subdued: the box appears in the lower right corner of the image, making it easy to edit out in many cases.

GRABBER

Mr. Monroe is an excellent programmer. His DISKID program for changing the serial number that DOS versions 4 through 5 attach to a disk when they format it is extremely useful. GRABBER is top-drawer as well, even if the advertising places it on the borderline between deliberately weakened "crippleware" and genuine shareware.

You load GRABBER by keying in the program name, followed by the path you want it to use when storing its images. If you fail to supply a path, GRABBER will pop up a black-and-white message informing you that it has not been loaded. When you do specify a path, the confirmation message appears in blue and gold.

GRABBER can be used with any monitor (CGA, MGA, Hercules, EGA or VGA). It can handle virtually every video mode and many, but not all, Super VGA cards. Super VGA is a wild and woolly area in which uniform standards have yet to develop. At this writing, Super VGA is pretty much video card-specific.

Once GRABBER has been loaded, you can capture any screen by holding down your Ctrl key and pressing the equals (=) key. (You can change this default hotkey if you like.) You will hear a beep, and GRABBER will tell you the name of the file it plans to use. Hit Enter, and the screen will be captured. GRABBER will beep again when it has finished writing to disk. You may also use your mouse (press both buttons for about two seconds) to activate the capture. This is important when using programs that completely take over the keyboard.

GRABBER can use both extended and expanded memory. And there is a command you can use to unload it from memory.

All GRABBER screens are captured to .EXE files. That means that you can simply key in SCREEN01.EXE, and the screen you have captured will instantly appear. This lets GRABBER offer a "slide show" capability. As the program's on-disk documentation points out, you can prepare a script for your slide show using a batch file that will display each screen for a given amount of time. One might use this when making presentations to employees or potential customers. You might use KDGraf to prepare a series of graphs illustrating key points in your talk, and use GRABBER to capture the screens and display them on cue.

The GRABBER package includes utility programs to capture and edit text screens. But the most important tools are those that let you extract and convert images from GRABBER's .EXE screen files to different formats. One utility, for example, will produce .PCX files, and another will produce .GIF files. In other words, if you have used GRABBER to capture a screen and store it in SCREEN02.EXE, these utilities can extract the image into a file in the .PCX or .GIF format. (We'll have more to say about graphic file formats in a moment.)

GRABBER is a well-planned, well-executed package. And, while the ad that appears on every captured image urging you to register is irritating, it's not a deal-breaker. Just be sure to get version 3.9 (February 2, 1992) or higher, since in the earlier versions the ad appears in the middle of the image. The registration fee is $59 or $29, depending on the amount of capability you wish to buy.

PCXDUMP

The .PCX graphics file format is as close as the graphics field has yet come to a universal standard. The format was created by ZSoft Corporation, makers of some of the leading PC paint programs. Over the years it has become so popular that virtually all graphics-oriented programs support .PCX files, almost by default.

PCXDUMP, from Denmark's Jesper Frandsen, takes advantage of that fact to let you capture many screens into .PCX files. The result is a very effective program that captures images, with no advertising message superimposed. However, the program will only handle VGA and Super VGA (SVGA) modes; unlike GRABBER, it does not support Hercules, CGA, or MGA screens. Since most people these days have at least a VGA system, however, this is not a major drawback.

Four hotkey options are included. One gives you a two-color file, one gives you an inverted (black=white, etc.) two-color file, and one gives you a 256-color (SVGA) file. All three of these options can be used with a mouse. The fourth option dumps an entire 256-color screen to disk, but does not let you use your mouse.

The mouse option is an added extra. When you activate PCXDUMP in one of the first three modes, you may use your mouse to crop the image you want to write to disk. Both mouse buttons are used, and you will soon get the hang of it. If you do not want to save an image, simply hit Esc. The program beeps when activated to let you know it is on the case; and it beeps again with a matching tone when it has finished writing to disk.

The program in its current version (3.70), however, still has a few rough edges. There is no command to unload it from memory, for example. And there is no way to tell it to put its saved files into a particular directory. It simply writes to the directory you are currently using.

Also, the mouse-activated crop lines are thin and a bit faint on some screens. On screens with a black background, the mouse lines are completely invisible. You may be able to compensate by controlling the colors used by the application that is generating the graphic, however. This is easy to do when creating graphs with KDGraf, for example.

The main point, however, is that PCXDUMP does indeed perform as advertised. And its deficiencies are easily overcome, if you know how to use DOS to copy and delete files. The author asks a shareware contribution of $5.

A crucial note!

Whenever you are dealing with graphics cards, it is important to remember that there are only the outlines of standards. In retrospect, the entire field appears to be at the same stage that the 9600 bps modem market was several years ago. Various manufacturers are currently struggling to establish their way of doing things as the de facto standard, but none has yet emerged.

For those of us trying to get the most out of our video hardware, this situation presents a real challenge. Plain VGA is pretty well set. But when you move into Super VGA, all bets are off at the present time. The hardware does indeed work, but you almost always need special video card-specific "driver" software to make it do so.

Western Digital's Paradise, ATI VGA Wonder, Headland Video 7, Tseng Labs, and Trident, for example, are among the leading high-performance video cards available at this writing. If you want to work at SVGA resolutions with 256 colors, you will need to populate your video card with 256K, 512K, or a megabyte of memory. And you will need a special driver, not only for the brand of card you use, but possibly for the specific model within that brand.

If this were not the computer field, one could easily say, "That's ridiculous!" Since it *is* the computer field, however, all you can do is shrug and say, "That's par for the course. Wake me when they get it all sorted out."

In the meantime, if you plan to work with your video hardware, there's a crucial tip you should know. First, try the program without doing anything special. But if it does not work, your next step should be to *turn off the computer*. Wait a moment. Then turn it on again and boot up with a "plain" DOS disk. (You can create a plain system disk with DOS's FORMAT command using the /S switch.)

All of the programs discussed in this chapter work. I've tested them personally on a 386 clone system with an inexpensive 512K video board that is compatible with the Paradise Professional. In some cases, as with DTP256, the results are breathtaking. But in one case I wasted literally *hours* trying to make something work. It had worked once before, and it should have worked again. But it didn't, no matter what I did.

My mistake was in assuming that a "warm reboot"—the sort you do with Ctrl-Alt-Del or by hitting the Reset button—would reset the video board. Apparently it does not. Or at least, it does not reset *my* video board. The problem was not solved until I finally had the inspiration to turn the system off and restart. From then on, everything worked like a charm.

So, if you experience problems using SVGA mode programs, check to make sure that the software has been installed properly. Then make yourself a plain DOS boot disk (**FORMAT A: /S**) and turn the system off. Put your plain boot disk in Drive A and turn the system on. Then try again. If things still don't work, the driver software may simply be incompatible with your video board. Rather than beating your head against the desk—or putting your fist through the monitor—contact the programmer to see if a driver exists for your particular type of hardware.

I want to emphasize that, while this is good advice in any case, it really applies to SVGA operations. Plain VGA work is very standard and fairly routine.

Graphic Workshop

Let's assume that you have produced a graph with KDGraf and captured it to disk with PCXDUMP, or with GRABBER and then converted it to a .PCX file. What can you do with it? The answer is, "Not much, unless you have a graphics viewing program." There is no way to even look at a graphic image from DOS. You can always TYPE a text file or use Vernon Buerg's LIST program to view it (Chapter 16). But a graphics file does you little good unless you have the right software.

In this case, the program to get is Steve Rimmer's Graphic Workshop (GWS). The registration fee for this widely available program is $40, and it is easily worth three times that amount. GWS has the ability to almost instantly show you the image in almost any graphics file.

A complete explanation of graphics files is well beyond the scope of this book. Indeed, the subject amounts to a book in itself. All you really need to know is that, when it comes to computer graphics, there are many ways to skin a cat. For one reason or another, different companies have come up with their own ways to put a graphic image on the screen.

The problem is that as a user, particularly a shareware user, you are likely to encounter all such formats. The genius of a program like Graphic Workshop is that it embraces nearly every format known to man or computer. It can show the images to you, and, even more important, it can convert a given image file to the other leading formats. For example, here are the formats GWS supports:

- Macpaint
- GEM/IMG
- PC Paintbrush PCX
- CompuServe GIF
- TIFF
- WordPerfect Graphics WPG
- Deluxe Paint/Amiga IFF/LBM
- PC Paint Pictor PIC
- Truevision Targa
- Windows 3 BMP
- Microsoft Paint MSP
- Encapsulated PostScript EPS
- Self-displaying EXE pictures
- Text files
- Halo CUT

Graphic Workshop works with bit-mapped graphic files, as opposed to "vector graphic" files. It will handle most of the popular formats, and it will do so in a simple, menu-driven environment which lets you do the following:

- View the images in the files.
- Convert between any two formats (with a few restrictions).
- Print them to any LaserJet Plus compatible or PostScript laser and many dot-matrix printers. Graphic Workshop can print color pictures to color PostScript and inkjet printers.
- Dither the color ones to black and white.
- Reverse them.
- Rotate and flip them.
- Scale them to larger or smaller sizes.
- Reduce the number of colors in them and do color dithering.
- Sharpen, soften and otherwise wreak special effects on them.
- Crop them down to smaller files.
- Scan in completely new files, assuming that you have a supported scanner.
- Adjust the brightness and color balance of the color ones.

Using Graphic Workshop

The program will handle image files of any size. It will use extended or expanded memory, if available, as well as disk space. GWS supports almost all of the leading video cards. If you have a CGA, EGA, stock VGA, or Hercules card in your system, Graphic Workshop will probably be able to detect it and set itself up accordingly. If you have a Super VGA card, however, the program must be configured to use it. (A selection of SVGA drivers is provided.)

But where is an IBM clone user likely to get a copy of an image created on a Macintosh or a Commodore Amiga. One answer is certainly communications. When you go online with CompuServe or GEnie, for example, you will find thousands of images created by Mac and Amiga users, as well as thousands more done by DOS users. By downloading these files to your system, you automatically overcome any disk file format incompatibilities, although these days, some Mac disks can be read by DOS systems and vice versa.

With the image on your disk, the next step is to view it to see what you've got. GWS makes this easy. Simply copy the image file into the GWS directory on your hard disk and key in **GWS**. You will see a list of files on your screen with a reverse highlight cursor. Move the cursor to the file you want to view, and press Enter. GWS will do the rest. The image will be on your screen in moments.

At that point, you can decide whether you want to resize the image or convert it to some other format. Or you may simply wish to print it. Graphic Workshop has easy-to-enter function keys for all of these operations and more.

Graphic Workshop simply has no parallel in the shareware world. It is equivalent in every way to a commercial package like HiJaak. And, as a purchaser of HiJaak, I can tell you that GWS is easier and more satisfying to use.

Desktop Paint and DTP256

At this point, let's assume that you have captured to disk as a .PCX file a graph from KDGraf. You have looked at it in Graphic Workshop, just to make sure that the file does indeed contain the image you had in mind. Now you want to "play" with it. Perhaps you want to add some text, or perhaps you would like to clip out or insert other images. The program to use is Desktop Paint (DTP) from Steve Rimmer's Alchemy Mindworks, Inc.

This program will simply blow you away. I undoubtedly found it easy to use because I own PC Paintbrush IV Plus, for that is DTP's inspiration. If you yourself have never used a paint program, the learning curve may be a little steeper. But the only real requirement is that you have a Microsoft-compatible mouse. Using a paint program without a mouse is like trying to play the piano with several fingers in splints.

I do not want to mislead you. DTP lacks many of the advanced features of PC Paintbrush. It operates only in black and white, and due to some programming language limitations beyond Mr. Rimmer's control, it places severe limits on the size of the image you can clip out and save or place on your "clipboard." But Mr. Rimmer assures us that he is working on overcoming this problem. In the meantime, Alchemy Mindworks has produced DTP256, a Super VGA version, that produces 256 colors and lets you control the red/green/blue balance of each one.

For a quick example of the kinds of images you can edit or create with DTP, see Fig. 15-3. All of the elements shown in this figure are supplied with the program. I merely did some cutting, pasting, and fiddling.

For those who *do* know paint programs, DTP offers cut, spray paint, text (several built in typefaces in several font sizes), paintbrush, roller, erase, line drawing (three widths), and editing or painting at the pixel level. There is, as yet, no ruler or image sizing function. But you can set gradient and fill patterns and bring up a grid.

If you are a new user, here are a few hints and tips. First, the File menu will let you open a currently existing file. (The program comes with EXAMPLE1.PCX.) Second, the "scissors" is your "select" tool. Move the mouse pointer to a portion of the image when the "scissors" is active, press a mouse button and drag the mouse to generate a box containing the portion of the image you want to work with. Then access Edit to clip or copy. Access Desk to get to the clipboard, and you should see the boxed image. Now, "Export" the image to a file. Then close your current file via the File menu, and open the image clipping file you have saved.

The main thing to remember if you are a new user is that you are not dealing with a blank tablet. You can move only within the boundaries of the image you are working with. If the image is too large or too small, use Graphic Workshop to resize it. At this writing, you cannot do so within DTP.

DTP256 is even more powerful. But don't bother getting it unless you have a Super VGA card with at least 256K of memory, and, preferably, 512K or 1 MB. If you have a card compatible with Western Digital/Paradise Plus or Professional, ATI VGA Wonder, Tseng Labs 3000 series, Trident 8900 series, or Headland Video

Fig. 15-3. Image from Desktop Paint.

7 or 1024i, then you will find the necessary software drivers accompanying the package. And you will have a ball working with 256-color images.

Oceans of clip art

The reason clip art is called "clip art" is that for many years, collections of printed images have been available to advertising agencies and other firms wishing to create professional looking ads and artwork. The images are supplied in books, and they are designed to be clipped out and pasted into a mechanical. The mechanical is then photographed, and from the negatives, printing elements are made to produce the final ad or brochure or whatever.

All manner of graphic devices are available—from a pointing finger to Master-Card and Visa symbols. There are also lots of line drawings of typical business situations. Two people talking, an executive pointing to a sales chart at a meeting, three people talking, and so on. The art is generally uninspired and quite run-of-the-mill.

Much the same could be said of the electronic clip art that has become available in recent years. The motto of many seems to be "Have scanner, will upload." This would not pose a problem were it not for the fact that by their very nature, graphic images occupy a lot of disk space, even when "ZIPed" or otherwise compressed.

One can easily spend scores of dollars downloading files from an online system or purchasing disks from a disk vendor, only to find that little, if any, of the images are good enough to use. On the other hand, every now and then you strike gold. And that not only makes it worthwhile psychologically, it also makes it worthwhile financially. For when all is said and done, when you have viewed and rejected scores of image files, electronic clip art is still much cheaper to obtain than the cost of hiring a commercial artist.

The image in Fig. 15-4 offers a good example of what I mean. The screen shot was taken while Steve Rimmer's Desktop Paint was active, editing one of a series of clip art images dealing with the months of the year. Never in a million years could I draw something like this. Yet I can download it from an online system, or get it from a disk vendor and then modify it to suit my needs using Graphic Workshop and DTP.

Fig. 15-4. Clip art example.

There are much simpler images available as well. One collection I know of, for example, offers four or five representations of the word SALE. Use Graphic Workshop to view and select the one you want. Then use the same program to crop the image and blow it up or shrink it down. Copy the file into your DTP directory and use Desktop Paint to customize it to your needs, if necessary. Print it out and paste it into the mechanical of your ad, or whatever.

You will need to practice a little with the various programs, of course. But once you get the hang of things, you can download image files, clip out the portions you want, size them to your needs, add text, shading, and basically do anything you want. It is important to be aware of the learning curve, though. You are not going to be able to do all of these things if you have just purchased a computer. But with a little practice, you really can become a graphics master. Besides, don't tell anybody, but playing with graphics really is fun. Worst case, you won't end up with what you want, but you will have learned a great deal.

Draft Choice

I can't draw my way out of a wet paper bag. But I know superb software when I see it, and Draft Choice from TRIUS, Inc. is unquestionably in that category. The program was written by David Schulz, of As-Easy-As fame, to offer computer-aided-design (CAD) capabilities on an ordinary personal computer, as opposed to an expensive engineering workstation.

It runs on CGA, MGA, and EGA video systems and supports HP Laserjets and compatibles, Epson dot-matrix printers and compatibles, and HP pen plotters. Other features include zoom, window, scale, rotate, mirror elements, lines, circles, polygons, boxes, arcs, bezier curves, cubic splines, and more. There is even an option to create your own fonts, a slide-show playback option for animating drawings, mouse support, and scores of other features. Just look at Fig. 15-5 for an example of what Draft Choice can do. (Hint: Only half of the house was actually drawn. The other half was simply replicated and flipped using a Draft Choice feature.)

Draft Choice also imports and exports files to AutoDesk and other standard formats. The program comes with a variety of prepared drawings, including the one shown in Fig. 15-5, to demonstrate its capabilities. I could go on at length, but for now, it is enough to say that when you load and run Draft Choice, you know immediately that you are in good hands. It feels like you're driving an expensive sports car—but it's shareware.

Conclusion

Computer graphics can be among the most rewarding of all applications. But it can also be among the most frustrating. I suggest that you approach the field with a sense of humor and with a lot of patience. You cannot expect to become a graphics master overnight, any more than you can expect to master the ins and outs of communications in a few hours.

However, as with communications, mastering graphics, or at least gaining a measure of competence, can be enormously rewarding. The software tools discussed in this chapter will be a tremendous help to you along the way. You really can prepare a graph, clip it out, view and size it, edit the image, and incorporate it into your business publications. And if you need to draw anything—from a set of

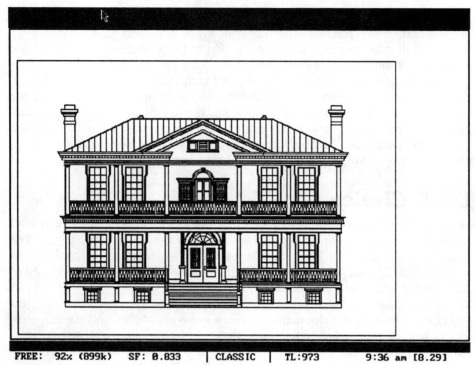

FREE: 92% (899k)   SF: 0.833 | CLASSIC | TL:973   9:36 am [8.29]

Fig. 15-5. Draft Choice "Classic."

blueprints to a simple roadmap—you will find that a program like Draft Choice makes it easy.

The message is to use the technology. The VGA/laser printer systems that have become the current entry level standard are capable of so much more than just word processing and text production. The programs profiled in this chapter will show you the way.

16

Crucial utility programs

AT ONE TIME OR ANOTHER, ALL OF US HAVE CONSIDERED A QUESTION LIKE, "If I were stranded on a desert island, which five books would I want to have with me?" The computer equivalent would be, "If I were condemned to sit in front of my machine all day, which five utility programs would I want to have with me?"

A utility program, as its name implies, does something useful. It doesn't produce text or calculate spreadsheets. It helps you use your system. As you would expect, some utilities are more useful than others. And some are absolutely essential. Thus, while I'd have a real problem picking the five books I'd want to spend the rest of my life with, I know exactly which four utility programs I would pick.

They are: FANSI Console, CED, LIST, and QFILER. You have probably never heard of any of them. But once you try them, you'll be hooked and, like me, you will refuse to use a computer without them. (If I'm going to a friend's house to work on his machine, I take these programs with me like a doctor carrying a medical bag.) All of them are shareware, available from the usual sources and from Glossbrenner's Choice.

In this chapter, we're going to introduce you to these four crucial programs. Then we'll look at a shareware program that will help you learn the most important computer skill of all—touch-typing.

FANSI (Fast ANSI) console

The "console" in computer-speak consists of the screen and the keyboard. The easiest way to describe FANSI ("fancy") is to say that it gives you complete control over both. The program has scores of features. Indeed, one of its advantages is

321

that it incorporates within a single framework the functions of dozens of small utility programs. (You will find a copy of the main FANSI driver and several related files on the disk accompanying this book.)

For example, FANSI significantly speeds up the keyboard. With FANSI loaded, your cursor will zip across the screen when you press an arrow key or the space-bar. The standard DOS cursor is sluggish and recalcitrant in comparison—you almost feel that you have to coax it where you want it to go. FANSI lets you control your screen colors, re-assign keys, and capture everything that has appeared on the screen to a disk file, even though it scrolled off into space a long time ago.

I'll have more to say about these features in a moment. But first, there is one feature that is so important that you will use it constantly: one-button scroll recall. At the touch of a single key, you can put your system on hold and scroll back through the screens that have already been displayed.

One-button scroll recall

For example, suppose you have a subdirectory containing 100 or 200 files. You key in **DIR** and watch as the filenames scroll by. Midway through the list, you glimpse a file you don't recognize. But by the time that fact registers in your mind, the filename has scrolled off the screen. Or suppose you're online with Compu-Serve or GEnie. The electronic mail messages people have sent you appear and scroll off into space. Only then do you realize that you've forgotten to turn on your comm program's capture buffer.

In either case, with FANSI loaded, you can easily scroll everything back again. Simply hit your Scroll Lock (old-style keyboards) or Pause (enhanced keyboards) key to instantly put everything on hold. A reverse video bar appears at the top of the screen indicating that FANSI has been invoked. Then use your arrow and paging keys to scroll back through the information that has already been displayed.

You can print the information one screen at a time with your Print Screen key. Or you can use another FANSI feature to clip out the information you want to save and write it to a file. When you've finished, just hit Scroll Lock or Pause again to release the display, and things will continue right where you left off.

It is impossible to over-emphasize how important this is or how often you will use the scroll-recall feature. The closest you can come to something like this with DOS is to key in **DIR | MORE** to pipe the output of the DIR command through the MORE filter, causing the information to be displayed one screen at a time. You can also enter a command like **TYPE filename.ext | MORE** to display a text file one screen at a time.

Even so, once a screen has disappeared, it is gone. And DOS can do nothing for you should you want to redisplay electronic mail messages or anything else that has scrolled off the screen in an applications program.

The FANSI instruction file on the enclosed disk contains cookbook instructions for quickly implementing one-button scroll recall on your system. The main things you need to know at this point are that FANSI is loaded by including a line in your CONFIG.SYS file, and that the number of screens you can recall depends on the amount of memory you allocate for the purpose. The version of FANSI supplied here (3.01K) makes full use of extended and expanded memory. (If you use FANSI, do not use ANSI.SYS. FANSI replaces the ANSI driver.)

FANSI can also be loaded "high" with the DEVICEHIGH= command in DOS 5. It goes without saying that you need a 386SX or better computer with, usually, 2M or more of memory to do this. See Glossbrenner's *DOS 5*, Chapters 8, 9, and 10, for a complete explanation. The point is that if you have extra memory, neither the FANSI driver nor its screen recall feature need cost you much in the way of conventional "640K" memory.

Other FANSI features

The features covered so far only scratch the surface of what FANSI can do. I don't want to overwhelm you, so let's just hit a few of the highlights. Among other things, FANSI can

- Speed up the screen display by as much as a factor of 10. When you key in TYPE filename.ext to display a text file, it will flash onto the screen. You can then use FANSI's scroll-recall to call back the pages and review them at your leisure.

- Automatically blank one or two screens (to prevent burn-in) after the number of minutes of inactivity you specify. You don't want to have your monitor end up looking like the display of an automatic teller machine with some phrase permanently burned into its phosphors.

- Expand the type-ahead keyboard buffer to 255 characters. The standard PC keyboard software allows only 15 characters. You may never hear the computer beep in protest again as you fire in more keystrokes than it can handle at a given moment.

- Lets you increase (or decrease) the keyboard key repeat rate to produce a much more zippy response from your arrow, paging, and any other key you keep depressed to accomplish a task.

- Make the Caps Lock key like that of a regular typewriter so it unlocks when you hit a Shift key.

- Completely customize your keyboard, whether you want to alter the meaning of one key, swap two keys, or use the Dvorak keyboard layout.

- Make DOS's "bell" (beep tone) as long or as short as you like.

- Generate audible key clicks. (Good for cheap keyboards that may not click themselves.)

The complete FANSI package

The full FANSI package occupies the better part of two floppy disks. (The shareware manual alone is over 250 pages long.) Consequently, the disk supplied with this book contains just four components of the complete FANSI package. In addition to the FANSI 3.01K driver, there are FANSISET.EXE, SEND.EXE, and DEJA-

VU.EXE. The documentation file on the disk will tell you how to get started using each of these FANSI components.

But, if you are in a hurry to start, load FANSI by incorporating the following command in your CONFIG.SYS file:

`DEVICE=FCON301K.DEV /R=50`

Make sure that the file FCON301K.DEV is in your root directory so DOS will be able to find it when it processes CONFIG.SYS. The switch /R=50 sets aside enough memory to save 50 screens.

Give it a try. Reboot your system with your new CONFIG.SYS. If everything is as it should be, FANSI will produce a banner as it loads in. When the DOS prompt has appeared, enter a few **DIR** commands to get some screens into the buffer. Then press your Pause key. A reverse highlight banner should appear across the top of the screen. Use your arrow and paging keys to scroll back through previously displayed screens. Return to DOS by hitting Pause again or your Esc key.

You can use FANSI to mark off portions of the scroll recall buffer to be written to disk. But often it is faster to use DEJAVU.EXE. Just key in **DEJAVU file name.ext**, and the program will write the entire screen buffer to the file you have specified. You can then use your word processor to locate and edit the text you want.

FANSISET and SEND

Next, try the supplied FANSISET program. Key in

`FANSISET filename.bat SEND`

This will activate FANSISET.EXE and take you to a series of menus offering you the option of setting various FANSI features. If you want FANSI to speed up your keyboard, for example, you will discover that you can use the KEYRATE setting on the FANSISET keyboard menu. (A setting of about 40 ought to put the right amount of pep into your cursor.)

Make your selection(s) and follow the instructions for leaving the program. FANSISET will then create a batch file using whatever you have chosen as your `filename.bat` in the previous command. This file will contain all of the necessary escape sequences and codes to set things up the way you want them.

Each sequence will be preceded by SEND, to call the supplied SEND.EXE program responsible for transmitting them to the system. Naturally, you can incorporate these SEND sequences in your AUTOEXEC.BAT file (use your word processor to insert the batch file FANSISET has created), so everything will happen automatically each time you boot up.

Finally, it is important to be aware of the terms SET and RESET. In computer talk, they do not necessarily mean "on" and "off." Instead, they refer to two different states. The FANSI manual uses these terms frequently, so you'll want to keep the computer-speak definition in mind when you encounter them.

You will have a lot of fun exploring FANSI. Just be aware that the program has so many features one can easily be overwhelmed. My advice is to survey things to gain an idea of the kinds of things that are possible, then concentrate exclusively on the ones that are of interest to you. You can always learn to use the other features later, if the need arises.

Registration information for the full FANSI package, with printed User and Technical manuals, can be found on the accompanying disk.

CED, the DOS Command EDitor

One of the most aggravating error messages is "Bad command or filename." DOS produces this message whenever you type a command incorrectly or tell it to do something with a file that it cannot find (usually because you made a mistake typing its name). Most of the time, you have little choice but to retype everything from scratch. DOS does assign editing commands to the function keys, but with the possible exception of F3, which recalls the last command, they are next to worthless.

Wouldn't it be great if you could recall a command and edit it as you would a line of text in a word processor? If you could make full use of the Ins and Del keys to insert and delete letters and words? How about being able to recall and, in effect, re-issue a command you entered five commands back?

Well, that's what Chris Dunford's CED ("said") has been doing for users since 1985. (Mr. Dunford has generously placed the program in the public domain.) Six years later, Microsoft introduced a utility called DOSKEY as part of its DOS 5.0 package that does the same thing. There isn't space to discuss the differences between CED and DOSKEY, except to note that the latest version of CED matches everything DOSKEY offers and more.

If you are a new user, you will find that DOSKEY does an acceptable job. But like most Microsoft utility programs, DOSKEY is workmanlike and uninspired. In fact, I'd call it clunky. However, CED, like the best shareware software, sparkles. It's fleet-footed and is designed with the kind of intelligence and professionalism that make you wonder whether maybe Microsoft assigns its newest programmers to writing the utilities for DOS.

Define your own commands

In addition to setting up a "circular command buffer" that you can use to recall previously issued commands (just hit your up or down arrow keys), CED also lets you define command synonyms. (The DOSKEY term for this is "macros.")

For example, if you want the system to give you a directory every time you key in d (instead of DIR), you can load CED and key in **CED SYN d DIR**. From then on, each time you hit an upper- or lowercase d followed by Enter, your computer will act as if you had keyed in **DIR**.

Space prohibits a complete list of CED's other features. But you should know that as good as CED is, the commercial version, PCED ("professional CED") is even better. Among other things, it offers an online help command, the ability to automatically log to a file every DOS command issued in a session, a "learn" mode that lets you save to a file the synonyms you have defined during a session for reloading later, and much else besides. The documentation for the public domain version is on disk. PCED customers receive a typeset manual. In both cases, the doc is well written and complete.

Vernon Buerg's famous LIST.COM program

If I could have only three utility programs, instead of the four or five hypothesized at the beginning of this chapter, after FANSI and CED I would have to have LIST-.COM by shareware wizard Vernon Buerg. Mr. Buerg has contributed many wonderful programs over the years, but LIST is undoubtedly what he will be remembered for, just as Ward Christensen is remembered for XMODEM, despite his many other contributions.

The basic operation of LIST is quite simple. You key in `LIST` followed by the name of the file you want to look at. The program takes over and displays the file. You can then zip to the bottom of the file by hitting the End key, return to the top via the Home key, or scroll or page through the contents to your heart's content.

But there is so much more. One of the features you will use most frequently is the FIND function. Simply hit **F** and respond with the string of characters you want to find. LIST will look for a match and take you there. To repeat the search, hit **A** for Again. When you find the section you want, you can clip it out and write it to another file.

Filters, tabs, line feeds, and FIND!

LIST can also filter your files. If you want to expand tab characters, remove backspace characters (usually found as part of words that have been underlined by their creator), add line feed characters to lone carriage returns, or strip the high bits and control characters from a file created by programs like WordStar or PFS:Write, LIST can do it in a flash.

Just bring the file into LIST, set the appropriate options, and follow LIST's procedures for marking lines and dumping text to a disk file. The program includes a command to let you create a version of itself (''clone'') with all of the options and colors set to your preferred defaults.

You can also freeze the top half of the display and scroll through the rest of a file in the bottom half. You can ''shell'' out to DOS to run another program or do something else, and return to LIST with DOS's EXIT command.

Anytime you want to look at a text file, or any other kind of file for that matter, without taking the time to load your word processor, LIST is the program to use. In fact, it's a good idea to ''path'' it so LIST is available at all times, regardless of where you are on your system. You might make a subdirectory called LIST, put all of the files associated with the program in there, and then add `C:\LIST` (or whatever) to the PATH command in your AUTOEXEC.BAT file.

QFILER—''Quick Filer''

The first time I used a PC, I felt like I was drowning. I had no idea what was going on, and every time I would enter a command, like DIR, the system would seem to leap out of my hands and out of my control. With the faster systems that we all use today, I'm sure the feeling is even worse for a new user. You key in **DIR** and—whoosh!—scores of filenames flare onto the screen, challenge infinity, and are soon gone.

FANSI puts a stop to that. CED gives you control over your DOS commands. And LIST lets you peer into and search through any file. But for the ultimate in file management and control, the answer is Kenn Flee's QFILER. With a program like this, and one or two other utilities, there is no need for Microsoft Windows and all the complex baggage it brings with it.

The version of QFILER current at this writing is 7.6A (8/13/91). And, as you might expect after seven major and many minor revisions, it has become quite powerful indeed. Fortunately, the power never gets in your way and never detracts from QFILER's main purpose. That purpose is to give you complete control over your files, in much the same way that FANSI gives you complete control over the keyboard and screen.

The major features

QFILER can do lots of things. It can display a directory tree of your subdirectories and log you onto whichever one you pick. That's handy, but the best way to use QFILER is to "path" it. Make a subdirectory called QFILER and include it in the PATH statement (**PATH C:\;C:\QFILER;C:\LIST**... etc.) that should be part of your AUTOEXEC.BAT file. Then, whenever you want to work with the files in a given subdirectory, go to that location and just key in QFILER.

A screen similar to the one shown in Fig. 16-1 will then appear, with the files listed in the left window. You can cause the program to present your files in

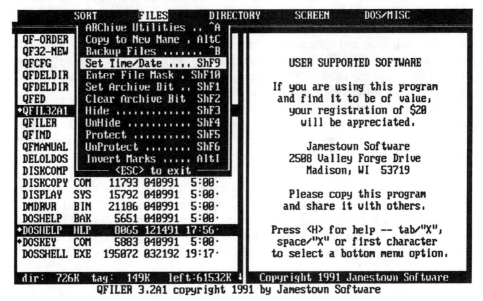

Fig. 16-1. A typical QFILER screen.

unsorted or sorted order. For sorted order you can specify name, date, size, extension, or inverted sort. One way or another, your files end up in a nice box that you can scroll, page, or mouse your way through.

As you move through the file list, a reverse highlight bar tells you which file QFILER is focused on. You can then hit S for "Show" and QFILER will display the contents of the file on the screen. QFILER will automatically call Vern Buerg's LIST program, if you have placed C: \ LIST (or whatever) in your path. If you don't have LIST, QFILER uses QFLIST.EXE, which offers the basic LIST-.COM features.

Let us assume that you have looked at a file and decided to get rid of it. In fact, let's assume that your mission is to clean out old and unnecessary files. You've got one right now, so exit LIST by hitting Esc and "tag" the file in QFI-LER. A diamond will appear to the left of the filename, and the entire filename will be highlighted.

Continue the process. Scroll through the list, looking at and tagging the files you want to get rid of. When you have tagged all of the disposable files, QFILER will let you delete them en masse.

Similarly, imagine that you want to copy a number of selected files from a directory on your hard disk to a floppy. Simply run through the QFILER list, tagging the files of interest. Then tell QFILER to copy all tagged files to a given location (like A: or B:). You will be prompted every step of the way. When the copying is finished, a directory of your target drive or directory will appear in the right window.

Yes, that's right. QFILER can show you two file directories at once. And you can move between them by using your right and left arrow keys. You can also tell QFILER to show you a different directory in each window at any time.

Notice the pull-down menu in Fig. 16-1. You can use menus like this one to control QFILER on a point-and-shoot basis. Or you may enter commands. The FILES menu shown in Fig. 16-1 lets you do all kinds of things to files, including changing their date and time stamps, and making them invisible to the DOS DIR command. The DIRECTORY menu (not shown) will let you create or remove directories, or use the DOS 5 XCOPY command to copy entire directories, including the subdirectories branching off them.

There is much more to say, but space is limited, so let me close this discussion of QFILER with a note about its handling of archive utilities. To use these features, you will have to have copies of PKARC, PKZIP, LHA, and any of the other compression programs you want to use. And they must be pathed so QFILER can find them.

But once this has been done, you can use QFILER as a "front end" to these programs. That means that you can select, say, a file ending in .ARC and "zoom" in on its contents. A list of the files contained in the archive will be displayed in the right window. You may then select the files you wish to extract or view. Similarly, you may tag the files you want to place in an archive and tell QFILER to do it for you.

Touch-typing with PC-FASTYPE

Few things are more satisfying than writing a computer program that—at long last, at 3:00 in the morning—makes the machine do what you envisioned it doing twelve hours and many cups of coffee ago. But programming, like bodywork on your car, major plumbing jobs, and French cooking, is best left to the professionals and inspired amateurs. They have the tools, the experience, and the skills to do it well.

As a computer user, particularly a new computer user, the single most important computer skill you can master is touch-typing. Coming from someone who types for a living, I know that admonition sounds like Tommy in the rock opera of the same name insisting that everyone learn to play pinball. But typewriting really is the universal computer language. The more fluent and facile you are, the more easily you will be able to use any computer and any computer program.

So, to heck with hunt-and-peck. As I have said from the beginning of this book, a computer is nothing more than a tool. And, as with any tool, learning to use it means mastering certain physical skills. Fortunately, computers are not only designed to accept typewritten input, they are also superbly suited to teaching typing skills.

I learned touch-typing at night school some 25 years ago, and then as now, most of a student's time is spent in drills. The instructor clicks a stopwatch and everyone begins typing from a page of text. When the stopwatch is clicked again, students count up the number of words they have typed and the number of errors, and thus calculate their accuracy and speed in words per minute.

PC-FASTYPE features

None of this is fun, but it can be much less onerous if you let your computer handle everything but the typing itself. For a computer, presenting you with text to type and comparing the keys you hit to that text, timing the entire process, and calculating your accuracy and words per minute is child's play. This is undoubtedly one of the reasons why there are lots of typing instruction programs on the market, most of them with list prices of around $50.

I haven't looked at all of them, of course, but they would have to go a long way to beat PC-FASTYPE, with all of its power, its features, and its registration fee of $25. Written by William J. Letendre, PC-FASTYPE requires a computer with a CGA, EGA, or VGA screen. (A monochrome version is also available, but not from Glossbrenner's Choice.)

PC-FASTYPE will work properly regardless of the clock speed of your computer. The program does not interfere with the system clock, and it can be used with either the original style PC keyboard, an old XT-style keyboard, or an enhanced ("101") keyboard.

PC-FASTYPE's operating theater is a detailed color graphics picture of your particular model of keyboard that occupies about two thirds of the screen. The top third of the screen contains the characters or words you are supposed to type.

```
his home town at mid-day carrying a
lighted lantern.  When he was asked to
                                  **
account for such a strange conduct, he
^
said that he was out just looking for
an honest man.
```

Fig. 16-2. A PC-FASTYPE exercise.

(See Fig. 16-2.) A typing rhythm sound beeps in the background as the character you are to type next changes color and blinks on the keyboard. (The sound can be turned off, if you prefer.)

If you hit the wrong letter, an X briefly appears over the incorrect letter and a video game-like sound is issued. There are other details, depending on whether you select the beginner, intermediate, or advanced levels.

When the drill is over, hit any key to see your statistics and an analysis of your performance. As you can see from Fig. 16-3, the program presents your raw speed, the number of errors, and your computed speed, a figure that is calculated by subtracting from your raw speed a penalty for each error. The number of characters in the drill, number of keystrokes entered, and percentage accuracy are also given. The program can also be told to keep a log of your drills, making it easy to chart your progress.

There are other nifty features as well. You can turn the metronome and all other sounds on or off, request that no letters be shown on the key tops, and specify how many characters (from 10 to 99) you want the program to present in each Beginner's drill. You can opt to work on numbers, special characters, capital letters, words, three- or four-letter groups, or phrases; or create your own drills and record them to disk. You can opt to concentrate on just the "home" keys, and you can ask the program to outline the keys that should be hit with each finger.

The program includes lots of help screens and easy-to-use menus, and there is a well-written manual on the disk, including a tutorial about typing techniques in general. (Registered users receive a professionally-printed, bound manual.)

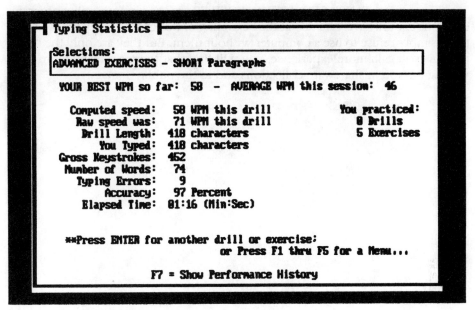

Fig. 16-3. Checking the results in PC-FASTYPE.

Of course, no training program will be effective if the trainee does not participate. So you will have to practice. But I can tell you, it's one heck of a lot more fun learning to type by computer than on an old manual machine with a hovering instructor and a stopwatch. Give it half an hour a day for two weeks or so, and you'll soon find that you're "in the groove." From then on, all of your PC operations will be easier, and you will become even more comfortable with your keyboard as time goes on.

Conclusion

Utility programs are one of the joys of public domain and shareware software. As you gain more experience using your equipment, you will begin to say, "I wonder if there's a way to do thus and so?" In almost every case, thousands of people will have wondered the same thing, and several of them will have written utilities to accomplish the feat. All you've got to do is track them down (CompuServe and GEnie are good bets here, since you can search for files electronically), then reach out and take them.

As a new user, the main message PD and shareware utilities should convey is twofold. First, you are not alone. Literally millions of people have had the same experience and felt the same frustration you have as you get to know your system. Second, you are far from helpless. There are software tools and utilities of every sort that can give you complete control over your system and your files.

To my mind, FANSI, CED, LIST, and QFILER are the top four utility programs everyone should have. As I said at the beginning of this chapter, they are so crucial that I simply refuse to use a computer without them. But they are only the beginning. As you gain more experience, you will find that there are many more gems waiting for you in shareware collections and in the public domain.

17

Fun and games

TALKING ABOUT SHAREWARE WITHOUT MENTIONING GAMES AND OTHER recreational programs would be like discussing Thanksgiving dinner and leaving out the pumpkin and mincemeat pies. We've had our vegetables, meat, and mashed potatoes. We've worked hard. Now it's time to relax for a just a moment and have some fun.

And what fun you can have! As with every other category of shareware, game programs range from the awful to the spectacular. And I do mean *spectacular*. The quality of the graphics, sound, music, and animation found in the best shareware games these days is breathtaking. They are easily on a par with the latest "16-bit" Nintendo and Genesis offerings, and, because they are shareware, they are a lot cheaper.

Although a number of games can work with lesser equipment, most offer peak performance with what has become the entry level hardware configuration: VGA, hard disk, mouse, and at least 640K of memory. Many can make use of expanded or extended memory and a joystick, if available.

In this chapter, I'd like to take you on a brief tour of some of the best games going. We'll start with Power Chess and Glencoe Blackjack. Then we'll enter Hugo's House of Horrors and touch base with Hugo and Penelope in their second adventure, Hugo II, Whodunit?.

The program will help you develop the skills and techniques you need to be successful at the blackjack tables. As Mr. Granger says, "You cannot play blackjack by the seat of your pants and expect to win . . . By utilizing these strategies you can lower the house percentage from around 6% to close to 0%! Often in a session the money is made on the secondary bets (splitting and doubling down), while the regular play ends up in a push. With a firm knowledge of the basic strategy, you will know when to make these bets.''

And these are just a few Apogee titles. All are offered the same way. Shareware users receive the first volume, a fully functional, complete, and challenging game. If you like the product, you can register and receive the additional volumes (stories or scenarios) for as little as $10 apiece. At this writing, I believe I would recommend *any* Apogee Software Productions product, sight-unseen.

Your children will get a kick out of Word Rescue, a top-quality arcade game with an educational purpose. And you will find yourself playing Picture Puzzle, a superb game for turning pictures into jigsaw puzzles that you re-assemble using your mouse. (You can ask for a puzzle with as many pieces as you want.)

Crossword Creator Professional is next. This program makes creating your own crossword puzzles a snap. You can then print the puzzle and clue list, or print the completed puzzle. If you've got kids, they'll also love the coloring book and connect-the-dots artwork offered by Rolf W. Demmerle. They are supplied as .PCX files, which you can view and print using Graphic Workshop (Chapter 15), the commercial program Print Shop, and many other programs.

Power Chess

Power Chess from New-Ware Shareware Products may well be the ultimate chess game. In the first place, it offers excellent graphics and is simple to play. Select a piece with your cursor and hit Enter. Then move the cursor to the target location and hit Enter again, and the piece will be moved. The computer will take ten seconds or more to think, and then it will make its move. After several moves, your screen will look like the one shown in Fig. 17-1.

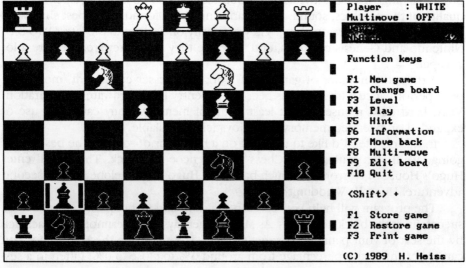

Fig. 17-1. Power Chess.

As far as I'm concerned, that's the essence of good chess software, but Power Chess offers so much more than ease of use. It follows and fully implements the international chess rules, and it tracks a lot of information likely to be of interest to a real chess enthusiast (playing time for Black and White, index of the last 21 moves, index of all possible moves concerning the position on the board, announcement of a checkmate in *n* moves, and computer hints for the next move.)

You can retract a move at any time, and you can call up a number of standard opening moves automatically. There is also a library of games and interesting board positions which you can load and add to, if you feel so inclined. It is very easy, for example, to set up a board to match the board you may have read about in the paper or in a chess magazine. Power Chess is even available (to registered users) in several languages.

If you are concerned about the futility of playing chess against a computer, as I am, you will be pleased to know that you can control how long the computer has to think about a move. You can allow anywhere between ten seconds and 1000 hours. Obviously, the less time you give the machine to analyze every possible move, the better chance you have of winning.

There are lots of other features as well. Power Chess can work with a CGA or Hercules monochrome card, but it looks even better on an EGA- or VGA-equipped system. You will need at least 512K of free DOS memory.

Glencoe Computing's BlackJack!

Blackjack, as most people know, is the casino game in which you try to get as close as possible to "21" without going over. Like Reversi ("GO"), chess, and poker, blackjack has long been a favorite of shareware and public domain programmers. But rarely do you find such a thorough (and thoroughly enjoyable) implementation as that offered by Donald L. Granger's Glencoe Computing. His BlackJack! program does far more than simply cut and deal the cards.

For one thing, it gives you a choice of casinos to play in (Glencoe's Golden Palace, Bally's Park Place, Peppermill Hotel, and Caesar's Palace). That lets you get accustomed to the slightly different rules at each gaming house. If you want, you can simply pick a casino and start playing. (See Fig. 17-2.) But if you want to go further, BlackJack! can accommodate you. The program offers nothing less than a tutorial and training tool to develop and polish your blackjack-playing skills.

For example, Mr. Granger advises that "You are not out to see who can get closest to 21 without going over—you are out to BEAT THE DEALER! This concept is overlooked by many novice players, and it leads to fatter wallets for the casino bosses. Although getting close to 21 is often the best strategy, it's just as important to know when to sit back and let the dealer beat himself."

The program will help you develop the skills and techniques you need to be successful at the blackjack tables. As Mr. Granger says, "You cannot play blackjack by the seat of your pants and expect to win. . . By utilizing these strategies you can lower the house percentage from around 6% to close to 0%! Often in a session the money is made on the secondary bets (splitting and doubling down), while

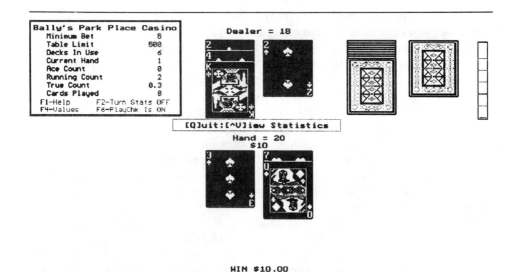

Fig. 17-2. Glencoe BlackJack!.

the regular play ends up in a push. With a firm knowledge of the basic strategy, you will know when to make these bets."

There is far more to Glencoe's BlackJack! than we have space to tell you about here. The main message is that it is both an excellent game and an excellent training tool, and the one capability doesn't interfere with the other. The program is designed to be a totally accurate simulation of casino play. And, with some effort on your part, it can take you to any level of play.

As the manual points out, the program does not claim to offer a sure-fire "system" for beating the casinos. "To become a proficient player you will have to spend many hours practicing basic strategy and, if you desire, card counting. If anyone tells you anything different, don't believe it. These skills simply cannot be learned overnight." But you can begin playing and enjoying BlackJack! immediately.

The registration fee is $30. The program requires an EGA, VGA or Hercules-compatible graphics adapter. It will not run on a CGA or MDA system.

Hugo's House of Horrors

One of the most venerable traditions in computer gaming, and world literature, for that matter, is the "quest." A hero (you) is given a mission of exploring some strange venue with some particular goal in mind. As you progress through various locations, you look for and collect various objects. The objects—a black rod, a bird cage, a pocketknife, etc.—help you overcome obstacles and challenges that lie ahead. And by collecting them, you boost your point total.

Along the way, you key in commands to the computer—and it responds, almost as if another person were sitting somewhere inside your monitor. You might ask questions to have the computer more fully describe your surroundings.

Or you might tell it to "get" some object. The computer might respond, "You're not close enough," or "I don't see any tasty food," or "OK." If you enter a word like ABRACADABRA, it might say, "That is a very old magic word and it does not work here." Or it might say, "Getting desperate, aren't we?"

The interactive approach described here was first implemented in a game called Adventure. Adventure was created in the mid-1970s by Will Crowther of MIT and Don Woods of the Stanford Artificial Intelligence Laboratory (SAIL). It was originally designed to run on a DEC PDP-10 minicomputer. But, along with VisiCalc and DOS, Adventure was among the very first programs Microsoft offered on the original IBM/PC.

David P. Gray's Hugo's House of Horrors (HHH) is a game in the same tradition. Hugo's mission is to explore a haunted house in search of his sweetheart, Penelope. Before he can rescue her, however, he must solve a variety of clever puzzles and challenges, often using items he collects along the way.

But, unlike the classic text-based Adventure, HHH makes full use of sound and graphics. Thus, when you want Hugo to move some place, you do not have to enter a command like GO SOUTH. Instead, you use your arrow keys to move Hugo through a three-dimensional space. (See Fig. 17-3.)

For technical reasons, it is impossible to reproduce the actual EGA/VGA images here with the same crispness and clarity you will see on your screen, so

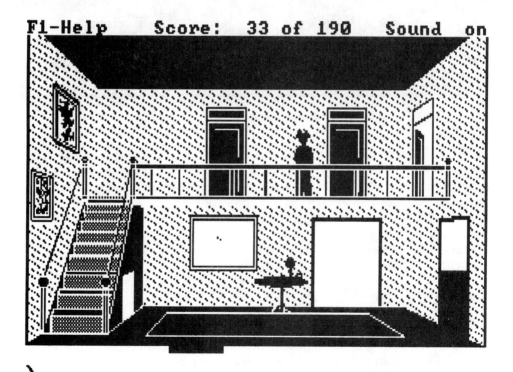

Fig. 17-3. Hugo's House of Horrors.

you will just have to take our word for it. HHH is both colorful and clear. It's also terrifically funny. As you can see from Fig. 17-4, the program narrates the story, though you can also key in questions and commands. It also offers unexpected comments. For example, where the stairs join the back wall in Fig. 17-4, you can key in LOOK and be told that there is a whistle on the floor. Key in GET WHIS TLE, and the program will respond "I wonder what that's for." I could tell you, but I don't want to spoil the surprise.

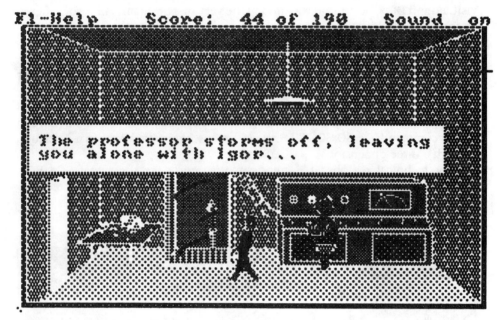

Fig. 17-4. Igor shrinks Hugo down to size!.

You will need a hard disk and an EGA/VGA system to play HHH. The requested registration fee is $20, and it brings with it a free hint booklet, a free self-running version (so you can sit back and watch Hugo do his stuff), and a free new game (when available). HHH has proved so popular that Mr. Gray has created "HUGO II, Whodunit?" In this game Hugo and Penelope visit a country chateau and end up solving a murder. As with HHH, the music, the graphics, the characters, and the surprises are terrific.

Commander Keen
from Apogee Software Productions

A text file supplied with Commander Keen, Volume I, "Invasion of the Vorti-cons," says that never before "has the shareware market seen a game of the quality of Commander Keen. Ultra-high-speed EGA scrolling graphics and animation at 40 frames per second.'' Small wonder that the program immediately rocketed to the top spot on the Shareware Top Ten list maintained by the Association of Shareware Professionals—and remained there for nine consecutive months (April 1991 through December 1991). Here's the setup, freely adapted from on-disk materials.

As Commander Keen, you play the role of Billy Blaze, eight-year-old genius. Billy builds an interstellar ship when not working at home on his college fast-track degree. Among other household objects, Billy uses his Nintendo joystick for flight control and his mom's vacuum cleaner (heavily modified) for his ship's ion propulsion system (with pile height adjustment).

At the first hint of galactic trouble, Billy dons his brother's football helmet and becomes—ta-da—''Commander Keen.'' The Commander's first adventure takes place on Mars, where the Vorticon invasion force is massing for the conquest of Earth. While Keen is exploring Mars, the Vorticons steal pieces of his ship and hide them within their cities.

Keen's mission is to recover all the pieces of the ship and repel the Vorticon invasion. This involves exploring many dangerous cities, packed with diabolical traps and hideous creatures, both of Martian and Vorticon origin. You will use your pogo stick to reach high ledges and jump over deadly pits. Your ray gun can be used to stun the Vorticon invaders.

This shareware episode is the first in a Commander Keen trilogy. The other two, ''The Earth Explodes'' and ''Keen Must Die!'' are available for purchase when you register Volume I with Apogee Software Productions. Each volume has completely unique graphics and animation. Volume II takes place on the immense Vorticon mothership, where you'll need to stop the destruction of Earth by disabling the eight deadly ray cannons aimed at Earth's greatest cities and wonders. Volume III takes Keen to the dangerous Vorticon home planet, where you'll explore huge caves, battle the top Vorticon ninja fighters, and discover the secret of the Grand Intellect.

The Commander requires 520K of free DOS memory to run, and you will need an EGA/VGA monitor. Each volume is $15 if purchased separately. But if you buy all three episodes at once, the cost is just $30 and your package comes with a hint sheet, a cheat mode password, and a new bonus game from Apogee. You will also be able to call the Commander Keen hints line or mail questions to Apogee for assistance.

Goodbye Galaxy

I was so impressed, I called Apogee to rave about their material. Scott Miller, the company's president, said, ''If you thought 'Vorticons' was good, wait till you see 'Goodbye Galaxy.''' Mr. Miller sent it to me, and he is absolutely right. Specially composed music, support for the Ad Lib sound board, an opening that makes you think you're watching a movie, multiple skill levels, more creatures, hundreds and hundreds of screens, joystick support, and more make it a super program. (See Fig. 17-5.)

Fig. 17-5. Commander Keen: Goodbye Galaxy.

Duke Nukem and Crystal Caves

Inspired by the instant success of the original Commander Keen, Apogee programmers produced Duke Nukem. Duke's mission is to stop Dr. Proton, a madman bent on ruling the world with his army of Techbots. As Duke Nukem, you'll chase Dr. Proton deep into the Earth, then to his lunar space station, and eventually into the Earth's nuclear-ravaged future. This Sega Genesis-style game features dual scrolling playfields, with huge 3-D backdrops. Duke jumps and somersaults—he can even cling to ceilings—as he escapes traps and battles Dr. Proton's robot guards.

Other features include four-way scrolling levels, cinematic effects, demo mode, built-in hint mode, arcade sound effects, joystick support, high score chart, save/restore up to nine games, unlimited continues, keyboard reconfigure, sound on/off toggle, cheat mode, and much more.

You will need a hard disk and an EGA/VGA machine operating at a speed of at least 10 MHz to play this game. Additional Nukem episodes are available when you register. According to Apogee, Duke Nukem was voted ''Staff Favorite'' by the reviewers at *PC Magazine*. At this writing, it holds the Number One spot on the ASP Shareware Top Ten Chart.

In Crystal Caves, another leading Apogee game, you enter an underground world of treasures and traps as the intrepid Mylo Steamwitz. As you progress, you enter cave after cave gathering treasures and evading a multitude of devilish hazards. Crystal Caves incorporates elements of Nintendo's Mario Brothers, Commander Keen, and Indiana Jones. As with all Apogee games, a high priority has been placed on solving ingenious puzzles built into the game.

Fig. 17-6. Duke, you're going in!

Variety is also evident in Crystal Caves. On some levels Mylo will even walk upside-down. Other levels have such low gravity that the recoil from Mylo's laser pistol can knock him into other dangers. Some levels are without lights, and others are packed full of falling hammers, egg-dropping alien bats, free-roaming slither eyes, and web-shooting alien spiders. Each level has unique graphics.

For the young and young at heart

The shareware world is filled with excellent games. Increasingly, really imaginative educational programs are showing up as well. If you have children, you will particularly enjoy Word Rescue and Picture Puzzle, since you can play these games along with the young ones. For slightly older kids, you might use Crossword Creator Professional as a way of making it fun to study key facts. And for the very young, there are coloring book and connect-the-dots drawings you can print out.

Word Rescue

Word Rescue is another Apogee Software Productions product. It is designed to teach spelling, logic, word meanings, and reading—all while being as compelling as the best arcade games. The graphics are great (EGA/VGA), and there is support for Ad Lib and Sound Blaster boards. Three levels of play are available, covering ages four through ten and up.

The central character is a child (boy or girl, you choose), who must rescue the stolen words from the Gruzzles. The Gruzzles can't read, and they don't want

342 FUN AND GAMES

anyone else to read. So, they've stolen the words out of all of the books. Benny Bookworm needs the child's help, but he also helps himself by dumping buckets of slime on attacking Gruzzles, when asked to do so. He also appears, umbrella in hand, floating down like Mary Poppins to rescue the child when he or she makes a misstep.

The game is played by jumping up to reach a question mark box. On contact, the box reveals a word, and all the other boxes reveal pictures of objects. The player must then locate and jump up to the picture that matches the word. (See Fig. 17-7.) If a Gruzzle appears, the player hits the spacebar, and Benny Bookworm appears out of nowhere to dump a bucket of slime on the villain. (Assuming Benny has any slime left. But that's another story.)

Fig. 17-7. Word Rescue.

Picture Puzzle

Picture Puzzle from Daniel Linton, Jr., is one of those programs you like the instant you run it. It feels right. It works right. And when you discover one of its many features, you think, "Why, yes, of course!"

What Picture Puzzle does is take a picture and fracture it into jigsaw puzzle pieces or "tiles." The tiles are all rectangles, but that's okay since you can control the difficulty level by opting for anywhere from four to 1400 pieces. Pictures are reassembled by selecting a piece with your Microsoft-compatible mouse and then selecting a new location.

When you click on the new location, the tiles involved will switch places. Each time you succeed in placing a piece next to its proper mates, the grid lines dividing those tiles go away, and you are rewarded with a musical tone. When the picture has been completed, the program plays a little tune. (Sound can be turned on or off.)

Figure 17-8 shows Picture Puzzle in operation. The picture is displayed, and then divided into pieces. Then the pieces are scrambled, as in Fig. 17-9.

Fig. 17-8. Picture Puzzle "Pooch" gets divided into pieces.

Fig. 17-9. Can you put Pooch back together?

If you need help, you can pop up a miniature version of the completed picture in one quadrant of the screen. The program is smart enough to keep track of the area you are working in when you call for this help, and to pop up the miniature in a different area. It also keeps track of your statistics (number of pieces moved, number of moves, etc.), should you want to engage in competitive puzzle solving.

Picture Puzzle can load several types of picture formats. These include its native format (.PUZ), PC Paintbrush format (.PCX), CompuServe "Jif" (.GIF), and .SAV. To use .GIF files, you will need Bob Montgomery's VPIC.EXE (version 2.1A or higher). Files ending in .SAV are created when you opt to save a puzzle before you have completed it.

At this writing, the program only supports $640\times350\times16$ resolution. That means any pictures that are 640 pixels wide by 350 pixels high with 16 colors, and are in one of the above formats, can be loaded and used by Picture Puzzle. Registered users receive a version that supports VGA and Super VGA resolutions, plus ten new puzzles.

I asked Dan Linton how he came to write Picture Puzzle. He told me he wrote the first version for a friend. The friend had a little girl who loved playing with the mouse, but could find few programs that suited. The resulting program was so popular that Dan returned to the keyboard and perfected it. And boy did he succeed.

With graphics by Gary L. Sirois (GLS), this is a truly addictive program. You know you shouldn't be spending time playing with it, but you think, "Well maybe just one more tile. I've almost got it . . .''

Crossword Creator Professional

Clearly, there's not much point in creating crossword puzzles for yourself. But there are lots of times when doing so for others can be a lot of fun. You might create a puzzle to help your kids study a particular subject. Or you might create a puzzle as a unique gift or birthday card. It could even be an interesting promotional gimmick. Sending out crossword puzzles geared to your business along with your brochure, for example, might be a good way to attract your customers' attention.

Whatever the purpose, Brad Kaenel's Crossword Creator Professional makes it easy. The program can generate a puzzle holding up to 36 columns by 23 rows, with clues as long as four lines each. When you have created your puzzle, you can print it out on most major brands of dot-matrix, ink-jet, and laser printers. The puzzle itself will print on one sheet; your clues will be printed separately.

Coloring book and connect-the-dots pictures

Finally, there are coloring book images and connect-the-dots pictures from Rolf Demmerle. These are simply charming. Just the thing to print out and hand to your child while you finish up some things in the office. (See Fig. 17-10.)

It is such a good idea, I wondered why no one had thought of it before and asked Mr. Demmerle how he came to produce these images. He told me that he

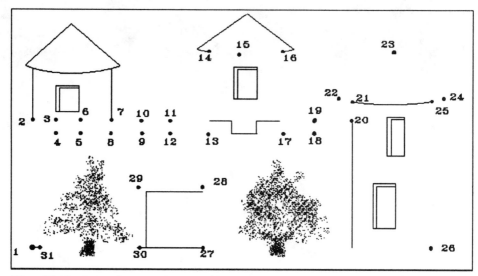

Fig. 17-10. One of many Connect-The-Dot drawings.

had done one or two of them for fun using the commercial program Print Shop. His daughter enjoyed coloring them, often requesting the same picture again and again. Realizing that other parents might have the same need, he produced a portfolio of coloring book and connect-the-dots images and made them available as shareware.

All of the images are supplied as .PCX files, so you can use them with a wide variety of paint programs. If you simply want to view and print them out at various sizes, you can use Graphic Workshop. If you want to alter or customize them, use Desktop Paint. Both of these outstanding shareware programs are discussed in Chapter 15.

Conclusion

It has been a central theme of this book that shareware can fill virtually all of your software needs. So it is appropriate to end with this brief discussion of games and recreational software. After all, none of us can live by word processing, spreadsheets, and databases alone. We need something for the child within. The programs discussed here deliver. In quantity and in quality.

But these are just a few of the top-quality programs of this sort you will find in shareware and public domain collections. You will have a lot of fun exploring them. Just watch out for the really good ones, since the better a game is, the more addictive it will become. And pretty soon, you'll find that you're not getting any work done!

Appendix A

Installing the supplied software

THE DISK ACCOMPANYING THIS BOOK CONTAINS SOME REALLY WONDERFUL programs—programs that will immediately start saving you time and effort while offering an excellent introduction to the kind of imaginative, quality programming you can expect from the shareware world.

Program summary

You will find documentation files for each package on the disk itself. But here's a quick summary of the supplied programs and what they can do for you.

DM Lite

Directory Master Lite from Marc Perkel puts *you* in charge of your hard drive and your files. Simply key in **DMLITE** and your files will appear as a list in a window. (Please see Fig. A-1.) You can cruise up and down the list, tagging the files you wish to copy, move, or delete. Those operations can then be completed in one fell swoop on the tagged files. This is much easier than typing in, say, **COPY** seven different times followed by seven different filenames.

If there is a file you want to view on the screen, you can easily do so. Simply move the pointer to the filename and hit your **V** key to "view" it. This makes it easy to view .DOC and .TXT files without spending the time necessary to load your word processing program.

You can enter a command to change to a different disk drive or to focus on a different directory path. You can tell DM Lite to show you just *.TXT files or use

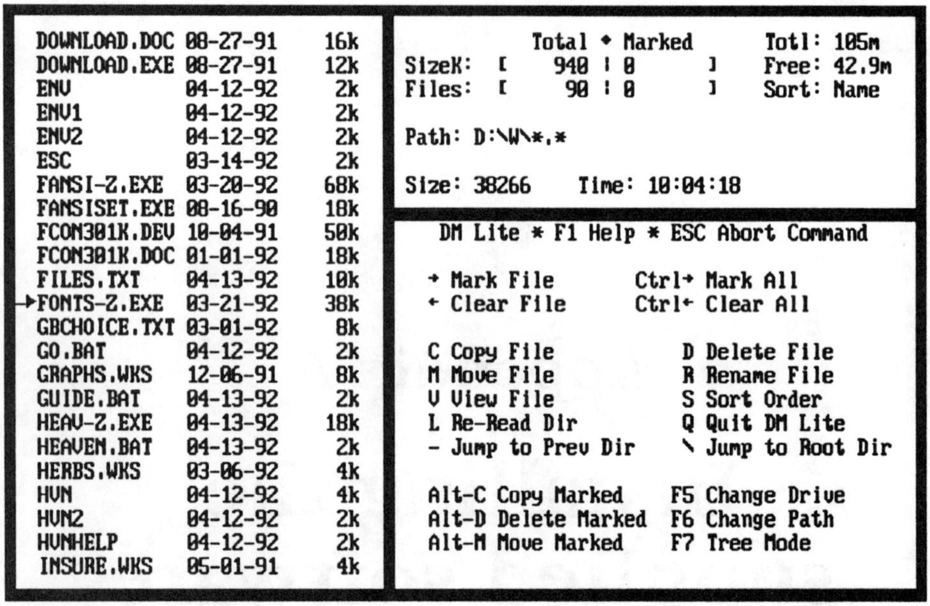

```
DOWNLOAD.DOC 08-27-91   16k              Total * Marked       Totl: 105m
DOWNLOAD.EXE 08-27-91   12k     SizeK:  [    940 ! 0       ]  Free: 42.9m
ENV          04-12-92    2k     Files:  [     90 ! 0       ]  Sort: Name
ENV1         04-12-92    2k
ENV2         04-12-92    2k     Path: D:\W\*.*
ESC          03-14-92    2k
FANSI-Z.EXE  03-20-92   68k     Size: 38266    Time: 10:04:18
FANSISET.EXE 08-16-90   18k
FCON301K.DEV 10-04-91   50k  ┌─ DM Lite * F1 Help * ESC Abort Command ──
FCON301K.DOC 01-01-92   18k
FILES.TXT    04-13-92   10k     * Mark File        Ctrl* Mark All
→FONTS-Z.EXE 03-21-92   38k     * Clear File       Ctrl* Clear All
GBCHOICE.TXT 03-01-92    8k
GO.BAT       04-12-92    2k     C Copy File        D Delete File
GRAPHS.WKS   12-06-91    8k     M Move File        R Rename File
GUIDE.BAT    04-13-92    2k     V View File        S Sort Order
HEAV-Z.EXE   04-13-92   18k     L Re-Read Dir      Q Quit DM Lite
HEAVEN.BAT   04-13-92    2k     - Jump to Prev Dir  \ Jump to Root Dir
HERBS.WKS    03-06-92    4k
HVN          04-12-92    4k     Alt-C Copy Marked   F5 Change Drive
HVN2         04-12-92    2k     Alt-D Delete Marked F6 Change Path
HVNHELP      04-12-92    2k     Alt-M Move Marked   F7 Tree Mode
INSURE.WKS   05-01-91    4k
```

Fig. A-1. DM Lite Sample screen.

some other specification. You can make, delete, and rename subdirectories, or display your directories as a "tree" and move among its branches. DM Lite is simply a super program.

PD

PD or "Pick Directory" is another Marc Perkel gem. Its purpose is to make moving around a disk drive as easy and painless as possible. The first time you key in PD, the program will create a file called PD.PIC containing a "picture" of your disks and their subdirectory layouts. From then on, you can move to different directories by cursoring up and down a graphic tree.

As you move from directory to directory using the graphic tree, an alphabetized list of all of your directories appears in a window at the side of the screen. You can hit your Tab key to switch to that window and look for your target directory alphabetically.

You can make, delete, or rename directories with PD. You can even operate from the command line, keying in PD followed by just the first part of a directory name. PD will search its list for the closest match and switch you to that directory. Thus, you might key in **PD PAC** to be taken instantly to the PACIFIC directory shown in Fig. A-2. Without PD, you would have to key in a command like CD\ED\PACIFIC to accomplish the same thing.

Marc Perkel's PD program, in short, can save you from ever having to type in CD\ again.

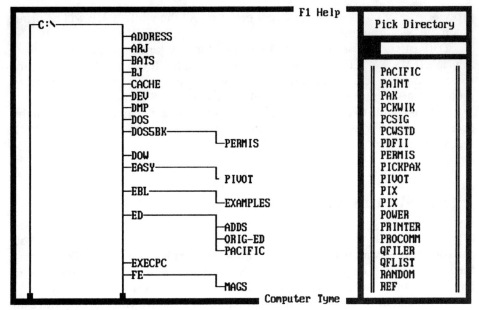

Fig. A-2. Pick Directory Sample screen.

WHEREIS

Marc Perkel has also contributed WHEREIS.EXE. This utility will search through your entire drive looking for the file or files you specify. You will find it most convenient when you cannot remember the complete name of a file. Thus, you might key in **WHEREIS *.PIX** to have the program report the location of every file ending with .PIX. You might also look for all files created before or after a certain date.

Please note that the program PIPEDIR.EXE that is supplied here is the same as WHEREIS.EXE. PIPEDIR is required by the Pick Directory program. I've supplied a little batch file called WHERE.BAT that copies PIPEDIR.EXE to WHEREIS.EXE.

DMP

This program is presumably pronounced "dump," as in the common computerese expression "dumping a file to the printer." It is a full-blown print spooler that is designed to let you get back to work as soon as possible after you issue a print command.

DMP sits in memory waiting for someone to send a file to the printer. When it sees this happen, it steps in and accepts the file on the printer's behalf. Depending on available hardware, DMP temporarily stores the file in memory or on disk and pays it out to the printer whenever the CPU has a spare moment.

This means that, with DMP loaded, you can tell PC Write (or any other word processing program) to print a file and be back at work in seconds, instead of being forced to wait until the printer has finished. You can even leave your word processor and go on to some different program. All the while, DMP will be printing in the background.

DMP offers lots of options and will spool to any kind of memory you have available (EMS, XMS, DOS), or spool to disk if need be. It can also be used to turn the contents of a screen into a text file. All you have to do is issue a command to redirect DMP to put its output into a file instead of sending it to the printer.

DMP is simple to use. But be sure to read the 37-page manual (supplied on the accompanying disk) to learn how to use all of its features. You will find that DMP is a real timesaver.

FANSI Console

Just as DM Lite gives you complete control over your drives and files, FANSI ("fancy") Console gives you complete control over your computer system. You can use it to vastly increase the speed with which text is displayed, while boosting the responsiveness of your keyboard. FANSI can make your CapsLock key operate like that of a regular typewriter so that it unlocks when you hit a Shift key.

FANSI can do many other things as well, but the feature you will find you cannot live without is "one-button scroll recall." With FANSI loaded, you can put the system on "hold" at any time and use your arrow and paging keys to recall and scroll through previously displayed screens.

That means, for example, that you can key in DIR and let the system display the files in a rush. Then just toggle FANSI on by hitting your Pause key and scroll back through the directory list at your leisure. This feature alone will save you hours of time and untold frustration in the course of a year.

UTILS-Z.EXE

To round out the program side of the accompanying disk, I've included four additional utilities that you will find quite helpful. These can be found in the self-extracting archive file (explained later) UTILS-Z.EXE. They include COLOR.COM, a program that makes it simple to change your foreground, background, and border colors. As long as either FANSI or DOS's ANSI.SYS is loaded (via your CONFIG.SYS file), COLOR.COM can change your screen colors in a twinkling.

You may want to experiment with a color combination you like and then include a command like COLOR 2,4,14 in your AUTOEXEC.BAT file. Doing so will set your preferred colors automatically each time you boot up. You may also wish to use your AUTOEXEC.BAT file to turn off your keyboard's NumLock key. For this reason, I have included NUMOFF.COM and NUMON.COM.

Finally, it can be very helpful to be able to rename a hard disk directory. DM Lite and PD both have this power, but the supplied RENDIR.COM is even quicker. All you have to do is key in RENDIR, and the program will prompt you for the name of the target directory. Key that in and you will be prompted for the new name you would like to use.

Elfring Soft Fonts

You will want to see Chapter 14 and Fig. 14-1 for more details on the incredible Elfring shareware soft font package. There was room for only three fonts on the accompanying disk (Black Chan 12 point, Black Chan 14 point, and Broadway 18 point). Nevertheless, they make an impressive demonstration of Mr. Elfring's artistry, and you will find yourself using them to create special memos, announcements, and printouts right away. Also supplied on the accompanying disk is the Elfring download program needed to get the soft fonts into the printer. The complete Elfring Soft Font shareware package can be found on Glossbrenner's Choice disk Laser 1.

Writer's Heaven and PRDEF.DOC

As explained in Chapter 9, Writer's Heaven is a package of macros designed for use with PC Write Standard Level. You may or may not wish to use the entire package, but every PCW user will find something of value in Writer's Heaven. You may wish to incorporate its pop-up notepad, for example, or its address grabber and envelope printer. The file PRDEF.DOC offers insights and tips for using fonts with PC Write. (PR.DEF is PC Write's printer definition file.) You are sure to find it helpful.

MAGS and PHONES

These are two Glossbrenner-created databases for use with File Express. (See Chapter 10.) They are designed to both illustrate FE features and to be of use in actual practice. Emily and I use MAGS to keep track of our magazine subscriptions so we don't inadvertently renew a publication before its time. And we use PHONES to produce our own phone book for the office. With File Express and PHONES, we can generate a new, up-to-date phone book in minutes. (And we do, at least once a quarter.)

Worksheets

Last, but definitely not least, you will find a collection of worksheet (.WKS) files designed to be used with As-Easy-As (or with Lotus 1-2-3). The worksheets include: HERBS.WKS, TUTORIAL.WKS, INSURE.WKS, LEASE.WKS, and GRAPHS.WKS. The HERBS and TUTORIAL worksheets were created especially for this book. They are fully explained in Chapter 11. Though it is not essential that you do so, you may wish to load As-Easy-As and these worksheets as you read that chapter. The other three worksheets are supplied by Trius, Inc., creators of As-Easy-As. They will automate the calculation of insurance premiums and lease payments, and GRAPHS.WKS will put on an impressive demonstration of the program's graphing capabilities.

General hints and tips

The installation process is a matter of making an appropriately named directory on your hard drive, copying one of the supplied files into it, and then keying in a single command that will cause that file to extract a copy of its contents. We will take you through the process step-by-step in a moment. First, however, there are a few tricks and procedures you will find useful for nearly all the supplied packages.

All of the program packages discussed above are supplied with their own documentation files. So be sure to look for files ending in .DOC to get instructions on setting up and using the programs. Naturally, you will want to run and start playing with the programs immediately.

But at some point, please take a moment to print out and read the appropriate documentation. You can enter a command like **COPY** *filename.doc* **PRN**, if you like. Or you can use the little version of LIST.COM found on this disk to look at any .DOC file on the screen with a command like LIST *filename.doc*. Or you can load the .DOC file into your word processor and look at it and print it from there.

Next, please remember that many of these programs are shareware. Thus, if you like and use a program on a regular basis, you are honor-bound to send the programmer the requested registration fee. This is something you will really want to do. All of the programmers represented here are good people who deserve your support. They, in turn, will support you with updated versions, help, and assistance. But you've got to register to qualify.

Finally, don't forget what the book said about the PATH command (Chapter 4). If I were you, I would create a directory on my hard drive called UTILS. (Go to the root directory with the command **CD** and then key in **MD UTILS**.) Then I would make sure that my AUTOEXEC.BAT file contained the line **PATH C:\UTILS** at the very least. (You will want to have other directories in your PATH as well; see Chapter 4.) Then, I would copy the programs I wanted to use into C:\ UTILS.

That way, a program like DMLITE.EXE or PD.EXE would be accessible to me, regardless of where I was on the disk. In fact, as we work through the installation process, I'm going to assume that this is what you want to do. If you disagree with this approach, you are certainly free to make changes.

Surveying the disk

When you put the accompanying disk in a drive and key in **DIR**, you will see a list of files like the following, without the annotation:

DMLITE-Z.EXE	Marc Perkel's Directory Master Lite
PD-Z.EXE	Mark Perkel's Pick Directory
DMP-Z.EXE	DMP print spooler
FANSI-Z.EXE	FANSI Console
UTILS-Z.EXE	Selected utility programs
FONTS-Z.EXE	Several Elfring fonts
GBCHOICE.TXT	Commercial for Glossbrenner's Choice
SELF-EXT.TXT	On-disk instructions
GO.BAT	Displays on-disk instructions

LIST.COM	Used to display the above .TXT files
HEAV-Z.EXE	Writer's Heaven for PC Write, Standard Level
PRDEF-Z.EXE	Insights to PC Write's PR.DEF control file
MAGS-Z.EXE	MAGS database for File Express
PHONES-Z.EXE	PHONES database for File Express
WKS-Z.EXE	Worksheets for the As-Easy-As spreadsheet

The magic of self-extracting files

As you will notice, many of the files on the disk have names ending in ''-Z'' and file extensions of ''.EXE.'' This is a convention I have adopted to indicate that the file in question is a self-extracting archive file. This means that when you key in, say, **DMLITE-Z** and hit Enter, the program DMLITE-Z.EXE will begin to run and extract the contents of the archive onto your disk.

You will see this more clearly once you have a better idea of what each self-extracting archive file contains. In the listing that follows, notice that the name of the archive is given first (''DMLITE-Z.EXE''). Then there is a list of the files the archive contains (''NAME''). For each file, the ''Original'' size is given, followed by the ''Packed'' size and the compression ''Ratio.''

Thus, the file DMLITE-Z.EXE will ''self-extract'' its contents, which are the files DMLITE.DOC and DMLITE.EXE, when you key in DMLITE-Z and hit Enter. You may either copy DMLITE-Z.EXE into a directory on your hard disk and perform the extraction there, or you may simply key in **DMLITE-Z B:** to cause the program to extract its files onto the disk in Drive B, or **DMLITE-Z C:\TEMP** to put the extracted files into C:\TEMP. In other words, you can direct the program to extract its files to a different location. Here's the list of the archive files on the disk and their contents:

Listing of archive : DMLITE-Z.EXE

Name	**Original**	**Packed**	**Ratio**
DMLITE.DOC	12304	4622	37.6%
DMLITE.EXE	40974	38526	94.0%
2 files	53278	43148	81.0%

Listing of archive : PD-Z.EXE

Name	**Original**	**Packed**	**Ratio**
PD.DOC	9663	3462	35.8%
PD.EXE	29267	28118	96.1%
PIPEDIR.EXE	11515	11076	96.2%
WHERE.BAT	30	30	100.0%
WHEREIS.DOC	1305	550	42.1%
5 files	51780	43236	83.5%

Listing of archive : DMP-Z.EXE

Name	Original	Packed	Ratio
DMP.COM	22553	14079	62.4%
DMP.DOC	101592	31999	31.5%
DMPNEW.DOC	9554	3704	38.8%
OMBUDSMN.ASP	629	369	58.7%
PF.COM	1021	800	78.4%
REGINFO.DOC	6785	2583	38.1%
XMBLOCK.COM	818	660	80.7%
7 files	142952	54194	37.9%

Listing of archive : FANSI-Z.EXE

Name	Original	Packed	Ratio
DEJAVU.EXE	6868	6611	96.3%
FANSISET.EXE	17675	17108	96.8%
FCON301K.DEV	49642	30440	61.3%
FCON301K.DOC	18540	7022	37.9%
SEND.EXE	6548	6296	96.2%
5 files	99273	67477	68.0%

Listing of archive : UTILS-Z.EXE

Name	Original	Packed	Ratio
COLOR.COM	512	370	72.3%
COLOR.DOC	2358	935	39.7%
NUM.DOC	342	196	57.3%
NUMOFF.COM	12	12	100.0%
NUMON.COM	12	12	100.0%
RENDIR.DOC	571	297	52.0%
RENDIR.COM	640	265	41.4%
7 files	4447	2087	46.9%

Listing of archive : FONTS-Z.EXE

Name	Original	Packed	Ratio
BC120RPN.USP	15150	6598	43.6%
BC140RPN.USP	19387	7793	40.2%
BW180RPN.USP	29488	8245	28.0%
DOWNLOAD.EXE	12053	7761	64.4%
DOWNLOAD.DOC	16206	4762	29.4%
ESC	1	1	100.0%
SAMPLE.BAT	1089	544	50.0%
SAMPLE.TXT	752	341	45.3%
8 files	94126	36045	38.3%

Listing of archive : HEAV-Z.EXE

Name	Original	Packed	Ratio
ENV	297	119	40.1%
ENV1	276	103	37.3%
ENV2	297	119	40.1%
GO.BAT	28	28	100.0%
GUIDE.BAT	8	8	100.0%
HEAVEN.BAT	90	81	90.0%
HEAVEN.DOC	32926	10215	31.0%
HVN	3414	1613	47.2%
HVN2	1371	677	49.4%
HVNHELP	1355	537	39.6%
LTR	343	166	48.4%
NOTEPAD	71	55	77.5%
README	1275	618	48.5%
13 files	41751	14339	34.3%

Listing of archive : PRDEF-Z.EXE

Name	Original	Packed	Ratio
PRDEF.DOC	40246	14834	36.9%
1 file	40246	14834	36.9%

Listing of archive : MAGS-Z.EXE

Name	Original	Packed	Ratio
MAGS.R0	4166	868	20.8%
MAGS.DTA	2552	619	24.3%
MAGS.HDR	266	145	54.5%
MAGS.REP	2352	285	12.1%
MAGS.IXH	1089	193	17.7%
MAGS.IX6	613	73	11.9%
MAGS.IX1	1813	378	20.8%
MAGS.S0	1525	429	28.1%
MAGS.SCR	2	2	100.0%
9 files	14378	2992	20.8%

Listing of archive : PHONES-Z.EXE

Name	Original	Packed	Ratio
PHONES.DTA	1464	178	12.2%
PHONES.HDR	703	258	36.7%
PHONES.IX6	370	52	14.1%
PHONES.IXH	1109	204	18.4%

PHONES.LRA	4	4	100.0%
PHONES.PRN	1333	466	35.0%
PHONES.QSS	4023	207	5.1%
PHONES.R1	5931	1345	22.7%
PHONES.S0	2732	707	25.9%
PHONES.SCR	2	2	100.0%
10 files	17671	3423	19.4%

Listing of archive : WKS-Z.EXE

Name	Original	Packed	Ratio
HERBS.WKS	3608	1256	34.8%
TUTORIAL.WKS	3634	1364	37.5%
INSURE.WKS	2332	866	37.1%
LEASE.WKS	2808	1128	40.2%
GRAPHS.WKS	7425	2246	30.2%
5 files	19807	6860	34.6%

A general procedure

All right, let's get down to cases. My approach on receiving any shareware or public domain program is to put it into a "holding area" and test it out before doing anything else. If I like a program, I copy it to my UTILS directory. Since UTILS is part of my DOS path, the program then becomes accessible from any location on the system.

Since you probably do not have a UTILS subdirectory, create one now. Get to the root directory of Drive C or Drive D with the command **CD**. Then key in **MD UTILS**.

Now key in **TYPE AUTOEXEC.BAT**. If you receive a message "File not found," it means that you do not have a file by that name on your disk. Here is a three-step process for creating one:

1. Key in **COPY CON:AUTOEXEC.BAT** and hit Enter.
2. Key in **PATH C:\\UTILS** and hit Enter.
3. Hit your F6 key and hit Enter. DOS will report "1 File copied."

Now key in **AUTOEXEC** to run this little batch file and set your path. (The next time you boot your system, the file will be run automatically.)

If you discover that you already have an AUTOEXEC.BAT file in your root directory, you will probably have to use your word processor to alter it. If a line beginning "PATH" exists, key in ;**C:\\UTILS** to add the UTILS directory to your path. If no such line exists, key in **PATH C:\\UTILS**. (Note that DOS requires a semicolon to separate directory names in the PATH line.)

The next step is to make a directory called TEMP. This will be your holding tank and staging area. Make sure you are in the root directory by keying in **CD**. Then key in **MD TEMP**.

Now, just to make sure we are all playing with the same deck, log onto Drive C, key in **CD\TEMP** to change down to your TEMP directory. Then put the accompanying disk in Drive A. Key in **A:** to log onto Drive A.

Now you are ready to extract the files on the accompanying disk and to put them to use immediately.

An extraction example

You are now on Drive A. Start by keying in **DMLITE-Z.EXE C:\TEMP**. That will cause the files in the DMLITE-Z archive to be extracted into C:\TEMP. Once the process has finished, go take a look. Key in **C:** and then **DIR**. You should be in the C:\TEMP subdirectory and your DIR command should reveal two files: DMLITE-.DOC and DMLITE.EXE.

Run the program by keying in **DMLITE**. You will see something similar to the screen shown back in Fig. A-1. Play with Directory Master Lite as you like. Make sure the pointer is on DMLITE.DOC, for example, and hit **V** to view the file. When you are finished, hit Esc to return to the DM Lite screen. Then hit F7 to enter Tree mode. Hit Enter to jump to the directory shown and exit Tree mode. Then hit F7 again to see a list of all of the directories on your drive. Move the pointer to one of them and hit Enter to move into it.

When you are finished playing around with DM Lite, exit the program by hitting Esc. Then key in **COPY DMLITE.DOC PRN** to print out the documentation.

What next?

I'm going to assume that you like DM Lite and want to be able to use it from now on. So, while you are logged onto C:\TEMP, key in **COPY *.* C:\UTILS**. That will copy the files into UTILS, where they will be accessible to you from anywhere, thanks to the PATH command.

Next, clean out C:\TEMP. Make sure you are indeed logged onto C:\TEMP by keying in **CD** and watching the screen as you "check directory," or simply key in **CD\TEMP** and do a **DIR** to look at the file list. Then key in **DEL *.*** to delete all of the files. DOS will ask you if you are sure, and, thanks to the fact that you have checked beforehand, you are. So go ahead and authorize the deletion. (Always check your location before using the **DEL *.*** command.)

Now you're ready for the next program, PD-Z.EXE. Follow the identical procedure. Log onto C:\TEMP. Then key in **A:** to log onto Drive A. Then key in **PD-Z C:\TEMP** to extract the Pick Directory files into C:\TEMP. Key in **C:** to get back onto Drive C and play with PD. Note that the first time you run PD, you will be asked for the letters of the drives you want it to record in its PD.PIC file. So key in **PD** and respond to the prompts. (Specify only your hard drives, not your floppies.)

Play with the program. If your path has been set to C:\UTILS, you can even key in **DMLITE** and use its file viewing feature to look at PD.DOC. (If you are not sure about the PATH, key in **PATH C:\UTILS** and hit Enter to set the path from the command line. Then key in **DMLITE**.)

There is one small twist regarding the Pick Directory package. As noted above, PIPEDIR.EXE and WHEREIS.EXE are the same program, but only PIPEDIR.EXE is supplied. To create WHEREIS.EXE, simply key in **WHERE** to run a little batch file that will copy PIPEDIR.EXE to WHEREIS.EXE. You may now run WHEREIS as a separate program.

As before, enter **COPY *.* C:\UTILS** to copy all of the files in \TEMP to \UTILS. Then enter **DEL *.*** to clear out \TEMP in preparation for the next program. You will want to follow essentially the same procedure with DMP-Z.EXE, FANSI-Z.EXE, and UTILS-Z.EXE.

Using the other programs and files

The remaining files on the disk are FONTS-Z.EXE, HEAV-Z.EXE, PRDEF-Z.EXE, MAGS-Z.EXE, PHONES-Z.EXE, and WKS-Z.EXE. For the Elfring soft fonts package (FONTS-Z.EXE), I suggest creating a separate directory called FONTS. Get to your root directory with the command **CD**, then key in **MD FONTS**. Go to Drive A and key in **FONTS-Z C:\FONTS** to extract the files into C:\FONTS.

Log onto C:\FONTS and key in **SAMPLE**. This runs a batch file that downloads the three supplied fonts to your laser printer and prints the file SAMPLE.TXT. You'll have a lot of fun doing this, but your next step should be to read the documentation file, DOWNLOAD.DOC. Use your word processor or key in COPY DOWNLOAD.DOC PRN to print out a hard copy.

As you know from the survey presented above, the remaining files extract into Writers Heaven and PRDEF.DOC for PC Write, two databases (MAGS and PHONES) for use with File Express, and a clutch of worksheets (HERBS.WKS, TUTORIAL.WKS, etc.) for use with As-Easy-As. PC Write, File Express, and As-Easy-As are widely available through shareware channels, including Glossbrenner's Choice (Appendix B). I suggest you wait until you actually have installed these programs before extracting these files.

Conclusion

Every effort has been made to ensure that the disk supplied with this book performs flawlessly. However, we do live in an imperfect world. Should you find that, possibly due to compression in shipping, the disk cannot be made to turn in its envelope—or if you get any kind of error message when trying to install the software—please do the following.

First, if you are a brand new user, see if you can find a more experienced person to help you. There are ways to free up a stuck disk, for example. Or there may be some point that is not clear to you, that someone with more knowledge of DOS can help you with. If that fails, or if no experienced user is readily available to help you, send the disk to Glossbrenner's Choice with a brief description of the problem you are having. We will check the disk ourselves, attempt to diagnose the problem, and send you a free replacement. Mail your defective disk to

Installation Problems
Glossbrenner's Choice
699 River Road
Yardley, PA 19067-1965

Appendix B

Glossbrenner's Choice Order Form

THIS BOOK HAS BEEN DESIGNED TO HELP YOU BRING THE POWER OF PERSONAL computing to your business as easily and inexpensively as possible. Consequently, while all of the programs discussed are available from user groups, mail order firms, and online systems, you may find it convenient to order from Glossbrenner's Choice.

Disks are $5 apiece for 5.25″ or $6 for 3.5″ media, plus $3 per order for shipping and handling. There's also a special Business-Pak offer that will save you 35% off the programs that are essential to nearly every small business or professional office.

You may use the order form that follows or a photocopy of the order form. Or you may simply write the disk names and your mailing address on a sheet of paper.

Disks are listed in chapter sequence. Each entry begins with the disk name (CORE 7, FE 3, etc.), followed by the name of the program or programs it contains. If you need more information on a given program, please check the relevant chapter. A special "book order form" is supplied for those wishing to order copies of other Glossbrenner books.

Glossbrenner's Choice Order Form
for readers of *Glossbrenner's Guide to Shareware for Small Businesses*

Please complete this form (or a photocopy) and mail it to the address given below.

Name_____

Address_____

City_____State_____ZIP_____

Phone (____)_____

Payment [ ] Check or Money Order made payable to Glossbrenner's Choice

       [ ] Mastercard/VISA #:_____ Exp:_____

       Signature:_____

Mail to: Glossbrenner's Choice
          699 River Road
          Yardley, PA 19067-1965

Order Summary

Glossbrenner's Choice Disks
Check off names of the disks you want on the back of this form and record the amounts below.)

Number of Disks	*Price*
____ 5.25" disks x $5 per disk	_____
____ 3.5" disks x $6 per disk	_____

Special Offer   Glossbrenner's Choice Business-Pak
Includes PC-Write, File Express, ProComm 2.4.3,
As-Easy-As, and MORFORM at a 35% savings.

11-disk set, 5.25" format ($35)	_____
11-disk set, 3.5" format ($42)	_____

Replacements for disk included with this book

Small Business Shareware disk, 5.25" format ($2)	_____
Small Business Shareware disk, 3.5" format ($3)	_____

Disk Total
Pennsylvania residents, please add 6% Sales Tax.
Shipping: $3.00 to U.S. addresses, $5.00 outside the U.S.

_____
_____
_____

Book Total (from Book Order Form)

_____

Grand Total Enclosed

_____

Glossbrenner's Choice Disks

Please check the disks you want. Record the total number of disks in the space provided on the reverse side of this form.

Chapter 4   Software Basics: DOS, Windows, and Applications
____   CORE 7   *MarxMenu*

Chapter 9   Word Processing
____   PCW 1   *PC-Write (Program Disk)*
____   PCW 2   *PC-Write (Help/Spell/Conversion)*
____   PCW 3   *PC-Write (Printer Disk)*

Chapter 10   Database
____   FE 1   *File Express (Program Disk)*
____   FE 2   *File Express (Supplemental)*
____   FE 3   *File Express (Supplemental 2)*
____   FE 4   *File Express (Documentation)*
____   BIZ GRAPH 1   *ExpressGraph*

Chapter 11   Spreadsheet
____   AEA   *As-Easy-As (Lotus 1-2-3 clone)*
____   Pivot   *Sideways printing of AEA spreadsheets*

Chapter 12   Communications
____   COMM 1   *ProComm 2.4.3*
____   COMM 2   *ProComm 2.4.3 Utilities*
____   COMM 10   *PKZIP, LHARC, and PAK*

Chapter 13   Accounting and Money Management
____   Cash Control   *Check-writing program*
____   Medlin Accounting (GL/AP/PR/AR/Invoicing)

Chapter 14   Printer Productivity Tools and Techniques
____   GRAB 1   *Grab Plus Program Disk*
____   GRAB 2   *Grab Plus Add-ons*
____   LASER 1   *Elfring Fonts, CHART, and KEYCHART*
____   LASER 2   *TSR Download, Jet Pilot, Quicksoft Font Selector*
____   LASER 3   *QFONT, Fontloader, STP (Save-a-Tree Printer)*
____   LASER 4   *Laser Letterhead Plus (Disk 1 of 2)*
____   LASER 5   *Laser Letterhead Plus (Disk 2 of 2)*
____   Mail Machine   *Produce labels for mass mailings*
____   Pony Express   *Calculate shipping costs/delivery schedules*
____   PRINTER 2   *LQ and ImagePrint (dot matrix)*
____   PRINTER 4   *OnSide - Sideways printing (dot matrix)*
____   ZipKey   *Instant access to U.S. zip codes and area codes*

Chapter 15   Business Forms and Graphics
____   CAPTURE 1   *PCXDUMP and GRABBER*
____   CLIP 1   *Clip art collection*
____   DTP   *Desktop Paint*
____   DTP256   *Desktop Paint for super VGA*
____   Draft Choice   *Computer-aided design program*
____   GRAPHICS 6   *Graphic Workshop*

	KDGraf	*Create snazzy business graphs*
____	KDGraf	*Create snazzy business graphs*
____	MORFORM	*Business forms design (Disk 1 of 2)*
____	MORFORM	*Business forms design (Disk 2 of 2)*

Chapter 16 Crucial Utility Programs

____	CORE 1	*FANSI, CED, and LIST*
____	CORE 2	*FANSI Documentation*
____	CORE 4	*QFILER*

Chapter 17 Fun and Games

____		Coloring Book and Connect-the-Dots Pictures
____		Crossword Creator Professional
____	VGA GAMES 1	*Commander Keen and Crystal Caves*
____	VGA GAMES 2	*Duke Nukem*
____	VGA GAMES 3	*Goodbye Galaxy*
____	VGA GAMES 4	*Hugo's House of Horrors*
____	VGA GAMES 5	*Hugo II - Whodunit?*
____	VGA GAMES 6	*Picture Puzzle*
____	VGA GAMES 7	*Power Chess*
____	VGA GAMES 8	*Word Rescue*
____	VGA GAMES 9	*Blackjack! by Glencoe Computing*

GLOSSBRENNER'S CHOICE GUARANTEE: If the disk supplied with your book, or any disks you order from Glossbrenner's Choice, prove to be defective, we will replace them free of charge. Simply mail the disk(s) to: Glossbrenner's Choice, 699 River Road, Yardley, PA 19067-1965.

Windcrest Books assumes no responsibility for this offer. This is solely an offer of the author, Alfred Glossbrenner, and not of Windcrest Books. Please allow 1 to 2 weeks for delivery.

Order Form for Glossbrenner Books

Please complete this form (or a photocopy) and mail it to the address given below.

Name_____

Address_____

City_____State_____ZIP_____

Phone (_____)_____

Payment [ ] Check or Money Order made payable to Glossbrenner's Choice
              [ ] Mastercard/VISA #:_____ Exp:_____

Signature:_____

Mail to: Glossbrenner's Choice
               699 River Road
               Yardley, PA 19067-1965

-- All prices include shipping and handling --

DOS 5 by Alfred Glossbrenner. In a review published on Prodigy, computer columnist Lawrence J. Magid writes, "Alfred Glossbrenner has done the impossible. He has written an advanced guide to DOS 5.0 that's also easy to read. *DOS 5: An Advanced Guide to Putting Microsoft's Breakthrough Software to Work for You* is the best of the breed."
   DOS 5
   Random House Electronic Publishing, 868 pp.
   Includes 3.5" disk containing "The Programs
   DOS Forgot^{tm}" ($52.00) $_____

Glossbrenner's Complete Hard Disk Handbook by Alfred Glossbrenner is the book the *New York Times* called "the most comprehensive and readable treatment of conventional hard disks that we have ever seen." *PC Magazine* calls it "impressive...The book's language is clear and concise, with easily understood technical descriptions...a thorough index makes this a book you'll want to keep close at hand for ready reference."
   Glossbrenner's Complete Hard Disk Handbook
   Osborne/McGraw-Hill, 787 pp.
   Includes two 5.25" disks of crucial
   hard disk utility programs. ($42.95) $_____

The Complete Handbook of Personal Computer Communications--3rd Ed., by Alfred Glossbrenner has been hailed as "the Bible of the online world." *Database* magazine awarded the book four terminals, its highest rating. "The thing I like most about Glossbrenner," the reviewer wrote, "is that he is one of the few technical writers who seems to have a sense of what the average person wants and needs to know... Not only is the book itself invaluable, Glossbrenner never leaves you hanging and provides sources and contacts for all kinds of related information."
   The Complete Handbook of Personal Computer
   Communications--3rd edition
   St. Martin's Press, 405 pp. ($20.95) $_____

How to Look it Up Online by Alfred Glossbrenner was written in 1987 as a companion to "The Complete Handbook." It is intended for those with the time (and the money) to master and use professional-level online information systems like DIALOG, BRS/Orbit, Nexis, Dow Jones News/Retrieval, and NewsNet. According to the *PC World* review, "Glossbrenner's knowledge of the on-line universe appears to be encyclopedic, and he presents it in enjoyable, lucid prose."

    How to Look it Up Online
St. Martin's Press, 486 pp.   ($17.95) $_____

The Information Broker's Handbook by Sue Rugge and Alfred Glossbrenner is designed to tell you everything you need to know to start a professional research service. Sue Rugge is widely regarded as the "world's first information broker." Since she founded the profession in 1971, her seminars and cassette tapes have introduced thousands of people to the field. This book distills her knowledge and insights to help you decide whether you've got what it takes to be an information broker and to get started in your own business if you do.

    The Information Broker's Handbook.
Windcrest/McGraw-Hill, 380 pp.
Includes 5.25" disk with vital broker
business forms, contact points, etc.   ($31.95) $_____

Glossbrenner's Master Guide to CompuServe by Alfred Glossbrenner will tell you everything you need to know to make the most of the popular CompuServe Information Service. *PC World* said, "Whether you already subscribe to CompuServe or are just considering it, you'll appreciate Glossbrenner's inside tips."

    Glossbrenner's Master Guide to CompuServe.
Brady Books/Simon & Schuster, 432 pp.   ($21.95) $_____

Glossbrenner's Master Guide to GEnie by Alfred Glossbrenner presents the in's and out's of using the General Electric Network for Information Exchange (GEnie). GEnie's motto is "Stay online longer, for less." Subscriptions are $5 per month for virtually unlimited non-prime time access.

    Glossbrenner's Master Guide to GEnie.
Osborne/McGraw-Hill, 616 pp.
Includes 5.25" disk containing Aladdin software
to completely automate your GEnie sessions.   ($41.95) $_____

For shipments outside the US, please add $2 extra per book. $_____

Pennsylvania residents, please add 6% sales tax. $_____

Book Total $_____

Index

Special Zoom/FaxModem Discount!

... for Readers of *Glossbrenner's Guide to Shareware for Small Businesses*

Zoom/FaxModem AFC internal
Regularly $109. Special price **$79**. (Save $30.)

Zoom/FaxModem AFX external
Regularly $129. Special price **$89**. (Save $40.)

Zoom/FaxModems let you send and receive faxes directly from your computer -- and print them on plain paper using your own printer -- for less than $100. But that's not all. You can use the same modem to connect with bulletin boards and online systems like CompuServe, GEnie, and MCI Mail at the industry standard speed of 2400 baud.

With the Zoom AFC (internal) and AFX (external) FaxModems, if the file's on your disk, you can send it to virtually anyone via fax, electronic mail, or direct upload. And you can do it fast! As *Computer Shopper* (November 1991) noted, "Only two modems. . . outperformed the pack. Of these, the Zoom modem was clearly the better performer . . . roughly 8 percent faster than the pack and 16 percent faster than the slowest modem tested."

The fax software bundled with these units also lets you "broadcast" fax transmissions to groups of people. A transmission scheduling feature lets you take advantage of low evening long distance rates. "Add to that a solid 2400 bps modem and a seven-year warranty," said *PC Sources* (November 1991), "and you get a lot for your money."

Zoom modems have always offered superior performance and value. But now, they offer something else as well -- a special discount available exclusively to readers of this book. The Zoom AFC is an 8-bit card that plugs into an empty slot inside your PC. The Zoom AFX is an external unit about the size of a paperback book, and is cabled to one of your serial ports (COM1, COM2, etc.). Among other things, both units offer the following features:

- Group III, Class 1 Send/Receive Fax (9600/7200/4800/2400 bps fax send and 4800/2400 bps fax receive).

- Hayes-compatible data modem (2400/1200/300 bps).

- Both fax and data (terminal program) software.

- Dual modular phone jacks, so you can plug your telephone into the modem.

- Seven-year warranty -- the longest in the industry!

To order your FaxModem, complete the coupon and mail it to Zoom Telephonics, Inc.

Zoom/FaxModem Offer

To order, simply check off the unit you want (AFC internal or AFX external), tear out the coupon, and mail it to Zoom Telephonics, Inc. (Sorry, no photocopies will be accepted.) Zoom will ship the FaxModem to you directly. Please allow two to three weeks for delivery. Prices quoted include shipping and handling.

Please send me:

☐ Zoom/FaxModem AFC internal IBM-compatible 2400 bps modem with fax and data software............ **$79**

☐ Zoom/FaxModem AFX external IBM-compatible 2400 bps modem with fax and data software............ **$89**

Name:_____

Address:_____

City:_____State:_____ ZIP:_____

Phone: _____

Payment Method: [ ] Check   [ ] MasterCard   [ ] VISA   [ ] American Express

Card Number:_____ Expires:_____

Signature:_____

Mail your completed coupon to:

> **Zoom Telephonics, Inc.**
> **207 South Street**
> **Boston, MA 02111**
> **(800) 631-3116**
> **(617) 423-1072**

Save $10 on the
Electronic Computer Glossary!

An award-winning resource, now available on disk at a special price for readers of *Glossbrenner's Guide to Shareware for Small Businesses..........*

Everyone connected with computers has experienced the problem of not knowing the right computer term or definition. Now, the electronic version of Alan Freedman's award-winning best-seller, *The Computer Glossary*, provides the solution.

- Over 5,000 definitions of computer terms.

- Easy-to-understand and complete definitions for everyone from novice to industry professionals. Covers micros to mainframes, LANs, computer graphics, communications, UNIX, HP, DEC, desktop publishing, PCs, Macintosh, workstations.

- DOS tutorial and commands.

- Easy to install, easy to use.

- Updated twice a year.

- Charts, specifications, vendors, diagrams, and more.

- DOS, Windows, and Mac/HyperCard versions available.

- Regularly **$29.95**. Only **$19.95** for readers of this book.

To order your copy of the *Electronic Computer Glossary* at the special price of **$19.95**, just complete and mail the form on the back of this page. For more information, call or write:

The Computer Language Company, Inc.
5521 State Park Road
Point Pleasant, PA 18950
Phone: 215-297-5999
FAX: 215-297-8424

Finally! The meaning of virtually every computer term, on disk!

Please send me one copy of the *Electronic Computer Glossary* at the special price of **$19.95** in the format checked below:

[   ] DOS 5.25"   [   ] Windows 5.25"

[   ] DOS 3.5"   [   ] Windows 3.5"

[   ] Mac/HyperCard

Name:_____

Company:_____

Address:_____

Address:_____

City:_____State_____Zip_____

Phone:(_____)_____

Payment: [   ] Check Enclosed   [   ] VISA   [   ] MasterCard

Credit Card #:_____Exp. _____

Signature: _____

Mail your completed form to:

The Computer Language Company, Inc.

5521 State Park Road

Point Pleasant, PA 18950

Laser Cartridge Savings!

Readers of *Glossbrenner's Guide to Shareware for Small Businesses* can **SAVE 10%** on their first **Super Cartridge** or **Cartridge Recharge** from The Laser Group, Inc. The Super Cartridge for HP LaserJets and compatibles is specially designed to be recharged again and again, and comes with a lifetime guarantee.

The Super Cartridge - "Rechargeable by Design"

Special Price	$62.95 + $2.50 Shipping
Regular Price	$69.95 + $2.50 Shipping

Laser Cartridge Recharge

Special Price	$31.45 + $2.50 Shipping
Regular Price	$34.95 + $2.50 Shipping

To take advantage of this special laser cartridge offer, complete and mail the order form on the back of this page. Or call **The Laser Group** for more information at **1-800-LASER12**. Be sure to ask about getting a credit for your old cartridge when you buy your first Super Cartridge from The Laser Group.

10% Savings for Readers of
Glossbrenner's Guide to Shareware for Small Businesses

To take advantage of this special 10% discount offer, check one of the boxes below and mail your completed form (and empty cartridge if you are ordering a recharge) to **The Laser Group, Inc.**

[   ] Please send one rechargeable Super Cartridge for my laser printer at the special price of **$65.45** ($62.95 + $2.50 shipping).

[   ] Please recharge the enclosed laser cartridge at the special price of **$33.95** ($31.45 + $2.50 shipping).

Name:_____

Company:_____

Address:_____

Address:_____

City:_____State_____Zip_____

Phone: (_____)_____

Payment: [   ] Check Enclosed   [   ] VISA   [   ] MasterCard

Credit Card #:_____ Expiration:_____

Signature:_____

Send your order or requests for additional information to:

The Laser Group, Inc.
223 Palmer Court - Suite 100
Dekalb, IL 60115
1-800-LASER12 (1-800-527-3712)
1-815-748-5823 (Voice)

Join GEnie® Today!

Money-back offer for readers of *Glossbrenner's Guide to Shareware for Small Businesses*

Stay online longer for less with GEnie and enjoy a world of information, communications, education, and entertainment.

The monthly subscription fee of just **$4.95** includes unlimited access to over 100 GEnie*Basic services during non-prime time. Send and read electronic mail, get valuable information in more than 40 bulletin boards, check the top news, shop in the GEnie mall, get stock quotes, research topics in our continuously-updated encyclopedia, and much more for one low fee. **It's the best deal going!**

But GEnie is much more than this. GEnie has hundreds of additional services available to you from only **$6 per hour**. Download files from our libraries, with more files than other major services. Exchange information on a variety of computers and software packages. Play graphical games and compete against other GEnie members who are online at the same time you are. Chat with people. Educate yourself and your family with our online courses or get help from our tutors. There's lots going on in our telecommunity.

GEnie offers access to world class information sources like **Dow Jones News/Retrieval, the Official Airline Guides, Charles Schwab Brokerage Services,** and data from the world's largest databases.

And if you're not completely satisfied, just ask and we'll close your account and return your $4.95 fee at any time during your first month.

Sign up for GEnie free!

To sign up, follow these four **easy steps.**

1. Set your communications software for half duplex (local echo) at 300, 1200, or 2400 baud.

2. Dial toll-free in the USA 1-800-638-8369 (in Canada, 1-800-387-8330). Upon connection, type **HHH**.

3. At the U#= prompt, type **XXX11111,AAAAAAAA** and press the **Enter** key.

4. Have a major credit card ready. In the USA, you may also use your checking account number.

If you need additional assistance in the USA or Canada, call 1- 800-638-9636. From outside this area, call 1-301-251-6415. Or write to us at the address below.

[ ] **YES,** I want to learn more about GEnie. Please send me more information.

Name_____

Address_____

Address_____

City_____State_____ZIP_____

Mail completed coupon to: GEnie, 401 N. Washington Street, Rockville, MD 20850

There's one word for the support you get on CompuServe:

Personal.

CompuServe, the world's most comprehensive network of people with personal computers, is also a worldwide network of people with answers to your hardware and software questions. You'll find quick solutions and information from thousands of members, including product developers.

All you need to get started is your computer, a modem, communications software and a CompuServe membership. To get a free introductory membership, complete and mail the form on the back of this page. Or call **800-524-3388** and ask for Representative 300.

Act now and you'll get a free CompuServe membership along with a $15 credit good toward exploring CompuServe's support services!

Put the world
at your
fingertips.

Join the world's largest international network of people with personal computers. Whether it's computer support, communications, entertainment or continually updated information, you'll find services that meet your every need.

Your free introductory membership will include a $15 usage credit. To get connected, complete and mail the card below. Or call **800-524-3388** and ask for Representative 300.

CompuServe®

☐YES!

I read *Glossbrenner's Guide to Shareware for Small Businesses.* Send me my FREE CompuServe Introductory Membership including a $15 usage credit.

Name:_____

Address:_____

City:_____State:_____ZIP:_____

Phone:_____

Clip and mail this form to: CompuServe
P.O. Box 20212
Dept. 300
Columbus, OH 43220